P9-BJR-233

SHALOM
PRESCOTT, ARIZONA
LIBRARY

LINE FIVE
THE INTERNAL PASSPORT

*Jewish Family Odysseys
from the USSR to the USA*

Based on the *Line Five* Oral History Project

created under the auspices of

THE WOMEN'S AUXILIARY
OF THE JEWISH COMMUNITY CENTERS OF CHICAGO

Edited by Elaine Pomper Snyderman and Margaret Thomas Witkovsky

CHICAGO
REVIEW
PRESS

Library of Congress Cataloging-in-Publication Data

Line five, the internal passport : Jewish family odysseys from the USSR to the
  USA / edited by Elaine Pomper Snyderman and Margaret Thomas
  Witkovsky.—1st ed.
        p.   cm.
      ISBN 1-55652-156-1 : $22.95.—ISBN 1-55652-155-3 (pbk.) : $12.95
      1. Jews—Soviet Union—Biography.   2. Refuseniks—Biography.   3. Jews,
  Russian—Illinois—Chicago—Biography.   4. Immigrants—Illinois—
  Chicago—Biography.   5. Oral biography.   6. Soviet Union—Biography.
  7. Chicago (Ill.)—Biography.   I. Snyderman, Elaine Pomper.   II. Witkovsky,
  Margaret Thomas.
  DS135.R95A152   1992
  947'.004924—dc20   92-15843
                                                                          CIP

© 1992 by The Women's Auxiliary of the Jewish Community Centers of Chicago

All rights reserved

Published by Chicago Review Press, Incorporated
814 North Franklin Street
Chicago, Illinois 60610

First edition

5 4 3 2 1

Printed in the United States of America

To those who shared their stories; may their odysseys of yesterday lead to bright affirmations tomorrow.

Photo captions for front cover, reading clockwise from top left:

1. Zelig Michlin, father of Tsilia Michlin Goldin, born 1876; *schochet, mohel,* and *cantor.* Picture taken pre-1930. He died of starvation in the winter of 1945.

2. Lilia Shafran showing early evidence of copy editing skill.

3. Paulina and Naum Ginsburg on vacation in the Caucasus, 1967.

4. Genya Simkina, mother of Tsilia Michlin Goldin, 1881–1950.

5. Portrait of the Samaravitsky family, taken in 1931. Julia Zissman, 2 years old, is in her mother Maria's arms. From left to right, standing are: Uncle Paul Samaravitsky and his wife Sofia; Uncle Alexander and wife, Aunt Sonja; Uncle Moshe Levitan and wife Aunt Liza; Julia's father, Izrail Zissman. Seated, from left: Grandmother Samaravitsky, Cousin Paul (son of Sonja and Alex), Uncle Isaac, visiting from New York City; Cousin Isaac (son of Paul and Sofia), and Grandfather Samaravitsky.

    Soon after the photo was taken, Paul Samaravitsky was arrested and within three days was shot. No explanation was given. Moshe Levitan was arrested without explanation and disappeared.

6. Tatyana Ochakovsky, a fervent Young Pioneer when she receives an achievement award on Recognition Day, 1972.

Photo captions for back cover, reading clockwise from top left:

1. The winner and champion . . . Alex Blinstein. The young man who endured an unusually deprived childhood became student boxing champion of the USSR in the mid 1970's. Sports allowed him to travel, expand his intellectual horizons, and complete his engineering studies.

2. Julia and Rudolf Umantsev on their honeymoon at the Black Sea, 1949.

3. Grandmother Perle Rubenshtein and Granddaughter Luba Radunsky, 1957.

4. Izrail, Nella, and members of the Radunsky family at graveside of Izrail's parents, Minsk. Photo taken shortly before Izrail and Nella emigrated in 1990.

5. Yanina Estrina and Kim Nayman on their wedding day in Gomel, July 30, 1983.

6. Wolf Estrin, Yanina's father. The Geiger counter in his classroom laboratory signaled the radioactive fallout of Chernobyl several days before official news was released.

CONTENTS

FOREWORD

With the demise of the Union of Soviet Socialist Republics (USSR), the opening of archives, and the accessibility of eye-witnesses, scholars have begun the task of recording, analyzing, and presenting the experience of the Jewish nation in the lands of the former USSR from 1917 to 1991. This enterprise, the enterprise of nurturing memory through historical retrieval, is vital.

However, the Jewish experience demands that other methods, as well, serve as the basis of collective memory. The Jewish experience, itself, gives birth to another means of understanding and recording the past, a means that emerges not out of Israel the nation, but rather out of Israel the family. The Jewish people have long seen themselves as a family. Thus, when the history of the Jewish nation begins with the Book of Shemot-Exodus, the first lines read, "These are the names of the sons of Israel who came to Egypt with Jacob, each coming with his household: Reuben, Simeon, Levi, and Judah; Issachar, Zebulun, and Benjamin; Dan and Naphtali, Gad and Asher. The total number of persons that were of Jacob's issue came to seventy, Joseph being already in Egypt." To be a member of the nation liberated from slavery hundreds of years later, is to be a child of one of the twelve tribes. For the Jewish people, life is with family. This sense that *people* is to be understood as *family* never wanes with national growth, with demographic development, or with entry into the land. God and Israel are regularly portrayed by the prophets as husband and wife, as family. The prophet Amos speaks to "the family," not the nation "brought up from Egypt" (Amos 3:1).

The essential story of the Jewish family is one of exile and redemption. Exile and redemption is an almost never-ending cycle. This cycle has been understood as a family story. To the observer, to the nations of the world who stand from afar, People Israel's experience is national in nature. However, the inner life of the Jewish people, the way in which she experiences herself has been as family, rather than as nation.

This book comes to answer little questions. When the Jewish family is reunited after much rupture, the Jewish family behaves like all other families behave. After separation, there is a desperate need to know, to fill in the abyss, to find out what happened on certain dates to family members. To be family means to be flesh, one to the other. Family defines itself by the experiences of each of its members. The intimate link between family members means that no one member's life is complete without access to and experience of the other's life. The family of the Jewish people has little idea of much of its members' experiences over the past 75 years in the USSR. Family stories are critical to Jewish self-understanding.

The Jewish families you will meet in this book have the same names as most American Jews, lived on the same streets as the parents and grandparents of most American Jews, certainly lived in the same cities. Beginning in 1881, the family was severed. The mass migration that followed, the *pogroms* that ensued in the wake of the assassination of Czar Alexander II, began the process. But, in 1917, with the rise of the Bolsheviks, a long dark night descended over the family Israel, over all the families of the Jewish people in the Bolshevik lands.

What is it that family members want to know of each other? What really happened when American Jews had nightmares, dreams, and fantasies about their brothers and sisters in the lands of the Communists? What did our brothers and sisters eat? Where did they shop? What were different years and decades like? What happened during the Holocaust when the Nazis invaded Byelorussia and the Ukraine, and hundreds of thousands fled or were evacuated East? What was it like to live during the Stalin purges? What was it like for a six-year-old to go to school and discover Jewishness for the first time? What was the nature of discrimination in the workplace? What was the nature of social intercourse with non-Jewish Soviets? How did people cope from day to day? What were the defense mechanisms? What were the flights of fancy? What were the small and petty little corruptions and stratagems that made life bearable? How did women deal with women's needs, so utterly neglected in the social system that was to have liberated women? What was the nature of daily life? Memory is built of details; gas, electricity, phone service, the post, transportation, how were all of these organized or not organized? Were there different seasons when food was more or less accessible? Were there different regimes under which life was better or worse? What were the recreational activities? What were the little beauties that made life a bit better? Who was murdered and by whom? Who died in unknown prisons, were buried in nameless graves and unmarked fields? How does Jewish consciousness move from childhood to adolescence and then develop in adulthood? How does one learn to read between the lines; to live underground as a Jew and publicly as a Soviet?

These are the questions, the little questions, that our book comes to answer. *Line Five: The Internal Passport* is a passport to the inner life of the members of the Jewish family. Each story is collected family by family, just as the Bible records the stories of the families of the twelve children of Jacob. "Line Five" is a passport into the mind and soul, into the seemingly petty and insignificant details that fill in the gaps that the historian and the demographer, the anthropologist and the political scientist must, of necessity, overlook.

Yehiel E. Poupko
Director of Judaica,
Jewish Community Centers
of Chicago

EDITORS' PREFACES

The fifth line of the Soviet Citizen's Internal Passport stated the nationality of the bearer. The republic of birth for all citizens was recorded on that line—all citizens that is, except Jews. Whether they were born in the Ukraine or Russia, Moldavia or Byelorussia, it said the same thing—*Evrey*—Jew.

When we began this undertaking, we knew that only an oppressive regime could impose such a cruel distinction on a national minority. What we did not anticipate was that before the book would go the press, the Soviet Union would be no more. Ironically, one memoirist predicted the event, but even she did not foresee how quickly the rusted-out structure would collapse. Nor did we quite anticipate the magnitude of the project. Though the challenge seemed to increase with each testimony, we don't claim that the book is even a blink in the eye of events leading to the collapse of the Soviet Union. If, however, these personal accounts bring to life the struggle for dignity that was as important as life itself to the people we heard, then we do not betray the testament entrusted to us.

Meeting these long-lost members of our diversely scattered family, reliving with them the fateful events that shaped their lives, we were transformed. Although we were strangers, the fact that they could still trust after living in fear so long, is a great tribute to their humanity. Certainly this was more than a lesson in history. It became part of my life experience. There was one other revelation. That fifth line is part of any passport, even if unstamped, of anyone who has experienced prejudice, whatever the bearer's religion, race or country of origin. For this reason I believe these memoirs must be read not only as the raw material of history, but as the truth of the human heart. Those who wish to pursue them in depth will find the original transcripts and tapes archived at the Spertus College of Judaica Asher Library/Chicago Jewish Archives and at the Chicago Historical Society.

Whatever the reader finds of interest and value in this collection is thanks to the fifty people who were willing to search through sometimes tragic memory or wounded spirit to recover their unique portion of the past for future generations. Whatever error, despite our care, that may appear in these memoirs, we accept the blame.

E.P.S.

The intent of this project was to interview newly arrived Russian-Jewish immigrants to the Chicago area. Approximately 9,000 were expected during the years 1988 through 1990; the Women's Auxiliary felt it was an important historic time and the commitment was made to preserve the memories of as many as possible. The documentation of previous waves of immigration left many questions.

Our sampling is relatively small. We interviewed fifty people, aged from ten to eighty-four, comprising nineteen families. Some of these families cover three generations. Approximately one-third of the families interviewed wished to remain anonymous because of relatives who had not yet been given permission, or did not intend, to leave the Soviet Union. We regret that we had neither time nor personnel to interview everyone who evinced an interest in participating.

We were struck with the responsiveness of those interviewed. Our interviewers grew with the task, using an outline of questions to explore the memoirist's histories. One gentleman agreed to an interview and then, after a few questions, refused to answer any more, saying, "I think I will write my own book." We wish him well.

Our sampling includes families who have lived, at one time or another, in towns and cities across the length and breadth of the Soviet Union: from Alma-Ata to Zvenigorodka and Zhitomir; from Kiev to Kharkov, Kuybyshev to Krasnoyarsk; and from Surgut to Pogranichnyy and Tselinograd. The variety of their experiences is fascinating. Some of our memoirists merit a book of their own but we were constrained by time and space.

There were problems common to all, but many individual differences. Difficulty in obtaining a higher education and admittance to institute or university affected almost all the adults interviewed. The harshness of the compulsory military service was experienced by most of the men. Anti-Semitism was experienced, to a greater or lesser degree, by everyone. We have tried to retain the flavor of the most dramatic expressions of the general experience, while stressing individuality.

The courage and humor expressed by these new Americans was impressive. Courage—to take their lives up by the roots and move to an unknown country with a difficult language and no guarantees as to job or income. Humor—in the way they faced the problems there and how they approach the confusing way of life here: there is a wry undertone to many of their answers. Since for me life consists of continued learning, this project has brought me insight, joy and knowledge. We recorded such wonderful stories but think of what we may have missed!

M.T.W.

ACKNOWLEDGMENTS

Because of the sponsorship of the Women's Auxiliary of the Jewish Community Centers the Line Five Oral History Project and this book came to fruition. The following people made vital and noteworthy contributions.

Carole Latimer, WA/JCC past president, for fostering the concept; Phyllis Grossman, president, for shepherding the project.

Rabbi Yehiel E. Poupko, JCC director of Judaica; Allen Siegel, M.D., Yale Holocaust Oral History interviewer; Zvi Gitelmen, author of *A Century of Ambivalence* and professor of political science, University of Michigan, for their help in training and education.

Fran Grossman, director of the JCC Family to Family Program; Nancy Dove, director of marketing, and her staff; Henrietta Williams and Svetlana Berger, interpreters, for their expertise and time.

The Oral History Project Committee: Nancy Carson, Sylvia Delman, Judy Ex, Susan Gensen, Ruth Goodman, Margot Hirsch, Saralyn Levine, Laurie Lieberman, Karyn Lutz, Ellie Meyers, Gail Neiman, Sharon Rowe, Cecille Shure, and A.J. Straus, each of whom contributed uniquely and generously.

Sarah Krive for her dedicated, fine work of transcription and translation, ably assisted by Krista Schmitz; Debbie Goldsmith for her contribution to the cover graphics design.

Philip Pomper, professor of Russian History, Wesleyan University, and Merle Lurie, for their historical and linguistic expertise.

Harlan Haimes, JCC president, for his interest and encouragement.

Special thanks to Jerry Witkovsky, JCC general director and Perry Snyderman, past president, who believed in the book from the moment it was conceived.

We are indebted to the memoirists who so generously shared their treasured family photographs. Since many were prohibited from taking their photos with them, we are all the more grateful for these visual records.

We wish to make special note of the work of Bruce Mondschain, whose sensitive and artistic photography allowed us to represent some of the memoirists as they appear today.

E.P.S. and M.T.W.

PART I

PASSPORT
TO REPRESSION

1

GRANDMOTHER AND GRANDDAUGHTER
An Overview of a Century

TSILIA MICHLIN GOLDIN AND YANINA ESTRINA NAYMAN

TSILIA MICHLIN GOLDIN was born soon after the turn of the century, her granddaughter, Yanina Estrina Nayman, in the middle. Their recollections span the spectrum of historical events from civil war and *pogroms* under a new Bolshevik regime, up to the Chernobyl explosion.

TSILIA MICHLIN GOLDIN
Not by Bread Alone

Tsilia Michlin Goldin can't remember an easy time in her life. She was born in Bobruisk in czarist Russia and bore witness to the bloody civil wars and pogroms *that broke out in Byelorussia after the Bolshevik Revolution. Members*

3

of her own family barely survived grave injury; her brother was shot in the face, her parents brutally attacked and beaten.

When she was twenty, she moved to Gomel to find work and there met her future husband Mendel (Mikhail), a foreman in a woodworking shop. Their religious wedding was illegal, so they married in secret.

At the outset of World War II, evacuated to Uzbekistan, the young mother of three labored in the cotton fields in a rural area while Mendel served in the military near Leningrad during the blockade. She and her children were bloated from starvation, and people around them were dying in appalling numbers from the inhumane conditions. If the war years consisted of hardship and terror, the postwar years were not much better.

On returning to Gomel, the Goldins discovered their home had been destroyed by bombs. During the privations of the following winter, Tsilia's father died of starvation. Five years later, a self-serving neighbor exploited Mendel's illness and Tsilia's fear of authority by usurping the house that she had hired him to help rebuild. The Goldins were allotted one room for the family. In time Tsilia planted and harvested a vegetable garden and raised chickens to sustain her family.

Tsilia had arrived in Chicago just one year before the interview. She emigrated with her youngest daughter Raisa and son-in-law Yefim Krugman and their two sons, Julian and Mikhail. Her older daughter Fira lives in Haifa with her husband and children. At eighty-three, despite the difficulties endured in her long life, Tsilia has clung to values acquired from her parents and grandparents. And despite the loss of many of her own dreams, she cherishes high aspirations for her children's future. She exemplifies a family whose Judaic observance was its pride, whose legacy is a rich tapestry of memories and lore.

Tsilia's grandfather, a cantonist in the czar's army, and a legendary figure because of his steadfast beliefs, set a peerless standard. Her father, a shochet *and* mohel, *constantly risked his life and imprisonment to practice the* mitzvot *[commandments].*

Tsilia's grandfather served in the czar's army from age twelve until he was discharged at thirty. Although the practice in those days was forcible conversion to Christianity of such youths, he remained Jewish.

Today, despite the fragility of age and the stamp of a hard life, the impression Tsilia conveys is one of strength and a remarkably sweet serenity. One abiding sorrow remains—the loss of her daughter Clara who, at thirty-seven, died from complications after a crudely performed abortion. Clara's daughter, Yanina, and husband Kim live in Skokie with their daughter Katya.

With the Krugman family Tsilia lives in a modest apartment furnished with recycled but immaculate appointments. Yefim and his older son Julian both work. Mikhail, the younger son, is in Jewish secondary school. Raisa plays the piano for preschool children's classes.

Denied an education because of the political climate around her, Tsilia was the least educated of her siblings. Nonetheless, she made sure her own daughters were well educated. She recounts her family history stoically, her face impas-

sive, except for two joyous memories. The effect of each—one from the past, one recent—transfixes her face. Soon after the war at a time when life seemed hopeless, she was able to fulfill a dream for her daughters' futures—to buy a piano—so that they could all become proficient musicians. Now, more than forty years later the musical heritage endures in Clara's daughter Yanina, who taught music and drama in Gomel.

Another heritage also endures. Just after coming to Chicago, her grandson Mikhail has made a decision that links him forever to Tsilia's father and grandfather.

A Poor Family

I was born in 1908 and grew up in Bobruisk, in Byelorussia. There were eight children, three brothers and five sisters. Originally there were ten, but two died. My father Zelig Michlin earned his living as a *shochet* and acted as a *mohel*.

Our home was pretty big, one of the most beautiful houses there. There were five rooms. There were ten children, parents, and grandmother, and quite often we had visitors from nearby towns because my father was considered very learned and was a very respected man.

Ours was a big family, a poor family, and I was the oldest girl. I had an older brother who studied and was a religious Jew. All my brothers became *shochets* like my father.

Although political changes were going on around us, our family was not political. Our life was the synagogue and family and prayer, but not much else. After the Revolution came the civil war and foreign occupation, and during these times many Jews fled and hid in the forests. We did so too and lived underground for four years, until 1922. First there was a German occupation, then Polish occupation, and then German again.

When the civil war ended I was thirteen, but I had to take on the responsibilities of the household because my mother Genya Simkina became ill. During the Polish occupation my older brother was shot—a bullet struck one side of his face and passed through the other side. Perhaps from the shock, my mother developed a heart condition. My brother, who was then twenty, didn't die, but it took him a long time to get well and recover his ability to talk.

A *Pogrom* Strikes Near Bobruisk

Between 50,000 and 80,000 people lived in Bobruisk; perhaps a third to half were Jews, maybe more. Russians and Jews lived quietly, but if something went wrong, the Jews were always blamed. I recall *pogroms* between 1920 and 1923. In one of these our family suffered.

My father set out one day dressed in his best clothes. He was a ways from home and suddenly noticed in the distance an angry mob approaching the town, so he looked for a safe place to hide. He found some workmen building a house, and he joined them as if he were part of the crew. But the mob approached, and one of them noticed his clothes and shouted that he was a Jew. The mob grabbed him and tore off his clothes, and they beat him terribly—his ribs were broken and his whole body so severely injured that he spent two years in bed. My mother was also injured because they came to the house and beat her. The younger children and I hid out in a tent near the hospital with my older brother (who was a *shochet* by then) because we were afraid to be with anybody else. I was twelve years old. After *pogroms*, people—Jewish people—were carried to the hospital in dreadful condition, bleeding, without arms or legs, with noses and ears cut off. Until then we had lived in a *shtetl* outside of Bobruisk, but after that we moved into the town of Bobruisk.

Defying the Ban against Religious Practices

It was dangerous to perform religious rituals in the 1930s, and the government persecuted people who performed them. Although he risked getting ten years' imprisonment, my father continued to perform them because of his beliefs; he did it for his people. He did not take money for circumcisions but did them as *mitzvot*.

The Night the Police Raided Our Home

My father was persecuted for being a *shochet*. Sometime between 1936 and 1938 he was imprisoned for a short period. Several times the secret police unsuccessfully tried to arrest him for performing a ritual slaughter. Once the police arrived at our house after *Shabbos* at about eleven o'clock or midnight. They began a very thorough search, turning the house upside down. This search went on from midnight until eight o'clock in the morning until they had torn everything apart.

They continued the search until finally they gave up in disgust. All night the officer in charge sat in a chair to supervise the investigation. No one had paid any attention the night before when, before their very eyes, Father took off the jacket he used to protect his clothes while slaughtering the animal and placed it over the back of the officer's chair. The jacket held the instruments they were looking for. No one even mentioned checking in the pocket of the jacket. No one even thought to look there! On this occasion my father was spared.

Neither School nor Job for a *Shochet's* Daughter

There were Jewish schools in the early 1900s, but in 1925 the government closed them. Until then Jews had gone there to study Yiddish and Jewish culture.

Non-Jewish people would laugh at Jews when they spoke Yiddish. Because of this some Jews stopped giving their children Jewish names and began to lose their culture.

I wanted an education, but because I hadn't finished primary school, I couldn't continue. Because my father was a religious man and a Jew, his children were denied access to the public school. The authorities knew that my father wouldn't stop his religious practices. And of course the Jewish schools had been closed. My dream had been to get an education and become proficient in something so that I could teach, or I would have liked to become a tailor, to work with clothing. I couldn't get into a professional school, and my family could not afford to bring in someone who would give me private tutoring. So it was impossible for me to receive a formal education.

In Bobruisk I couldn't find work because I was the daughter of a *shochet,* and those were the years after the Revolution when religious people were prosecuted and their children were not allowed to attend public schools. Right after the Revolution my older brothers went to Yiddish school, which the government still allowed. When those schools were closed, I had no place to go. Years later my younger sisters were able to go to school, but I was caught in that middle period when nothing was open to me.

So, in 1930, I went to Gomel, the second largest city in Byelorussia, which is maybe three hours by train from Bobruisk. I went to stay at the home of my mother's sister. I thought there I would be able to find a job.

At my aunt's house I met my future husband, Mendel Goldin. It turned out he was a very distant relative on my uncle's side. I had been in Gomel a month, maybe three weeks looking for work. To make a long story short, Mendel came to visit his relatives, and there at my aunt's home we met. I was happy. He was young and handsome, and interesting and nice.

Married in Secret

Because we had a religious wedding in synagogue, I had to get married in secret. If we had been caught, my husband would have lost his job. Only my uncle and several very religious witnesses attended; not even my parents were there. Afterward, we had no party or celebration. This was in 1930, and there wasn't much money to spend, and I wore a dress I made myself. I was the only one in the family to have a religious wedding. My sisters had civil ceremonies performed according to Soviet law.

The family remained in Bobruisk until 1941, though I lived in Gomel. My husband supervised a shop that made by-products from lumber. My life was hard. During the years between 1932 and 1941, I was pregnant four times. One child was stillborn—I think because I lifted heavy boxes during the pregnancy. I had three little girls: Fira, who now lives in Haifa, was born in 1932, Raisa was born in 1941. Clara was born in 1938 and died in 1975. My husband was always out working, and I had to look after the family. Also, I kept some chickens and raised vegetables.

War and Survival

When the war broke out, Mendel, a man in his forties, went into the army and my family came to Gomel. My parents, my sister, and her family joined me and my three children. We began our relocation to Central Asia, going on foot much of the time. Raisa was only three months old. When we traveled by train, German airplanes would drop bombs. We managed to get to a rural area of Uzbekistan to a village where we began working in the cotton fields. There was no money and almost no food, just cotton.

When we would go to work, the children would stay with my mother. There was a lot of sickness—malaria was common. We lived in a barracks with a lot of other adults and children. There was a little bread to eat and not much else. One kilogram of bread cost 150 rubles. Officials would distribute the bread, one-half kilo for a worker and 100 grams for a child per day. Because they couldn't stand the conditions, a lot of people committed suicide. Cotton was needed for the army, but the people who worked in the fields had nothing. The soil was so poor that only cotton, no vegetables, would grow there.

Just about every family lost a relative from illness or starvation—a child, a parent, a brother. Almost everyone ended up bloated from malnutrition. I was young and strong, and because my husband would save some money from his soldier's pay and send it to me, our family was able to survive. My husband's brother lived in Moscow and also would send a little money. But still the children were bloated from malnutrition.

During the war Mendel served on the railroad. He was near Leningrad during the blockade. His job was working with explosives. He was part of a special group that would go into occupied territory and explode bridges and roads so that the enemy couldn't use them. Right after the war he came home very, very sick. He was not tortured or wounded in the fighting, but on his return he began to suffer from a skin disease; his skin was peeling off. The conditions they lived in were the cause; they didn't take their clothes off for months or bathe or eat properly. There were a lot of people who died not because of bombs or mines but because of disease.

On our journey back to Gomel we traveled in cattle cars. The trip took almost a year, and by the time we reached home, it was winter. We arrived home in February 1945, three months before the war was over, but we had left Uzbekistan in 1944. We were traveling with my sister's family, and my sister became very sick, with a temperature of 104 degrees. We had to leave her in Moscow because they couldn't figure out what kind of disease she had. So, including her children, ten people of our family were left in my care. Raisa had broken her leg and had to stay in the hospital, and we had no food or money. On top of that, when Mendel returned he was very sick and could not work for a year.

A Strange Reversal

When we reached Gomel we found that our house had been blown up and we were homeless. Many other people arrived home to the same situation. Our family ended up living in the kitchen of a neighbor's house. We were on the ground floor and had to keep a blanket over the door because winter in Russia is terribly cold. We also had a blanket over the door to separate us from the others living in the house.

During this terribly cold winter, my father died of starvation in 1945. Sitting in the kitchen without any food, one day he just collapsed and died. My sister eventually got well and returned to Gomel. She helped me to buy a cow, and with that we survived. We had milk but no food, no clothes, and my husband was very ill. A year later, when he recovered, he returned to the woodworking factory though he could not do manual labor. After the war he had to walk about six miles in all kinds of weather to get to the factory. Then the factory gave him a horse so he could ride to work.

Five years later we moved into our rebuilt home. Before the war, the whole house had been ours, but now there was one more family with us. The people whose home we had stayed in helped us rebuild the house, which cost a lot of money. Although the man helped us, we did most of the work. This other family was to get half of the house, and the other half was to be ours. But this family, Jewish people also, claimed the house and gave us just one room. There were four children in their family and two adults. They had a boy who had been shot in the war and had lost a leg.

All in all, there were some big problems. They cheated us, and we were very unhappy. From 1950 on, the five of us lived in a single room. I felt horrible because I was left illiterate and couldn't do much. Those years were horrible.

A Dream of Music

I always dreamed of having a piano for my daughters. I felt it would be good for their education. My oldest daughter had a very good voice, and the musical training would give all three a good background.

My fifteen-year-old daughter went with my sister to Bobruisk to buy a used piano for 2,000 rubles (about $30 in today's money). It was a lot of money at that time but not an extraordinary sum, just a lot for a family where the husband had been sick in bed for a year. I wasn't employed. My sister paid for it, and gradually over time I paid her back. The piano came from Germany, brought to Russia by people who probably took it from an abandoned home. After the war many people brought things back that way.

My daughters all studied the piano and eventually were able to study music at the university. They all became teachers.

When the children grew up it got a little easier for us. Fira went to work every day. I was already helping out a little; we had a big garden. And the children went on for college educations.

Fira studied music; she had a beautiful voice. So she set off for Minsk though, as she was a Jew, it was difficult for her, but she finished her studies anyway. My middle daughter, Clara, set off for Leningrad and attended the university. She also learned to sew. She finished her studies with gold honors medals. She was very capable, and she worked very hard. She died when she was thirty-seven years old. She died "under the knife." The doctor was responsible for her death.

Mendel worked until 1965 and died in 1970. Our house was demolished in 1982, and I got a nice apartment where I lived alone for the six years before we left the country.

The Dilemma of Trying to Maintain the Tradition

If I hadn't been Jewish, obviously life would have been easier. My children were very talented. They always wanted to go to the university and wanted to go on for advanced degrees. They wanted to study and be learned people. Because they were Jewish their opportunities were limited.

I wanted to maintain the Jewish traditions, and this I did as long as it was possible. For a while we could get meat from a *shochet* in another town and would stand in big lines just to get a chicken. Then he died around 1975; there was no one left who could perform kosher slaughtering. From then on I had no meat on the table, only vegetables and fruit. Though I was unable to get kosher meat or matzah on Pesach, still I tried to observe as best I could.

There were people in another town who made matzah illegally, and sometimes we were able to get some. Some people even made the matzah at night in their own homes and would distribute some to the other Jews in the neighborhood.

Unfortunately, I could not pass the Jewish traditions and language on to my children because it was persecuted. It was laughed at. It causes me much pain that my forty-nine-year-old daughter cannot say a word of Yiddish. She understands everything but cannot speak the language. My husband and I always spoke Yiddish, but the children didn't because they were afraid, afraid of being persecuted.

I'm Jewish because I was born that way, and that's the way it should be. I'm from a very religious family. I think that Jews should continue to be Jewish and try very hard to follow Jewish law, to study as much as they can. I derived my strength from my love of my children and the family. I just wanted to keep them together. And I carry in my heart the hope that for them things will be better, that they will have a better life than I did.

In Chicago, last year my grandson Mikhail started to attend Jewish school, and at the age of sixteen willingly asked on his own to be circumcised because he "wanted to be a Jew." I was impressed and very surprised that this young boy made this decision. I was very worried about him, that at his age something might

Zelig Michlin, father of Tsilia Michlin Goldin, born
1876; *schochet, mohel,* and *cantor.* Picture taken
pre-1930. He died of starvation in the winter of
1945.

Mendel (Mikhail) Goldin, born in Gomel 1899;
died in 1970. Picture taken about age 19.

Yanina Estrina and Kim Nayman on their wedding day in Gomel, July 30, 1983.

Tsilia Michlin, born near Bobruisk in 1908, photographed at about age 25.

Yanina's mother, Clara, on the right, with her sister, Fira. Photo taken about 1961.

go wrong, but everything went well. He doesn't know any Yiddish words, but he has a Jewish heart.

YANINA ESTRINA NAYMAN
Passage to Dignity and Pride

Caught up in the necessities of daily life, Yanina, twenty-nine, is neither encumbered nor driven by the past. Legends and lore passed on by her elders were absorbed when she was a child and perhaps transformed as things can be in a child's mind, but the essence remains. The most painful memory is the death of her mother, who, when Yanina was thirteen, died under the knife of an inept abortionist.

She is quick to point out, however, that a loving, supportive family sustained her as she matured, even as an adult when she had to contend with a crisis that most would consider the stuff of a futuristic nightmare.

Neither her father, a physics teacher, nor Yanina knew what had occurred when the Geiger counter suddenly began sounding off rapidly in her father's classroom. At the moment he called to warn her, Yanina, the mother of a child under two, was caught up in meeting her institute studies deadline. Her dilemma, to complete her class work or flee with her daughter Katya, was almost unbearable. She managed to get through the crisis, and with her husband Kim, determined to emigrate no matter what the sacrifice.

Four years later, at the time of the interview, the Nayman apartment, immaculate and orderly, reflects Yanina's energy and sense of purpose. Though the furnishings are the castoffs of others, she has painstakingly restored them.

Katya's adjustment has been rapid. Her mother had taught her to read a little Russian. Now even before starting first grade, she has taught herself to read English. Today, in the family musical tradition, she studies ballet.

The friendship of two American families means a great deal to Yanina, as does the opportunity to learn more about being Jewish in a land of religious tolerance. Here even the Orthodox Jews, whose unfamiliar ways she can respect without wishing to conform to them herself, are free to practice their beliefs with dignity and pride.

While attempting to master English, earn a living, and first learn the ropes of day-to-day life in Chicago, Yanina was also preoccupied with the process of bringing over from Gomel nine members of her family. The phone had rung and she was (speaking transatlantic) hearing anxiously that their name seemed to have been overlooked.

Countless phone calls and letters later, Yanina has succeeded. She and her husband Kim not only assumed the debt of bringing the family over but also the inconvenience of housing a crowd in a small apartment until apartments for the new arrivals can be found. The joyful reunion is their ultimate reward.

Life Was Good

When I was growing up in Gomel, it was good. I had very good parents who loved me very much and always paid attention to me and to my needs. I have a brother who is eighteen years old now. He is still in Gomel with our father.

My father teaches physics and astronomy. In Russia there are only public schools, and all grades from first to tenth are in one school. My father taught in the eighth, ninth, and tenth grades—the older children.

My mother was an engineer in a candy, sweets, and cookies factory. She was responsible for keeping the machinery running. It was a hard job considering all of her family duties, eight hours a day. I was in kindergarten and then elementary school, and my grandmother and grandfather on my mother's side, and my grandmother on my father's side, all helped out too. I was the only granddaughter.

Family History

I grew up knowing my grandmother—my father's mother—who had her own house in Gomel. When I was born, my grandmother was already retired, but I know that she had been a salesclerk in a food store. Her husband died much younger. She often talks about her husband, about how he loved her and how he was a very good husband and that when he died in the war, she never got married again.

On my mother's side, my grandmother didn't work. She had three daughters, and you could say she worked at home. My grandfather was in the army during the war. He was very ill and it was difficult for him to work. He worked a little in a factory, something with wood. I never knew exactly what he did because he was already retired when I was old enough to understand.

And my mother's grandfather, my great-grandfather, had lived in Bobruisk. He did the circumcisions on the newborn Jewish boys. In my house there were not many Jewish traditions; my parents and grandparents knew very little Yiddish or the other traditions. But my Grandmother Tsilia was born into a religious family, and she always kept kosher. She had separate dishes, and she fasted on Yom Kippur.

What They Told of the Second World War and Afterward

During the war, my grandparents on both sides were evacuated. Grandmother Tsilia was in Uzbekistan, and my father went with his mother to Siberia, which is very far away and very cold. Once my father went out, maybe to look for firewood. He was young and got lost. For a long time they couldn't find him, and because he was out so long he froze some of his fingers. He didn't lose them, but they don't look the same as the others. He still went on to become a mathematician and a physicist. He can do anything.

Family Stories

My mother studied the cello, but she was sick often, and the instrument was quite heavy, so eventually she stopped. But her two sisters had advanced musical educations. My Aunt Raisa taught conducting, choir, and singing at the music college in Gomel, and my Aunt Fira, the oldest sister, who is now in Israel, was a music teacher. She is now retired. My mother graduated with a silver medal. My grandmother thinks she deserved a gold medal but that because of her Jewish nationality she received a silver medal. But still, that's very good—all A's.

Then she took and passed the entrance exams at the Leningrad Institute of Food Technology. In a big city there are better universities, better institutes, better education. She studied there five years, and then she came back to Gomel and found a job. She was an assistant supervisor of a food shop in a piston factory. I don't remember much of what my mother was like. I was just a kid when she died.

Living Conditions

When I was a one-and-a-half years old, my parents bought an apartment. Basically, it had two little rooms, living room and bedroom with a small kitchen. And I lived in this apartment until I came here to the United States. In Russia, getting an apartment is a big problem. When I was thirteen my mother died and my father remarried, and he went to live in his wife's apartment and left our apartment for me.

But many of my young friends live with their parents, and it can create many problems for both children and parents. It is very expensive to rent an apartment, and young people usually can't do it because they get paid very little.

I lived on the fourth floor of a five-story building. Identical buildings were all around. Gomel was almost destroyed during World War II, by bombs and because the Germans occupied the city. In the city there were many one-floor houses, but later there were some tall buildings but not like in Chicago! I think maybe the highest was twenty floors. But the five-story ones are more typical.

Growing Up Jewish in Gomel

I knew that I was Jewish when I was very young because I remember one time, when I was maybe seven or eight years old. One boy called me this name—you know, in Russia they call you a bad word—*zhid.* I've never forgotten this. So I always knew that I was Jewish, different from others. There were many other Jewish children around, but I knew that Russians, or Byelorussians, did not like me. Of course, there were conversations at home about these matters. I don't remember exactly what was said, but I remember that my grandmother always said she did not want her granddaughters to marry Russians or Byelorussians. I think almost every Jewish family feels the same way. They don't want their children to marry a non-Jew. I heard it from both grandmothers and from my father.

While growing up, I was expected to do some things at home. And when my mother died, my father and I took over all the housework. My brother was only three and a half at that time; he went to preschool then.

When my mother was alive, I remember holidays we'd spend together. Our family was close. My mother had two sisters, and they were very close to each other, so we saw each other quite often.

Jewish holidays were celebrated, not by my parents but by my grandparents. We had matzah, but in the last few years it was very difficult because there was not even one temple or synagogue around. So if you wanted matzah, you had to go to Moscow or another big city and buy it. It was very expensive. But my grandparents sent some to us so we had it. I don't ever remember being at a seder. But in my grandmother's house she observed the traditions.

Aside from being called a bad name, I don't think I knew anything about being Jewish. I didn't know any history of the Jewish people or anything like that. We didn't have any Jewish books or films about Jewish people, like here.

At work everybody knew I was Jewish. And I would say it with dignity so that they wouldn't see that I was afraid that I'm Jewish, so they wouldn't say bad things about Jews behind our backs. Sometimes people would say bad things about another Jew. So I would say, "I'm Jewish," then they would feel respect and fall silent and say, "No, no, no, you're a good Jew." And then they wouldn't say things like that in front of me.

Here in Chicago my husband and I saw a film about Jewish people. We were very glad, but when we saw a film about the Holocaust, we cried. I don't remember exactly how I learned about the Holocaust, but in Russia people knew about this. There wasn't much in the history books, but both my parents and I knew about it. We knew about how Jewish people had it very bad during World War II, but about early history we didn't know anything.

A Musical Education

I wanted to become a teacher, but I don't remember when I decided to do this. I attended two schools, music school and regular public school. Then for four years I went to a music college, and then I went to the institute. I studied the piano—we had our own. My parents bought it for me when I was six. It was a small spinet, made in the Ukraine.

I started music lessons when I was six. My aunt, my mother's sister, taught me. I practiced a lot and liked it. I practiced sometimes one hour, sometimes two, but at other times I was lazy.

I had no trouble getting the education I wanted. I always studied very well. In Russia, the highest grade you can get is a five—*pyatorka*. I always got fives. I remember one time the teacher gave me a four, and I thought that it was because I was Jewish. But I can't say that it made any trouble for me.

My Mother's Sudden Death

My mother had not been ill before she died. You won't be able to believe what it was—it was after an abortion! It wasn't from an infection. It was a bad doctor—I don't know how to say it in English—he made a hole. I was not at home; I was at summer camp, and they didn't tell me exactly what happened. But I know that after the operation she was alive but she could not eat, and she was very, very ill, and then she died. They came and got me at camp and took me and told me.

Many women got abortions in Russia back then. I didn't hear of other deaths from abortions. But I knew that many women had more than one abortion during their lives. Of course, there are no contraceptives in Russia. I know that for my mother it was her first abortion.

In Russia, all medical procedures are paid for by the state. Upon death of a parent, they pay a pension for the children, very little, but it depends on wages earned. I remember that for my brother and me, my mother's pension was maybe ninety rubles, maybe less. When I was eighteen, it stopped for me, and they paid only thirty-six rubles a month for my brother.

The Wedding Celebration

I met my future husband when I was twenty-one, and I knew him about five months before we got married. My grandmother lived near his mother, and they introduced us. Our wedding—oh, it was big and nice! In Russia, we sign a marriage certificate. This takes place at a municipal organization that keeps records about all marriages, divorces, births, and deaths. You come there with relatives and friends, and the special woman in charge says some words and congratulates you, and you sign some papers. That's it. The woman is something like a judge, but not really. And then, our parents and my husband rented a big hall and cafe, and we had a big party. We had many relatives come from other cities, so we had about 140 people. It was very expensive.

We didn't get gifts in Russia, but in more recent years people mainly gave money because they didn't know what newlyweds wanted, and anyway, there was nothing in the shops.

We didn't know when we got married that we would want to leave the country.

But then we saw that life there was not getting any better; it was just getting worse and worse. And then there was Chernobyl.

The Chernobyl Disaster

My father—it was lucky that he heard it. At school they had a Geiger counter, and he called me. You know, it happened on a Saturday and on the following Monday he called me from work and said, "Yanna, don't let Katya go outside for a long time. And wash her arms and face several times, more often than usual." Of course, he didn't know how bad it really was. He just saw the counter that was clicking very quickly; before Chernobyl, it was just a slow click. The accident happened the twenty-sixth of April, 1986, but the government didn't tell us anything. We didn't know anything. They called people and told them to go to the May Day parade and had children go to the parade and stand out in the sun. I remember it was very hot. My father told the children to go to the parade too, and they stayed almost two hours under the sun.

Then, maybe May 3, they told us Tunnel Two had an accident, but that it wasn't so bad, that we could stay in Gomel, and everything would be OK, and that it wasn't dangerous for children. But it was terrible! People in the government took their children and grandchildren away from Gomel, and others began to talk about this and to realize that maybe the accident was a very bad one. But who had relatives in another city? Who could leave?

That year I finished at the institute, and it was time for the examination. If I did not sit for the examination, I would lose the five years I worked in the institute. I didn't know what to do. It was terrible. And Kim, he couldn't just leave his work, and besides, we had no money to leave.

So Katya, a year-and-a-half old, stayed in my mother-in-law's house for a month, because I was in Minsk. For a whole month she didn't go outside. I called her every day, and I cried because I didn't know what to do. And the day I took the last exam, that same night I came to Gomel, got Katya, and went to Leningrad where I stayed almost two months. Then my vacation ended, and if I didn't want to lose my job, I had to go back. But after the accident, we didn't buy any milk for the whole rest of the year. We just gave Katya canned milk because they always mark on the can which factory made it. We also didn't buy any beef, because the cows eat the grass and we felt it was dangerous. Instead we ate chicken. The uncertainty was horrible.

The accident happened during the night from a Friday to a Saturday. In Chernobyl they evacuated people on Sunday. But on Saturday, officials knew, but even in this city, right next to the nuclear power station, the children were playing outside, and eating outside, and were hanging around outside!

Gomel was not evacuated at all. Some little villages near Chernobyl were evacuated, but not Gomel. How can they evacuate 500,000 people?

Now we know that it was very bad and that it is getting worse, because we got a letter from our parents and they say the government is paying the people in

Gomel extra money so they can pay for health care. Still, there is no food in the shops. And all fruit and vegetables became radioactive.

Emigration: A Process

We didn't plan to leave Russia, not right away, until after Chernobyl. It was difficult to leave; we had to have an invitation from Israel or America to leave Russia. But we didn't have one. In 1988, my relatives got an invitation for themselves and then for us. My Aunt Raisa, my mother's sister, got an invitation for us from Israel. We received the invitation in December, and then in May we left Gomel. My aunt also lives in Chicago now.

When we got the invitation, we went to OVIR and we went through paperwork and documents, and our parents had to write that they gave us permission, and so on. It was OK.

We took a few clothes, and we sent one box of books to HIAS in Vienna, and they sent it on to New York and then Chicago for us. We knew we needed pillows and blankets and some clothes. When you fly, there are restrictions on what you can take, and we knew that in Italy there would be restrictions. From Italy to the U.S.A., you can only have two bags per person. So since we were three persons, we could have only six bags.

In Transit: Destination Unknown

When we arrived in Vienna, we knew that we wanted to go to the United States but we didn't know if it would happen. Everybody has a choice, then it depends on whether you receive refugee status from the American Embassy in Italy.

Refugee status means a lot. Without this status I think only a few people can get here. Unless you have rich relatives who can support you, you won't receive help if you can't find a job, and relatives can help only so much. Of course, many Russians don't have any relatives here at all. We didn't, for instance. We are the first from our family, so for us it meant everything.

Refugee Status: "Like a Lottery"

When we were in Italy, we didn't understand anything. You might receive refugee status or you might not; it's like a lottery. Nobody really knew, almost every Jew was in the same situation. In Italy many were refused by the American Embassy. Nobody really understood how the Americans determined if you were a refugee or not. We filled out many applications, had interviews. Some people who were refused refugee status by the United States went on to Israel; others stayed to wait. Sometimes they would reapply, and sometimes a second time they'd be refused refugee status. Some people waited until they were the last immigrants in Italy. I know one woman who stayed in Italy ten months. She was refused for ten months, and then finally she came to the United States. The Joint Distribution Committee was willing to pay for her stay in Italy!

Our Name Is Called

In Vienna, we were met in the train station and asked, "Israel or the United States?" Then we spent two weeks in Vienna, after which we were sent to Italy where, all in all, we spent almost two months. There we were scheduled for an interview at the American Embassy. At the embassy we spoke with the consul. After a week, we heard, "Nayman, you will fly on the twenty-fourth of July," and that was it!

We were able to get refugee status. In our case, they didn't pay any attention to Chernobyl. I'm not sure why they gave refugee status to us. They even bought us tickets. We were met in New York and spent the night there, and then we took a plane to Chicago.

When we landed in Chicago, we were met by the people who had signed for us. They had relatives in Gomel, and so we asked them to sponsor us; they had been here only six months themselves. It was difficult for them, but they did it. They met us in the airport with a sign "Nayman," because we had never seen each other before. And we stayed at their house only six days before we rented an apartment and began to live here on our own. By the time we got to America, it was financially very difficult. When we had been here a month, Jewish Family and Community Service came and gave us a check and helped us. They said that our guarantor would let us stay in their house for a month. But we could not stay with these people that long. They were five people, three of them children, in a very small apartment. Still we were very grateful to them for keeping us six days.

For three months we received money only from Jewish people, nothing from the government. For three months we received money for rent and food. They also gave us Medicaid and a counselor, as well as the I-94 visa that gave us work permits, the right to get green cards.

When we were in Italy we didn't have $1,500 a ticket for each person, so now we are repaying HIAS. We repay them a little amount every month.

Realities: The Best and Worst

There were times when I was crying. With refugee status, I think that because we received help only from Jewish Family and Community Service [JFCS] and from the Jewish Fund, we didn't get assistance from the U.S. government. For the first few months we received Medicaid through the JFCS. We use Mount Sinai Hospital, which is very far away.

I have only one wish right now—to find a job. Because if you have a job here, then everything's OK. Of course, there are some problems, but you can live very well.

My husband is so-so about his job at the kosher sausage factory. It is hard work. He's not afraid because it's hard but because there's no future. He's young, and imagine the idea of working until retirement just washing meat! He is the only one in our household who works. He hopes I can find a job so he can go study. He wants to study English. In Gomel he worked in a shoe factory. There's no real shoe factory in Chicago. Only a little one, where they make ballet shoes. You can't earn enough money even for an apartment. So now he has two jobs—at the meat factory and delivering pizza. But at least each week he has one day off.

I think the worst time for me in Russia was when my mother died. The second bad time was when we first came here. We slept on the floor. Nobody called; the phone was silent. I cried because I missed my family; I felt so lonely. But luckily my grandmother came ten days after we got here.

Now I've finished a course and am looking for a job. I worry that I've spent $4,000 on computer training and won't find anything. I've already sent out eighty resumés!

Arrangements for Those Left Behind

We are making arrangements for my brother, my father and his wife, and other members of the family. I will go to the embassy the twenty-fourth of October. Then the embassy will send us an application, and we'll send it on to Washington. Now my relatives have a case number and are in the American computer. Of course, now we will have to pay for them, and this takes a lot of money. We have nine people, so probably we will have to pay around $12,000. We don't know how we will manage it, but we will.

Learning to Be Jewish in the Country of Immigrants

My grandmother had to raise her children without any Jewish education. My generation had even less—nothing.

I want Katya to know that she's Jewish and to be happy about it, to have dignity. We felt this way in Russia. Sometimes my family would discuss it, knowing that many famous people are Jewish, that there's a pride in it. But we really didn't know anything about Jewish traditions and customs. Then we came here, and now we have two Jewish families who are our friends; they are very good friends, and they are helping us to learn Jewish traditions. I don't want her to have just Jewish friends, especially here in America with lots of nationalities and immigrants. It's a country of immigrants, so she has to learn to play with everybody. But, of course, I want her to marry someone Jewish.

2

HEROIC SERVICE
TO A GOVERNMENT
THAT CHOSE TO FORGET

THE GINSBURG/FRIEDGAN FAMILY

DR. NAUM GINSBURG, a cardiologist, and Dr. Paulina Shmilkina Ginsburg, a pediatrician, met and married in Kiev in 1934 when both were medical students. Their recollections portray a child's view of a *pogrom* in her town and the financial upheaval following the Revolution. He recounts the Soviet army's disarray at the outset of World War II from the view of a young chief of a medical unit. She describes the privations of a young mother evacuated to the East. From the Revolution to the Chernobyl disaster, their narratives reveal the power of their personal relationship, their devotion to work and country, and the impact of events of their time on educated Jews.

Their older son Isaac and his wife Lyuba recall a childhood in which anti-Semitism becomes more entrenched and Isaac lives through the trauma of losing his job. Lyuba recalls painful childhood encounters with anti-Semitism during World War II. Their daughter Anna and her husband Alex, seeing a limited future, led the exodus from Kharkov. Mark, eleven, fourth generation of a remarkable family, is in process between two cultures.

DR. PAULINA SHMILKINA GINSBURG
A Plan "To Become Something"

Paulina Shmilkina Ginsburg remembers the time when her family owned a home and business. History has documented how soon after the Bolsheviks seized power, the government confiscated private property and businesses, and in the aftermath, spasmodic violence erupted. The young parents and their five-year-old fled from pogroms *that struck their Ukrainian village. Impoverished, the family's best hope for the future resided in the child, Paulina. She was "to become something." For her that meant a medical career. Her father, forced to work on a* kolkhoz *in order to allow his daughter an education, vented his frustration by labeling the government* burvasy, *an insult coined of Yiddish and Russian, meaning people without shoes, or an inept government.*

Years of mandatory separation from her husband Naum before, during, and after the war exacted a toll on Paulina's health and spirits. They were reunited during a miraculous meeting in a train station in 1944 and, later, on an idyllic two-year family sojourn in Soviet-occupied Germany. The return to Kiev in 1948 was marred when she found she must share a kitchen with a hostile neighbor who incited the KGB against the family.

The former honor student at the Medical Institute of Kiev ingenuously charts the growth of Soviet anti-Semitism, revealing its effect on her career and that of Naum, a highly decorated Soviet Army medical officer who attended the military top brass. When their son Isaac is ready to enroll at the institute in Kharkov, their home from 1953 on, his hopes for a medical career have been dashed. Later he is fired from his military college post during a wave of anti-Semitic fervor, a reaction to Jewish emigration and the Israeli Six-Day War.

Whatever her other concerns, today Paulina has one great sorrow. In 1988 she and Naum, their sons Isaac and Boris, and their wives and families were poised to go. But when they received the emigration documents, Boris and his family were excluded. For this twist of fate there is no accounting, except perhaps the shoddy work of some burvasy.

Since the interview, the retired couple visited Israel to confirm the excellent adjustment Boris and his family have made. For they too live in a free country.

Earliest Memories

I was born in Zvenigorodka near Kiev in 1913, but I remember nothing about my birthplace because when I was four years old we moved to Boguslav. My father had been born there and because of his business stayed there. Until we moved, he came to visit us or we went from Zvenigorodka to visit him. It was not far.

Before the Revolution my father was an owner of a big store and we owned a house. But after the Revolution, the government took the store from us and the house, too. After that we rented a little room.

Father had owned a flour business. The flour came from the mill to my father's store, and he sold it. When the government took away this store, they took everything else away as well. At the time *kolkhozy* hadn't been organized yet. Father then worked with some kind of private commercial dealings—I don't even know how to describe it exactly. He traveled a lot, to Moscow. He sold things, like flour. He became a salesman and bought in one place and sold in another, where he had contacts with people. He bought the flour from peasants and transported it to Moscow, to Kiev, and other big cities, and sold it there.

The Horrors after the Revolution

One of my earliest memories is a *pogrom* in the village of Boguslav. *Pogroms* began soon after the Revolution after we joined my father in Boguslav in 1919. I was five and a half. We suffered, of course, because the violence was mainly against Jews. Some of the Russian population helped us. One man, Krashchinkov, who rented the first floor of the house to my father, saved us many times. He would hide us in the basement.

At this time in the Ukraine there were several groups, like gangsters: *Mosno, Zelyonij, Pekljura*, anarchist-nationalists. They tore up apartments, stole things, and killed people. They burned the houses.

On the village square I could see the bodies of people who had been hanged. Jewish people, hanged just because they were Jewish. I was so afraid I couldn't sleep. My parents took me away so I wouldn't see any more of those terrible sights. When the violence intensified, Papa ran with us and we hid in little villages.

When I was six years old, I started the *gymnaziya*. Then the *gymnaziya* became a school, and I went to school. My grandmother, my father's mother, Sima, lived with Father, Mother, and me at the time. My younger sister was born after my grandmother died, and she was named after her.

I knew when I finished grade school, I must continue to study. I was supposed to become "something" in the family. I remember how later the Soviets took everything away, and Papa became, basically, nobody. Because Papa didn't have any kind of specialty, he had to go work at the *kolkhoz* in Boguslav. These were organized in the early years of Soviet government, for people who had nothing. They made everyone collective farmers.

So he went to work as a collective farmer, and he got a document of proof of this, and that's why I could study. Then in 1927 I left the village for Kiev. Before I went to medical school, I was required to perform some kind of labor to be allowed further study. I needed a paper that proved I worked somewhere, since I wasn't from a family of farmers or workers. So when I was fourteen years old, I went to work in a knitwear factory for about one year. I worked at a weaving machine with spools and needles and spun thread. After that I had earned the document that permitted me to go to medical school. In 1927 I arrived in Kiev. I had finished school, then worked, and gone on to medical school. I moved three times. First I lived with my aunt and uncle, Father's brother, next I lived one year in the dormitory of the medical school, then my father left his work at the *kolkhoz* and came to Kiev, so I lived with my father. He came to work at a big factory that made things for the military, for ships.

Matzah Was Illegal

When I was growing up, we spoke Russian though my mother spoke good Yiddish. My grandmother and grandfather were very religious. My father also performed religious services in the home, even in the 1940s.

When we were still allowed to celebrate the holidays in the 1920s, we traveled to the home of my mother's parents in Zvenigorodka. We would have matzah for Pesach, and when my grandfather asked the Four Questions, I replied in Yiddish. But in Kiev there was no matzah, not in 1927. It had become illegal. In Boguslav, it was also illegal, so my mother baked matzah at home. Even in recent years it was illegal in Kharkov. People there received matzah from Riga or Moscow. Nobody could go to the store and buy it.

Medical School, Marriage, and Honors

When I started medical school, there was no problem that I was Jewish. It was normal, and I was treated like the other students. About 20 percent of the class was Jewish. I don't remember what the population of Jews in the area was. It didn't matter to me. At the institute there were a lot in our group. Teachers treated us alike, and I felt that I had the same opportunities. I graduated with honors.

I went into pediatrics because I like children. It was also easier to get into the pediatrics department than in some of the other departments. The competition was about eight students to one spot. There was a better chance, it was a surer thing, so I applied there. I worked in the medical school. In the medical school there were two specialties, pediatrics and gynecology. I chose pediatrics.

My friends were mixed, some Russian and some Jewish, but mostly Jewish people. We weren't political.

I was already in my first year of institute when I met Naum. It was in 1929. My parents had moved to a new apartment. Naum's relatives were my parents' neighbors, so they met first. It was just a coincidence, but Naum likes to say he was encircled! We decided to get married after about two years.

Married Life under a *Burvasy* Government

I never joined *Komsomol*. I didn't think anything at all about socialism because I simply didn't know anything different. My father, however, spoke very negatively about it. He called the government *burvasy*—people who have no shoes, a bad government. We didn't have enough money, and we lived in one room. The apartment had more rooms, but about four families lived in the apartment. My father, mother, my sister, and I all lived together at this time.

Naum and I got married December 2, 1934. There wasn't any kind of wedding party. We went to ZAGS and signed the papers, and in the evening we went to the movies. Then Naum went home to his place, and I went home to mine. We didn't have our own apartment. After some time passed, my aunt, who lived in the same apartment as my family, felt sorry for us. "This isn't right that the husband and wife don't live together," she said. And she invited us to live with her in her room.

Naum finished his studies at the Medical Institute of Kiev in 1936, and I finished in 1938. At that time he was sent to work in a little town called Stary Oskol, and after I graduated, I went with my son to where my husband was. Isaac had been born in Kiev while I was a student, in the hospital where Naum's uncle worked. Although we were treated like everybody else, Naum, an A student, was allowed to come and go at the hospital any time. He says, "We gave birth together." I remained in the hospital seven days, and afterward my mother and father took care of Isaac. By the time I graduated, Naum had become chief of the hospital in Stary Oskol, and that's why I was given medical orders that allowed me to go to the same place.

We were young, so everything seemed good. Things didn't seem so hard, though this wasn't a good time for the country. In 1937 one of the biggest processes to kill people began. Then everything got bad. There weren't really any Jews who remained around us. We left Stary Oskol and lived with my family in Kiev.

Prewar Anti-Semitism

Because Naum was a good student, he should have been able to continue his education. But at that time, when the government was increasing pressure on the Jews, he wasn't allowed to get his Ph.D., and he had to go to work in another city. Suddenly equal education for Jews was changing. I joined him in Stary Oskol in 1938, and we were together until 1940. We came back to Kiev and he began to work on his Ph.D., which takes three years in the Soviet Union. He was working with a famous medical professor in Kiev, Dr. Gulovits. At that time we didn't have an apartment. We lived with my parents.

In June 1941, just after the war began, Naum enlisted. I had been practicing medicine. On July 5, 1941, Naum accompanied us to the station: Isaac and me, as well as my parents and sister. We all boarded a cattle train heading east, but we didn't know where. Naum stayed behind to serve in the army. The trip was dangerous. Frequently we would get out and hide to avoid the firing, then board again; this went on for the entire journey. Finally we reached Stalingrad, which is now Volgograd. All the people on this train were herded into the sports stadium with other refugees. We were there no less then two days. My sister was married by then, and she was pregnant. We sold everything that we had with us so we could buy some bread.

Meanwhile, my sister's husband went into the army, too. He had been a student in teachers' college but hadn't graduated yet. So he joined Naum and worked as an assistant to him.

When we went to Stalingrad, I had to take charge of the family. I was making the decisions. My father was horribly depressed at that time. After two days we left by ship for Astrakhan, on the Volga River by the Caspian Sea. We traveled very slowly. When we arrived in Astrakhan, I set off to find work and a place to live. After some time, Naum learned where we were through my uncle in Moscow, who received letters from us. People who served in the war were given a certain document for supporting the family. So Naum was able to send us this document for our support.

We stayed in Astrakhan until the German army came to Stalingrad in 1942. Then Astrakhan was bombed horribly. By ship we again escaped to the east—to Uralsk, and then to Guryev, also on the Caspian Sea. We were there three weeks. Then we went to Bashkiryev, to the little village of Rayevka near Ufa, because at that time my mother's sisters lived there. This is an autonomous region of Russia, the Bashkirian Autonomous Republic. We lived here about one year with my aunts. We had very little room.

We were on a *kolkhoz*. One aunt worked as an accountant/bookkeeper so we could survive. I wanted to practice medicine but couldn't because they didn't have a medical office, but I did some work and was paid in food. Then we moved to Buguruslan, where I found work at the clinic there.

The time we spent in Buguruslan is a bad memory. I was terribly upset. I worried a lot. My son was sick with bronchitis. The work there was hard—there was a lot of horrible work without let-up. My sister had already had her baby, and we lived together. There wasn't enough money or food.

In addition to what I said before, at that time I began to feel anti-Semitism. I couldn't imagine the end of the war would ever come.

A Miraculous Meeting

In 1944 I became very sick. My sister and her husband, who now lived in nearby Sorochinsk, decided to send me to Moscow for medical consultation. I was to go to Sorochinsk first. That night, along the way, I had to change trains in Kuybyshev. The Kuybyshev station was so crowded with military personnel and civilians I couldn't even buy a ticket. I sat there for twenty-four hours and waited. I kept staring at all the military officers in the station. At last I couldn't help telling my feelings to an old lady sitting next me. "It would be so nice to find my husband here," I said. The old lady very quickly set me straight. "In reality such a thing can't happen."

I put the thought out of my mind and went to get a drink of water, when suddenly someone behind me came and put his arms around me. I was terrified!

Then in another moment I realized it was Naum! I really couldn't believe what had happened. But it was very nice that it could!

After I recovered from the surprise, we set off together for my sister's and I learned how the meeting came about. Naum had come to Buguruslan on leave, but he had only ten days—not enough time to wait for my return. In fact, the night I first arrived at the station in Kuybyshev, Naum passed through Kuybyshev on his way to Buguruslan. There, when he learned that I was on my way to Sorochinsk, he went to find Isaac at school. Naum surprised him there. Then he took Isaac and my mother, and they went to Kuybyshev where he found me still waiting at the station.

We were together for just a few days, and then we went to Moscow. I stayed there for a consultation in the hospital. Naum went back to the army. The doctors in Moscow diagnosed a problem, but it was a mistake, considering what we learned later. So they didn't perform surgery or treat my condition. It was stomach ulcers.

In 1945, when the war ended, Naum reappeared in Buguruslan and accompanied us to Kiev. My father didn't work by this time, but my sister and I worked. We all lived together. Naum very much wanted to continue working for his Ph.D. but was unable to receive permission to leave the army at that time. He was assigned to serve in Weimar with the occupying Soviet force.

My father was very sick with high blood pressure. From the time of the Revolution on, he no longer felt like a free person. Life for him was very hard. He was sixty-eight years old. His blood pressure was very high, and there was not enough medication.

I went to work in Kiev at the Kiev Regional Children's Polyclinic and Hospital. I was there about a year before we went to Germany. I saw children there who were just exhausted, who had various children's illnesses. But sometimes there were children who came from other cities who were malnourished. In Astrakhan there had been a high death rate from the measles, because the children couldn't acclimatize.

Reunited in Occupied Germany

When he got to Germany, Naum received permission, as most people did, for the family to join him. He was in Weimar already working as the chief of a hospital when we arrived in May 1946. For us it was a much better and easier life, because there was food and a nice place to stay. Not just an apartment but a house! Even after the war we didn't have such a nice apartment back home as we had in Germany. A famous antifascist doctor had lived there who had killed himself during Hitler's time. His widow lived on the first floor, and we lived on the second floor. Her children lived in Argentina. The *frau* wasn't Jewish but she too was antifascist, a beautiful lady.

We were happy because we were together after a long time apart and now the war was over. Also, I felt my husband's support. Before *I* was the support, and now I felt very free. Many times we had been separated, so now we were together and didn't think about such matters as political problems. It was a second honeymoon.

I did not feel anti-Semitism from the German people who communicated with me. Their behavior was good.

The house we lived in had three levels. The professor's widow lived on the first level. We lived on the second level; on the third level lived two women, one German, one Russian who worked at the hospital.

In Germany we had five rooms, a big hall, a bedroom, the children's room, a living room, a *kabinet* for my husband, a big kitchen, bathroom, a special room for a refrigerator. Every day I cooked. There was already furniture there. I kept it up very well. I was afraid to damage this furniture. At that time the Germans didn't have enough fuel, and when it was cold we invited the *frau* into our apartment. In Russia we had one room, and in this room was everything, and the whole family all lived in it. We had no refrigerator; we cannot compare. Even now, people who live by Soviet standards that are OK don't live as well as we did then. We remained there until the summer of 1948.

When I arrived I studied biochemistry and began working in the laboratory of the hospital as a biochemical doctor. They didn't need a pediatrician at that time. Soon I began working again and continued for a year and a half.

I trained in a hospital training laboratory in Jena, about twenty-five kilometers from Weimar. Then I worked in a clinic for children. Professor Ibrain, a very famous professor, practiced in this clinic. He interviewed me, and I knew the answers to his questions, so he knew I understood. I had studied some German, so I knew enough to communicate.

Isaac learned German because everyone else around him was German, except for a few Russian children. In Jena where we lived there were maybe three Russian children.

In Weimar there were many Russian soldiers and officers. The chief of the army and his officers stayed there. The Soviet division was located in Jena. This was at one end of the city, and we lived near Naum's hospital at the other, separate from the others. In Jena there was a school from first to fourth grade, and in Weimar from fifth to tenth grade, so Isaac went to the fourth grade in Jena. He then went to fifth grade at a Russian school in Weimar.

Boris was born August 11, 1947, in the hospital in Jena. In Germany where Boris was born, we had a separate room and he was with me. In Kiev there had been one big room where many women gave birth together at the same time. In Russia the children were kept in another room, sometimes two in one bed.

Conditions were advanced for the care of mother and child in Germany, but in the Soviet military hospital in Germany then, there were no gynecologists assigned. In that respect the care was better in Russia.

My parents and my sister stayed in Kiev. The economic situation changed, and things were very bad at that time. Even now in the Soviet Union I don't think anyone lives as Russians did after the war!

So I sent packages from Germany, and my husband sent money. After the war anti-Semitism in the Soviet Union worsened. It began in 1946, and by 1948 it was a very dangerous time for Jewish people; 1948 was the time of cosmopolitanism.

We wanted to go back to Russia because my parents and sister were there. I thought while I recovered from surgery my mother and sister would take better care of me. It was also important for us to go back to Russia and be with the family, and Naum wanted to be with his teacher in Kiev. In truth, we might have remained in Germany until the army left, because the generals liked Naum's care so much.

I had the surgery for my stomach ulcers about May 1948. Oddly enough, because of it, my husband got permission to return. He had been taking care of the generals and the military chief who didn't want to let him go back to the Soviet Union. When the chief came to see me in the hospital, I asked him for permission to go. Right then he agreed to let Naum leave.

The Kitchen and the KGB

We returned to Kiev to the same apartment, which had six rooms, to the same room. After serving in the army, Naum was allowed a second room. In these two rooms lived our family, my parents, and my sister and her husband who received a third room. They had a boy who was born during the war, in 1942, and a girl born right as we returned. My mother took care of the whole family then, the cooking, the cleaning. My sister and I both worked. She was a doctor of chemistry and worked at a clinic. We both stayed out of the kitchen!

Despite the comparative luxury we enjoyed in Weimar, it was not a problem to live together with our family. It was the other families that were difficult. There was one kitchen for everybody to use, and there was only cold running water. Another room was completely destroyed during the war. We went to a bathhouse once a week. I think that the most important thing is that two of the neighbor families had struck some sort of deal with the Germans. After the war they remained in the same apartment, and they were very anti-Semitic people. In the Soviet Union at that time, anybody could write to the KGB and say that other people were bad, and the KGB would investigate. So it was terrible and Naum began to have some problems with the KGB.

I was afraid that because the kitchen was open to everybody that someone could poison the meat. Also, my mother and I were afraid that when we went into the kitchen this one woman would begin to hit us. Her name was Eugenia Maslinikoya. She wrote many letters to the KGB, and the judge knew her but was afraid of dealing with her.

But because Naum worked in the hospital at this time, they didn't do anything, although they kept the papers on file. This continued the whole time we lived there, and that's why we left this apartment in 1953.

After the Doctors' Plot

In 1953 anti-Semitic tension was very strong, and if something was wrong or somebody thought something was wrong, they could do anything to Jewish doctors. Although the tension was very strong, I didn't have any problems. I was practicing pediatrics at the time. In Russia there are separate medical offices and hospitals. People come to the medical office and say that they don't feel very well and want to stay at home. The doctor can treat them and give them a permit to stay home. But when their health is too bad, they can be sent to the hospital with a prescription. For children it's the same thing.

"Easier to Breathe" after Stalin's Death

I was not a supervisor but a regular doctor, so I did not feel so much pressure from the government. I took care of sick children and talked with the parents, so it's not like my husband who was chief of staff. We lived separately because Naum went to Dnepropetrovsk in 1951. We moved there in 1953. It was easier to breathe after Stalin's death.

In 1954, the year my father died, we moved together to Kharkov, in the northeast Ukraine. We remained in Kharkov until 1989. Naum was unable to earn his Ph.D. until 1962, while he was chief of the therapy department. Our living conditions then were much better. In Dnepropetrovsk and in Kharkov we had two rooms in a separate apartment. We had a refrigerator now and no neighbors spying in the kitchen! After that my mother came to live with us. She took care of the family until the last two years of her life.

I continued practicing medicine in Kharkov. There I didn't feel anti-Semitism toward me personally. We didn't see anti-Semitism in the streets but would read things about it in newspapers. I didn't feel it until Isaac wanted to enter the institute in 1953. When Jewish students enter, they feel how bad it is, and their parents feel it too.

I could not work in a major hospital because of anti-Semitism. Instead I worked in the office at the polyclinic. When patients came to this office, I might give some prescriptions, and then they would go home. If they felt good after that, they did not return to the office. So I could not follow up on patient care or treat them. For doctors it is better to work in big hospitals.

Emigration and Enemies

Everyone was afraid for many years, and nobody talked about political things, because anybody could be a KGB agent. So at this time I didn't know anyone who was trying to emigrate or who was involved with dissident activities. But later, in 1973, I worked with a doctor whose niece emigrated to Israel in 1974. This doctor, her name was Brunina, had some unpleasantness after this. She shared an apartment with another family, and the husband in that family was a military officer. The officer, or maybe somebody else, told the KGB that she was listening to Radio Israel, so she had a problem with the KGB. And this doctor was held in a building by the KGB for about twelve hours. They yelled at her and threatened that if she continued listening to the radio, she would be put in jail. Afterward she was released and that was the end of it. And during the Six-Days War the Russian doctors were told that if they cared enough for Russia, they would go to Egypt and beat Israel.

Isaac listened to the radio and criticized the Soviet government. Naum didn't like it, but I let him say what he wanted. But we said that he must be very careful and not talk about it in public.

We began thinking of leaving when Isaac was fired from his job at the military college, in 1976. This is a time when people began to emigrate from the Soviet Union. Naum was very disappointed. He didn't think that could happen to Isaac. Some other professor in his college had been fired, but he couldn't imagine that it could happen to Isaac because he was in a strong position. When it happened and he couldn't find a job, Naum went to the party committee and told them. But after some time he understood that they wouldn't really help. He began to think about leaving, but he couldn't because he had been in the army a long time and not enough time had passed for them to let him go.

He did not know military secrets. He was a doctor! And Isaac couldn't leave because he had been teaching in a military college so he also was supposed to know military secrets. It was a shock for us that Isaac was fired. But after some time he began to work. Then everyone calmed down. By that time I was retired and worked part-time as a consultant.

Chernobyl and the Environment

In general, the radiation was in Kiev. Some relatives were in Kiev, so when it happened, my niece with her child came to Kharkov and lived there maybe one month. They had some tests done. All the members of the family had some tests, but they didn't feel sick. But some doctors I had worked with who went to Chernobyl had some problems with their blood. There were changes in the blood—anemia.

Of course, everybody was angry with the government. At that time people could talk publicly about it. At first the government didn't inform people. Many days later they gave information. Then there were other questions: Why did they build a nuclear power station where there was such good agriculture in the first place? Why was the construction quality so bad?

Isaac believes the cover of the reactor was not strong enough. Some parts were destroyed. But pollution in the Soviet Union is so great that maybe radiation is not the worst thing. And there are many manufacturing plants that cause strong pollution. Yes, and many other disasters. Many people in the Soviet Union know today that in the Ural Mountains in the 1950s they had a nuclear disaster like Chernobyl, but it was kept secret at the time.

Our granddaughter, Anna, said, "Let's get out of here." Isaac didn't talk much about it because he was afraid Naum was ill. Naum was very bad at that time because of a heart condition, and I was afraid to move him. But Anna and Boris, they talked about this. And Isaac also. And then Anna wrote to a friend in Israel without telling me, to send the invitation. We received the invitation in 1988, the same year my mother died.

The News, Good and Bad

It took about two months to get the visa. I had some mixed emotions. Not only did Naum not feel well, our younger son didn't receive the necessary documents. Boris was the only one in the family who didn't. Everybody else did, even the parents of Anna's husband. Then, only after some time, a friend who was in the United States brought an invitation, but it was too late and Boris couldn't come here. He had to go to Israel.

Because my son couldn't come with us, we are destroyed because we are one family. But we hope that we can be together in the future.

We made decisions. Naum didn't tell anybody he was unhappy, and I tried to make him feel better. Anna saw it and so she cried, and when he saw that, he understood that he must be strong, and so he became strong because he didn't want to destroy our plans. He became braver for the sake of Anna.

An Assessment: Past, Present, and Future

For me the worst time was the war. The best time was my youth, when I studied, when I graduated from the institute and had children.

The precious things I was able to take—my children! My grandchildren. The family pictures. I had a ring from my grandfather. It's not very valuable, but I had to leave it there. The customs officer didn't permit it. I gave it to Boris for my sister.

We raised our children to be honest, decent, and hard-working, to have a good attitude toward people, to value friendship and family support.

Isaac is now looking for work. Boris, my younger son in Israel, is a mathematician. He has his Ph.D. In the Soviet Union he was a professor in a college. In Israel now he works as a rental agent because of the language problem. He must learn Hebrew. We are planning a trip to Israel. Anna bought the tickets for us, and we have applied for the passports. I think we may receive them soon.

The surprise for me when I came here was freedom. You don't have to be afraid to say what you think. Also, there are nice friendly people who are helpful and kindhearted. At the community center there are volunteers who want to help. Such very friendly people. You cannot find the same in the Soviet Union.

DR. NAUM GINSBURG
Healer and Hero

The hardships that ensued after the Revolution did not deter Naum Ginsburg from his aspiration to become a doctor. He was a gifted student and in 1936 graduated from the Medical Institute of Kiev first in his class. However, he and his fellow Jewish classmates were to share the same fate. They were denied access to study for a Ph.D. Naum had to part from Paulina, his young wife, also a medical student, and their baby son, to assume a medical post with the railroad in Stary Oskol. This out-of-the-way assignment ultimately allowed him the special privilege of staying out of the war. He disregarded the privilege.

At the outbreak of the war he volunteered for one reason: to fight fascism. Inevitably he became chief of staff at one facility after another and survived, despite injury, some of the fiercest action of the Soviet war theater, including Stalingrad. His numerous honors and war decorations attest to his dedication and steadfastness.

The Soviet military mop-up after defeated German forces led Naum's division to Odessa where he saw the pitiful survivors of the Jewish population. He also witnessed the environs of Lublin and the machinery of Maidanek, the death camp. He saw no Jewish survivors in Lublin.

Naum's stellar wartime achievement behind him, in 1948 he returned from Germany to face cosmopolitanism in Kiev. He lost his post at the hospital there and chose to relocate. He further suffered slurs that Jews did not fight in the war. The anti-Semitic climate of Dnepropetrovsk troubled him, and he left for Kharkov in 1953. It was only in 1962 that he attained the long deferred Ph.D.

Today, the distinguished, soft-spoken cardiologist reflects without self-pity on a life of service to a country that evinced a kind of cruel amnesia toward dedicated public servants like himself.

Before the Revolution

I was born in Zhitomir, near Kiev, April 8, 1912. My father graduated from Kiev University in pharmacy in 1903 and had his own pharmacy in Zhitomir, a town of about 200,000. We lived in an apartment. My mother didn't work. My sister Manya, who was two years older than I, became a professor. She studied chemistry and later received a Ph.D in biochemistry.

Before the Revolution we didn't feel anti-Semitism because most of the people who lived in Zhitomir were Jewish. The doctors and the pharmacists were mostly Jewish. Grandfather lived in Ananev, and his two brothers were doctors. My grandfather was a math teacher in a *gymnaziya*, and my father received a good education. In that time in Russia there were percentages of Jewish people who could go to medical school and university, and my father was a war hero from the war with the Japanese, so he could go. My uncle also took part in the war. He became a very famous doctor. My mother's family was from Lithuania.

I remember my mother telling me how when she married, in honor of the wedding, her father, who owned an iron factory, laid down iron tiles on the street from the synagogue to the house. To symbolize hope for the couple's strong life, he paved this temporary road for the wedding party.

My father's family came to Zhitomir from Kiev. In 1903 my uncle moved to Zhitomir and started his practice as a doctor.

Before the Revolution my father had the pharmacy, and we lived very well. After the Revolution, the government took the pharmacy and things became difficult, so we moved to Pulino. My father, mother, and sister moved into a one-room apartment. We lived on the salary my father earned at the pharmacy. I went to grade school in Zhitomir and finished in Pulino. The men—my father and I—moved to Pulino, and the women—my mother and sister—stayed in Zhitomir because my sister had to finish school there, and my mother remained with her.

The distance between these two towns is about twenty miles. My sister Manya went to Kiev and enrolled in college in 1927–28. Later she earned a Ph.D. Mother moved to Pulino in 1927, when my sister graduated and went to pharmacy school in Kiev.

The Revolution and Change

After the October Revolution there was a lot more anti-Semitism. My father couldn't find a job because he was a Jew. Pulino, near Zhitomir, was a very small town in the Ukraine. Even before the First World War there were a lot of German people, so the government of the town was German. In 1918 the Germany army had been in these places. The Jewish people fled to places where there were Germans because they were afraid of *pogroms* and they felt safe with the Germans.

Only a Few Judaic Remembrances

Although I had been circumcised, by the time Isaac was born, Jews weren't allowed to be circumcised in the Soviet Union.

Some Jewish holidays were celebrated by the family. Because my mother was from Lithuania and my father from the Ukraine, they spoke mostly Russian at home. They spoke different dialects of Yiddish.

The only Jewish ceremony I recall was when my cousin got married and there was a *hupa*. My father was not religious.

Komsomol and Jewish Youths Clash

When I was in grade school in Pulino, on the Jewish holidays the *Komsomol* people would fight. They forced the Jewish children to work in the gardens, in the fields, so they couldn't observe religious holidays. So these children and I would fight the *Komsomol* leaders. We went around to houses on bicycle and posted notices that all Jewish children should go to celebrate the Jewish holidays. After that the government talked with the parents, and there were problems. Some children were expelled from school. I was too. But my father had lived in the town a long time and talked to the chairman of the school, and then I was allowed to return.

Medicine Was a Family Tradition

After grade school, I knew I wanted to be a doctor. I was from a doctor's family. So all the time I planned for this, and my father talked about it, but I was very young so I studied by myself, then went and took the medical school tests in Kiev. In general I got all A's, but in the Ukrainian language I got a C. Anyway, I was in the fourth category. The first category was workers and farmers; the second, children of workers and peasants; the third, civil servants; the fourth, children of civil servants; and the fifth, all others. In 1930 I worked on a newspaper, then entered medical school in 1931 and graduated in 1936.

Politics and Purges

In the college there were a lot of political subjects and political organizations, like *Komsomol,* which I never joined. I didn't like the political stuff. But I liked medical school. These were difficult years. There were some students who didn't have any education before but got in because they were members of the Communist party.

In the years from 1921 to 1939 there were political trials. Some professors were fired from their jobs. There were some good students, but they could do nothing because they might be killed. The trials were beginning in 1932–39. I wasn't very afraid because I was young. But some of my friends were involved.

In 1934, during the trials, some people were expelled from the institute. For example, a fellow student, Kishinzon, was put in jail, and then he was killed in jail. He didn't do anything. They said he was a Trotskyite. He was only about twenty.

We couldn't discuss these things openly, only with close friends. My friends were good kids, mostly Jews, the kind who never joined the *Komsomol.* Two of them became famous professors, Mina Epstein and Ephim Lihtenshtein. The first one was a doctor, and the other was in biochemistry. We were friends after medical school. We used to play chess. Bunya Zamekovsky was chess champion of the Ukraine. Two of them have died already, but Mina is still alive.

A Ph.D. Is Postponed

I was first in my class and was doing really well, but no one Jewish could go on for the Ph.D. After college we all had to go serve somewhere, so I went to a little station town called Stary Oskol to work as a doctor for the railroad. My professor, a famous Soviet Jewish professor, Max Moysevich Gubergritz, helped me. I worked in this town for four years, and then in 1940 I could go back to school. The war began in 1941.

Paulina and I had been married in 1934. She was still in medical school at that time. Isaac was born in 1936 in Kiev. In 1938, when she graduated, Paulina moved to where I was. Our son Boris was born in 1947, in Germany, where I had been stationed after the war.

Outbreak of the War

I volunteered for the army during the first days of the war, June 30, 1941. I didn't have to join the war because, after I had graduated from the medical institute, I worked as a doctor on the railroads. But when the war began, I thought that everyone should fight fascism. So I went to the military office to enlist.

Paulina and Isaac went to the Far East. Many civilians went East because there was less fighting there.

Early Military Losses

The army was badly organized. The First 253rd Division was formed near Nikopol in July 1941. The next month, August, near Krivoy Rog, our division was hastily organized, poorly armed, and couldn't fight against the Germans, and so south of Krivoy Rog our division was defeated. After that defeat the remainder of this medical unit became part of the Ninety-ninth Division, so I was sent there. I was chief of the medical battalion in the division, a captain. All medical school graduates receive a military classification. I was not required to carry a weapon.

We went with the front lines of the army, southwest of Kiev. Then we crossed the Dnieper and went southeast of Kiev. I was in the reserves. From the reserves they made the regular army. In the town of Krasny Ulich, fighting was going on, but our army was very bad. The Soviet army ran from the Germans. They lost a lot of people, and in the hospital I was very busy.

The Command to Become a Party Member

Because I was a chief of this battalion, the commissar said as an example I must join the party. In any case, if I didn't join I thought that the KGB (in the army it's SMERSH) could arrest or hurt me. The commissar wanted me to join the party because there was a panic and many people were deserting, so I would serve as an example for others not to be afraid. In the army there were practically no commanders of my level—commanders of battalions—who weren't in the party. So I joined at the end of 1941.

At army activity meetings, they wrote minutes of what was said. The chief, Commissar Pisetsky, was Jewish, from Zaporozhe. He was afraid and burned the papers of the meetings, party records.

Many people were afraid because the army was badly organized, so they deserted. Most of these people were from the East—Uzbeks, Kirghizis. I didn't know of any Jews who were deserters. Commissar Pisetsky was killed during this time.

I was unable to be in touch with my wife. But I wrote letters to my uncle in Moscow. Finally I got a letter from my mom and sister in August of 1941. They were in Astrakhan, a city on the Volga River. They had moved there from Stalingrad.

The Encirclement

Starting in October of 1941 our troops became active for the first time, and we made an attack. It was the first time I'd ever seen German soldiers and tanks, and the German army was retreating. Then the Soviet army moved into the Ukraine, and our troops went to Kharkov. It was the spring of 1942, and this was called the Iz'um-Barviemkov Circle.

I worked in a divisional hospital. We didn't do specialized operations—there weren't specialists—just general surgery. But operations were done on all patients who had been wounded—in the chest, stomach, head, anything.

The wounded who couldn't be moved were taken care of right on the front lines. The ones who could be moved were given medicine and then just transported to the hospital. If they couldn't fight anymore, they could go home to their families.

All kinds of guns and artillery were in use, and bombs were dropping. There were constant air raids. The medical group led the transport of injured in the division, and the injured who were being helped at the medical areas were rounded up. There were people who were emotionally destroyed. We had one doctor, a dentist, who had taken part in the war with the Japanese at Khalkin-Holl in 1939. He received the Red Medal of Honor. After that encirclement, he buried his Red Medal of Honor in the ground and tried to swim across the Donets River and defect. After that they swore at him. He was depressed for a long time and was terrified of the Germans. I thought about my family, that I had to remain alive—that's about it.

In May of 1942 the German army made another attack, and they succeeded in surrounding us; about 100,000 troops were encircled. (One army is four or five divisions. One division is about 10,000 troops.) This included the Fifty-seventh, the Sixth, half of the Ninth, the Pushkin tank corps, and many other parts that fell into this trap.

We were encircled in a little city near the Donets, in the Iz'um region, southeast of Kharkov on May 18, 1942. The encirclement lasted forty-eight hours. Our division fought its way out of the encirclement. To get away, we looked for an opening, and this was across the Donets River. When we crossed the river, that day many of the medical people were shot with machine guns. Many people perished. The Jewish doctors who served with me were Kriycher, Kaminer, Eisenberg, Kreicerov, and many others.

During the period of the encirclement I thought about my family, and I was afraid that the family would lose me. I didn't do much thinking, though, because those were very hard times. Many people needed surgery.

When we broke out we were happy, but some people were very sick because they had to go through cold water. The Germans didn't follow us across the border of the Iz'um region, and they didn't come farther. They made communications that they were strong on this position. The firing was very heavy, but they stayed. In this place winter went into May.

Of course, after we broke out, I believed I would find my family. But we couldn't correspond. There was a break in the mail service because the military addresses kept changing. So for three weeks there was nothing, but after that I started receiving letters. They were reassuring letters that everything was all right, that everything was good, basically to calm me down. Before, I got letters from my uncle in Moscow about the family saying, "They can't find a place to live." Then I started receiving letters directly from them and could calm down.

On to Stalingrad

The troops moved on to Stalingrad; I went there in October of 1942. We were stationed north of Stalingrad, at a factory where they made tractors. In the beginning the Germans were very strong, and they killed a lot of people. Some of the Soviet troops were killed, part of the medical corps, some of the doctors. Transportation across the Volga is very difficult because it's a wide river. The Germans would fire across the river, and people would be killed trying to cross it.

The winter was very cold and hard. In January of 1943 the Germans began to lose their position. They began to die. March 2, 1943, the German army began to give up. The Russian army encircled and destroyed the German army. Three hundred thirty thousand German soldiers were encircled and surrendered. These soldiers and officers couldn't do anything. People were moved to the POW camps. The road was very difficult; many of them died.

There was never any time away from this. The first time I could see my family was in 1944.

The Train Station at Kuybyshev: A Surprise

In the winter of 1944 when I was stationed on the bank of the Volga, my wife was very ill. I received a letter about it. They gave me ten days' leave, and I went to see my family. No one knew that I would come. She had left to see her sister who now lived in Sorochinsk, and she had to change trains in Kuybyshev.

At the Kuybyshev train station we met. I saw her first. She could not see who it was when I hugged her, and I frightened her terribly! I was with her for a week.

After Stalingrad, we went to Kursk. We were pushing the Germans. During this time, June 1943, I was shell-shocked. We were near Svedlovo. I didn't go anywhere else for treatment. When two or three days later I went back to work, we were in Svedlovo. The Eighth Contingent, led by Chukov, was sent to become part of the First Ukrainian Contingent.

Of course, we were feeling better and better. By this time I became a major. I received the Order of the Red Star of the First Level, two medals for the Battle of Stalingrad, and one for the Battle of Berlin. I stayed with the army all the way to Berlin. After that we crossed to Poland.

Jewish Population Remnants

When we occupied Odessa, we saw the first Jews. There weren't German soldiers, but mostly Rumanians. We drove through the West, then the southern Ukraine. First we went to Krasny Rog, and then through Odessa. Our division was a bit north of the city, but we went into Odessa. Though we were there only twenty-four hours, we saw old Jews, sometimes with children, who weren't killed thanks to the fact that Odessa was occupied not by German but by Rumanian troops who, for money, didn't kill them. They were in very bad condition, thin, their clothes torn. Jews came out when we arrived, and we saved them. In Poland we tried to help, but it was horrible.

Near Lublin, we didn't see any Jews, only camps. We saw the equipment they used to kill people at Maidanek. It was a death camp. We didn't see any Jews.

We were in Lublin, then on the banks of the river for quite a while, south of Warsaw, then to Poznan. Poznan had been encircled by a German officer corps. Then we went to the Oder River. The buildings were more or less preserved. There was absolutely not the kind of devastation that there was in the Ukraine. The people mostly hid, but some met the Soviet army well.

Before the war it was well-known that ghettos existed, that camps for the extermination of the Jewish population existed. We knew even before the war that the Germans, in 1933 with the coming of Hitler, started to kill Jews.

Treating the Enemy

When we would surround the Germans and come across a wounded German officer, we were forced to help him so he could be interrogated by our commander. That was extremely difficult, because for my comrades and myself, it was simply disgusting to help him. I had to help him because of my medical training, because I was a doctor and the army needed information that the German officers knew about military equipment and so on. I didn't treat them myself, but I watched. After the surgery, members of the Soviet army took them away.

When the war had ended, the inhabitants of Berlin—even tortured children—started crawling out of their basements; we gave them medical treatment.

Once in Berlin, we were in the Berlin Zoo and saw a monkey that had been shot in the arm. We did some surgery, and after that, many years later, I saw a movie in which this episode was mentioned, except that after the surgery in the movie the monkey was presented to a famous Soviet marshall. It didn't really happen that way; the Germans ate the animals in the zoo.

Hospital Chief of Staff in Weimar

In 1945 I received the Order of the Great Patriotic War, First Level. Then we went to Weimar. At this time, because I was a physician, I became the chief of the hospital staff in Weimar. Because Buchenwald is near Weimar, I saw the concentration camps. Then our hospital moved to Jena, a suburb, where we remained until 1948. In 1947 Boris, our younger son, was born.

While there I studied how medicine is organized in German hospitals, and there were some good professors there. I was studying electrocardiology. My wife studied biochemistry. She had major surgery for stomach ulcers performed on her in Germany. It was very important because in the Soviet Union at that time they couldn't do that kind of surgery.

Cosmopolitanism in Kiev

From 1948 to 1953, all Jewish people were affected by anti-Semitism because the Soviet government tried to fight the intelligentsia and Jews under the term *cosmopolitanism*. From that period Jews felt pressure from the government.

In 1948 I had an assignment to go the military hospital in Kiev and work as a therapist in this hospital. I was a colonel by the time I went to work in this hospital.

After the war there were many people in the army, political people, who told Jewish people that they didn't take part in the war. This was the first time I felt it personally. I began to sense myself as a Jew again, as different, after I got out of the army.

In this period, I was fired from this hospital and sent to another hospital in Dnepropetrovsk, on the Dnieper River in the Ukraine. The family stayed behind in Kiev because Isaac had to finish high school. In the Soviet Union, as you may know, to rent an apartment is not so easy, so they just had a little room. In 1952 for a Jew it was very hard to work as a doctor; people didn't trust Jewish doctors because of propaganda.

The propaganda increased with the Doctors' Plot. I had a couple of friends involved. One of them, Vovsi, I knew in Germany, a very famous Russian Jewish doctor, the head of doctors in the Soviet army. As chief, he inspected the hospitals. He was the cousin of Mikhoels who was on the Jewish committee during the war, who contacted America so America helped the Soviet Union during the war. Then Mikhoels was killed. When Vovsi came to visit to see how things were going, we had a party for him at our home.

We were all absolutely positive that the Kremlin doctors, including Vovsi, were in no way guilty of the charges that they were killing people. Moreover, I knew many of them. Like Vovsi, they were all honorable people and good doctors, and the charges were clearly fabricated. In addition, we Jewish doctors who had served in the army were suddenly mistrusted and investigated. At this time I was working in Dnepropetrovsk. When Stalin died, everyone knew it was only made up.

After the Doctors' Plot, I didn't want to work at the hospital in Dnepropetrovsk anymore because it was very anti-Semitic, because it was dangerous. So I moved to Kharkov, a town in northeast Ukraine, in November of 1953.

In Kharkov I was the chief of the therapy department until 1969. And then I went to the army sanatorium. Then I worked as a doctor in the Kharkov clinic. And in Kharkov while I was working in the hospital I got my Ph.D. in 1962. In 1963 I received two more titles; I became a full colonel and Colonel of the Doctors of the Ukraine.

Discrimination against Jewish students who wished to enter medical school began in 1948. It was very hard to become a Jewish doctor. I wanted Isaac to become a doctor. I had gone to school in Dnepropetrovsk and thought maybe he could study there. He had graduated from high school in 1953 and wanted to become a doctor, but it was impossible.

For the Future Generations

I decided to come to the United States because of the children, grandsons, granddaughter. We knew there was no future when Isaac was fired from his job at the Military College for the reason that he was a Jew. He had two masters degrees and a Ph.D. And they meant nothing. Other professors were also fired from the school because they were Jews.

Even at that time in 1976, I wanted to come to the United States, but I couldn't do it because I had been in the army, and my son had been at the military academy, so we couldn't leave.

I applied in 1989; we applied as a whole family. But we really wanted to leave in 1976. So it was more than ten years that we wanted to come.

Of course, in 1952 when Stalin was alive, things were worse. After Stalin died things became a good deal better. The government didn't do anything. Some people say there is anti-Semitism in the United States. But what is the difference? In the Soviet Union, you have the government's anti-Semitism, not just the people's. The government didn't try to help things.

Chernobyl

We first heard about Chernobyl from some of our relatives in Kiev. After the first of May the government informed everyone by radio. Some members of our family, who live in Kiev, came with their son who was in high school, and they lived with us for a while in Kharkov.

The fact that the government hid it from the people, that the May Day parades took place with children in them and the children were exposed to radiation, that's a crime. Kharkov is about 600 kilometers away from Chernobyl, but the wind was blowing the other direction, so we weren't exposed as much. In Kharkov there was only a little radiation, but still more than before. We were worried about exposure. In central Kharkov the government washed the streets every morning because of the radiation. But they did it for themselves, not for the people, because in the central part of the city is the Central Committee, so they washed only those streets. And they gave incorrect information on the radio; they downplayed the seriousness of it all.

America Did Something for Us

Here everything differs, day-to-day life, life in general, the way people relate to each other; everything is better than it is in the Soviet Union. People are very nice to us, and we feel that it's good for us. We didn't do anything for America, but America did something for us. One thing that is hard is finding a job here. My grandchildren have found jobs very fast, but my son can't, and I haven't.

Captain Naum Ginsburg, third from left in front row, chief of the medical battalion of the 99th Division during World War II. Picture taken in 1942. He went all the way to Berlin with this unit.

Lyuba Khoroshkiya, right foreground, with her parents, Merel Stolyarova and Boris Khoroshky, and older sister, Yevgenya. Photograph taken in 1937 in Friedrichhofka, the Ukraine.

Paulina Ginsburg's mother, Esther Friedman
Shmilkina, holding great-granddaughter, Anna, about
1960.

The Friedgan family on vacation in Yalta, 1982.

The Ginsburg/Friedgan family at Naum and Paulina's fiftieth wedding anniversary, 1984.
First row: Lilya and Boris Ginsburg (now in Haifa); Paulina and Naum; Isaac and Lyuba
Ginsburg. Second row: Leonid and Michael Ginsburg; Mark Friedgan, Alex and Anna
Friedgan.

Dr. Naum Ginsburg with military
decorations earned in World War II. Photo
taken prior to emigration in 1989.

Mark Friedgan, school picture taken in Kharkov circa 1985.

ISAAC GINSBURG
Standing Taller

Born into a family of doctors in Kiev in 1936, Isaac Ginsburg had to reconcile his aspirations, after the Doctors' Plot uproar, with the realities of an intensely anti-Semitic society. He graduated high school in 1953 but heeded the advice of his parents, who counseled him against applying to medical school. Since rejection was virtually assured, he would certainly have to enter the army, a perilous alternative for an intellectual young man, even more so if he were Jewish. He lowered his sights to engineering but found that he and his Jewish peers were met with ingenious strategies to hinder attainment of higher degrees.

Nonetheless, Isaac completed two master's degrees, one in mathematics, the other in mechanical engineering. His heartbreaking persistence led to attainment of a Ph.D. in 1968, "Stress Analysis of Shell Structures." This event went unnoted at the Military College of Kharkov where he was an assistant professor of mechanical engineering. With characteristic optimism he reflects that his dismissal in 1978 with several other Jewish faculty members was not all bad. According to Soviet law, he could not emigrate for five years after leaving work at a job where he might have access to state security secrets. The Ginsburgs emigrated eleven years later.

Here in Chicago, Isaac observes that the Jewish community supports its members, whereas its absence, as in Kharkov, necessitates that each individual struggle alone against the impact of anti-Semitism.

Both he and Lyuba are improving their English skills, a prerequisite for finding work in their profession. While the entire family is thankful that four generations have immigrated here, Isaac shares his parents' sense of loss that his brother Boris resides with his family in Israel. Meanwhile, he works part-time at a community college tutoring mathematics. Out of the formidable family reserves of optimism that sustained him during his struggles against an oppressive regime, Isaac Ginsburg still draws strength.

A Surprise Visit from Father

During the war we were evacuated to Boguruslan, in the East, near the Ural mountains. I remember that the war years were hard. There was not enough to eat. Once, in 1944 when I was eight, my mother was ill and had already begun a journey to her sister's home in Sorochinsk. I was at school when all of a sudden my father appeared. What a surprise! It had been three years since I had seen him. He was in a military uniform, and I ran into his arms. I insisted that he come with me so he could watch me ski. This area was very cold in winter, but my father came to the mountain with me. I had little wooden skis that were made by hand. He waited and I went on the mountain, but it was very cold. He had just come from Poland, I think, and after a short time, he said he was very frozen and we must go back. After that we traveled to Kuybyshev, and he surprised Mother at the train station.

After that my father returned again, then all of us and my mother's parents took the long train trip back to Kiev in 1945 after the war ended.

A short time later we moved to Weimar, which was a big change for me. I think in these years *where* we lived was not important. For me, it was important that I was with my father. He was able to spend some time with me. Sometimes he'd go with me to the cinema or theater, but most of the time he worked very hard.

Coming of Age

I began to understand something about anti-Semitism when I was in high school in Kiev. At that time in the Soviet Union, the period of cosmopolitanism against Jewish people had begun. I knew some of the "bad" people about whom they wrote articles. They were our friends or in our family. So I began to understand that something was wrong.

For instance, although the doctors were freed after the Doctors' Plot of 1952, the attitude toward Jewish people, and Jewish medical professionals was not very good. In the Ukraine especially, Jewish students were not admitted to medical school. For this reason I entered a polytechnic institute. To do so I left Kiev for Dnepropetrovsk, where my father was working at that time. There I became a student in the engineering college. Later when my father moved to Kharkov, I moved there too to study at the Kharkov Polytechnic Institute.

My Eyes Are Opened

Boris Goldstein, my uncle (Father's sister's husband), was a very great biochemist in the Soviet Union and was recognized outside of the country as well. At first when he stated his opinions, I didn't understand him.

Most students learned that only one way was right, Lenin's way, and that all others were bad. If something happened in other parts of the world, it was hard for schoolchildren or institute students to understand what was happening. Whenever we listened to the radio or read the newspapers (there was no TV then), only one kind of slogan could be heard.

Boris Goldstein spoke infrequently and only in private gatherings. Others like him were imprisoned for those same kinds of comments. He opened my eyes, especially when we learned about the Doctors' Plot. We lived in a neighborhood of doctors and knew they were good people. They would not do anything bad to others. We just knew that what the government said about these people was not right. I wasn't really afraid, but I began to understand that for Jewish people in my country there was no freedom.

The Army Was the Ultimate Fear

I never applied to medical school because my mother didn't think I had a chance of getting in. If a student graduated from high school and didn't go right into the institute, he was required to enter the army. So she was afraid and wanted me to apply to the institute. The army in the Soviet Union is hard for any young man, but to be in the army as ordinary soldiers is especially hard for Jews. There is a lot of anti-Semitism, a lot of crime and severe beatings. I knew of people who died from these beatings. We had a relative who died, but it was in the 1970s. Living conditions in the army were like living in a bad jail. Most institutes at the time had a military department. All male students had to do some military service. After our fourth year, during the summer, we were required to serve. I was lucky because I had to serve only one month. Before, longer service had been required. This was the most difficult time in my life.

The students were divided into tens. The sergeant was uneducated, hated educated people, and was very violent; he gave orders that made no sense. Once we had a forty-minute rest period in a forest where there were many pine cones. He ordered us to pile them in one place and then in another. Though we had already worked hard, he made us repeat the task. He treated us like slaves. We lived in a little tent with a bed made of wood, in which ten of us slept. If one needed to turn, the others next to him had to turn too.

This was our schedule: we had to stay up late and get up early, run about two miles, and then go to the gym and do exercises. Only then did we have breakfast; the food was terrible. Right after breakfast, we had to study. But one class was nearby, and the other was some distance away. We had fourteen minutes to run all the way and make it on time for the next class. Still, because my physical condition was good, army life was not as hard on me as on some of my friends. In our group from the institute I had three Jewish friends who were not in such good physical condition, so they had trouble jumping over hurdles. They were forced to keep training while others ate breakfast. The sergeant made it harder for them.

I Become a Serious Student

The first year and a half at the institute, I did not work hard. But then I realized that in order to graduate and get a job, I had better work harder. I graduated from the institute with good grades. Although I began working, I still wanted to go to medical school, but in the Soviet Union, you cannot go on to another school after you graduate from the institute; you must work. Medical school didn't have night classes, so I had no choice. I went to work.

Mathematics interested me. After some years I entered the evening mathematics department in the university and began studies. Then I took a different job and had more time to study, so I was able to earn a master's degree from the university. I liked my work because it was scientific and logical.

I Marry the Head of the Class

I met Lyuba in 1954 in our second year at the Kharkov Polytechnical Institute. She was the best student in our class. It was important to me that my wife be Jewish because by that time I had formed an opinion about what was happening in the Soviet Union. I think Lyuba thought as I did.

We had a good wedding! We went to the wedding palace and then we had a party with our friends and relatives. But we had no Jewish rituals like we've seen here in the last year, like the *hupa*. At that time all the Jewish observances were dead. We had no synagogue in Kharkov.

We had a few weeks for a honeymoon, but not right after the wedding. We finished our course first then visited Leningrad, Moscow, and Kiev.

After we were married, we lived with my parents and my brother Boris. And after Anna was born, in 1959, there were six of us. My father's mother came to help. After she died, my mother's mother came to stay. In 1966, we got a one-room apartment, and Lyuba, Anna, and I lived there.

Disappointed But Not Surprised

Again we felt our Jewishness when, after some time, we had to do our internships. All students have to do this. Because we were good students, we had the right to choose the place. Lyuba and I wanted to go together to Leningrad for a month-long practice. The professor wanted us to go with him too because he needed help on his dissertation; I especially could help him. But despite this the chairman decided that other people would go to Leningrad and we would go to a little city named Kramatorsk. So we were disappointed, but I was not surprised. I understood the rules.

When we graduated from the institute in 1958, we could not go on for our Ph.D.'s. Jewish people were not admitted, especially in the Ukraine, though in other parts of the Soviet Union, students could go, for example, to Siberia. People who graduated from those parts could go on to work on their Ph.D. But in the Ukraine you could not, all because of anti-Semitism. Even if you passed your exams with all A's, if you were Jewish, the local party office of the city (which was connected to all educational institutions) would refuse you admission. Only the president of the institute could decide otherwise, but most of them didn't want any problems with this office.

Lyuba and I got work at the same company. The chairman of the company's personnel department, who was on the commission to select graduates of the polytechnic institute, was Jewish and he invited us. So we went to work in Kharkov.

Lyuba worked there about a year. I worked there a few months then went to another company where I worked about five years, a coal-mining institute that did projects for the coal-mining industry. I worked in the vibration laboratory.

I was not satisfied with my work in this company. I had friends on our work team, which was all Jewish, who wanted to work for a higher degree. While we were at the company, our team attended the university and worked on our Ph.D.'s too. We could not attend the institute. The chairman at our company was sympathetic and spoke with the chairman of the engineering college. He also wrote a letter to the institute and arranged for us to take these exams. If he hadn't, nobody would have paid attention.

"Special" Conditions for Jewish Students

The institute chairman agreed to give us a chance to take the exams. Everyone who works on a Ph.D. must pass three exams: in foreign language, philosophy, and his area of specialization. All of us passed the foreign language well; this was English. And the second, philosophy. Maybe by then they realized that five or six Jews had passed the written exams. They began to set special conditions. There were two professors, and the third man was the chairman of the party department. We were told they couldn't give us a date to take the exam, that they were very busy, that we should come back in a month. When we returned at that time, they gave us permission, but we were told we must take oral exams. Afterward, only two of the three professors said we passed, so they held up the grades. It took about two weeks before they made a decision. Most of the grades were C and unacceptable.

We had studied by ourselves, not in any night classes. When the exams were not judged fairly, it was like a blow to my head. I was young. I had known it would be difficult, but it was even worse than I'd imagined. After a few weeks I was able to go to another institute in another city. Until then, I felt very bad.

By 1968 my Ph.D. dissertation was completed and accepted at Kharkov State University. The subject was stress analysis of shell structures used in aircraft, in missiles, in vessels, and in the building industry, too. Some had military applications, but now many of them have civil engineering applications, such as sports arenas.

My work did not change after I completed my Ph.D. I was an assistant professor but couldn't progress either in title or salary level, because I was Jewish. I gave lectures and worked on the scientists' team. Russians or Ukrainians who received a Ph.D. suddenly rose to the next level. But I worked at the same salary level for about ten years. Of course, I was offended, but the work was interesting. I understood that in that country only one thing could happen—I could be fired. And in 1976, I was!

There were many Jewish professors employed there because the chairman who established it was a smart man. He understood that he could make a good college only with good professional teachers. He hired many good Jewish scientists who could not find jobs elsewhere. For a few years, it became a very strong military academy. It was actually a college that was equivalent to an academy. In the Soviet military, there was one missile academy, one tank academy, one aircraft academy. Then there were military colleges in different places, in many cities. But the chairman of our military college very quickly raised its level so it seemed like an academy. Not every college can grant a Ph.D., but ours could.

Personnel Changes

In 1969 our chairman retired. The new chairman changed some of the staff. The atmosphere in the college deteriorated, and then a third chairman came. His commissar, chief of party politics, was very anti-Semitic. At that time the first Jewish people had begun to leave the Soviet Union.

The government asked Keldish, president of the Soviet academy, how long it would take to fire all the Jewish scientists, and he said he would need about ten years. So at this time they began to fire good Jewish people from these places. Most of the Jewish professors at the military college, including me, were fired.

I was not disappointed because I wanted to leave the Soviet Union, and I could not do it because of my work in this department in the military academy. I needed to have stopped working there more than five years previously to be cleared. But you see, it's very hard for a Jewish scientist to leave his job because to find another job is very hard. I didn't even try to apply to emigrate in the 1970s, because if I did, I would lose any chance to find a job, and I knew I could *not* get a permit.

I found a job three months later at Kharkov State University, at a civil engineering institute. My former department chairman at the military engineering academy, Brislavsky, was no ordinary Russian. He had left the academy because the Jewish professors were fired. He agreed to work in the civil engineering institute if they would allow him to hire whomever he wanted. He hired me and I worked with him there until I left the Soviet Union.

A Voice from Afar

Only the Voice of America gave us information about Afghanistan, Sakharov's arrest, and Shcharansky. The information the Soviet government issued was lies. It was surprising that some of my good friends who were intelligent did not understand that what the government said about Sakharov was a lie. We discussed this many times. It was after Khrushchev's speech in which they revealed the truth of what Stalin did that people who had a brain understood that what they believed before was a lie!

What Did *Glasnost* and *Perestroika* Change?

Glasnost and *perestroika* did not change anything. What I know now from letters from my friends, even when things are changing in other places in the Soviet Union, in Kharkov there's little change, except that the shelves in the shops are empty.

In 1987, when we saw that our friends who had been refuseniks for ten years received a permit to leave, we realized that we had a chance too. My daughter's best friend, also a refusenik, had relatives who lived in Israel. She received a permit to go there and sent us an invitation. We received it in March of 1989, and we decided to take a chance on getting a permit. We applied on April 1, 1989, and received permission at the end of May. We left in August 9, 1989.

LYUBA KHOROSHKAYA GINSBURG
The Family Shield Was Love

Lyuba Ginsburg was born in 1935 and lived with her parents, older sister, and younger brother in Volochissk near Friedrichhofka in the Khmelnitskiy region of the Ukraine. Despite a limited education, her father had been "literate enough" to be the editor of the newspaper of that region. Lyuba's parents were from poor families with many children. Her mother who grew up in the Odessa region had told her how they had hidden in the cellar while marauders struck. When the pogrom *died down, the family left their hiding place and found their dwelling in shambles. But they considered themselves lucky because some of their neighbors had been attacked or killed.*

The Second World War triggered a period of separation and hardship for the Khoroshkiy family. Lyuba's father was sent to Byelorussia, and her mother and the three children were relocated to Zatobol'sk, Kazakhstan. The village turned out to be a stronghold of anti-Semitism, where people blamed the Jews for Stalin's harsh farm collectivization policy, which had led to mass starvation in the early 1930s. Lyuba's husband Isaac points out that the roots of the hate for Jewish people predated the Soviet Revolution by centuries and that the Kazaki killed Jews en masse in the Middle Ages.

Though the Khoroshkiys survived the war, suffering the same fate as their Russian neighbors, their privations were compounded by anti-Semitism.

Years later, as a gold-medal graduate who was denied the opportunity to choose her school and later at the Polytechnic Institute of Kharkov, Lyuba experienced a more insidious form of bigotry. The most painful incident occurred when she and Isaac, her future husband, had the opportunity to study in Leningrad. In 1957 a professor invited them to go with him to Leningrad to assist him with his Ph.D. research. Isaac notes that Lyuba was the top student in the class, and both of them excelled in math. The opportunity for the young couple to gain such experience while living in one of the great cities was irresistible. Permission was denied for no reason.

Lyuba was not allowed to go on for a Ph.D. after earning her B.S. in mechanical engineering from the Polytechnic Institute of Kharkov in 1958. Both had trouble finding work but were hired at the Shop of Structural Cranes in Kharkov. She and Isaac were married in 1957, and daughter Anna was born in 1959.

In the sixties and seventies more information about the outside world filtered into the Ginsburg home through Voice of America and the BBC. Lyuba was surprised and troubled by the revelations, especially because the Soviet press continued to publish distortions and lies.

Reflecting on a life of early deprivation but rich in family devotion, Lyuba's eyes well with tears, not of sorrow but of joy. Until recently the Ginsburgs lived with Anna, her husband Alex Friedgan, and their son Mark. Though acutely aware that there are problems with language and in finding employment, she is nonetheless thankful that the family is in a land where they no longer need be second-class citizens.

My Memories of World War II

We were evacuated to Kazakhstan when war broke out. For the first year my father lived with us, in Zatobol'sk, a village near Kustanai. My father went to war in 1942 and remained until it ended. My mother was all alone with us children. It was a very difficult time for all of us because we didn't have enough food or clothes; we were always hungry. The government gave us a special ration card, but we received only two small pieces of bread, some flour and vegetables, very small portions and not regularly. My mother worked in an office as a typist and secretary during the day, and in the evenings she sewed clothes for residents of this village, rich Russian people who were evacuated from the Don during the period of collectivization. They hated the Soviet government, and they hated Jewish people.

The Other Enemy

I remember the day when my father left for the war. In the middle of the night my mother woke up because she felt something out of the ordinary. Smoke was coming into the room. She opened the door and went outside. Somebody had blocked our stovepipe, and we could have suffocated.

When I started school in 1943, I was the only Jewish child in the class. Many of my classmates called me a *zhidovka*. Very often they hit me. My teacher who had emigrated from occupied territory arranged for us to go together to school so she could protect me.

Once some big kids took my little brother, six years old, and hung him upside down by his feet from a horse. Even though the horse wasn't going very fast, my brother was afraid and cried. My mother came back from work and saved him. Otherwise there wasn't much she could do because neighbors were unfriendly and mean-hearted.

My sister was one of two Jewish children in her class. All the Russian children hated them for no reason. I remember once some Russian children ordered a very big, angry dog to attack me. The dog jumped on me, and I was very frightened. A Polish woman working nearby saved me from it.

My mother had many difficult episodes in her work and life at that time: my sister had tonsillitis, and then she and my brother became ill with scarlet fever; Mother developed boils on her whole body and could not put on clothes, so she could not go to work. My sister and I went to the market and sold some of our things to buy bread and milk. We sold some clothes and a kerosene lamp with a glass to cover it. We kept together, we three children and our mother. She tried to protect us and would say, "When the war ends and Father comes back, things will be much better."

Toward the end of the war, we received no letters from Father for a long time and feared he had been killed. At last when the war was over, we received a letter that while in Byelorussia he had been injured. When the war was over, he came to Zatobol'sk. I remember the day very clearly. It was the beginning of July 1945. The whole family went to the train station at Kustanai to wait for him. When the train arrived and we saw Father step down, what a happy day for all of us!

After he arrived we stayed there a month because we didn't have clothes to travel in. We didn't have *any* clothes, but Father had brought fabric, and Mother had brought a sewing machine from home to make a living. Now she used it to make clothes for all of us—me, my sister and brother, and for herself, and we returned to Bobruisk by train.

Postwar Recovery

At first we lived in one small room, but after that Father was allowed a basement apartment. It was damp and not well heated, with two rooms, one small and the other larger, but my parents fixed it up. We lived there until 1953.

After the war times were better. Father worked in the planning department as a planner for reconstruction. Mother worked, and we went to school. I was in the third class, my brother in first and my sister in seventh. Still, this was not an easy time because in Bobruisk there had been much damage from war battles and German occupation of Byelorussia. We had special ration cards and were given some bread, meat, and flour, but it was not enough. Potatoes and herring were our main diet.

In the spring my sister and I would collect potatoes that had fallen during the harvest. From these we made pancakes. But they were not good potatoes; they had started to spoil because they lay on the freezing ground all winter. In the 1950s rationing ended and we were able to buy food at the market. Only then did we stop going hungry.

Second-Class Citizens

When I graduated high school, I waited for a year for my gold medal but I didn't receive one. When I went to my teachers to have my diploma signed they asked me why I did not receive a gold medal. I said I didn't know, but one of my teachers was Jewish and explained that it was because I was Jewish. From this time I began to question and to think more deeply about the political situation, about national politics in the Soviet Union. I began to understand who Jewish people were in Soviet society.

The Job Assignment

When I was a student at the Polytechnic Institute of Kharkov, I experienced prejudice. Isaac and I met there, and we both experienced it. We met in our second year and studied in the same class. When we had exams with certain teachers, they treated us as second-class people. Some teachers that were anti-Semitic tried to show us that we were a lower level of person. When we wanted to go to do our internship in Leningrad, we were shown this again.

At the time I graduated school, I received the "red diploma," which meant I had earned the opportunity to choose my job assignment. When we received a list of jobs from the personnel department, it turned out we didn't receive what we wanted. I would have liked to have gone to Leningrad, but that was out. I wanted to work on my Ph.D. at a science institute in Kharkov. We looked for work there, but a person from the department we applied to did not accept us because we were Jewish. But at another institute, also in Kharkov, there was a person from the personnel department who was Jewish also and who offered us engineering work. And so we went.

We both received jobs at a large Kharkov factory, which manufactured cranes for the building industry. I was a design engineer for the metalworking shop in this factory, doing special features, punches, drill jigs, special metalworking jigs. My husband was a draft engineer in the metalworking shop. I worked several months, then I took a leave of absence because I had a baby. I stayed at home and took care of my daughter for several months. After that I began a job, also as a design engineer, in the project bureau of an engineering company that was very close to my house. I could get to work in fifteen minutes on foot. I worked on several projects for the mechanization of manufacturing process. We designed projects, for example, for an automobile tire manufacturer and for small bearing manufacturers.

The "Thaw"

In 1962 Solzhenitsyn published *One Day in the Life of Ivan Denisovich*. I read it and was surprised because I didn't know about the *gulag*—that so many people were in the *gulag* and that there was so much suffering. We also read several stories in the magazine *Novy Mir* (*New World*), edited by Tvardovsky. They published a few of Solzhenitsyn's stories. Among our family and friends we passed around these magazines and discussed them. People were getting agitated with what they were reading. At that time it was not dangerous. It was the time of Khrushchev's *ottepel'*, thaw. There is a novel written by Ilya Ehrenburg with this name. We were receiving new knowledge about our life and I began to think more, to criticize life, the government, all the political organs in the Soviet Union. I was a member of a trade union, but we spoke of these matters only with our family or friends in private, not in the wide circle.

In the late 1960s we were starting to see Sakharov's publications. We listened to the Voice of America and the BBC from Britain. We had more knowledge about the world. In 1973 some of our friends went to Israel. We couldn't leave at that time because Isaac worked in a military factory.

The Melting Point

In 1973 after the Yom Kippur War took place there was increased anti-Semitism in the Soviet society. It surrounded us, the word *zhid*, so that we must get out of the Soviet Union. We heard this on the streets, the bus, the train. We had in my company many people that were big anti-Semites. They lived in Kharkov during the time of the Second World War, and some had supported the fascists. At this time in the Soviet Union they began to support the Arabs, and they could talk louder about their feelings against the Jewish people.

In the late 1970s they had the trial of Shcharansky. We heard about it only from Voice of America and BBC. In the newspapers were other things. We felt uncomfortable. We knew that our life might change, but *we* couldn't do it. We couldn't speak out against this wrong information, against this order, because we could be imprisoned like Shcharansky. We were afraid.

Shcharansky was released in 1986. It was the beginning of *perestroika*. We heard about Chernobyl, the beginning of May, ten days after it happened.

The Memories Remain

As bad as the war was for all people, we also felt the hate of the Russian people around us because we were Jewish. I couldn't choose the institute I wanted, and I couldn't choose where I would work. Many times I felt I didn't go on business trips to other countries because I was Jewish. I created the projects, and other people went in my place to Italy, France, Cuba, Hungary, Bulgaria.

The best times in Russia were living with my family, living with my husband. When we got married, we were so happy on this day! Even if in our work, in our society, we did not have an easy time of it, I can't think about bad times in this period in our life. Here I miss only my job and the friends and relatives I left in the Soviet Union. I also miss my parents' graves.

ANNA GINSBURG FRIEDGAN
Leading the Way

Though Anna deplores the institutionalized thinking of the Soviet educational system, the spunky, guileless math major is living proof that an individual given thoughtful parental upbringing and perhaps a courageous teacher can see through the opaque totalitarian scrim. Not all her Jewish peers did.

Anna was born in Kharkov in 1959 and acquired a typical Soviet education. She attended kindergarten, then at seven went to school. She became a member of the Oktyabryata *(a Communist group for young children) and then a young* Komsomol'ka *(member of the Communist Youth Organization). An adored only child, she enjoyed the care and concern of her grandparents Naum and Paulina and her parents, Isaac and Lyuba. She is credited by the entire family with initiating the drive to emigrate. She is employed today as a computer programmer for McDonald's.*

No Individual Thinking

From the very beginning everyone is organized into a group. When they're young they have to think like their teachers, and then when they are grown up they have to think like society wants them to think. No individual thinking.

If you only *thought* about politics, you could go to jail. The only group students could join at college was *Komsomol,* and they could remain members until age twenty-eight. My friend's brother thought about politics and about being Jewish. He was expelled from the university and could not graduate!

I can't tell exactly when I changed my views about our life. When I was growing up I listened to my parents, and when I was fourteen I went to the mathematics school. The students and some of the teachers in this school were different. Mark Donskoy, a history teacher, was Jewish. He taught us about World War II and what happened to the Jews. This was not in the textbooks. Approximately one-third of the students were Jewish; it was not all new to us because everybody knew something from parents and grandparents. But because it was taught to us in the school, it was a big deal.

At home my parents talked a lot about politics and about the emigration situation as it evolved. In 1973 when I was fourteen, emigration started to the United States. I knew that people who wanted to leave were treated badly. First, my father's friend tried to leave. He was fired from his job. There was a meeting where everybody was brought together to discuss how bad he was. Even if his coworkers didn't think so, they said this. He was embarrassed publicly. Then he had to pay a lot of money to leave.

When we finished school, one of my friends wanted to go to Israel. People who were friends with her didn't call her because they were afraid. They didn't talk with her. It was terrible for me. I could not understand this! She was ostracized by Jews as well as non-Jews. Now she is in Israel; she left in 1977 or '78.

My Father Was Fired

One thing that had a major impact on me was in 1976 when my father was fired from the military academy because he was a Jew, not because he was not competent. At the same time, several Jewish professors were fired. I was worried about the family, because it was a difficult time for us, not only economically, but the morale was very bad. Maybe it was then we first thought about leaving. But again, we could not, because of my father's secrecy level. He could not find a job, then finally he did, but it was a bad experience. For the first time in my life I really felt insecure. It always remains a worry to me that it could happen again.

My Career

From the beginning, as I was growing up, I wanted to be a mathematician. My father helped me in this choice; I didn't consider anything else. I had very little problem getting into the university because at Kharkov University there was a better situation for Jews than at other colleges, and many Jews were there.

Mathematics students have to work very hard. There are not too many people in the competition for admission. After you study so hard and then graduate, you don't receive a very big salary. That's why it was good for Jews. I had a friend who studied with me. At first she tried to go to the polytechnical institute. She was in my school and she had very good grades, almost all A's, but she could not go just because she was Jewish. The next year she went to the university.

When you graduate from college, you cannot go to a company to be interviewed. This was the first time I knew for sure that I was Jewish. All the better students were Jewish, yet none of them could go to the good companies, nor could they stay at the university to do research. Many people wanted to hire these students, but their personnel departments—almost every one—are run by people who worked in the army. They just directly asked us, "Do you have a woman who can work but who isn't Jewish?" It was a shock for us.

At first I thought that I could do research, but then when I understood I could not, I went to a company and began to work. In the university I had some computer training but not enough to be a programmer. Most of the people who worked in my department were Jewish. They were very good programmers, and I received very good training.

A Push Broom and Quality Picking

I worked from 1981 until we left in 1989. But in my first years I didn't do much professional work. That's what happens to most Soviet engineers and scientific people. At harvest time, the company sends you to a collective farm. I worked like a slave in the fields harvesting potatoes, tomatoes, cucumbers, watermelons, corn! In Russia this is not done with machinery but by hand! People who supervise you are always uneducated people. The farm was terrible. Then in the winter, you had to go and build buildings, or clean the streets. I had a push broom!

This happened throughout the country! There's one popular comedy about how a famous professor put his card in a sack of potatoes. It read, "These potatoes were quality-picked by [the professor]."

An Introduction by a Friend

I met Alex in 1978 when I was on vacation in Sochi, in the Caucasus. We were introduced by our mutual friend. I had studied with this friend in high school, and Alex studied with him in college. Meeting on vacation was very nice. We were married in April 1979, in Kharkov. There was no religious aspect to this, none at all!

Childbirth in a "Better" Hospital

When I was in the hospital to have my child, November 9, 1979, I felt the care was very bad, though I was in one of Kharkov's better hospitals because of my grandfather. Hygiene was bad; there were three women in a room, four or five in some rooms. Again, this was in a *good* hospital. In others it would have been ten or twelve. There was one shower on the whole floor for ten rooms. They handed the babies to us to feed them and then took them away. A nurse would carry three or four babies in her arms, not even in a cart.

I was in the hospital two weeks because I was sick. I had a problem because of this care. My water—they broke the membrane before they had to. And during the delivery, they made a cut that didn't heal properly.

My Son: A Family Project

I was attending the university, so when I brought the baby home my mother and my mother-in-law had a difficult time! We lived in one apartment—two rooms, a kitchen and bathroom—my mother, father, Alex, Mark, and I. All of my family was very helpful to me. I was able to study and graduate from the university without any trouble. In the morning I fed Mark, then my father or Alex brought the baby to my Grandmother Paulina who lived near the university. After classes I came to pick up Mark.

Chernobyl and Its Impact on Kharkov Life

I read the paper and listened to the radio about Chernobyl. My aunt from Kiev came to us with her son. She called before, to tell us she wanted to come, but we didn't know exactly what had happened. It was scary. In Kharkov there was not much radiation, but many people were worried. From Kiev and especially from Chernobyl, people began to come and live in Kharkov. It caused trouble for people because of the apartment shortage. You had to wait in line at your company for an apartment usually for many years. Then when Chernobyl happened, these people came to Kharkov and occupied apartments that were for people who lived in Kharkov. Working people were not happy about it!

I didn't take special precautions because of the radiation. We were told in Kharkov not to worry about it. We worried a little, but not much. As the years went by I didn't want to go to Kiev because I knew that in Kiev there was a lot of radiation.

A Different View of the World after *Glasnost*

After *glasnost* I found out some things about Russian society that I didn't know before. Many good books were printed, and I read one by Vasily Grossman written in 1963. This was the most exciting book for me. It was about Jews and World War II, and about camps, about Stalin, Stalingrad. It was such a different view of the world for me. I believe it has been translated into English. A Russian ideologue said about this book that it could only be published after 100 years.

Nationalistic Struggles Threaten

It was good that Sakharov was released, but I didn't think that there was a big change in Soviet society. We could read more about everything; just *Pamyat* could say more. I think that's what these people think is democracy—that you can fight with each other! Armenian with Azerbaijan, Uzbek with Tatar. National fights, not democracy! I believe that while the Communist party remains and provides this, nothing will change. No, I cannot see how the Soviet Union can stay together though it has economic interconnections. Maybe different republics can exist without each other, but they need help from other countries. *All* the Soviet Union needs help.

The United States or Israel

I knew that I wanted to leave. I talked a lot with one of my friends, because she had a brother who left in 1974 when he was twenty-two and went to Israel. He married an American Jewish woman who lived in Israel. Then he worked in a company that had a contract with the United States. He lived in the U.S. about ten years. His children were all born here. When the oldest girl had to go to school, he returned to Israel, though he did not have an easy life there, because he believes that Jews have to have a Jewish education in Israel.

We didn't try to leave before 1979 because my father was in the military academy and because of his security clearance we could not even think about applying. Then emigration was closed. When Gorbachev came and *perestroika* began, he said that those who have relatives can go out when they want. Because my friend's brother was in Israel, she and her mother wanted to go there. But they could not; they were not allowed. They had a lot of trouble and tried for three years to leave. Finally, emigration began again, and they left in December 1987.

In 1988 I called my friend in Israel and asked her to send me an invitation. We received it in March 1989. Then I began a little bit to *nudge*, to persuade my family—not a lot, but a little. I cannot say it was hard to persuade anyone, because everybody believed that we had to go. It was a difficult decision, especially for my grandfather and grandmother, because my uncle didn't have the same invitation. Finally he went to Israel, so our family is divided now.

My father was fired right away, because he was a professor in a military college. He could not teach Soviet students because his ideology was not "good" anymore. He was fired on April 1; we left on August 9. When we received permission to emigrate, we all had to leave work. At my job it was not too much trouble because one year earlier my boss had left for New York. And, at the same time two more people from my department were leaving. Now the department doesn't exist!

We took with us most of the books that we had. We took a lot of things that I believed we needed here. I had information from my friends that when you come, you don't have anything! Like sheets and towels, everything. There was a short period before we left when we could send parcels, but on July 15 it ended. We sent a lot of what we had, so when we came here we had clothes and dishes.

In customs we didn't have any trouble, but we didn't try to take such things as my grandfather's uncle's gold medal from the university. We knew customs would not have allowed us to take it.

When we left, we could change ninety rubles into dollars. So for that we got $120. For a child, it was forty-five rubles. Then when we came to Vienna, we were met by people from *Sohnut* who gave us money. I came here instead of Israel because I believe that America is a more democratic society.

ALEX FRIEDGAN
In Exchange for Wheat

Alex, born in 1959, is dispassionate while recalling life in an empire out of synch with the times. The anti-Semitism he experienced as a boy is given little weight. Clearly the problems of acquiring a decent education and establishing a rewarding career had greater significance. He became a mechanical engineer after earning his Ph.D. at the All-Ukrainian Polytechnic Institute of Kharkov in 1987.

Today he is a computer programmer working hard to raise the family standard of living while sponsoring his own parents' immigration. Asked about the pressures on the multigenerational Ginsburg/Friedgan family who had lived almost two years in a materialistic society, Alex did not deny they existed. At the same time, however, he appreciates that it was economic pressure the West brought to bear on the Soviet government that made it possible for himself and his family to emigrate.

Soon after the interview, the Friedgans moved to their own townhome, and Alex's parents arrived from Kharkov.

Not to Tell Your Parents Your Problems Is a Russian Thing

While growing up I was reminded a couple of times that I was Jewish. This happened more on the playground than at school because I was one of the first students. They called me names and pushed me around. Sometimes just one person, sometimes more, not often, but it was not the best thing to have happen to you. I didn't tell my parents about it. I believe that was the code of behavior— never tell your problems to your parents. It is a Russian thing. I don't know how it is here, but over there, children have a more separate life from their parents.

During the school years I had a couple of best friends. I had one Jewish friend and one Russian friend. To this Russian boy it didn't matter that I was Jewish. It didn't mean anything.

The difference between our family and non-Jewish families was, I believe, cultural. My family read books. They understood the situation in the country. They let me hear their discussions about the country only when I was more or less grown up. I believe being Jewish is more like a level of consciousness, a cultural level.

We had vacations together as a family; we went to the Black Sea, most of all, to a small place near Yalta, because we had a place to live there. It was not a dacha. The company where my grandpa worked, as I understand it, had a couple of houses there so they could rent them. My grandfather Anatoly was the head of a company that installed telephone cables. Those are nice memories.

I would say I received the average school education, average urban school, because the level of rural schools is much lower. In school we had only one program, so there was nothing to choose from. I was good in mathematics, physics, and science. I didn't like literature that much. I'm a more technical person.

To Avoid the "Mistakes" of the Past

I talked with my father when I was ready to go to the institute, and we decided not to aim too high because of the lessons of the previous generation. So I went to a technical institute and didn't go to a university. Actually, I wanted to go to Moscow University, but we decided not to try for that because in 1952 my father (an honor student at school as I was) wanted to go there and they didn't accept him. At that moment the pressure on the Jews was the highest.

I graduated from the Kharkov Automobile Institute in 1981 with a master's degree. I wanted to work at the same institute because I had been there for two years already in a research position. We had some results at that moment, so my chief told me that the research I had done was a fourth of the Ph.D. The head of the institute thought otherwise, and they decided to take another student.

So, I started to work at the Hoist and Crane Conveyer Company and worked there until I emigrated from Russia. I did get my Ph.D. in evening school. While I was working I went to evening school at the All-Ukrainian Polytechnical Institute in Kharkov, from 1983 to 1987. Because I could not use the research I had done before, which was in another area, it took a while but I earned my Ph.D. there. My dissertation was on stress analysis of metal structures of cranes.

At a Dead End

I decided to leave Russia because I didn't see any future for me. I had reached the highest level that I could. It was a dead end for me. I would say that it was a dead end because of the anti-Semitism.

When the Gorbachev *glasnost* policy began, I was a student. I already knew some things and I could guess about the rest, so what I learned wasn't really "news" but information. At first I thought maybe it could help the country. But now I don't think that anything can help.

Gorbachev is asking for help from the West. But they have to give up the empire. Only then can they move in any direction economically or politically. I don't know whether they want to give up that. All the other countries gave up their empires 100 years ago; they live and prosper, but the Soviet—they want to be a great country, the greatest empire. I believe they're crumbling because they are an empire!

Chernobyl—The Ultimate Stupidity

I learned about the Chernobyl disaster from the Voice of America. I believe it was May 2, about a week afterward. Stupidity. I thought it was a stupidity. We were pretty far away so it didn't concern us personally as a disaster. It was trouble for the region, but it wasn't the prime concern of ours. I could worry about the food supply, but there was nothing I could do about that. There was no way to check products. I had more emotion about it there, but I can't find the words in English to express what I felt. It's a poor country. The feeling was they never *ever* can do anything properly.

The Other Side of the Iron Curtain

The trip from Russia to this country was both pleasant and difficult. I had seven people whose things had to be moved and organized, and we had to rent the apartment. But it was really nice to see Italy and Vienna, where we stayed for nine days. We walked around the city and saw the people. The people are different on this side of the Iron Curtain. They are prouder and have more self-esteem. You can see that they are more confident in the way they conduct themselves.

I started to work in January. Since I had studied English before, I knew it pretty well. I had some problems because the pronunciation differs from the one that I learned.

I miss my parents. I miss my friends. Most of them are in New York, some in Israel. Those in Israel like the life they live now. They had a chance to settle in before the Persian Gulf War. We called afterward; they were OK. They are in Haifa. Right now it's very hard because they have to assimilate and the country has to adjust.

The better the country it is, the less stable family life is. If life is very hard, people must think about the basics—food, things like that. If life is easier, people have time to think about their own pleasure.

I do believe that the battle for Russian Jews to emigrate was very important. I heard about it on the radio, and my father used to say, "Russia sold its Jews for wheat." And it was very important. We knew that somebody needed us; somebody was trying to help us.

MARK FRIEDGAN
Changing Places

Mark's adaptation to his new country was easier in terms of language than the other family members but harder in terms of independence. He finds his parents are more protective in Chicago than they were in Kharkov. While he does not carry a burden of anti-Semitism with him, he concerns himself more with the day-to-day challenge of blending in with his classmates.

Early Memories

I was about eight years old and in third grade when I found out I was Jewish. It wasn't really different. I had about thirty friends, and about five of them were Jewish.

When I was little we lived near a military school, so the neighborhood was like a military neighborhood. There was the military campus, the training grounds. That's mostly where I hung out. We lived in a house nearby because my grandpa taught there. Then we had to move because my grandpa wasn't teaching there anymore and the house was for military school trainers.

Then we moved to the house where my great-grandma, Paulina, lived. She was on the first floor, and we moved to the fifth floor.

Celebrations

We celebrated the Ninth of May, Victory Day. The First of May was really good because there was a big parade and I usually got a lot of presents. You know those Macy's parades in New York? It was about that big. They even had balloons, but the balloons weren't that big. We did not celebrate any Jewish holidays.

School Days

I started school when I was six; I skipped fourth grade. In first grade, we studied math, Russian, reading and writing, art, music, gym. I started Ukrainian in second grade. Our school went from first grade to tenth grade, all the grades. It was too small for all the children at once, so there were two shifts: from eight to twelve noon and from twelve-thirty to six in the evening. In first grade you go from eight to twelve. In second grade you go from twelve to six. All the even grades were in the evening, and the odds were in the morning.

The school in Russia had a swimming pool; that was a big advantage. And we learned to speak and write Ukrainian. It's a little bit different than Russian; it's like Polish.

In music class the teacher played the piano, we sang songs, and we learned notes and took tests. But I also had private lessons in music and English.

The English I learned in Russia helped me a lot because all I had to learn here was the accent and that was about it. I had the grammar and vocabulary.

Before, in Russia I had three school years and three teachers, and here I've had two school years and seven different teachers who teach different courses. There the teacher taught every one of the main subjects, math, English, Ukrainian or Russian.

Some things about schools are different. In Russia I had two really good teachers. They had an assignment notebook where they wrote down behavior. They expected more from me there. Here I bring homework home once a week, not as often as there. Still, I learn more here. There are more subjects here. The other thing is that in Russia I was only up to the third grade. But in third grade we learned the math that we are doing here now in sixth grade.

School is OK; it's easy. I hardly have to study to get good grades. Math is easy. Science is a little bit harder. On English tests I usually get A's. I've never gotten a B on an English test here.

I can't be one of the best right now because there's the HEP program, the Higher English Program. I'm not in it because you have to get good grades in English for three years to get into HEP.

Free Time There and Here

My best friends are still in Russia. We liked to collect things. You know Bazooka bubble gum? They have those small little comics in them. We had a different kind of bubble gum, and we collected the inside papers from that. I began to find out about this in second grade. In third grade I started collecting them, and I became like the master person for trading. I really have a lot of them.

In this country I like television, Nintendo. The library is pretty good, and I like to play on the computers. They have a lot of good stuff like golf. I had to write a report for school on the computer.

In Russia we did not have computers. The only fun things in school were the pool and the gym. I did have a lot of homework, every day. I also had swimming lessons. In second grade I tried ice skating. I quit after two lessons because the teacher was mean, and also because I didn't really like it. I've been roller skating here. I'm pretty good at it.

My Freedom There and Here

When we were going to leave, my friends thought I was really cool. They thought that I was going off on a big adventure. I didn't actually care about leaving Russia. When I was there, I was free to do anything. Here I'm not because my parents think I'm really small, but I'm eleven years old!

3

DEDICATION, WORK, AND HOPE

THE A. FAMILY

TWO GENERATIONS OF the A. family have dedicated themselves to medical and health care. Inda has devoted herself to specialization in breast oncology, her husband Lazar to veterinary medicine, their son Anatoly to surgery, and his wife Lia to pediatrics. To protect Lia's family in Russia, the A.s chose not to reveal their name. The older generation has left the good and bad of the past behind them in a desire to keep the family united. The hard-working younger doctors, though lacking the traditions of the past, are sending their two children, born in Odessa, to Jewish religious schools in Chicago. Their optimism about the future was recently celebrated with the birth of a son they've named Jacob, a first-generation American.

INDA G. A.
A Life of Purpose

Although Inda G. A. resembles, in some way, other Jewish women of her age and country of origin, she does not share the Yiddish vocal inflection or the distinctive gestures of those who emigrated to the United States earlier in the century. Her narrative was given in Russian and translated into English by her son Anatoly. A few days later in a follow-up interview, her daughter-in-law Lia translated.

The small apartment, housing four adults and two children, is neat, furnished with utilitarian used furniture. On the day of the interview the living room was decorated with colorful paper chains and balloons. The family has just celebrated the birthday of Leon, seven, son of Anatoly and Lia. Adorning the walls of the dining room are Leon's artwork and Hebrew exercises from Jewish day school. Natalie, two, attends day-care. Anatoly and Lia have been studying intensely to pass medical exams to qualify for residencies—he in surgery, she in pediatrics.

In some ways, this daughter of a religious Jewish family achieved what her parents had hoped the Soviet educational system would allow. She became a physician and surgeon, specializing in breast oncology. Merely to survive the ordeals of World War II took courage and great strength. To become a doctor during wartime conditions took even more. But after achieving her degree and gaining recognition in her specialty, she found herself thwarted when she might have achieved greater heights in her field.

The most difficult memory for her concerned the circumstances in which her entire family perished during the German occupation of her native town, Dunaevtsa, in World War II. All the Jewish inhabitants were killed in a single barbaric act. (In A Century of Ambivalence *by Zvi Gitelman there is a picture of the monument in memory of the victims erected at the site of their martyrdom.)*

Another painful memory was the propaganda effect of a well-publicized allegation during Stalin's regime. In late 1952 a group of Jewish doctors in Moscow was accused of conspiring to poison Kremlin officials. Though Inda lived in Odessa, the so-called Doctors' Plot cast a pall over her career for a significant number of years.

Today, Inda A., sixty-nine, is a Russian immigrant studying English like many who are less educated. She has geared up, however, with her characteristic sense of mission to assume the traditional role of a babushka *[grandmother]. She and Lazar will help their son and his wife by caring for the children while the young doctors try to build new careers in their adopted country.*

At the time of the interview, she and her husband were in Chicago on a recently expired visitor's visa, hoping to receive permanent visas. [Editor's note: Subsequently they were granted asylum, and the young doctors are now in residency.]

Everybody Becomes "Equal"

I decided to become a doctor when I was a child. I liked medicine very much and felt I needed to be a doctor. My parents wanted me to have a good education because they themselves didn't have the opportunity to become doctors. When my parents were young, in czarist Russia, the Jews had to live in the Pale of Settlement. Jews were restricted from living in the cities and couldn't receive an education. But after the revolution, the slogan was "Everybody is equal." At the beginning of Soviet power my parents believed that Jews would have equal rights. It was true before the Second World War, at which time I was able to enter medical school.

I was born in 1921. My parents Nuchim (born 1889) and Chana G. (born 1895) and our family lived in Dunaevtsa near Khmel'nitskiy, the Ukraine, 400 miles northwest of Kiev near the Polish border.

My mother didn't work but stayed at home to raise the children. My father worked as the chief of a store that distributed merchandise to workers' organizations. After the Revolution, goods that were taken from the rich were sent to such stores to be given to those in need. It was the beginning of communism, and there was no selling. Everything was in the hands of the government. The store was a storage place where a worker's organization could apply for coats, for example. It was just for clothing.

My brother Usher was born in 1924. He was very bright and wanted to build, to be involved in engineering. He was the best in his class in mathematics.

Communism: The Promise and the Threat

After the Revolution the family did not talk about politics at home because everyone thought it had changed things for the better. One could study and learn and attain positions or occupations commensurate with one's level of education.

In the 1930s when Stalin was killing people who held high positions in the party, no one from my family was killed. But because of what was going on, my family did not feel secure. Every night when my father went to sleep, he prepared things in case someone came during the night to arrest him and take him to prison. In preparation, he laid out matches, salt, and clothing that he would need if they picked him up because there would be no time to gather necessities. They would come for him and that would be it. Of the people who were arrested when I lived in Dunaevtsa, I don't remember any that came back. I can't say for sure, though, that none did because in 1939 I went to Kiev to study, and after the war started I did not return. There was a short period of rehabilitation after the death of Stalin in 1953, when those who survived were able to return.

Medical Studies during the War

I lived with my parents until 1939. Then, at the age of seventeen, I left to study medicine. I began in Kiev, continued in the city of Novosibirsk (near Lake Baikal in Siberia), and finished in the eastern part of Russia at the Medical Institute of Alma-Ata (in Kazakhstan, which borders China). When the war broke out in the western portion of the country, the government relocated us in order to protect the students in essential fields. I was part of a cadre—students who began studying in Kiev—that was relocated to the east.

Dunaevtsa was very close to the Polish border, and when the war started it was occupied by the Germans for some time. During the entire war I received no mail. Only after the war was I able to visit. There were various rumors. The first time I was relocated I knew nothing, but when we were farther east, we heard stories, although no one knew exactly what was going on until after the war.

We didn't think about ourselves. We hoped our parents would be alive and that the war would finish soon. Each month the propaganda was that the war would be finished in another month or two and that soon everything would be OK. We never thought about anything else except our relatives and our work.

Wartime Conditions

Nobody helped us; we were ragged and hungry. America sent parcels to Russia, but it wasn't enough. It was very hard, but everything went toward the war effort. All industries worked for the front and produced nothing for civilians. But none of us cared how we looked. In Novosibirsk the winters are very cold, and there was nothing in the store to buy. We went to the open-air market where everything was very expensive. We bought one pair of boots, *valenke* in Russian, made of wool, hard wool. Another girl and I took turns with these boots. She wore them one day and I, the next day.

During World War II, students at the Alma-Ata medical institute lived in confined space, six or seven to a small room. Even after the war it didn't improve because the country was destroyed. There was no transportation. We lived near the hospital, about five blocks away and so went there on foot. In those days I always woke up early, while it was still dark. To get food for breakfast we students stood in line. Food was not only scarce, it was very bad. We would be hungry all day. A very small cafe served the area, and to get food there we had to show our ration cards. After standing in line perhaps thirty minutes to an hour, we might leave without getting served because we had to get to class on time. Sometimes one of us would get in line earlier and would help the other. When we were served, we received hot water, and something resembling tea (nobody knew what it was), and a piece of bread. There were many people around me in the same situation. It was only hope that kept us strong.

There was limited access to textbooks. We had one book to five students. Sometimes we read together. We had a lot of practical classes, and our professors' lectures compensated for the lack of books. The lectures were excellent, better than the books. The professors were well educated, and all spoke five languages.

We medical students lived in the *obshchezhitie*. The buildings of the medical institute and of the veterinary institute were on the same street on the same block. So Lazar, who attended the veterinary institute, and I lived close to each other. We met on the street. Lazar was from Odessa. You know, the people from Odessa are special. They are strong-minded and do what they set out to do. When he saw me, he made up his mind. Lazar and I met in Alma-Ata and were married six months later in July 1943. He had a good character; not everybody was able to be like that. Maybe he liked that I was so different from him. He's alert, energetic, and makes a lot of friends. I am different, quieter, and happier to be at home.

We Must Part for a Year

Near the end of the war I received my orders to go to Moldavia. I graduated from medical school in 1944. Male doctors were assigned to military service, while female doctors were sent to a free area of Russia. Because of the lack of physicians, many of whom were killed during the war, I was sent by the commission of the medical institute to the liberated part of Moldavia. Lazar and I had to be apart. We worked hard and didn't have much time to write to each other. We knew we wouldn't be able to meet again until after the war. I wasn't able to leave until 1946 when another doctor was sent to replace me. When Lazar finished his education, he was told he could go to Moldavia, but he wanted to go to Odessa where his family was.

My Family's Fate

When the country was freed from the Nazis, I found out what happened to my family. They were killed by the Nazis in 1942. They were thrown into a mine with 1,000 other Jews from that area. My entire family, my father, mother, and brother, were killed. Unless they were hidden, no Jew remained alive in Dunaevtsa. After the war, in 1945, I returned to my native town, and there were people who were not Jewish—Russians or Ukrainians—who saw everything, and they told the story of what occurred. After the war Jewish people from the neighboring towns collected money and built the monument that now stands in front of the mine.

I was one of four girls from Dunaevtsa who started out as roommates in Kiev. When the war started the others went into the army. I was the only one who was lucky enough to go to Novosibirsk to continue my medical studies. After the war, I learned they were still alive and were able to finish their medical education. But all of their parents were dead.

Assigned to Moldavia

When the war ended, so much had been destroyed that it remained a struggle just to find food and a place to live. Doctors lived as close as possible to the hospital because they had to get there on foot. As a young doctor, I examined twenty or more patients in a typical morning. On an exceptionally hard day I saw sixty or seventy before going in to perform surgery. After that, I would go back to the polyclinic to check up on postoperative patients and then later in the evening, I would return to examine and check in new patients. During this period I was doing my own research and was one of the first physicians to administer testosterone (the only male hormone available in Russia) to women with breast cancer, using injections and oral medication. In one case this treatment helped a patient in the final stages of breast cancer to survive three more years.

Oncology is a very discouraging specialty. To get satisfaction from my work was difficult. Oncology patients usually died. It was difficult and disheartening, but I was very compassionate and did my best, and that's why the patients liked me. I was the only doctor in the area, but I had been a good student and had benefited from good teachers. The patients trusted me, knowing I did my best for them. I continued to be the only doctor at the district hospital of Moldavia for some time.

We Are Reunited in Odessa

When Lazar went back to Odessa in 1946, I returned as well so that we could be reunited. He had continued studying in Alma-Ata after I was required to go to Moldavia and had graduated from veterinary school. Although we had known each other only half a year, that was enough during wartime. At the very beginning, we lived for a short time with Lazar's mother, and then we rented different apartments over a period of seven or eight years. In Russia everybody rents apartments; nobody owns an apartment. The reasons for the temporary places were the poor living conditions, small rooms, and the lack of a kitchen or a bathroom. It was just after the war, and the buildings that had been destroyed had yet to be rebuilt. Several families could be living in a single apartment. Nevertheless, we kept trying to better our living situation.

Our Son Is Born

Anatoly was born in Odessa eleven years after we were married. He is our only child. Our way of life and cramped living conditions discouraged us from having more children. It was hard to raise children.

My own parents had been very religious. They raised us according to the traditions and observed the religious holidays. My grandfather was a member of the synagogue, of the *shul*. But since it was a Communist country, it was difficult for me to fulfill the religious rules because doing so would have compromised my position.

I observed the holidays I remembered from childhood. I made *hamantaschen*, and we went to Lazar's mother's home for Passover, but holidays were celebrated only at home.

The Doctors' Plot: Moscow to Odessa

When I first started practicing medicine, it didn't matter that I was Jewish. After the war attitudes toward Jews changed many times. Right after the war there wasn't major anti-Semitism. It increased until Stalin's death with a peak in 1952 and 1953. There was a time in 1952 when nobody would go to Jewish physicians. It was the time of cosmopolitanism. It was at this time that nine physicians from the Kremlin hospital were tried because of the so-called Doctors' Plot.

Although it supposedly took place in Moscow, the newspapers published a terrible rumor that spread across the country like circles in water: that Jewish doctors were trying to poison the whole population! The impact was felt strongly in Odessa where there was a high percentage of Jewish doctors. Most doctors felt that the situation throughout the country was becoming worse. In 1953 it wasn't officially claimed that Jewish doctors had to be fired, but patients, especially in out-patient departments, hardly went to them. A Jewish doctor could wait for eight hours and see no patients, unless the patients were Jewish. It was terrible on trains, trolley cars, or buses. I heard of Jewish doctors being thrown off the bus, even if it was moving. Many preferred to walk rather than to ride and take the chance.

A professor at the hospital where I worked recommended me for a position as a teaching assistant in surgery at the Institute of Medicine. Later he told me that unfortunately he couldn't help me because I was Jewish. I would have liked to teach. If I had been accepted, I would have been able to start my dissertation on breast cancer, but this was only possible ten years later.

I began by doing general surgery but became interested more and more in oncology of the breast. For almost twenty years I specialized in that field. Patients came to me from all over the city and other cities as well.

Last year I worked in the out-patient department. I did not continue to perform major surgery; I felt I was too old. Instead I saw patients and acted as a consultant in oncology for doctors with unusual cases from all over Odessa. One day a week I performed minor surgery that didn't require general anesthesia.

After Stalin's Death

After Stalin died, for a short time everyday life became easier. People were not as afraid of being sent off to a prison camp to die. The situation in the country wasn't so awful. It wasn't so hard to get food. But for a Jew like my daughter-in-law to get an education, and for me to move up in my occupation, was still very difficult.

Attitudes changed a little, but not much. The attitudes of neighbors varied; it depended on their education and their attitude toward other nationalities formed in childhood. If your neighbors hate you, they call you a *zhid*. If you have a good attitude, they like you as a person. I was a friendly person and liked to communicate, and so the neighbors' attitudes toward me were good.

Once I could have joined the Communist party, but no one in my family was a member. Now, it is difficult to explain why I didn't think about politics, but at the time I was just starting medical studies and had no time to think about politics. My not joining would not have been held against me.

The problem was that when I had a goal, to attain a higher position in the hospital, I was thwarted, my ambitions cut off. Nobody said it was because I am Jewish. They would come up with an explanation for why I didn't get the position. It was a cover for anti-Semitism. The slogan was that all nationalities had the right to do what they wanted to do, but under the table the government did what *it* wanted to do.

I Didn't Want to Emigrate from Russia

At my age it was difficult to emigrate to another country. I was satisfied with my work, I had money. It is difficult to go to another country where you have no money. But Anatoly and his family came to Chicago in December 1988, and the anti-Semitism increased in Russia. Nobody knows where this will lead. We left everything in Russia. Emigration is not an easy situation.

Our family applied together to leave Russia two years ago. We applied first in 1980, but for some reason we were ignored. Since that time the attitude between the countries (Russia and the U.S.) has changed. A new U.S. president was elected, and Brezhnev changed his policies toward the Jews. Yet, we didn't try again until 1988. Anatoly and his family received permission, but Lazar and I did not. They left Russia in 1988 and came to the U.S. through Austria. We came here as guests in October 1989. We left everything in Russia, and it's impossible to go back. We've applied for political asylum in the U.S.

When your children live with you, you try to live with the difficulties. When your children are gone, you don't want to remain in a dangerous situation. The neighbors changed; they stopped being friendly and treated us as enemies. Because the Jews of Germany were well educated in 1933, the general population resented them; the situation in Russia in 1990 is similar. In 1933 the Jews who thought it was a temporary situation put their lives in the fire. Russian Jews don't want to repeat that mistake.

The instability there makes it impossible to predict what will happen. All our friends are trying to leave Russia. They write to us, "It is very dangerous, don't come back. Stay there."

Because I received my education at a Soviet school, my attitudes differed from the beliefs of my parents. Never in my life did I ever believe that I would live somewhere where it would be possible to return to Jewish traditions.

LAZAR A.
Life Consists of Small Events

A large man of few words, Lazar A. was reluctant to be interviewed. His daughter-in-law Lia translated. He perceived his history as nothing out of the ordinary, yet at the age of six months he recovered from a wound in the head from grenade shrapnel and when a little older, he observed how his mother ingeniously fed the family using the by-products of sunflower seeds. Undoubtedly it was painful to dredge up some of the old memories.

He describes the back-breaking efforts of a young student to further his education in Odessa when he worked almost around the clock in a "workers' faculty" arrangement so that he would qualify to enter an agricultural institute in veterinary medicine.

But his life was not all hardship and tragedy. At the age of sixty-nine, almost fifty years after the events, he remembers with a smile his courtship of Inda in Alma-Ata, Kazakhstan, during the cruel conditions of the Second World War— how they had just enough money to purchase the two necessary marriage license stamps and one seemed to disappear. Had they not retrieved it, who knows when the marriage might have taken place!

After a rigorous life as a veterinarian traveling to rural areas around Odessa to care for livestock for most of his career, and later, as an agricultural inspector, Lazar finds himself adapting to an entirely different world. His concerns about anti-Semitism remain, even here in the United States. He questions whether Jews can be safe anywhere but Israel. Because his son and daughter-in-law and two grandchildren are in Chicago, Lazar and Inda followed their hearts, heedless of other anxieties.

Life Was Hard

Sarah and Anya were my sisters. One was older, the other younger than I. They are in Russia today. Until the war began, we lived together. My mother did not work. My father was a worker at the docks. Life was hard. There wasn't enough food in Russia in 1921, when I was born. In 1933 and 1937 many people died for lack of food. We ate sunflower seeds and the husks leftover from the seeds after the oil was pressed from them. The husk of the seeds was used in the bread. In 1921, when I was six months old, Odessa was beset with riots and government power was gone. We lived near the market. One day someone tossed a grenade, and two fragments lodged in my head. They operated and removed them; I still have the scars.

I Remember My Grandparents

My earliest memories were that life was hard, that there wasn't enough to eat. My grandmother's name was Chana, and my grandfather was Boruch. I think even then the family name was A. They lived in the town of Ananev in the Odessa region. My grandfather was a glazier. They did not live with us. My father was religious. He went to synagogue, laid *tefillin*, and observed the Jewish holidays. I went with my father to synagogue, and I went to a Jewish school until it closed when I was about eight and in the second grade. I remember when I was very small they hid the matzah on Pesach and gave us presents. My parents kept a kosher home and used different sets of dishes for dairy, meat, and Passover foods.

From stories told to me in childhood by my grandparents, I knew that there were *pogroms*, that it wasn't a good thing to be Jewish. I remember the word *Jew* was unpleasant when they said it. Everybody tried to hide it. During my school years I had Russian and Jewish friends. During childhood kids don't speak a lot about it, but when I got older it was different. I had my first problem when I was eighteen years old after finishing high school, when I applied to enter an agricultural institute.

Joining a Workers' Faculty

I always liked animals and decided when I was young to work with them. When I was older I wanted to go to the agriculture institute, but had to complete a special program to be able to do so. In Russia there were worker faculties, night classes for working people. If you finished such a faculty as a worker, it was easier for you to enter the institute. So, I enrolled in a workers' faculty because it was the only way for me to get a higher education. Education was only available for workers; most young people couldn't afford to study. They had to work in the morning and study in the evening. It wasn't necessary to do this just because I was Jewish. But for Jews it was the only way. It was very difficult to enter the institute without spending a couple of years at a workers' faculty.

I studied at the faculty of the agriculture institute not far from my house. There they made things from wood and metal. I started working in small workshops, as an apprentice. I was sixteen and did what I was told to do. Because I had to be a worker to enter the faculty, I worked in the morning until 4:00 P.M. then took classes after six. I then went to this faculty for two years of evening study.

At the agriculture institute there were very few Jews. There were twenty students in my group, which was not the full faculty, and more than half were Jewish. Some of these students were only able to get a ten-year education, the equivalent of a tenth grade education in the U.S., because they had to work to support themselves. Most of them didn't enter the institute after that.

There were two organizations we could have joined: the professional union and the *Komsomol*, the Communist Youth Organization. As a Jew I couldn't join the *Komsomol*, but I joined the professional organization. After the two years, when I was eighteen, I was able to enter the agriculture institute without taking entrance exams. It was 1939, and by then it wasn't as large a problem for Jews to enter. I was in school when the war broke out.

Relocated in Alma-Ata When War Begins

When the war started the institute closed and was relocated in Alma-Ata, which is in the far east of Russia. My father, a dockworker, had to do war work and wasn't permitted to leave Odessa. My older sister Anna was a family doctor and served in the army at that time. They knew that the war was starting, and many people were taken, especially doctors. When the war broke out, Anna was already in the army, in Donbass in the middle part of Russia. I and my small sister and my mother were evacuated on a coal ship. It was dirty and uncomfortable; there wasn't enough room or places to sleep, but it was our only means for leaving Odessa.

It was the beginning of September when we started our evacuation. It was very dangerous because there were German submarines in the Black Sea, and planes were dropping bombs. From the Black Sea we entered the Sea of Azov, and then we switched from the ship to a train. My mother was evacuated with my sister to Tashkent. I went to Alma-Ata.

The people from Moldavia, which was farther west and already occupied by the Germans, came and said that they were killing Jews. Most of the Jews tried to escape, but some, who didn't believe it was the nature of the Germans to kill Jews, stayed and were killed. My cousin and I talked to people who escaped from Moldavia leaving everything behind. It was very difficult to leave Odessa, but my father had a seaport ID, and so the family was able to take the ship and leave. I think that more Jews would have been able to escape, but Jews who remembered when the Germans came in the First World War couldn't believe that the same people would kill them. They remembered them as being more tolerant than the Russians. So many Jews stayed, and whoever stayed was killed.

Education and Deprivations of Daily Life in Alma-Ata

The evacuation was very difficult because we had nothing. Like now, we left everything and came without anything. Life was very hard, a struggle. Out of twenty, five from our group went to Alma-Ata. Kazakhstan (Alma-Ata is the capital) had its own agricultural institute, and that's where we went. This institute and the institute in Odessa were connected to each other. Our classes, conducted in Russian, the national language, were taught in part by professors from Odessa and in part by professors from Kazakhstan.

There was no clothing available, no shoes, no pants, and nothing to eat. Once a day they fed us a soup, which consisted mostly of water, some pickles, and two or three kernels of corn. Bread was rationed to 400 grams a day. You had to have a ration card to get it. Students had cards but had to work at night to keep them. On the black market food and clothing were available, but it was too expensive. Nobody could afford it. A pint of milk cost a month's salary. I worked at night at a large meat warehouse. They made a broth from the meat, and we got to eat some in place of receiving wages. In the summer I went to the small villages nearby, working as a veterinarian, and I was able to get food for my family, flour or rice.

We Meet and Marry

The Odessa medical school was relocated to Alma-Ata also. The institute and the medical students' dormitory were very close. All of us students spent our free time together, dancing and talking. Inda had gone to medical school in Kiev, but she came to Alma-Ata from Novosibirsk. My friends from Odessa who were students at the medical school introduced me to Inda. One day Inda came to see me. I had torn my only pants, and she sewed them for me while I lay under the blanket. I fell in love, and soon after that we got married.

Inda was in the last year of study when we got married. I had two more years. The wedding reception took place in her room with friends. She had a little money, and I had a little money, and we made a marriage. It was a civil marriage. You have to pay money for the two stamps, which are like a marriage license, but when she went to buy the stamps, they were out of them. We couldn't be married legally without these stamps. So, I went to the bank to buy the stamps. It was summer and very hot in Alma-Ata. After I bought the stamps, I folded them and because of the heat they stuck together. When I brought them to the official in charge she said it wasn't enough, that we needed two. We had no more money to buy more. Somehow we took them apart and were able to be married. There was no money for a wedding trip. Even after we got married in 1943, Inda continued to live in her place and I in mine.

I didn't have to serve in the army during the war because the students of every cultural institute had a required card that exempted them from service. In addition, I had a heart problem and so wouldn't have been able to serve anyway.

When Inda finished school, because she was a doctor, they refused to let her stay with me. They sent her to the European front, which had been liberated from Germany, because there was a need for doctors. At the beginning of 1944 she left Alma-Ata and went to Moscow, the Ukraine and Moldavia. In 1945 when I finished my education, they sent me to the Ukraine, to Odessa. Eventually, in 1946 Inda was also able to come to Odessa.

Living Conditions in Odessa after the War

When we were first reunited in Odessa, we didn't have a place of our own and stayed in my mother's house. My father died during the war. He was working near an army airport and was killed during bombing. My mother was living with her younger sister in Odessa when she died at the age of eighty-four.

After the war, living conditions were very difficult; we had no apartment, so we had no opportunity to have children. I worked all around the Odessa region, and so I was never home. I was home less than 100 days a year.

The village around Odessa would call for help from the city when there was a sick farm animal or an outbreak of disease among the animals because they had no local veterinarians. They would call, and I would go to the village and organize treatment and immunization for the animals—chickens, cows, horses, pigs, or sheep.

Although working in the villages took me away from home and the poor road conditions in the villages made my work difficult, I was able to buy food in the villages while it was still scarce in the city.

I worked as a veterinarian for twenty years, until 1965, and until recent years made occasional visits to the villages. After 1965 I worked more as an inspector than a doctor, often traveling to the smaller cities where they didn't have as many experts in my field.

Forbidden Matzah

I tried to pass on Jewish traditions and Jewish religion to my son Anatoly, but there were no Jewish books, no Torah, and I didn't read Hebrew. Instead of teaching him through books, we talked to him about his grandparents and the traditions they upheld. We celebrated the Jewish holidays as well as we could in Russia. We celebrated Purim and some general holidays. Every year on Pesach we got matzah. There was a time when it was forbidden to have matzah, and we tried to get it from underground. Sometimes I took Anatoly to synagogue, but it was dangerous because you could lose your job if you went to synagogue.

Chernobyl and *Glasnost*

We only heard about the disaster at Chernobyl. We couldn't do anything; we just knew it happened. We didn't know then exactly what happened, and it's only become more clear now. It was near Kiev, not Odessa, and nobody in Odessa was much concerned about it.

Before *glasnost* I didn't hear of any Jewish religious teaching, but after *glasnost* they started talking about it and meeting together in a synagogue. They made small-scale demonstrations for Jewish education. I was interested in Jewish education and organization of schools for Jews. I even took part twice. Before, if somebody found out that someone taught Hebrew, the teacher could be brought to court. Only the people who wanted to go to Israel tried to study Hebrew underground. In Odessa there were only two or three people who knew Hebrew.

In the last five years, because of *perestroika* and *glasnost* people were able to leave the country more and speak more openly. After *glasnost* I didn't really learn anything I hadn't already known. We knew about most things but were afraid to speak of them. We knew if we said something wrong we would "disappear."

No Reason to Remain

When Anatoly and Lia left with their family, there was no reason for us to remain. It might have been better for Inda and me to go to Israel, but because the children came here, we did too. I left Odessa with nothing. Even our photographs were left with my daughter-in-law's father.

We have friends in Israel. There will be a time when all Jews here in the United States will go to Israel. Anti-Semitism here will increase. I read newspapers published in the United States—in New York—in Russian, in which there are a lot of anti-Semitic articles. They are making fascist signs on synagogues here just like in Russia. It's not that bad now, but it could get worse.

Family Closeness

We were family of the same blood around our mother, because the mother is the beginning of the family. A mother loves her children and tries to keep them together. When children grow up, they have their own families, but they gather in their mother's home. I think all families stay together because of children and grandchildren and warm feelings toward each other, even though every member of the family has a different character and different ways, some good, and some bad.

I hope that even though now is a difficult time, the children will work hard and reach their goals. We grandparents have decided to devote ourselves to the kids. We will stay at home with our grandchildren to give Anatoly and Lia the opportunity to study to become eligible for medical residencies. Life is a series of small events and obstacles, some not so small, that we must overcome as we work to make our families safe and secure.

The "A" family in Odessa: Lia, Anatoly, Inda, and Lazar holding grandson, Leon. Taken prior to Lia and Anatoly's emigration in 1988.

Lia, holding Jacob, who was born in Chicago in January, 1992; Anatoly, Leon, Inda, and Natalie. Photo © 1992 by Bruce Mondschain. All rights reserved.

ANATOLY A.
Real Politics Stayed Hidden

At the time of the interview, Anatoly A. was under tremendous pressure, as was his wife Lia. He had to pass the foreign students' exams to qualify for surgical residency and was striving to perfect his English. In Odessa he had been a practicing surgeon for several years, had earned a Ph.D., and theoretically had been in a position to rise at the hospital where he had been practicing. The family had lost out on opportunities to emigrate in 1978 and 1980. Lia explained the thinking process that led to their actual emigration, particularly concerns about Pamyat, *a nationalist organization that was becoming more blatantly anti-Semitic.*

The extent to which Anatoly had "paid his dues" in the USSR was recounted in Lia's history. He served on an emergency air service with thirty-six-hour duty stints and no regular hours. Still, at the time they left, his hard work and dedication had paid off. He was situated well on his career track, in line to become a department chief.

Though accustomed to restraint in discussing political subjects—the habit of a lifetime—Anatoly states his contempt for the political details dispensed in the Soviet press. "It was impossible to get any real information."

Unlike Lia, Anatoly suffered only routine discrimination in the form of quotas and having to take the low road rather than the high to attain a footing in his profession.

The young doctors send their seven-year-old son to a religious Jewish day school, though both have an ethnic rather than religious identity. When Leon announced to his father, after school one day, how the world was created, Anatoly felt obliged to present the scientific view. Thus, Leon will have the information necessary to come to his own conclusions.

I was born in Odessa, 1954. My mother was an oncologist. My father was overseeing the hygiene/health inspection of cattle. He inspected the villages that raised steers and checked the animals before they were slaughtered.

I believe my grandmother, my father's mother, took care of me before I started school. Then I went to *yasli*, a nursery school, until the age of four. After that I went to kindergarten. I usually had supper with my mother. My father was often away on business trips. I was an only child and did everything by myself. Nobody helped me. From time to time I remember I was afraid to be alone. Then I would phone my mother. Our neighbors had a phone, but we didn't have one until I was grown up. Sometimes I went to their home to watch TV, which first appeared in Russia in 1959 or 1960.

In Time I Got Used to the Idea I Was a Jew

I remember Pesach and Purim. I remember Purim because I liked to eat *haman-taschen*, and I remember Pesach because we spent it with my grandmother. I remember the matzah and the horseradish and the salted eggs.

When I was a child I didn't like being a Jew. I remember going up to my mother and saying I didn't want to be a Jew because the boys around me had decided that Jews were bad people. I wanted to be like the others. When I said I didn't want to be a Jew, she said, "You're a Jew." And I said, "No." My mother's cousin, a very clever woman, tried to persuade me that being a Jew was very good and that it was impossible to change a nationality. I don't remember if I cried. In time I got used to the idea.

The consciousness that I was a Jew, a particular kind of nationality, came to me much later, at the end of school, when I was about fifteen. In my family we didn't touch on this subject very often. It was a sensitive question. Talking about it a lot doesn't help you to live with the difficulties. You start thinking about it all the time and that doesn't help. If you live in such a community and wish to have a social life, you have to use the rules of the community.

Medical School Quotas

I don't remember discussions about politics until I became a student. In Russia, the official opinion given in the newspapers is just the opposite of what it really is. It's very difficult to get information about what's happening with the Jews. Everybody knew that only 5 percent of the students admitted to the medical institute were Jewish, the quota set by the Russian government. Everyone knew that once at the medical institute you would have a lot of problems because of being a Jew. The discrimination was not an open policy; no official would openly admit to it. You could go to the medical institute and say, "OK, I'm a Jew. Do you discriminate against Jews?" "No," they would say, "we like Jews." But you see, official people have two faces. When you ask them about Jews, they show you one face; but when you start to do something as a Jew, they show you the other face.

I chose chemistry originally. It was a very difficult course of study; I knew at that time if I succeeded in entering the university to study chemistry my only career choice would be teaching. It was very difficult to move in research in chemistry as a Jew. In science, your development depends on the institution, the type of research, the kind of teachers, the kind of people who surround you. Research didn't have any future for me because I didn't want to be a teacher. I was familiar with the field because friends of my parents were teachers. Also, teaching chemistry is not a specialty in Russia.

My next choice was to be a doctor. I can't say I wanted to be a doctor from the very beginning of my life. Maybe it was my family, the books that surrounded me, the friends of my parents who were doctors, or my mother's advice, but by the time I was fifteen I had decided to prepare for medicine.

I didn't encounter much discrimination. They discriminate against Jews in the acceptance process for medical school, but I passed all the exams and was able to enter. Maybe the chief of the medical institute at that time was a very good person. My wife Lia couldn't go to medical school in Odessa because of the quota system. Her father was afraid that she would be failed. My parents were afraid, too, but they didn't want me to leave Odessa. That's why I applied first to the institute in Odessa, but if I had failed I would have tried to attend in another town.

Learning to "Swim" during Internship

I was sixteen when I entered medical school and graduated at twenty-two. I got my diploma, but I had to do an internship. Then I had a residency of three years during which I worked as a physician. Since I was just a resident I had some "privileges." For example, if there were complications in a case, I had a "curator" who looked after that patient and I was not the sole person responsible for that patient. But after three years, you become a physician and work on your own. Sometimes when you perform an operation, someone watches you and tries to help, but that's not typical. Usually you enter the medical mainstream right after your internship, and you "swim" as well as you can. Other people only make a show of looking after you, but nobody really interferes. It's like here. Everybody's the same.

In the sixth year of medical school I specialized in surgery. From my second year on I had been a member of a research organization at my medical school. This research organization helped me to become a surgeon.

On holidays, we had one or two days off. The first of May and the seventh of October represented something of the history of Russia, but to me it just meant a day off. As a surgeon I usually worked long hours. I lived with my family until the end of medical school, and then I moved to another town. I stayed with them not just to save money but also for social support. My family was a great help to me.

I Wasn't Invited to Join the Communist Party

It's very difficult, virtually impossible, for a Jew to become a member of the Communist party. First of all, the Communist party is a career, and they don't want Jews to have a career. Second, future members are chosen by existing members who choose people like themselves. Third, I was too young for the Communist party. Since I didn't always show my desire to become an active member of the Young Communist League or Young Communist Party, I wasn't tracked for selection.

Not being a member of the party did not become a problem for me. I stopped thinking about domestic politics. There are two political forums in Russia: the international forum and the local forum, the day-to-day events in Russia. In the local forum nothing ever changes. Everyday they would say the same thing: "Work for Russia and we will look after you." Why pay attention to that kind of politics?

Sakharov: From Popularity to Disgrace

Real politics stayed under cover. They don't say anything about Jews or people who don't live like everybody lives. Such people were given the name "dissidents." They tried to keep news about dissidents quiet. Sakharov was a great person and originally very popular. When Sakharov stated publicly that the state of internal politics of the Soviet government is not good, immediately a lot of comments appeared in the newspapers saying Sakharov was a bad person.

Nobody told us what Sakharov's dreams and ideas were. Nobody, including me, knew what he wanted to do. When an announcement appeared in the paper that Sakharov was a bad person, you realized that he had done something against the government, and you knew he was digging a grave for himself. It was impossible to get any information, any real information from the newspaper, so no one has any information about political matters.

I knew that there must be another side to the story, but I didn't know what it was. I knew that this was a very famous person who was in research in nuclear physics and he was a three-star hero, but what he would like to say and why the government published this article against him, I didn't know. That's why internal politics were not interesting—because I knew in advance what would be said.

As a physician in my generation I had Ukrainian, Georgian, Russian friends. There were few Jewish physicians in my generation because discrimination against Jews in the medical field rose after Stalin's death. Depending on their character and education, our friends had similar reactions when they read the news.

Ukrainian Was More Important than English

I studied English before I started medical school, two or three forty-five-minute lessons a week. We read little articles and translated them if we could. Nobody encouraged us to learn English for future considerations. They paid much more attention to the Ukrainian language.

Why Emigrate?

In 1978 I first thought about emigrating. I was in Bilgradenstrof, about 100 miles from Odessa. The institute assigned me there. I was there for three years. We actually applied to leave in 1978, but it was too late; the door was no longer open.

I returned to Odessa in 1980 and worked as a surgeon in an emergency hospital. In 1980 they didn't even answer. People in Moscow could still get out, but nothing was moving in Odessa. In 1980 I applied to go to the U.S. because I thought there was no future for Jews in the Soviet Union. Emigration is something to consider when there is no opportunity to fulfill your dreams. When the option to leave is open, you have to at least try.

LIA A. A.
After a Dark Struggle

The designation "Evrey" on the fifth line of her Soviet internal passport blotted out Lia's high academic achievement. In the 1970s she clashed with authority every step of the way to achieve her life plan, to be a doctor. Her grandparents and her husband's mother, living in a different political era, had no trouble getting into medical school. But after December 1952, when Stalin accused nine Kremlin doctors, six of whom were Jewish, of the Doctors' Plot, anti-Semitism blossomed.

Lia faced an insidious system where teachers recorded lower grades to hinder particular minority students. In childhood, she was hurt by children calling her Evrey *or* zhid. *As she grew older, the pervasive prejudice that blocked Jews seeking medical careers forced her not only to work harder but also to confront the system. Ultimately the effort itself became a reward.*

To attend medical school Lia, an honor student, had to travel to Saratov, "halfway to Siberia," where the minority quotas were not as great a problem. It was a sacrifice leaving her supportive father. So, more than midway through the medical program, once more having achieved honors, she bucked the system to return and finish her medical studies in Odessa. When she was ready for her first medical assignment, the familiar inequities reappeared.

In the fall of 1986, just months after the disaster at the Chernobyl nuclear station, pregnant with her second child, Lia took advanced medical courses in nearby Kiev. Not only was the public uninformed of the public health risk from radiation, but her professors also seemed unconcerned. Only later did the truth filter through the media. Today she maintains a brave stoicism in the wake of that exposure.

But for Lia the decision to emigrate came with the emergence of Pamyat, *the blatantly anti-Semitic Russian nationalist organization. She was shocked when the Jewish cemetery where her grandparents and mother are buried was vandalized and beautiful stone monuments desecrated. It was then that she urged her husband to leave—just when he, as a young surgeon, was advancing in his own career.*

Though Lia's identity was forged through her struggle with the Soviet system, she acquired a more subtle cultural awareness from her paternal grandmother. After her mother's untimely death, Lia learned how to cook certain Jewish dishes, a kind of living remembrance of an otherwise buried Jewish tradition. After Lia married, however, her husband's mother observed Jewish holidays, especially Passover, which happens to be the young couple's anniversary.

Though Lia concedes no sense of religious identity, she admits she was pleased and surprised as a guest at the first Jewish rite of passage she attended in Chicago—a brit. She found the joy of friends and relatives on this occasion very moving—"the most bright feeling." Since then, the family celebrated a brit of their own when their son Jacob was born. When Lia enters a synagogue, she appreciates the welcome. But despite her remarkable progress in English, she feels unable to respond as she would like.

Only two and a half years after coming to Chicago with limited English proficiency, Lia has passed the foreign student's medical qualifying exam and is entering pediatric residency in a fine teaching hospital. Her impatience to attain economic independence for her family is an inevitable corollary of her life experience and her own independent character.

I was born in Odessa in 1958. My grandparents were doctors. My mother and father were engineers. They both finished institute studies in Odessa. My brother Mikhail, an engineer, is four years older than I. Except for a few years in Tambov, where my parents were assigned after their institute studies, I spent most of my childhood in Odessa. When my mother's father died and my grandmother was alone, our family moved back to live with her.

We observed no Jewish holidays until the last years when my father's mother lived with us. She told me about her childhood in a small Jewish city and how they celebrated the holidays. After I got married, my mother-in-law, who was also from a small Jewish city and a religious family, told me about them. But during my first twenty years I didn't know anything.

The Internal Passport

One reason I knew I was Jewish was my Soviet internal passport. Whenever you travel, everybody knows that you are a Jew. It looks like a present my brother sent me. It's a joke: the "Odessa Citizen's Passport." Here line by line, just like in the real passport, is listed your family name, your first name, your father's name, when you were born, and on the fifth line, your nationality. On my passport it was *Evrey,* which means Jew. Other passports might say Ukrainian or Russian.

I was five when I first realized I was Jewish. Among children you can hear, "Don't play with him, he's a Jew." It's difficult to appreciate now, but sometimes it hurts when a child plays with you and calls you a name you know is bad, but you don't know why. I was young when my mother died, and my father worked and traveled a lot, and my brother was studying at an institute in Moscow. I stayed alone at home most of the time and had no opportunity to talk about the confusion. It may have happened only once or twice in my childhood, but I remember because it hurt. I knew it was better not to speak of it and that it was better if nobody knew you were Jewish.

As a child, I didn't like my name because it was a very Jewish name. If I said it, nobody needed to ask my nationality. It was obvious. I liked my given name, but not my family name. I remember asking my father why he had such a name. But you can't change your name.

It's difficult to say whether I would have married somebody who wasn't Jewish. As I grew older I understood that I was Jewish. My friends were Jewish, and I never considered that I could marry someone who wasn't. I lived in Odessa, a city with many Jews. In my eighth grade class at school there were maybe twelve Jewish boys and girls. Moreover, many of the teachers were Jewish.

We knew that it was almost impossible for a Jew to get the gold medal, the highest award in the public schools. We accepted the Russian attitude and weren't afraid we'd be hurt because we were Jews. I had some Russian, Ukrainian, and Bulgarian friends, but most of my friends were Jewish because when there was a difficult situation the Russians would stay apart and not be involved in your problem.

This is the way it was, and when you understand what was going on, it was sort of satisfying. I knew I had a more difficult way, and my way was different from all others. I liked that I had to struggle more than others to succeed. I liked to be first, and I liked that I was able to be first, even though I was a Jew.

Halfway to Siberia

The Russian and American educational systems are different. In Russia you finish public school after tenth grade. If you wish to study medicine, you attend a medical institute for six years. One must pass an exam before being admitted to an institute, which is the equivalent of a college in the U.S. Then you spend three years on the job—a total of nineteen years.

Sometimes public school teachers would mark in the Jewish student's permanent record "good" instead of "excellent," even if all his marks had been excellent. I had all "excellent" marks from the time I was ten, and my father wanted me to get a gold medal because then I could enter medical school with only one exam. If I passed it with a mark of "excellent," I could enter medical school without any problem. At the end of the last year of school, the tenth year, I had all "excellent" marks. Still, my father had to talk with the principal because I was not on the list for those qualified to receive the gold medal. They averaged my score at the end of school and hid the true average. I had the top grades but did not receive the gold medal to prove it. As a result I had to take all the exams. That was my first obstacle.

The next problem was that to take the exams I had to leave Odessa to go to

Saratov, which is like traveling from New York to San Francisco, six hours by plane from my city. This was because I would never have been accepted into medical school in Odessa. Only one Jew was accepted in every group of twenty applicants for the Odessa medical school; the other nineteen could not be Jewish. In Saratov it was easier because it was halfway to Siberia from the European part of the country where there is a large Jewish population. Since Saratov was very deep in Russia, I think less anti-Semitism showed up there, especially fifteen years ago when I entered.

A Pretense Reveals the Truth

After the exams, I had scored an average of twenty. The maximum score you can receive is twenty-five. All who get twenty can enter medical school. But when they made a list of those who could enter medical school, my name wasn't on it. I sent my brother, who was also in Saratov, to speak for me. He pretended he was an applicant and said, "My name is _____ and I passed the exam with a twenty, but my name is not on the list." They said, "That can't be because we accept all boys with a score of nineteen."

My brother came back and told me, "If I were in your place, I could enter but you cannot." In this case they wanted boys more than girls! But, before my father left he talked to the dean of the faculty, who was Jewish. He showed him my diploma from school, and that stated that I had received an award, a *Grammata*, a certificate like a gold medal in special subjects, which was awarded for a perfect score in a given subject. I had a *grammata* for biology, chemistry, literature, and math, even though I had no gold medal. I went to the dean, and I was allowed to enter medical school, but I didn't receive either a stipend or my student ID.

For one year I studied without a stipend and without an ID. Only after that year did they agree to take me into the regular course because I had excellent marks in all my courses for the year. In the third year I received a higher stipend, awarded to excellent students. Students who don't do well don't receive stipends, and those whose studies are excellent receive a higher stipend, 25 percent more than others. After the second year I received only the higher sum.

I entered Saratov on a six-year program, but my family was in Odessa and didn't want me to stay in Saratov. However, in Saratov they had a lot of Jewish professors, and the academic level of the school was much higher than in Odessa. After 1953 or so there were no Jewish professors in Odessa, and the medical school was not better for it. I studied in Saratov and liked it much better than when I went back to Odessa. I liked the students, the teachers, and the professors, but I was lonely away from home. My brother's wife was originally from Saratov, and during my first year I stayed with her mother, but then I moved to a student dormitory.

There were six or seven of us from Odessa, all Jewish, who had to go elsewhere for medical school. We went back together to Odessa for our school vacations. It would take six or seven hours on a night flight. We would leave at nine in the evening and arrive at five or six in the morning.

Another Temporary Setback

I was twenty-two when I went back to Odessa. My father wanted me to come back sooner, but it was impossible. The institute wouldn't accept me. It takes two years to transfer. In Saratov it was easy; I filled out the application, and I was told that in Odessa they had agreed to take me. I said good-bye to my friends, left my address for them to write, and came home with all my belongings. But when the school year began, I was told there was no place for me, and I was forced to return to Saratov for another year. I spent four years in Saratov and two in Odessa.

After six years in medical school, I had a yearlong internship, which was like a seventh year of study. We had a chief of internship, and we worked at the hospital in different programs such as infectious disease, pediatrics, and gynecology. I was in the Odessa City Clinic 7. I had a good chief for my internship, and I liked my assignment. I worked with kids for two or three months in each different specialty such as hematology, infectious disease, early childhood development, and pediatric internal medicine. After this, when I was twenty-four, I took my exams, and was certified to practice pediatrics anywhere in Russia.

I Refuse My "Orders"

After you finish medical school you receive an "order" to go to a special place where you must work for three years. You have to repay your education by working in that place. The order resembles residency in the U.S.

I had some trouble getting my assignment. Again I was one of the best students but was not given a choice. I was assigned to a small village but didn't want to go there and wouldn't sign the order. Because I wouldn't sign, I didn't work for more than half a year. During this time I struggled with them to get permission to stay in Odessa. Finally, I ended up in an outpatient department in Odessa.

Did I ever think it was not worth fighting the system? No. Maybe that has to do with my character. Officials haven't liked me all my life because I won't sit back. I say what I want to say. Even here in America.

An "Old Maid" of Twenty-four

My future husband and I met through our parents' friends. We had studied in the same school and lived only one block from each other in Odessa. Most of our married Jewish friends met each other during their school or institute years. We met when I finished medical school, before I started my internship. Some of our friends met as we did, but I don't think this was most typical.

Most early marriages are during student years at the institute or university or medical school. I was twenty-four when I got married; the average is from twenty to twenty-three. The age when you marry depends on your education or what part of the country you live in. In the Baltic republic the average age to marry was twenty-five. In the Ukraine, twenty-one or twenty-two was the average age. So I was an old maid!

After we were married my mother-in-law invited us to celebrate Jewish holidays. Three or four times a year she prepared gefilte fish and different dishes from matzah, and even cakes from matzah meal. At Pesach we could get matzah in synagogue, and she prepared all the traditional dishes. (The traditions are a little bit different in Russia.) We observed the traditions most thoroughly on Pesach because we were married at that time, so every year we had a Pesach table.

Traditional Foods without Tradition

When I was growing up after my mother died, it was my job to do the cooking. I did what I could and knew how to make some Jewish foods like *latkes*. My father's mother taught me how to make gefilte fish and other dishes. I did it just for fun, not for the rituals. It didn't have to be shabbat or a holiday when I made chicken soup with *mandelen* or matzah balls. I just knew these foods from childhood and prepared them on any holiday.

Our Family Increases; Our Careers Rise

Our son was born when I was doing my internship. His father was in Kiev on his *ordinatura* [medical internship]. He was doing his clinical studies and got his Ph.D. there. He came to pick us up after the baby was delivered. He stayed a week and then had to go back.

I don't know why, but five years later, when I came home from the delivery after our daughter was born, I knew it was impossible to live in this country anymore. From appearances everything was going well for our family. I had a good job. I finished my three-year course and started working in a hospital as a neonatologist. I had a good salary. My husband finished his Ph.D. and started working in Odessa's largest hospital as a surgeon.

Anatoly had problems because he was a Jew and wasn't assigned work during regular hours. He was assigned only night shifts or shifts on *somaviation*, an ambulance plane service. Such cities as Odessa, which is a large city, have a lot of hospitals, medical schools, and professors. The quality of medicine is high. In the small towns in the Odessa region there may be no clinic at all. If there is a patient with difficulties that the regional doctor can't handle, he calls the large city and a special plane that takes doctors from the large city to the patient's home for consultation. If it's serious, the patient is transported to the large city hospital.

All doctors in large clinics have duties, and one or two days a month they are on call with the ambulance plane service. The clinic where my husband worked was the largest clinic in the region for doctors who worked only on this service. It was hard work, and nobody wanted to do it. He was the one on the staff that did it because he couldn't have gotten into the hospital any other way.

The pace was like that of a residency here—he could spend thirty-six hours away from home and return at twelve at night or later. Two hours after arriving home he might be called to go somewhere else. Finally, right before we left, he was able to start working regular hours from nine to six. He had received his Ph.D., and they agreed to take him on the regular staff of the clinic. It's prestigious for a clinic to have a doctor with a Ph.D. He might have been happy to stay, because at the time we were getting ready to leave, things were taking a better turn for him; he had a good salary and regular hours. In the future he might have been able to advance because they assigned him where he might have become a department chief. I was the one who raised the subject of coming to the United States.

Pamyat and Open Anti-Semitism

We saw that everything was getting worse around us. There was *Pamyat*, a nationalistic organization. Because Odessa is a very Jewish city, it has two or three Jewish cemeteries, and my mother and grandparents are buried in one of them. In Russia when you have money you try to build a monument in memory of the dead. It might be made of marble with something inscribed in Hebrew or in Russian. One day we visited and found broken monuments and broken graves.

My family's graves were not damaged. They just damaged the central aisle where the most prominent and most expensive monuments were. Jewish monuments can be very large; a Jewish star can be two meters high of black marble. Since the monuments are large, you can't see beyond the second or third row from the center aisle. I think they broke what was in the center so that everybody could see it was broken.

Around the same time, a park was built over another Jewish cemetery. They just took machines, leveled everything, and put trees there. How can you feel, and what can you say? It was just a job for some people, and they did it.

Like a Return to the Period of the Doctors' Plot

People couldn't read the true facts about the anti-Semitism behind the Doctors' Plot trial when it was happening in 1953. People who are still alive remember what went on then, like people being thrown off buses. Even now since everything has turned around in Russia, my friends and my husband's aunt write that it's dangerous to travel by train, tram, or bus because there is a lot of anti-Semitic talk and that they fear similar things will start happening again. I think it's become worse since we left because when we were there it wasn't as open.

My brother lives in Lipitsk, a small city in the middle of Russia, not far from Saratov. He doesn't write that he wants to leave. Most anti-Semitism is on the border near Poland—in the Ukraine, in Byelorussia where there are more Jews. In the middle of Russia, where there are one or two Jews in a city, nobody cares, but where there are many, it's a problem.

Chernobyl: How It Reached Us

I remember the Chernobyl nuclear station accident very well. We were going to go camping with friends in Riba, which is not far from Odessa, and were packing tents in our cars. The first of May is a labor holiday in Russia, and the whole country gets three days' vacation. My mother-in-law came to our home on April 29, the day before we left, and said, "Something happened in Chernobyl." She had heard it on the radio, the Russian broadcast, just news that something happened, as if something happened in the bakery. Nobody realized what was actually going on. So we took the kids camping and brought our own food. We stayed on the banks of the river and used the water from the river. We spent all three days outdoors. All three days, just days after the accident, when the radiation level was very high.

Kiev is twelve hours from Odessa by train. It's far, but not too far to have an effect, depending on the wind. They say the winds blew in two directions, to the south and to the north. In Sweden, all the Baltic republics, and a piece of Byelorussia, they received a high level of radiation. We were in the other direction, the Ukraine, and I don't think that it was very high, but the chances of our exposure were increased because we were outdoors and drank the water from the river and used it to prepare food.

That year I was pregnant with Natalie, and I was taking advanced courses. I spent three months in Kiev, 100 kilometers from Chernobyl, because nobody told me it was dangerous for pregnant women to go there. Now everybody knows that they have to take kids out of Kiev three or four months a year for their health. We have received letters from our relatives and friends from Kiev who wrote that they didn't know anything and stayed in the city during the entire incident. The kids ate wild fruits like strawberries and whatever else they did normally. Now the newspapers, television, and radio are reporting everything, but knowledge after the fact can't change what happened.

The government didn't educate the people as they should have at all. All those years that we were in Russia, even we doctors didn't know the danger. When I was pregnant with my daughter and went to take an advanced course in Kiev, I wasn't aware of the danger. The only thing that was said was after my course. When I was five or six months pregnant, the professor who gave me the exam asked me, "How do you feel about being pregnant here? Are you bothered or not?" I said, "No, I'm not." And she seemed to agree. I don't think she knew any more than I did.

Perhaps Anatoly and I knew more than others because he has a distant relative who works with atomic power stations, in the main office in Kiev. He got much more information, but he knew only levels of radiation, where it was worse, such as the river. But nobody realized how long it would continue to pose a threat for the population. They thought that when a year passed, everything would be OK, not that it would be worse from year to year. The last letter that we received from my friend in Kiev said that the government, through city hall, gave all the women permission to have three months' vacation, with two months' pay, to take the kids under twelve years old away from Kiev. But they can't solve the problem of the air.

Once we agreed to leave we needed someone to sponsor us. My mother's cousin left Russia ten or twelve years ago and lives in Chicago. We wrote to her, and she agreed to fill out the papers.

Natalie was born in September. In April we got the documents from OVIR, and in September we got permission to leave. The whole process, from the decision to permission, took a year.

Help from Many

We came December 20, 1988. When we arrived here we were met by Jewish organizations, and we received support from them. The first ten days, we had help finding an apartment, and the Jewish Family Service gave us a very good case worker who helped us get Leon into Jewish kindergarten.

It was at this time that we talked about having Leon circumcised. He was five-and-a-half then, but he understood a lot and knew that most of the kids were circumcised. I think we decided all together. My husband is a surgeon and didn't think that a boy has to be circumcised. He believes every part of the anatomy has a purpose, even the appendix. He agreed to the circumcision because there was a medical reason to do it, not just a religious one. Leon had a constriction when he was three months old, but in Russia they refused to operate on it. They just made a tear in the constriction. I think he should have been circumcised anyway, but in Russia it was impossible.

I Am a Stranger Here

Though I'm glad to be here, I miss Russia. Because everyone speaks English around us, I don't feel at home here. I don't like to go out. It's difficult to explain. You can't say what you want to say. It's not like home.

We're Soviet Jews, but we were Russian; we were not Jewish. Because we never practiced religion, we never did anything, we just knew that we're Jews. It's like a label. It's not our feeling; we never were an entity like here.

"The Most Bright Feeling"

It was a great surprise when our American friends the Shapiros took us as guests to a circumcision in a house that was not very big, but full of people. They were saying *mazel tov* and *simen tov* like a whole family. I can't explain it, but it was the most bright feeling that these people felt that it's all in the family, that it happened for them, that they got a new member. I like that the Jews are unified here. In Russia you never feel that you are a member of something large; you have your friends, your narrow circle, but there is no community. Here the Jews seem like a large family with something in common.

Now my English is better, but a year ago it was a major problem. When we came to the synagogue, everybody started to smile and talk and ask questions, but I couldn't answer because I couldn't understand. I felt that they wanted to do as much as possible to make us feel comfortable. We were surprised at so much attention and so much concern. Before I started studying so hard for the medical exams, I felt I could go to the synagogue near us. I don't feel as much like a stranger there as I feel in the street.

From Our Own Efforts

I hope that we'll pass our exams and start working, that we'll be able to help our children choose what they want. They will not have a problem with the language; their native language will be English, not Russian. I hope we'll have freedom to do as much as we can on our own, without any help—not our parents', not the Jewish Federation's, or anyone else's, so that what we have will be from our own efforts.

4

PROBLEMS IN THE BIOGRAPHY

THE UMANTSEV/SHAFRAN FAMILY

RUDOLF UMANTSEV and Julia Zissman Umantsev reflect the political awareness and vitality characteristic of those who live and work in a capitol. Had they not had "problems in the biography," they both believe they could have accomplished more. Certainly they would never have chosen to leave Russia had Russia not in so many ways abandoned them.

Their son, Alex, and his wife, Lilia Shafran, inherited the same problems, but Mikhail Gorbachev's policies provided them with an escape hatch. For them all the possibilities available in their adopted country are fulfillment of a shared dream.

RUDOLF UMANTSEV
Some Things Are Beyond Repair

Rudolf Umantsev's story is one of making things better, making things work, whether he was tutoring his future wife Julia in mathematics or making the best of a bad situation. During the war, he was sent unarmed to the front and did what had to be done. When anti-Semitism was high, he took a job beneath his talents and transformed it into an illustrious career.

Rudolf graduated from the engineering institute at a time when it was a plus for a manager to fire his Jewish employees, however competent or essential their contributions in the workplace, when Jews were sent as far away as possible from the desirable cities and were routinely disparaged in newspapers and journals.

An honors student, the young electrical engineer found work at a district company whose director was willing to take people with "problems in the biography." Specializing in repairing industrial equipment of all kinds, the small company did essential work in a country where everything seemed to be breaking down. Because his professional training was irrelevant there, Rudolf spent a year just learning the work. Nonetheless, he learned to like it and made contributions that went well beyond his immediate sphere. These include the invention of equipment to repair the engines of icebreaker ships, critical in keeping shipping open in the frozen seas of the North. In addition, he collaborated with other experts to become the editor of a textbook and other works in his field. Before he emigrated, Rudolf, who had risen to the top of his specialty, was granted permission for his writings to be translated into English.

In a sense Rudolf's forbearers had been exiled even before his own reluctant self-imposed exile to the United States. His maternal grandfather moved by decree to Irkutsk, Siberia, early in the second half of the nineteenth century. Born in the Ukraine, in the Pale of Settlement, Grandfather Chaim Lustig (1836–1934) had purportedly held student gatherings in his house, to read, exchange opinions, even protest within the circle against conditions in czarist Russia, activities presaging the roots of the revolutionary movement. Despite the hardships of Siberian exile, Chaim had nine children and led a long life.

Rudolf's father, Boris Umantsev, and mother, Fanya Mikhailovna Lustig, were both born in Irkutsk, Boris in 1893 and Fanya in 1898. Boris became a financial inspector after the Revolution. Fanya was a respected gynecologist and worked for fifty years. Rudolf was born in Irkutsk in 1924 but moved to Moscow at the age of three when his father, a former clarinetist with the czar's army orchestra, was given a plum for his Communist support, assignment to the capital.

In 1942 Rudolf, seventeen, was drafted into the army and had to join the Communist party. This was a time when Jews were prevalent in the organization. Indeed, for all schoolchildren, he recalls, there were a series of steps that would lead to Communist leadership: Pioneer, Komsomol, party membership, followed by governmental positions of various levels, and finally, general secretary, which was Stalin's title. Later on, another step was put in place, the first step, Oktyabryonok, named after the month of the Revolution. Oktyabryata were children from five to seven years old who automatically joined the early ranks. But not everyone could be a Komsomol member—only the best.

After his youthful indoctrination, Rudolf recalls praising Stalin to his grandmother, who listened patiently to the boy while he proclaimed, "This is our leader, the father of all nations, of all peoples!" She replied, clearly unimpressed, "No, he's a czar."

My Early Childhood

Our family moved to Moscow in 1927, ten years after the Revolution. My father was a Communist, working as a financial inspector for the company GOSTORG, a governmental trading company. At that time, everybody wanted to live in the center, the central part of Russia. After 1932 my grandfather and grandmother went to Moscow to live and stayed in our house. They spoke only Yiddish, so when I was ten years old I could speak a little Yiddish. Later I forgot it.

When I was born my family practiced Judaism in the home. In Moscow we lived near the synagogue, maybe 200 yards away, in the central part of Moscow— *Malaja Bronnaja*. That synagogue was the only synagogue in Moscow; now they call it the Moscow Choral Synagogue. Until recently, except for this synagogue, there wasn't any kind of Jewish house, except a small *shul*, also close to the place where we lived. My grandfather liked living quite close to the *shul* where he could go and pray and meet with people. There was a Jewish theater, too. We went to the theater until 1948, when the producer Mikhoels was killed.

I was circumcised at birth in Siberia. There it was absolutely unheard of to have a boy not be circumcised, just like in America. In our district in Moscow there were many Jewish families. About half of my classmates were Jewish. We celebrated the Jewish holidays until 1942 when my great-grandmother, Chaia, died.

Among children and teenagers, religion of any kind was not popular because of the Communist idea. When I was ten years old I was a Pioneer. All Pioneers wore a red tie. On the first day of fourth grade, all of us children came to school in white shirts and black pants. We stood in line and were each given a metal pin. Then someone gave a speech saying that we had to be ready for the *Komsomol*, the next step after Pioneers. In three or five years we had to become *Komsomol* members.

The Outbreak of the War Surprises Us

When the war broke out in 1941, it was a surprise, totally unexpected. I was a high school student, sixteen years old. The administration of my school gathered all *Komsomol* members, students fifteen to seventeen years old, and we were sent to Smolensk in the western part of Russia, close to the front. We were sent there to prepare a fortification against tanks. There was no shelter and one gun for 1,000 children. A student, slightly older and a little smarter than the rest of us, was in charge. We had shovels, only shovels, so we built a trench and a wall against the tanks. The trench was ten feet deep, ten feet wide, as long as we could make it, fortified by a twelve-foot width of barbed wire.

We worked there about a month and a half, through June and July. They separated us into districts, each with 1,500 children. One day two men came on horseback and said that the Germans were somewhere nearby, but they didn't know where. They told us to run away. Moscow was about 200 miles away, or 300 kilometers. We ran about fifteen or sixteen kilometers a day, to a railway station, Malyj Yaroslavets, halfway between Moscow and where we had worked. We went the rest of the way by train.

We got back to Moscow in August, within ten days. The situation was calm until October 16, when there was a panic in all of Moscow. The German army was approaching the city. Our family was evacuated to Siberia. I left by train with my mother. My grandmother was evacuated with my mother's sister's family to Novosibirsk, at the beginning of October. My father stayed in Moscow until December, when he was evacuated with his factory crew to Siberia where he spent the remainder of the war making military products.

At first I went with my mother to Kuybyshev, now Samara. We lived there one month. My father, with his factory, evacuated from Moscow through Samara. I made contact with him there. After a month, in January 1942, Mother returned to Moscow. I stayed with my father in Tomsk, where I finished high school. I was drafted into the army in 1942, a year later.

Food Was Scarcer than Gold

Once I sold a piece of gold to a governmental shop and got two pairs of socks, two pounds of sugar, and maybe five pounds of macaroni. Inflation was very high then, and there was a great shortage of food. Food was the price of life.

When I was first drafted, first I studied in the military school and finished this in May 1943. I was sent to the western front, the second Ukrainian front. From the Baltic Sea to the Black Sea, the area was divided into parts, maybe four fronts. I reported to my military place of dispatch on August 27 in Kharkov, when it was liberated.

I was the commander of about twelve soldiers, of a unit smaller than a battalion. We had two cannons. As an officer, I had to be a member of the party. I became a member in 1942 when nobody could predict how the war would turn out. It was an awful situation because the front was in the Moscow suburbs.

From 1943 to the end of the war I was a serviceman on the front, a lieutenant in the antitank artillery. We turned the Germans back around that time. In the summer of 1943 the Germans were held near the city of Kharkov. It was important to make a strong stand there because Kharkov is a major industrial city, perhaps more important than Kiev. The fighting in Kharkov lasted a year. I arrived just when the Red Army was starting to win there.

I was wounded in the leg in December and hospitalized in Moscow for six months. At that time my mother was in Moscow, and we saw each other often.

She was a gynecologist and worked for the hospital of the Department of Railway Transportation.

When I got well I had to go back to the front. This time I was sent to the third Byelorussian front, to Konigsberg. I served with the Seventh Guard Army, Seventy-second Division, Seventy-eighth Separate Antitank Battalion. I won medals for the liberation of Konigsberg, on the tenth of April, 1945; I was awarded two orders of the Red Star and other orders that are not very important. The English queen, Queen Elizabeth, gave belt buckles as a gift to all officers. (At first it was difficult to take military decorations out of the country. Later with documents it was possible to take them out.)

Demobilization

I returned from the war in 1947, during a total demobilization of the Soviet army. Those who wanted to go home couldn't get permission, and those who wanted to be with the army were demobilized and sent back. There was some reason for this. In Russia there's always *some* reason. Youngsters were in the army and gained a lot of experience, but they wanted to go back home to study and so on. The army leadership wanted them to stay in the army so that the army would consist of the younger generation. The older generation, which didn't see many opportunities in civilian life, wanted to stay in the army, but the government didn't see any reason to keep older people in the army.

Discipline after the war wasn't very strict in the Soviet army, and life was rather easy. It was a good, pleasant time. I served in the army, but basically I played soccer a lot. Our battalion stayed near the new border of Russia and Poland. After the war, Russia occupied eastern Prussia and Konigsberg, and this territory became part of Russia.

I Meet a Girl Who Needs to Be Tutored in Math

When I came out in 1947, I entered an institute. For people who served in the war it was easy to do. I studied electrical engineering. Julia and I met that same year; we were very distant relatives, maybe fifth cousins on both maternal sides. We met in the summer at our dacha south of Moscow. Julia went there with her aunt to visit her relatives.

Julia was finishing school, and her math was very bad. She was and is a poor mathematician, and she needed tutoring. For almost a whole year I helped her study mathematics. We mixed the work with fun. We studied math and got to know each other better. I got the idea very quickly that she was a very reluctant student in math.

We were married July 10, 1949. My mom delivered our son on July 10, 1952, three years later. So July 10 is an important date in our life.

The Rise of Anti-Jewish Attitudes

There wasn't a specific date when anti-Semitism began. Before World War II there wasn't much anti-Semitism in Russia. The idea had not yet developed. Stalin was busy struggling with his enemies, and religion wasn't his main problem. That's why one could be a Jew, observe Judaism, and celebrate holidays.

In 1949 cosmopolitanism started. The term was used to describe people who are worried, not about their country or their Communist leaders but about the world in general, who would like to talk with people from different countries, anybody, regardless of ideology. This generally referred to Jews. Cosmopolitanism was not a well-publicized trend or term. The Doctors' Plot of 1952 is well-known, but the origin of that incident was much earlier. In Russia cosmopolitanism is an absolutely negative word. In 1949 the Russian government and educational system started special departments responsible for generating ideas to try to separate people from the cosmopolitans, like talking about people from abroad whose ideas are harmful for Russia. Especially important was the use of such special departments in institutes and universities.

In 1948 things were changing. The Anti-Fascist Committee was dissolved, and the Yiddish newspapers were stopped. Purges began to occur in places like Birobidzhan. Then there was an execution [of Jewish intellectuals] in 1952. We didn't hear anything bad about Birobidzhan. It wasn't affected by this anti-cosmopolitanism campaign. After Stalin's death, some documents were released showing that there had been a plan being developed to relocate Jews to Birobidzhan after the Doctors' Plot, following the campaign to convince people that Jews are enemies of the Russians.

Cosmopolitanism Comes to Mean Jewish Nose

In Russian there is a bad nickname for Jews, equivalent in English to "Jewish nose." The expression, *morda*, means "face of a horse", and *zhid* means "Jew" in Polish. After this campaign, the terms *Jewish nose* and *cosmopolitan* became equivalent. For six months, from the end of 1952 until March 1953, at the death of Stalin, not a single newspaper was issued in Russia without a special story, a *feuilleton*, about Jews. Not a single paper, including *The Pioneer*, the newspapers for kids, starting from kindergarten! For writers, it was a piece of bread for them to write in newspapers about Jews.

A medical newspaper circulated in our family because my wife is a pediatrician and my mother a gynecologist. In it was a big front-page article, a story about a certain doctor, Aleksandr Yakovlevich, who was a respected man, a very good specialist, and liked by everyone. They found out that on his passport it said not "Aleksandr Yakovlevich" but "Abram Yakovlevich." That was his crime, to call himself Aleksandr instead of Abram.

In Russia nothing happened without some reason. If an article was issued, it was meant as a signal for people, the authorities at that hospital, to start a campaign. It meant that Yakovlevich was a dead man. You could do whatever you wanted to with a man with such a status. You could just simply sue him.

I was at the institute during this campaign, writing my thesis for the B.A. In a class of 120 students, there were nineteen Jews. In America a student who gets a degree has to worry about the future by himself. He must look for a job, for a future employer. The Russian system is absolutely different. Your institution finds a job for you. The institution is responsible because everything must be under control of the central government, which the institute administration represents. You can only get a job through the institutional process. An employer usually doesn't have the right to accept people without such an assignment.

At that time, all Jews in my department were told that we would get an assignment for positions far from our homes, in small towns far from central places—regardless of our grades or of the results of our study, regardless of everything. After getting our B.A. degrees, we became engineers. (Americans are sometimes confused why so many engineers come from Russia. Almost everybody in technical science, and even sometimes in natural science, is an engineer.) But we were told that we wouldn't even get engineering positions. I simply refused to sign up for the assignment.

At that time experienced Jewish specialists of all kinds had problems. Some couldn't find work where they wanted, others lost their jobs, and young people couldn't find work. Some brainless bosses thought that their main responsibility was to fire Jews, regardless of experience or position; even a world-renowned scientist might be fired. Sometimes bosses got promoted because of that sort of thing.

How They Spread the Word

In Russia personnel departments were staffed by the KGB or the army and were very well organized. It was only necessary to issue an article in a newspaper, with a couple of phrases, to signal everybody in all the companies and institutions. Each head of the personnel department who read the newspaper would see this phrase and get the intended idea. No call, no letter was needed. Just one front-page story, editorial, a couple sentences, a hint, between the lines in *Pravda*—that was more than enough. Then a campaign would begin in each place. They were able to cover an enormous country with one sentence, one small idea in the newspaper.

In spite of this, there were people who knew that Jews could be useful for their enterprises, that Jews could work hard, were not worried about difficulties, and were dependable. They tried to attract Jews to their small companies that did work that was not very important, just necessary.

I had excellent grades. I had a "red" diploma, only A's. Three out of 125 students had a red diploma in my program. I was the only Jew; the two others were Russian. The first went to work at Yushin, a company that makes aircraft. That is one of the biggest, most prestigious companies. Of course, he got an entry-level position, but he got it straightaway with lots of advantages. He was given an apartment, a big salary, vacations in resorts on the Black Sea, the Crimea. All big institutions in Russia have their special closed resorts, open only for members of that institute.

The second Russian participated in the Second World War. Boris Konstanti-novich had been a POW in Germany in a concentration camp. At that time his situation was almost that of a Jew because he was from some point of view like a Jew. (Anyone who survived the German prison camps was considered equiva-lent to a traitor. He was tainted by surviving capture.) He is a very close friend of mine, someone with whom I correspond. We went to work together. He found a job in a company and told me that this company would accept Jews and different people with, as Russians used to say, "problems in the biography."

The company dealt with equipment, big electrical equipment like motors, generators, transformers. Our responsibility was to repair this equipment. It wasn't a prestigious, well-known, or great place to work, but it was a necessary service. Everything in Russia was in short supply—equipment, wire, materials, motors. In America if something breaks, you can fix it or find new equipment and forget about the old. In Russia it is necessary to fix everything. Prior to the time of our arrival, it was a small company, absolutely unknown.

Ivan Pechurin, a Russian, was the head of the Communist section of the company. Each company must have a Communist organization inside the enter-prise. He tried to attract Jews who were very big scientists in engineering. Because he gave them work, Pechurin had big troubles with the director of the company. The director used to say, "What are you doing? Why are you creating a synagogue in our enterprise?" Pechurin told him, "Look at yourself. You survive because of those people. It's your neck. They feed you." That was the sense of it. Without the Jews he would be nothing, and the company would be nothing.

Some of the people I worked with would be known in America in the electrical engineering community: Alexander Mosyevich Moldavin, Ph.D. in mathematics; Alexander Yakovlevich Filin; Yakov Mosyevich Karstein. Almost all of the engi-neering staff were Jews.

When so many Jews are together in one place, it's impossible to live without jokes. Russians knew that the Jews were good, dependable, people they could talk to. For instance, in Russia it used to be necessary to go to special seminars or political meetings to study the history of the Communist party, structure, building socialism and communism. At these meetings almost the whole group were Jews. Why? Because Jews were engineers, because Jews were smart enough that they could understand the written material. The joke at these meetings was, "Why shouldn't we just talk about the Jewish holidays? Why talk about socialism?" In a different kind of place that kind of joke wouldn't have been accepted at all.

I Learn on the Job

Basically my job was to repair machinery, but I wasn't trained to do so. It was a completely new thing for me; I had to learn on the job. For almost a year I worked as a worker, not as an engineer, in order to learn all the details of the job. At first, it was frustrating, but then I realized that it was an interesting area where I could discover and study new things for myself and society.

One of our responsibilities was to fix the electrical motors of the large ships that clear ice in the Arctic. Such ships are necessary because Russia's large northern ocean border freezes during the winter. It is necessary to ship things along that route, even through ice. These ships were icebreakers that make a path for other ships.

The way we used to fix an icebreaker was to deliver the unit to Japan where they had the technology to fix them. You needed to cut the ship into two pieces and take out the motor to fix it. Our company developed the technology to fix the motor inside the ship without cutting it apart. This was difficult because in a ship there is very little space around the motor.

To fix a ship in Japan cost hard currency, gold. We got paid in rubles, which means nothing to the country. To pay in hard currency was a major financial outlay. There is a shortage of hard currency and a surplus of rubles. Because we saved money for the government, we received a reward of money that ended up going to people who had nothing to do with the project, just to government officials.

I Rise in My Field

I worked at the district plant in Moscow for thirty-five years and became a leader in the repair of industrial equipment. I became the editor of a major textbook in our field. The original version was prepared by the most famous person in this area, Rudov Genken, who was Jewish. The book is *The Repair of Electrical Appliances*. When he died, I became the editor. The editorial board asked me to update the book. When I was in the process of emigration, I got a letter asking for permission to translate this book into English.

Gorbachev's System Couldn't Be Fixed

Gorbachev showed everybody that the Russian variant of the socialist system cannot survive. But Gorbachev wasn't the person who asked the question, he just showed people the answer. Before him there were many people who tried to ask the question, Where are we going? Everybody saw that the system couldn't survive because people in Russian do not work. Companies, institutions, distribution system, collective farms—everything has fallen apart. Everyone steals to get something. There's a saying—"What's the way of the Soviet system? The government steals from the people, and the people steal from the government."

Gorbachev sensed that the economy was failing. He wanted to change the economic situation. He wasn't thinking about grand political changes. He wanted to fix it as if it were an electric motor: take away the broken part and replace it with a new part. Because it wasn't just a broken, damaged motor, but a system that was bad throughout, the changes had to keep going further and further.

What Might Have Been

Now, I compare the differences between my life here and my life there a couple of years ago, before this process of emigration started, when all things in our family were normal, when things in Russia were more or less good. I cannot compare my present situation with how it would have been in Russia. We hear how things are there from newspapers and letters. Clearly, I took the right path, so there's no point in regretting it. Now there are gangsters there—it's not safe. It's worse than in Chicago in the 1930s.

I arrived in the U.S. the seventh of May of 1990. Having lived my life out in the Soviet Union, I wonder what the point of a person's life is. I see that maybe in America I could have followed my pursuits, but there I couldn't reach my goals. It would be much better to start life in America, in a country with great possibilities. I know that I could have done something valuable with my life.

The Russian government at different periods tried to break apart and suppress Jewish communities. Now they do not care about Jews. They simply let them go. In all of Russian history, the government never tried to issue a statement against anti-Semitism, although it's a violation of the Russian constitution. That fact helped me make the decision to leave.

JULIA ZISSMAN UMANTSEV
A Reduction of Remedies

By the time Julia Zissman Umantsev finished medical studies, the young pediatrician had already seen an attrition of possibilities taking place around her. Just after the Doctors' Plot furor, she graduated from the Medical Institute of Moscow. After she had already been assigned to an esteemed research institute for the Ph.D., suddenly, without cause, she was relegated to the Maria Roscha, *the notorious red-light district of Moscow, a career plunge consistent with the climactic decline of opportunities for Jews. Despite the dangers on the streets, Julia cared for children of prostitutes for five years until she received an appointment to the prestigious clinic of the Department of Railroad Transportation where her mother-in-law, a gynecologist, headed a department. There, by contrast, Julia tended the children of railroad VIPs, sometimes in their dachas.*

Julia, born in 1929, grew up in the thirties when Stalin had begun his purges. Two uncles, one high up in the Communist party apparatus, were arrested unjustly. One was shot soon after; the other died in prison. Overnight their families and Julia's grandfather were consigned to the street. They took refuge in the basement of the same building her family lived in. Although the basement was often flooded, they lived there many years. One of the bereft families was exiled in Karaganda until helped by Alexei, the still influential former Archbishop of Moscow who was close to the Zissmans' neighbors, the Strausovs, a Russian Orthodox family. These good people helped Julia and her family escape the German bombardment of Moscow. She and her mother fled to Tashkent where they lived with an Islamic family, and Julia had to blend in by wearing a chadra and braided hair like the daughters of the family. Her mother worked two jobs, by day as bookkeeper for a large factory and by night in a slaughterhouse laundering workers' clothes. The meat bones that she was allowed to take home were vital in a situation where food was extremely scarce.

Again, thanks to intercession by the Strausovs, Julia's family returned from Tashkent to Moscow, where they took temporary refuge in the same basement as her mother's widowed relatives until their own room was available again.

In 1949 Julia married Rudolf Umantsev for whom she gave up a Russian boyfriend. Rudolf, an engineer, tutored her in math to help her prepare for the medical entrance exams. Their son Alex notes that Jewish students typically worked with tutors to intensify their skills because they had to be better qualified than Russians to enter the Medical Institute.

In the last years Julia lived in Russia, the quality of life for all citizens declined. After the Chernobyl disaster, Julia treated children suffering from radiation exposure. Though Rudolf had refused when she first wanted to emigrate, once Alex, their only child, left with his family, he relented, and they followed in May 1990. She and Rudolf live with Alex, Lilia, and their beloved little son Boris for whom she cares while his parents are at work.

An Influential Family Helps Raise Me

I was born in Moscow in 1929. My mother was a bookkeeper in a big factory, and my father worked as accountant at a big firm. Before the Revolution he had worked at a bank. We lived in a three-room apartment that my mother received from work. Two rooms were occupied by the Strausov family, and the third room by my family. At that time it was the custom to share care of all of the children in an apartment. The Strausov family took care of me and their own three, who were older.

The Strausovs were close relatives of the most important religious person of the Russian Orthodox Church, Alexei, Archbishop of Russia. Strausov was his secretary and a friend of my grandfather, who liked to come to the apartment to talk to Alexei about history, about Torah, about ancient Hebrew. Alexei knew ancient Hebrew, Aramaic, French. Grandfather Samaravitsky, my mother's father, lived nearby, and would come to visit the archbishop who also visited this apartment. Before the war, all types of religion were suppressed, not only the Jewish religion but the Russian Orthodox religion too. Many Russian churches were closed. The archbishop used to celebrate Russian religious holidays at our apartment. We would go to my grandparents while Alexei and the Strausovs held services in our rooms. On Easter, my mother would help prepare their foods.

At Grandfather's Kosher Home We Celebrate Jewish Holidays

We strictly observed all Jewish holidays at my grandparents' home with all the traditional dishes. Although my family didn't keep kosher, everything at my grandparents' was kosher. We always had matzah because my grandfather was connected with the synagogue. Some Jews didn't know what it was, but we knew.

In general we knew about Jewish traditions, but my grandfather didn't speak Russian very well, so he didn't tell us much about Jewish holidays. I used to pray, and everything was done during the holiday that was supposed to be done. I picked up much more information from Aunt Strausov who knew a lot about Jewish traditions and used to tell me about them. Because the Strausovs were Russian, I learned a lot about Russian religious holidays, too. Right after the war, I learned that being Jewish was not a good thing, and I began to understand the family worries.

I was twelve years old when the war broke out in Moscow. From the very first day there were horrible bombing raids. We used to find shelter in the Moscow metro where everybody would go with pillows, mattresses, blankets, everything, to spend the night or maybe a couple of days. Immediately after the war broke out, I was sent to a hospital to work as a nurse's aide. At that time people started to evacuate from Moscow, but my family couldn't leave because my mother was chief bookkeeper of a very big electrical plant. She had a lot of responsibilities and a large sum of money at home, the payroll for a month, which she couldn't deposit because banks had canceled all operations.

We Were Warned: You Jews Won't Survive the War

When the war broke out it became known in Moscow that the Nazis had a strong anti-Semitic policy and that they exterminated Jews in the occupied territories, even in the Ukraine. Our neighbors, the Strausovs, said that presumably they would be able to survive the occupation if the Nazis came to Moscow, "but you

Jews, you won't. We know what's going on, what the Nazis are doing with Jews, and you won't survive. You have to go, you have to leave." They helped our family leave Moscow when it was difficult even to get a place on a train going south from Moscow. We left Moscow in October 1941, a very dangerous time, when the Nazis were almost in the Moscow suburbs, and the front was so close we could hear the cannons.

I worked at the hospital from morning until night, and my mother also worked. When we got our chance to leave, my father took me immediately, right when I came back from work, and we left the house just as we were. We didn't know where we were going because they just pushed us into the wagon and that was it. We were supposed to go to Tashkent because that's where my mother's factory had been evacuated. We traveled for four months, not because of a slow train, but because we didn't have legal documents or tickets, though the people who helped us travel were friends of Alexei and tried the best they could. We stopped at a station and had to spend some time there living in the country, in a church. Winter came, and we had to stay in that town. My mother still had all the papers and documents of this factory and wanted to go where the rest of the factory workers were so she could hand them over to the head of the factory. To lose them could cost you your life.

When we got to Tashkent, Mother handed over the documents. She worked full-time at the factory, and at night she worked at a slaughterhouse, doing the laundry for the workers. She washed their clothes by hand, from seven at night until seven in the morning. Even so we didn't have enough money to live on. Food was distributed by ration cards at work, so she had to work another shift in order to get more ration cards. A blue-collar worker at the same plant would have different benefits, bigger portions, more ration cards, but my mother was a white-collar worker, so she had a different packet of benefits, much smaller, and not enough to feed the family. The meat from the slaughterhouse was sent elsewhere, to the front maybe. Sometimes we could get bones, though, which was important for our survival.

I Live Like an Uzbek Daughter

I was able to go to school because we lived with a very intellectual Uzbek family, very rich. The man, who was Muslim, had four wives. We lived in Tashkent with his main, first wife. He had another estate, with gardens, where the three other wives lived with their younger children. The main wife lived in Tashkent with teenagers who went to school. The children went to Russian schools, learned Russian, French, English. They taught music too. I attended the same grade as one of the man's oldest daughters, who was my friend. In the summer, all members of the family would leave Tashkent and go to the estate. To live there was something very special, except for working in the garden. I had to wear a *chadra*, the traditional Islamic dress for women. I, a Jewish girl, had to wear a

Muslim outfit! I had forty-two braids, the whole thing. You had to look like one of them, or you could be killed!

These people took us in because they loved my family. They spoke very good Russian. When we got to Tashkent there was some kind of law in effect so that people in those regions had to take in evacuees. My mother helped this man with his bookkeeping, and I worked in their garden. Because of that, he gave some rice and other food to our family for the whole winter.

The End of the War

Father came at the very end of the war. The Strausov family helped us get permission to get back to Moscow. We lived for a time in the basement with our relatives, and then we got our apartment back.

I was already in the tenth grade and wanted to go to medical college. It became clear, however, that this type of education was virtually prohibited for Jews, that colleges were closed for Jews. I got into the institute with the help of my husband, who tutored me in mathematics. I entered in 1948 and finished in 1954.

I met Rudolf in 1947, and we got married in 1949. I had been in love with a Russian boy who was in the tenth grade with me. The young man was not Jewish, and my mother didn't want me to marry a Russian. She was working all day long and didn't want to leave me home alone, so she sent me to the suburbs, to her cousin's family. I lived there for a while and met Rudolf who was a distant relative, related by marriage.

Rudolf was a good tutor. I also had other tutors in biology, physics, and chemistry. Those people worked for the institute I wanted to get into, and they knew what was necessary to pass the exams. I worked hard and passed them all with good grades. In my application I wrote that I wanted to be a gynecologist. But in spite of my good test results, they pushed me into a different department, pediatrics, which I didn't want to enter. At that time everybody wanted to become gynecologists, so even though I scored high on the tests, they wouldn't let me do what I wanted to do. Since they didn't have enough students for the department of pediatrics, I became a pediatrician. In time I found satisfaction in my work.

Is It Possible for Jews?

Inside our student community and among our teachers, I didn't feel outright anti-Semitism or any kind of different treatment. It wasn't open, but all the Jewish students, five or so among 200 students in our department, knew their place exactly. Because we were Jews, we knew that not everything was allowed. We couldn't go outside certain borders. For example, a Russian student could apply for any class and get in. They gave the places to the Russians first. For Jews it was a very sensitive situation; you tried to avoid being refused a place. Before applying for those sorts of things, we would try to investigate if a Jew could even get into a given class. We tried to talk to assistants, to people who worked in that laboratory, asking, "Is it possible for Jews? What's the policy?" It usually depended on the professor. If we found out a certain professor accepted Jews, then we would write applications and try to get into his course.

Alex was born in 1952, while I was still in school. My husband took care of him most of the time. He was writing his dissertation, so he could stay at home to study and take care of Alex. My mother helped on the weekends.

Because I finished medical college with good grades, I should have been able to get an assignment at that college, in the same department where I had begun research two years earlier. But when I graduated, it was a question of documents and formal application procedures and so on. My nationality was the most important thing. I was sent to *Maria Roshcha*, the red-light district of Moscow. I didn't want to accept the assignment, but I didn't have any other choice.

I Tend to the Children of the *Maria Roshcha*

In 1954 I graduated, and they sent me to the worst, most difficult region in Moscow inhabited by prostitutes and criminals. There was rampant theft and corruption; that area had the highest crime rate. The streets were completely dirty and poorly lit. I would go there at night, but I wasn't afraid. When a family knew that the doctor was coming, they would ask the people in the neighborhood, criminals and the like, to bring the doctor to them and see that the doctor was protected, not only against other people but also because the roads were slippery and dangerous. The stairs in the buildings were bad, and so they would carry my bag full of instruments. Sometimes when I answered calls, I would see a gang busy dividing its spoils. I would say, "Go away, I have to look at the child." And they would pick up their things and quietly leave.

There were different kinds of prostitutes—for example, those who worked at the railway station, at the markets or shops, and those who worked around the churches. Despite their lifestyle, they were excellent mothers. They liked me because I was a doctor, and I knew almost everybody from that society. They were good to their kids.

The Communist Party: Why Rudolf Joins and I Do Not

Membership in the Communist party wasn't possible for me, as a Jew. My husband became a Communist in 1942 when the situation was absolutely different. Now, being a party member is considered a privilege, and Jews aren't allowed. There was a time when I wanted to join the Communist party. With membership, I could have gotten a better position. At that time I worked for a clinic, and I might become head of the pediatric department. I was young, experienced, and full of energy. I had studied for two years at a clinic after the institute and earned a higher degree. Despite my qualifications, they wouldn't take my application.

During another period I wanted to continue my studies, but they wouldn't accept my application for many years until a special law was issued. The law said that a doctor could not work as a physician without taking continuing education courses. As a doctor, it is necessary to update your knowledge, but it was many years before I could do this.

My mother-in-law was the head of the Department of Gynecology of a very prestigious place, the clinic of the USSR Department of Railroad Transportation. Advancement there depends on the departmental structure. My mother-in-law let me know when there was a position open. It was the decision of two people, the head of one department and the director of the whole organization as to whether or not I could be hired. They accepted me, and I worked for this clinic for thirty-five years.

Conditions for a Working Mother

I got up at six in the morning. My husband left for work at seven o'clock, and I left at eight. For three hours I would have office hours. In the afternoons I made house calls. I wrote prescriptions, and the patient had to pay for them. The working day lasted six-and-a-half hours. In case of an emergency, of course, we had to work longer hours either at the hospital or at people's homes. In those cases, nurses would come out to help us.

Among my patients were kids of high-ranked parents who worked for the Department of Railroad Transportation, the children of the minister, vice minister. Sometimes it was necessary to go to their homes because they lived in dachas outside of Moscow. Sometimes I would stay there overnight with the children. If one of the children had to go to the hospital, then doctors from our clinic had to care for the child in the hospital, in spite of the fact that the hospital had its own physicians and pediatricians.

If I had a morning shift, then I got off at four. I'd get home at five or six because I had to do the shopping. If it was an evening shift, I left at one in the afternoon and got home at eight-thirty. I worked five days a week plus two Saturdays a month. I shopped every day, cooked, and did the cleaning and the laundry. I went to bed at eleven or eleven-thirty and had to get up at six.

In 1962 we got our own apartment, although we still lived with my father. It was a relief because it was large enough for our whole family. At that time living conditions changed a little bit. In the late 1950s and 1960s, I had to wash everything by hand. We had refrigerators, but no washers or dryers. Soon after we got a new apartment, we bought a washing machine.

In the Sixties, Dyed-in-the-Wool Anti-Semitism

In the sixties anti-Semitism was overwhelming, dyed-in-the-wool. I had a good, high-level education, but though I wanted to become head of a department or maybe change my place of work, I couldn't. Some of our relatives began to emigrate to Israel in the early seventies, and one, a physician, invited me. He said that he would try to prepare a position for me. During the Yom Kippur War anti-Semitism was less of a problem than during the Six-Day War in 1967. It wouldn't have been difficult, and I really wanted to try, but my husband did not.

We were interested in the domestic and national situation and listened to "Voice of America" and "Voice of Israel." When Sakharov was arrested and banished to Gorky, we understood and were on Sakharov's side (because we had family that knew him). Almost everybody in our family understood how bad it was, how unjust.

The Children of Chernobyl Come to Moscow

In 1986 a number of things happened. There was the Chernobyl disaster, and it was around that time that *glasnost* started. They were not connected directly, but the party congress was prior to the disaster, and so *glasnost* had been announced before the accident. Chernobyl was like an explosion for *glasnost*, a test.

As a doctor I was familiar with nuclear medicine, with treatment after radiation exposure. We treated children from the Chernobyl region who were affected by exposure to radiation. We saw them in Moscow five days after the disaster. They had various problems. They didn't send the worst to us; chemotherapy was done in other places that had special equipment. We tested the children with only a small degree of infection. The most common problems were changes in the blood. Their skin had not yet been affected; they just had minor blood problems. Radiation sickness is the kind of disease that evolves gradually. Now, those same children are in the most serious of situations. I continued to see these children up until the time I left. The blood changes in them have developed into leukemia in varying degrees.

The Question Was Solved

Later, it wasn't necessary to try to convince Rudolf to leave because when my son left the country the question was solved automatically. The place wouldn't matter, America, Israel, or the moon! We would leave the country to be with our children.

Portrait of the Samaravitsky family, taken in 1931. Julia Zissman, 2 years old, is in her mother Maria's arms. From left to right, standing, are: Uncle Paul Samaravitsky and his wife Sofia; Uncle Alexander and wife, Aunt Sonja; Uncle Moshe Levitan and wife Aunt Liza; Julia's father, Izrail Zissman. Seated, from left: Grandmother Samaravitsky, Cousin Paul (son of Sonja and Alex), Uncle Isaac, visiting from New York City; Cousin Isaac (son of Paul and Sofia), and Grandfather Samaravitsky.

Soon after the photo was taken, Paul Samaravitsky was arrested and within three days was shot. No explanation was given. Moshe Levitan was arrested without explanation and disappeared.

Pioneer Camp, Rudolf Umantsev on right, 1932.

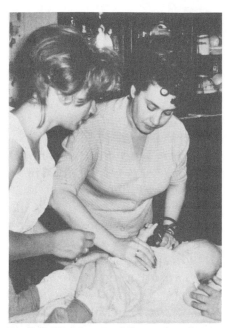

Dr. Julia Umantsev while employed at
the Clinic of the Department of Railroad
Transportation in Moscow where she
worked for 35 years. She often made
house calls.

Umantsev/Shafran family enjoying tea. From left: Julia; Lilia holding Boris; Rudolf; and
Alex, in their suburban townhouse, 1992. Photo © 1992 by Bruce Mondschain. All rights
reserved.

ALEX UMANTSEV
Contrasts and Comparisons

Alex and his wife Lilia arrived in Chicago in May 1988 with their little son Boris after an exhausting departure through Moscow customs, a stopover in Vienna, and almost six months of processing in Italy. Born in 1952, Alex still bristles at the unjustness of the Soviet system that tried to own the minds of its citizens, indoctrinating them from kindergarten.

Upon his departure from Moscow the authorities allowed him to take few personal possessions, prohibiting even his handwritten journal and Chumash, *the Hebrew prayer book that had been in his family almost 100 years.*

Alex finished institute studies and found a job that he never liked but where he could begin work on the physics problem in which he was interested. He decided to change specialties. In order to do this, he had to enter the two-year department at Moscow University. But there were two candidates and one vacancy. He passed all the exams with good grades. Although the other candidate, a Russian, received lower grades, he won the place.

Nonetheless, Alex persevered and became a physicist with a Ph.D. in solid-state metals research. Today he is pleased to be a researcher at Northwestern University. Now he can securely compare and contrast the Russia he knew with the America he knows. He and Lilia sponsored his parents' immigration one year after their own arrival. Together the Umantsevs live in a recently purchased suburban townhome where little Boris, a handsome, personable, and very confident preschooler, is being raised to be bilingual.

How I Learned in Russia That I'm Jewish

In America kids recognize themselves as Jews from the very beginning. But in Russia, I didn't recognize myself as a Jew until I was fourteen or fifteen years old. I heard this word—*Jew*. I didn't understand why kids called me a Jew or why it was bad. In Russian there are several terms to call a Jew, and they are not like nicknames. By that time, many of my friends were Jewish, and I started to understand that I belonged to the Jewish nationality, to a very old people, to the part of the world community with a very old and rich history.

The Moscow Synagogue is very old, very beautiful, with special details that helped to serve the religion in this difficult environment. For many years, Russia was trying to kill all religions, and especially the Jewish religion. We started to visit the synagogue during big holidays like Passover, Rosh Hashanah, Simhat Torah, when I was sixteen or seventeen. We also used to meet friends near the synagogue, and somehow I realized that this tradition was mine. This was something that I could say that I liked, that I understood. I was proud, and I am proud of being Jewish.

I can't say that it was my family that brought me to the synagogue. It was probably my friends and my own desires. I'm not sure that I really can explain all the details even now. In Russia, it was part of a child's education to teach them that there isn't anything like religion. The great idea, the Communist idea was that all people should be Communists; they should be the same, and most importantly they should belong to the working class. Organized religion was outlawed.

I recall the story when one man was imprisoned just for teaching Hebrew. He had a group of people who studied the Hebrew alphabet, words, trying to understand the Torah in Hebrew. He was imprisoned not for some kind of plot against the government but only for teaching the Hebrew language at the beginning level. I'm absolutely sure that people who gathered and tried to study Hebrew were not at any kind of advanced level. When I lived in Russia I only knew a few letters of the Hebrew alphabet.

I knew guys who were expelled from the institute because they visited synagogue. Once during Rosh Hashanah or Yom Kippur, we were at the synagogue, singing and talking with friends, and a man appeared who was taking pictures of us with a flash camera. Some of the pictures appeared at the institute where I studied. I don't remember if my picture was there, but we students were telling this story to each other—which photographs appeared and who was questioned about visiting the synagogue. The pictures appeared at first in the party committee of the institute.

All enterprises and institutes are governed by the government. They have a special party committee. It is very stupid that everything could be governed from a single place, but in Russia these things are customary. The first pictures appeared in this party committee, and then they were distributed to the departments.

Lilia and I Meet on a Ski Vacation

We met each other far from Moscow in a small, northern town in the mountains. Almost all of us were Muscovites. I was with my friend, with whom I worked at the institute and with whom I published a paper. Lilia came to see her friend who was with my same group. It was unusual that we met each other far from Moscow, though we both lived in Moscow. We used the same metro station in Moscow to get to work but only met 1,500 miles away from Moscow!

When Lilia returned to Moscow, I met her at the train station. We dated for a year, and then married. A year is not a very long time, but we were both in our thirties and had some life experience.

I Applaud after Our Wedding

You have to sign special papers and get a special seal on your internal passport when you get married. The passport plays a very important role in Russia. There is a person who is responsible for this procedure, who has to pronounce a special speech, congratulating the new couple. Usually it's a woman, and she has a special dress, with a ribbon with a Russian emblem on it, with the flag, with some kind of stupid thing. When she was pronouncing this speech, Lilia knew that I didn't like it and that I couldn't wait for the end of her speech. The official said, "Congratulations. It's the beginning, starting a new family; your family is the smallest part of the society . . ." and other stupid things. It was trivial, a substitute for a religious, beautiful ceremony that makes sense, substituting a religious idea with a Communist idea, with the idea that you belong to the state, that your life belongs to the state. When she finally finished, I applauded, which was absolutely unaccustomed, absolutely unnatural, but that was how I reacted.

Capturing the Minds of Children

Starting from kindergarten, you are indoctrinated with the Communist idea. Of course, this is difficult for everybody, not only for Jews, but it's more difficult for Jews because the Communist idea excludes Jews. Now people have simply thrown out almost the entire idea, all in one year. Everybody knew that this indoctrination was something very dangerous and unnecessary. It began with the renovation of history. In 1917 they threw out religion; everything started from the Revolution. Now people have grasped all that has happened, and they are in turn throwing out ideology and are coming back to a religious point of view.

Russian Nationalism

Now people are recognizing themselves as a Russian nation. They are trying to condemn Jews, and of course this process of recognition as a nation brought about more anti-Semitism. Even so, the most important point in Russia is simply food, not nationality.

To some extent, despite the war Jews feel themselves more protected in Israel than in Russia. They can see that the situation is bad in Russia and becoming worse, not better. Everybody needs food and protection, and those are two things that are in short supply in Russia.

The Idea to Emigrate

I wanted to emigrate ten years earlier than we did, when I finished the institute and started to understand things that were happening. I wanted to leave, but in

1979, at the end of the year, Russian policy changed. The government simply closed the gates, and I couldn't get out. For ten years I had to find some kind of occupation, work. I was lucky that I could.

When I met Lilia, we started to talk about things like that. We didn't talk much, because quickly we realized that we had absolutely the same opinion, and when you have the same opinion, you don't have much to talk about, you see? We were only waiting for the moment, but we were not sure that the moment would come.

The situation could change so quickly and drastically that the president of Russia wouldn't have anything else to say except "let them go." When that happened we were almost the first to leave. My cousins left Russia during Gorbachev's fourth "wave." Counting back to the Revolution, people number the emigrations; that was the fourth wave. It depends on the point of view. The first wave was after the Revolution, the next before the war and immediately after the war, the third in the seventies ending in 1979. Now this is Gorbachev's, the fourth wave. We really can call it Gorbachev's because he gave permission for it to take place.

At first, we saw very slight signs of change when he was trying to improve his image and get some kind of help from the Western countries. He permitted more contacts with Western countries. It was similar to the situation in the Seventies, the period that was called *detente*.

Boris Is Born and the Gates Open

Then later we got strong, very strong, clear signs. These signals came in the form of new treatment for refuseniks. Many of my friends were refuseniks. We got permission to leave the country, and Lilia delivered Boris almost on the same day.

Two days later, I went to OVIR while Lilia was at the hospital. I went each day to find out about her condition. Two days after she delivered they told me we had permission to leave, and if we liked we could get all documents, visas, and leave Russia as quickly as we liked. It was to some extent difficult because our son was so young. We had to wait for three or four months. He was exactly four months old when we were prepared to travel with him.

We had a lot of luggage, much of which was for Boris. We had special food, a Finnish milk. He had been drinking the formula for four months, and we thought it would be difficult for him to change foods. Living in Russia, you always try to get something that you can depend on, which usually meant trying to get some kind of Western food. We had a lot of special things for Boris, like clothing, socks, shoes. And we had a big baby stroller, which was old and awkward but very solid. (When we got to America we traveled a lot. I don't remember any other period of my life when I traveled so much!) His stroller was good protection; it was as if he were in a small tank.

Then, the second part of the luggage—I don't understand how it could happen.

I was able to bring my entire archive, simply everything I had in Russia. I had many books. Some of them, general books like novels, we sent to America to a friend of mine in Philadelphia who left a year before us. Only special books that I used at work were not sent by mail because Russian mail isn't very dependable.

Other than these books, I had some handwritten things. You cannot send handwritten things by Russian mail; it is absolutely prohibited. You can send them from city to city inside Russia, but not abroad. I used to write everything by hand, my thoughts, work that I've already finished. I didn't have a journal because I'm not so organized as to keep everything in the same journal. It was just separate papers collected by a paper clip. Each topic was set off by a paper. I also had some computer programs that I finished. They could probably be sent now, but it costs a lot and we don't have that kind of money.

We were nervous to some extent when leaving. We got into an incident at customs. I was very nervous, upset. I visited the office of the chief of the department trying to get the permission to send cargo, but I could not. I realized that I had to carry everything with me. I was angry and I lost my temper.

Before the day of your flight, you must pass through customs offices. You must show your luggage, open all your bags, boxes, everything you have and show it. They have a great list of things that are restricted, that you can't take out, or if you can, you cannot take out two things alike, only one. For instance, they restrict the amount of jewelry/valuables you can take. This category includes golden rings, earrings or chains, things that belong to women, or silver spoons and forks for the table. We didn't bring those items that day. We didn't bring all our things the day before.

The second category is anything written by hand. When you pass through customs, you cannot take your handwritten papers. Those are prohibited. You have to show your journal, your register, your diary, to officers, and then it is their choice to make a decision. They could look through everything, read it, and come to a decision. Or if he found something or did not like your face, then forget about it. It's up to his discretion to give permission or not. Why the concern with handwritten material? Russians are always afraid that somebody could take secrets out of Russia and bring them to different countries, to their enemies.

This is an interesting point that delves deeply into the Russian ideology—everything belongs to the state. You do not have your own property, your private property, which is something that appeared in Russia only during the last year. During the last year they started to talk about laws concerning private property. Before that, everything belonged to the state.

Just two months before we left there was a law that you had to get special permission to take each book with you. If a book were old, published before the war, before 1941, then you wouldn't be able to get permission. If it was a really special book, you had to take complicated special measures. Our *Chumash* was published in 1898, and I couldn't take it out. They wouldn't give us permission. My parents tried, and they couldn't. Nobody gave them permission because it was thought that it was a treasure and should belong to Russia. It's a bilingual

Chumash, Russian and Hebrew. On the first page is written "For use by Jews." Despite this fact, they wouldn't let us take it.

The third stage of leaving Russia is a document and visa inspection by the military. They also check absolutely everything you have with you. They didn't allow me to take my stamp collection, but I wasn't worried about that thing.

An awful incident occurred over the baby. Fifteen to twenty minutes before this inspection, Boris fell asleep. I asked them to let him be, not to touch the kid or the baby stroller because he was sleeping. They refused, and they started checking everything inside the baby stroller. We had to take the baby out. We had to wake him up. He started to cry. He was only four months old! His birthday was the twenty-eighth of September, and we left the country on the twenty-ninth of January. He started to cry, and he cried for three hours, until we reached Vienna. It was absolutely awful. I don't know what they were looking for—gold, something secret. There is a term that we use for this last procedure—we call it "the last piece of Soviet Russia". It is something that I will probably remember forever.

The final inspection took more than a day; they started at night. The luggage inspection alone took several hours. Afterward we had to go home and get our family and the rest of the things. Then we were waiting in a long queue. I didn't get any sleep for over twenty-four hours. It's a long and difficult procedure. This procedure needn't be an obstacle. If you're nervous about the procedure, then you have a different choice. You can leave everything. You can take just your passports, visas, and bags with some necessary things, and that's it.

Like Babylon

My first impression of New York International Airport was that it was something like Babylon. There were so many people, so many bags. So much was happening—just streams of people running. I didn't understand anything. I knew only that I had to pick up our bags and the baby stroller, to get out of that place. It was all a dream. New York is a symbol of America. I wanted to get some New York air, so I walked out of the airport, but I was only able to spend fifteen minutes outside the airport. I tried to understand what New York looked like, but it was difficult. It was so big. I remember one thing in particular. I was surprised that the airport was so close to highways. In Russia airports are always somewhere far out of the city.

The Major Difference between the U.S. and the USSR

The most important difference between Russia and America is the people. People have a different feeling, a different attitude toward you. This difference was, to some extent, surprising. In this case it was a pleasant surprise. Not only in all Jewish agencies that we dealt with, whose welcome was, to some extent predictable, but also in other situations, people were very welcoming. We somewhat expected that we would be accepted with good feelings by the Jewish community. But, even in streets, in shops, in public places, the American people were very friendly, smiling. If people knew that you'd just emigrated, they would try to ask you questions and talk to you. We felt that they were happy that we had come to their country.

LILIA SHAFRAN
Seeing it with Her Own Eyes

Lilia is extroverted, friendly, and laughs easily. Aside from the romantic meeting she and Alex had at a ski resort far from Moscow and memories of the beautiful monuments and parks in central Moscow where she grew up, Lilia's most vivid memories include the nightmarish process of dealing with OVIR, which she recounts with the same intensity as her husband described the educational barriers for Jews and the customs experiences at the airport. Their exodus from the airport in a way capsulized a history of heartless, vindictive officiousness.

Born in Moscow in 1953, Lilia was raised by her mother and grandmother after her parents were separated when she was a small child. When, after three years of trying to enter the foreign language institute, her goal of becoming an interpreter and translator was precluded, she studied proofreading and editing. Eventually she obtained work with a journal whose readers were in the hydroelectrical and nuclear power plant industry. It was at her office that she learned the true nature of the Chernobyl accident and was able to inform her family.

Without having discussed their desire to emigrate, Lilia and Alex were in total accord. They wanted their son to have a better life with greater possibilities. Lilia, pessimistic about her former country, prophesied the dissolution of the Soviet Union during the interview.

Lilia has maintained her maiden name, a tradition in her family, consistent with her approach of holding on to the good of the past, rejecting the bad. Today, one of the attainments that most pleases her is that she is a teaching assistant in the eighth grade at the Ida Crown Jewish Academy in Chicago, where she helps students with their English, math, and social studies. And thanks to Alex's parents who care for Boris when his parents are away, they can take off occasionally. These brief interludes allow them to relive a happy time in Russia, as when they drive into Wisconsin for a day's skiing.

Lilia's outlook is expressed in a brief statement of philosophy. "My life credo:

I prefer to think and then to do. Never to think people are bad until I see it with my own eyes. I do not like to believe any rumors."

My Education, in the World and at School

I became aware of politics at the time of the war of Israel and Arab countries. There was a lot of anti-Jewish talk in Moscow. It was thought that the Israelis did something terrible. "Aggressor!" This was the most common word at this time. The people on the street, especially Jewish people, understood that this was a big lie.

When I graduated from high school in 1970, I wanted to be an interpreter, to translate technical articles. I wanted to attend the foreign language institute because to graduate from this institute was very prestigious. For three years I tried to enter the Institute of Foreign Languages, but to do so I had to pass four exams with two B's and two A's. They couldn't give me a B on the English exam because my English was excellent—pronunciation, grammar, everything; Russian language—also excellent—and composition. So they gave me a low grade for Soviet history. The professor said, "You're not well prepared. I can't give you a B. I have to give you a C."

For three years I tried to get in with zero success. I worked at school, some secretarial work. When I was sick and tired of this, my mother said I must try something else because everyone needs a profession. I have a "humanities" kind of mind. I'm not good with technical science stuff, so I started to look for another option. I found nothing. My mother suggested that I go to a college connected with proofreading. My Russian language was very good, and I entered without any difficulty because it's just a middle-level profession. They don't think about anti-Semitism at this level. It's difficult to understand, but they just didn't want Soviet Jews to have a high education. They allowed us only a middle-range education. After this I started to work as a proofreader.

I Become an Editor for a Trade Journal

I worked for a trade journal for hydroelectric power stations and nuclear stations, like Chernobyl. The journal was connected with the Project Institute of Power Stations. It was a small national scientific publication with circulation of maybe 2,000. We published twice a month and abroad, bimonthly, because this institute did projects in the so-called Third World. The main readers of this journal were specialists.

To rise you needed to be a member of the Communist party and not Jewish. I started working there when I was in proofreading college and worked there twelve years. I had an unusual working life because I was promoted several times. I don't know why, because for the other Jews it was difficult.

Since we were part of the institute, we had the same job names as the engineers had, like project leader, senior engineer, and so on. When I began as a proofreader, I was called an entry-level engineer. My last description was chief senior engineer. I was promoted by job title and money. But the kind of work remained absolutely the same. It was interesting work for me. In the Soviet Union a lot of people work in technical fields, bright engineers, but they can't express their thoughts well. They write articles, but they are difficult to read, and it was an interesting challenge to try to correct that aspect.

My Friend Breaks Her Nose Skiing and I Meet Alex

I like downhill skiing, so I decided to go to the far north, near Murmansk. They have mountains, chairlifts, and it's very cheap to go there. It's not very comfortable to live, but to ski, it is good—a lot of snow, blue skies, but very cold. It takes twenty-four hours from Moscow to this town, Kirovsk, which is two hours from Murmansk. In 1986 I went with my girlfriends, four of us. Fortunately one of them broke her nose, because if she hadn't, I never would have met my husband! Three of us lived in one cabin, and she lived in a hotel. At one point we decided to visit her because we hadn't seen her for five days. One of us ran into her at the bus stop and saw that she was in bad condition. She had really broken her nose!

We went to her room and there were a lot of people there—maybe ten. Among those people was my future husband. My friend worked with him at the same institute and introduced us. We decided to meet the next day, all of us, to ski together. Before he left, he said he would get together with us when we returned to Moscow. We started to see each other, and then we married.

Our Wedding

It wasn't a Jewish wedding, unfortunately. It was small because we didn't have money to go to a restaurant or have a big wedding. Ten people came to my husband's apartment. We celebrated after the marriage, but the marriage itself was in the government office. Prior to the ceremony an orchestra, seven young women with violins performed Mendelssohn's "Wedding March." The people's deputy said the usual words, the same as in the church, in synagogue or under a *hupa*, and then she told us how to behave in the family—in the Communist manner! I wore a dark pink suit because I could use it everywhere and because a white dress would have been very expensive.

After getting married, we moved to my apartment. My mother died in 1980 and my grandmother in 1979, so I lived alone. It was small, with two separate rooms, a small kitchen, a small bath, and we had our own furniture.

My husband wanted to emigrate in 1979, to go to Israel. His parents asked him not to do it because they thought they would never find a job in Israel. They had a hard life. His mother was a pediatrician and his father an electrical engineer. They graduated from the institute at the time of the Doctors' Plot, the campaign against Jewish doctors and all Jews. Alex's father is a brilliant engineer, but he was only able to get an entry-level job in a small office. His mother had planned to stay at the institute and get her Ph.D., but instead she had to take a job. She wanted to be a gynecologist, but she had to become a pediatrician instead. When their lives had finally stabilized, they were afraid to move, so they asked Alex to stay. He was a good son, the only child. He loved them and couldn't leave them. He dreamed of emigrating for ten years before we would go. His parents came here in May, a year after us.

After the death of my mother, I started to think about emigrating because I was all alone. But I was afraid to do it alone, because I knew that it would be very difficult. When Alex and I met each other, we started to speak about it. In 1988 my husband's best friend suddenly left the country. They had tried to get permission to go to Israel, the Israeli visa, for eight years, and finally they got through. People had tried to send it from Israel many times during those eight years, but the Soviet government interfered, and the visa never reached them. At that point the door opened a little bit and they jumped through. Then suddenly it was closed again for three months. When it opened again, it became not a door but a gate.

When I was pregnant with Boris, both Alex and I made up our minds to leave. When we talked about it, we realized we had shared the same dream for a long time.

Chernobyl: Worse than Hiroshima or Nagasaki

We first heard about Chernobyl on TV, three days after the event. It happened on Friday, but they didn't tell us about it until Monday. As a result many people were exposed to radiation in the Ukraine. I learned more about it at work. People who worked in this field understood a lot better than other people what had happened and what was going to happen. They said that it is more of a catastrophe than Hiroshima or Nagasaki because it was more powerful. They also said that no one could stop the nuclear reaction, that it would go on and on. A concrete sarcophagus was built around the area, but contamination is still occurring underground. The radiation is getting worse and worse. Only now, four years later, do people understand.

Aside from the fire deaths, nobody died immediately. When people started to feel bad and lose their hair and teeth, and problems arose with their bones and their stomachs, they finally understood that it was caused by radiation and not something else. Nobody knows how many people are affected. I think it must be in the thousands, because not only the Ukraine was affected but Byelorussia, Lithuania, and Norway.

I know that now, four years after Chernobyl, the radiation level in the Ukraine, and especially in Byelorussia, is very high. A group of children from Byelorussia were sent to Israel, and all of them have radiation disease such as cancer. I also learned about it in the *Chicago Tribune* and from a woman whose friend is in Byelorussia and sent her son to Israel. Only Jewish children were sent to Israel; other children were sent to countries such as France and Finland.

I Didn't Want to Raise My Child in Russia

When I became pregnant, I decided I wouldn't allow my son to grow up in the Soviet Union. I couldn't think of it! I never believed Gorbachev. I knew that it wouldn't get better, that it would only get worse and worse, because when *perestroika* and *glasnost* started, they were only words and nothing else. I can't imagine how people believed him, how American people believed him. On his forehead it was written, "I am lying, I am lying, I am lying!"

I was sure that my son would feel the anti-Semitism more than I. My husband and I never discussed it. We decided immediately. We opened our mouths at the same time. In one voice we asked our friends who left to send us visas from Vienna because at that time it was possible to send visas from Austria. They left February 28, 1988. Our visas came May 7, 1988, in two months. It took four-and-a-half months to get permission from OVIR.

My Baby's Birth

Boris was born in a hospital. I had good care because the father of a friend of mine was close to the director of this hospital where I delivered my baby. I had some complications and stayed there ten days. After I delivered my baby, some of the placenta stayed in my body, so they had to keep an eye on me. On the fifth day there was a lot of bleeding that had to be cleaned up. I was given anesthesia during labor only because of my connections. Other women weren't given anesthesia. I was in labor sixteen hours. They gave me a spinal injection, and I felt nothing during the first fifteen hours. Then they said that was enough, and I was given no more anesthesia for the last hour.

"Prisoners" of OVIR

When my husband first made the decision to leave the country in 1979, he brought his documents to OVIR, the department of visas and permits. It is an awful organization, terrible. Their attitude later became more friendly, but ten to fifteen years ago, you can't imagine how they spoke with people who came to ask them for visas—as if they were prisoners! These people only came to ask for permission! It was terrible. The lines were very long. The first time you stood in line at OVIR was to sign up to get the application, and then you returned with your application and the necessary documents. You had to go and sign in and receive a number. Then you went home, and when it was your turn, a week or two later, you had to show your number; people wrote their numbers on the palm of their hand. If somebody wanted to go through this line without standing, he had to show his number. Some activists who kept the line would keep track of people's numbers. Your number depended on your place in line; it could be higher than 1,000.

In Moscow it was much easier than in other cities like Kiev and Minsk. The people I talked with told me that they simply paid money to get an application. Nobody knew if this person worked for OVIR. A person would say, "I can get you an application, but you must pay for this." The person who got such an offer to pay or stay in the line would think, What's better? To stay in the line, waste my time, probably two weeks, or to pay 100 rubles? Someone who couldn't pay had to wait. But it was also difficult to find a person who would offer you this chance, because they were also afraid. I suppose there could be an incidence where someone paid and never got it.

What Is in the Baby Carriage?

At the airport it was terrible, really terrible. On the very last day we had to go through the passport control and handbag control. We left the country when my son was four months old, and he was in the baby carriage, sleeping. The customs officer asked, "What is in the baby carriage?" I told him, "It's my baby." He said, "That is not the answer." I said, "What do you want me to say? What are you looking for in the baby carriage? I will tell you, I will answer." He said, "Pick up the baby." I decided not to argue with him. I picked up the baby, and he checked the baby carriage and found nothing, and then he said to put the baby back into the carriage. The baby cried for hours afterward.

Then he looked at my jewelry and started to weigh the jewelry for gold content. He said, "This, this, and this I can't allow you to take with you." There was one ring, one pair of earrings, and the gold watch with the gold chain. He said they were too heavy. The thinking in the Soviet Union was that gold would become more valuable from year to year. He thought I would be able to sell it for money.

My watch and chain were bought by my grandmother, and she gave them to my mother, who gave them to me. When they were bought, the price of gold was low. Then the price of gold in the USSR became higher, and then they started to look at the weight of your gold. It was a rule, if you're leaving the country: one wedding ring, one other ring, no diamonds, one pair of earrings, one chain. But they also put a limit on the value. Everything has to be very cheap. So it was impossible to bring the formerly inexpensive gold item that had become expensive. The customs officer said we're robbers—if each Jew takes a golden thing! For me they had a sentimental value, and there were similar things that we weren't allowed to take with us. We gave those things to my husband's parents.

I think now the customs officers have been ordered to be polite. With foreigners they will be the best, but with their own citizens, no. They are especially rude to Jewish people and worse to those who are going forever. I'm sure they themselves want to leave the country. That's why they were and are and will be like dogs!

We Leave the Darkness Behind

When we entered the Austrian Airlines plane, the stewardesses met us with a smile. They were so nice and so polite. When they saw my little son they ran to us and asked, "What do you need, how can we help you?" It was unbelievable. It was very pleasant to be around people with such good manners. In Moscow, they barked at you!

Two-and-a-half hours later we landed in Vienna in the big airport. Everything shines brightly after the darkness of Moscow, after the customs officers, after those faces. The faces in Vienna were smiling. Everything was unusual. The representatives of *HIAS* and *Sohnut* met us, and the *Sohnut* representative asked, "Who's going to Israel?" At that time everybody was going to America. A lot of people who were going to America had relatives from previous emigrations. Those who had relatives in Israel went to Israel. Where a person had relatives was the deciding factor. Some people had no relatives in the U.S. but had very good friends who said they would send them a visa and help them for a while; those people also went to America. Because a lot of people studied English but never Hebrew, more chose America.

HIAS people in Vienna sent us to apartments, to hotels. They transported us in a van. We had to stand in line to visit HIAS. There were a lot of people, but because of our little child we got in without any lines. We were told we'd have an appointment in two days at HIAS, for instance at 9:00 A.M. on Tuesday. The van would come and take us. Appointments started from 9:00 A.M. until ten at night. The HIAS people worked hard.

The Processing

They wanted our name, our children's names, what city we're from. Now it's different, but then we were asked the maiden name of our mothers, because they want to know if we were Jewish or not. They asked who would send a visa from the U.S.

From Vienna we went to Rome for one week. In Rome we were each given a caseworker from HIAS, and each family told their story—why they left the country, for what reasons, what happened. After the questions were answered in Rome, we rented an apartment in a small town near Rome, Ladispoli, and began waiting for the appointment.

We had an appointment in the American consulate, and we told our story—why we left the Soviet Union, how we felt the anti-Semitism in our family. In two days they made the decision to give us refugee status, and we were given the visa to the U.S.

My husband immediately began to send his resumé to universities all over America. He tried to make contact with people in charge of his specialty—theory of physics in solid-state metals.

Endless Possibilities

When I came here I studied to become a dental assistant. Alex is working in his straight specialty. He does the same as he did in the Soviet Union, and he's very proud.

Of course, I have dreams for my son. My husband and I will do our best to give him a good education, send him to college, the university, for a master's or Ph.D. I want him to be highly educated, to get a good job in the U.S., and to have a wonderful life. I want him to stay in the Jewish community, first of all. I want him to know from his early childhood that he is Jewish, that he must be Jewish. I want him to marry a Jewish girl. I don't want him to be Orthodox, but I want him to recognize himself as Jewish. I want to send him to the Jewish school to learn Hebrew, to know all religious rules, to learn how to celebrate Jewish holidays—I want him to know it all.

A Backward Glance

I miss my friends and the friends of our family, of my mother. I still recognize them as my best friends. They're still alive, and they can't leave the Soviet Union for various reasons.

Glasnost and *perestroika* were good for the Jewish people because the policies opened the doors of the Soviet Union, and Soviet Jews got an opportunity to leave. But the policies didn't give the Soviet people real reform. People had some freedom but didn't know what to do with it. The laws didn't change much. You could say, "Humph, I do not believe in Gorbachev." That was your freedom. Once you could not say, "I do not like Brezhnev," and people couldn't go to demonstrations. Now they can. But they have nothing to eat, nothing to put on, no clothes. The ruble is nothing! They can buy nothing with their salary. The salary is small, prices are big.

What Will Happen There?

I predict a breakdown of the Union first of all—I'm sure it won't be a union. It may be some separate states. Probably some of them will become part of other states—of Poland, Romania, Turkey—like Azerbaijan. I don't know. Nothing good will happen.

5

DIFFERENT VIEWS
OF THE SAME LANDSCAPE

NELLA AND IZRAIL RADUNSKY

NELLA RUBENSHTEIN RADUNSKY and Izrail Radunsky shared the same internal passport of Jewish stigma, yet each responded to the experience according to the dictates of memory and personal perspective. Nella, a lawyer, was schooled in the law but had known its abuses. Izrail, an artist, felt the lash of prejudice but dulled the pain by escaping to natural locales in harmony with his interior landscape.

NELLA RUBENSHTEIN RADUNSKY
Child of an "Enemy of the People"

The course of Nella Rubenshtein's life changed forever one night in 1936, when secret police shattered the sleep of her unsuspecting family and arrested her father. The packages his wife sent immediately after the arrest to sustain him until a trial went undelivered. He had vanished. Moishe Rubenshtein, thirty-

125

four, a factory leather worker, had been a loyal supporter of the Communist regime. His wife Perle, a bookkeeper, was twenty-eight; Nella was three. The questions surrounding the episode were never answered, but Nella was branded "the child of an enemy of the people."

Today, Nella, fifty-eight, lives in a teeming Chicago Housing Authority high rise, an unlikely place for a graduate attorney. Born in Minsk, Byelorussia, she practiced forensic graphology because as a Jewish lawyer she could not obtain work. She attained, however, a fine reputation for her forensic expertise, which otherwise went unrewarded. Her neatly groomed dark hair, simple, crisp dress, and calm manner mask the tragic experiences of her youth and lifelong struggle against a terrible stigma. Only when she speaks of these events do her emotions overcome her.

After surviving World War II in Kuybyshev, in the Urals, Perle Katz Rubenshtein and her daughter Nella nearly starved when they returned to the Katz home in Stary Konstantinov, a small town outside of Minsk. Perle's parents and most of the Katz family, including women and children, had been massacred by the Nazis. Their home had been bombed, burned to the ground. Perle was able only to rent a room in which water froze. Food was scarce. Anti-Semitic emotions were high. No sooner would Perle find a job than it slipped away. In despair the young mother thought she could end their suffering. But Nella, thirteen, wept and pleaded until her mother relented.

Perle and Nella traveled to Minsk where Perle's surviving brother, just back from military service at the war front, interceded with an employer on her behalf. Memories were still fresh from the war and heros were still honored, even if they were Jewish.

Despite her intelligence, top scores, and hard work, Nella could never overcome the terrible stigma that accompanied the state-instituted act that killed her father. In 1957 when she was already married to Izrail Radunsky, an artist, Nella and her mother received a letter "rehabilitating" Moishe Rubenshtein.

For more than thirty years the Radunskys endured the typical hardships of Russians as well as the additional hardships of Jews. The turning point was the Chernobyl explosion of 1986. This was the year before the birth of Rita, daughter of their son Michael and his wife Alla. The baby was born healthy but did not thrive. It was suspected that the available food, locally produced and contaminated by radiation, was the cause. Another terrible concern was that Michael, an accountant, was frequently assigned work in the city of Chernobyl. Once Michael and his family were able to leave, Nella knew that she and Izrail must follow.

The final ironic chapter concerning Nella's father came when the family was preparing to emigrate. An official demanded a signature of release from Nella's father. This bureaucratic blunder could arise only in a land whose government would suspend in perpetual limbo "a child of an enemy of the people."

Left Alone

In 1936 my father was subject to repression and sent away; we didn't even know where. I was three years old. My mother was twenty-eight years old. We were left, the two of us, alone. We didn't know anything else about my father, and my mother lived out the rest of her life alone with me. So, to put it briefly, in 1936 I was left fatherless forever, and my mother was left a widow.

My mother told me that my father was a very honest person. He was a good worker, and why they took him away, she never understood because, as we say, "without judgment or investigation" they came during the night, took him away, and didn't tell us anything. We never saw him again; our whole lives we lived in fear. I never told anyone that my father had been repressed, because for me that would have closed all doors. I wouldn't have been able to go to school anywhere or find work because everyone whose parents have been subject to repression are considered "children of enemies of the people." I went to study and always hid it, never telling anyone the truth.

The War and the Killing of Our Family

We lived with my grandparents in Stary Konstantinov until 1941 when the war began. Then my mother and I went to Kiev where her sister lived. During this time, probably in 1942, the German soldiers killed my grandfather and grandmother and my mother's brothers' wives and children, all the family. It was purely by chance we had left there and run away to Kiev. We arrived in Kiev, where my mother's sister lived, in order to take her and her children to Grandfather's house in Stary Konstantinov, but the Germans had already started bombing Kiev. So, we left Kiev and headed east with Mother's sister, and only for that reason the three of us remained alive. My mother's brothers were called to the front. They were soldiers throughout the war. The younger brother was killed on the front, and the other returned.

In Kuybyshev I Learn I'm Jewish

We all ran away on foot, then we were able to travel on some kind of transport trains. And that's how we made our way to the Urals. Throughout the war we lived in Kuybyshev. Mama worked there in a factory. We lived there during the war until it was over, together in one room with Mother's sister and her three children. They gave us coupons like food stamps, and for the coupons we could buy bread and other foods. There was bread and oil, and maybe meat. But because my mother and her sister and her sister's children worked at the factory, they got workers' coupons, which meant a little more bread, a little more oil. But for country folk there wasn't even that. Sometimes, maybe, there was meat or eggs for the children. We got sick, of course, caught colds. There wasn't much to wear. We wore socks we sewed ourselves and rubber boots. At work we had wet feet. Of course, it wasn't just Jews who suffered during the war. All the Russian people suffered, too.

Before the war, I don't remember knowing I was Jewish. I was a little girl. I learned for the first time that I was a Jew during the war, in Kuybyshev. It was there that we first heard the insults, that there were all kinds of *zhidi*, that Jews were hiding in the *taiga* [Siberian forests] and in Tashkent, while the Russian people were fighting. It was all untrue, of course; it was just anti-Semitism they thought up. My father's name was Moishe (Yiddish for Moses). When I went to school it was the first time I heard *zhid*. I couldn't bring myself to tell the other schoolchildren that I was Jewish. I changed my father's name to Michael so they wouldn't know I was a Jew.

The Cruelty of Survival

In 1945 the war ended, but we couldn't travel. Only in 1946 could we go back to the city where we lived before. In the winter we went back to Stary Konstantinov, but when we arrived, our house was not there. The Germans had bombed it and it burned down. There was just a big hole where our house had stood. All our belongings were lost. We barely survived that winter. It's impossible to tell the story of how we lived in a room that opened right out onto the street.

My mother and I rented a room from an old woman. It had a "summer" entrance. In Russia winter entrances have a kind of corridor, but summer entrances are like a porch that opens right out onto the street for when it's warm out. In the middle of the room we had a stove with a pipe that went out the window. We burned things in the stove, but our backs would freeze. There was no plumbing of any kind. We had to get water from the river, and it would freeze in the room. We couldn't even bathe; there wasn't a bathtub. The Germans had torn everything up, and in 1946 they still hadn't restored anything. We were really in a kind of torture. There was nothing to eat. There was real hunger. And my mother couldn't stand it anymore. It's hard to tell all this, and hard for someone who didn't live through it to understand what it was like. I was thirteen years old.

There was a stove with a pipe out the window. We kept that stove going. You could close the flue, and of course then you would die from the smoke. And my mother said to me once, "You know, let's close the flue and lie down to sleep, and then we won't have to wake up again." She said we could end all the troubles, all the problems. We could go to sleep and in the morning not wake up. And I started to cry horribly. I begged and pleaded with her not to do it. Somehow we got through the winter, and in the spring my mother's brother took us to Minsk. From that time, 1947, until our departure for America, we lived the rest of our lives in Minsk.

We Ran Out of the House

After that we went to Minsk, and my uncle helped my mother to look for a job. For a while we lived at the home of her brother. But after his first wife and two children died during the war, he had remarried. His new wife didn't want to see us, to give us anything to eat. I don't remember his first wife because I was a little girl and lived with my mother in Stary Konstantinov in the Ukraine, and her two brothers lived in Minsk before the war. I don't how things would have been if she had lived. He took himself a new wife, and it was hard for them too. They lived in one room. She said, "It's bad enough for us. There isn't anything to eat. What is she doing here with her daughter?" My mother couldn't stand this. She didn't want her brother to have problems with his new wife. My mother took me, and we went away without a place to go, without food to eat. We ran out of the house. His wife had hurt us. So we went wherever our eyes led us.

My mother's brother did help my mother to find a job. Wherever she'd go, they'd ask if she was Jewish. Then they would say, "The place is not available." They didn't want to hire her. She would call: "Do you need a bookkeeper?" "Yes, come over, let's see." She would come, they'd see her, and tell her the place was taken. But it was easier for those who fought at the front. Because her brother came back with medals and honors, and only because of this, could he help Mother find work.

There are many nationalities in the Soviet Union, and many people fought in the war, but if you take, for example, the medal "Heroes of the Soviet Union," Jews had the third most, even though there were fewer of them than other nationalities that took part. But even to get to that point where you would be given this medal was a big step, because they didn't want to give them to Jews.

The job my mother got had a place to live for the employees, and they gave her a room in a communal apartment that had a room for each family and a kitchen for everyone. We lived there until I got married. Years after we left and broke off relations, things improved between my uncle and his wife and us.

The Winter Coat and the Summer Coat

When I grew up and was already a young woman, my mother had two coats, a winter coat and a summer coat. We shared these two coats. When it got warm, Mama would wear the winter coat, and I wore the summer coat. When it became cold, she wore the summer coat, and I was given the winter coat to wear. In that way I could go to school to study. My mother always gave me the better coat.

In Kuybyshev my father's name had become Michael, and my whole life after that I wrote *Michael*, not *Moishe*, so nobody would guess. Even to get a library card you had to put down your nationality. When I went to college, they wanted to accept me. But after I told them my last name was Rubenshtein, they said everything was closed, that all the places were filled. I was a good student; I always tried.

I was seventeen years old when I started at the institute. I had a girlfriend in school whose father was a dentist; he treated the director of the institute where I wanted to go. He said that I was an orphan and that I had a very difficult life. He asked him to take my documents for this institute. The institute where I studied was part of the Institute of Forensic Examination, and there were only three Jews in the program.

I Settle for a Career in Criminology

I had a dream of becoming a lawyer, but I was not allowed to do so. Many times I tried to find a job as a lawyer, but I couldn't get one, simply because I was Jewish. I went to work as an expert on criminology.

I analyzed handwriting, false documents. People falsified signatures on documents, received money illegally, all kinds of things. I worked for the Office of Criminology, Criminal Investigation. I worked in the Handwriting Laboratory for Investigation of Handwriting and Documents. For instance, someone might come in and ask, "When was this document written?" And we could say whether it was written long ago or three years ago. Or, we might receive anonymous letters, where people would write all kinds of information. I would compare the signature on certain false documents with those of the suspects. This might reveal that the writer received money illegally, forged letters to people. If a person is a suspect, you analyze all aspects of the handwriting. It's a whole science.

I also worked on the establishment of authorship. For example, anonymous novels or poetry, you have to figure out who wrote them—Lermontov or Pushkin, for example. By analyzing the handwriting, character traits can also be established. In recent years that aspect of the science has been developing, and there are people who can determine certain character traits or nationality. That is, native language can be determined by text.

Seven or eight people worked at the same laboratory. There were many laboratories in the facility. They did chemical, physical, imprint examinations—from tires, legs, fingertips, knives.

Three Jewish people worked at the institute. I was the only Jewish person in my laboratory. The institute had about 100 workers. The people I worked with treated me very well, simply like a person. I don't mean to flatter myself, but they really loved me there. They treated me very well. The bosses were nice to me too but never did anything for me. They all treated me with a great deal of respect, but they never gave me raises or promoted me. In 1980, the boss of the laboratory where I worked was killed in an airplane crash. I was the oldest, most experienced worker, but they didn't make me head of the department. They gave the job to a young Byelorussian woman.

Marriage, Children, and Four Square Meters for Each

When Izrail and I met, I was twenty-three years old and he was twenty-seven. A friend we had in common introduced us on the street. It was the May First demonstrations. All the students were sent to the demonstrations. We formed a column and wove our way through the crowd with our friends, and somehow we met there. We've been married thirty-five years. We knew each other only six months before we got married. Izrail says his parents liked me a lot. He didn't want to wait for a long time.

Our wedding was at home for friends and relatives. It was very modest. We couldn't get married in a synagogue. There wasn't anything like that back then in Russia. No one did that. We did the civil ceremony at ZAGS and then had a party. We had seventy guests. I wore a pink dress, not a wedding gown. I still remember that! A tailor sewed it for me.

We did not get our own apartment right away; we lived with Izrail's aunt, and then with my mother in one room. Only in 1962, when we already had two children, did we get a little apartment with two rooms. The wait to receive an apartment was ten to twelve years. People who had six square meters of space were not allowed in line, but if it was less than six, they were allowed. So, we lived in one room, twenty square meters, me, my husband, mother, two children. So we each had four square meters. The problem was there wasn't much housing. After the war, people came from the country to Minsk to get apartments. I'm not against country folk, but everyone was pushing and shoving to get apartments. They didn't want to work on the collective farms. They wanted an easier life.

Luba was born in 1956 in a hospital. I had good care during my pregnancy and delivery as far as that was possible in Russia. I had no problems or complications when the baby was born. Six years later when I had my second child, our son Michael, we lived in one room with my mother, with a communal kitchen. The room was sixteen square meters. I had to go back to work so I wouldn't lose my job because for Jews to find work at all was very difficult. When I was pregnant, they gave me a leave of two months after the birth. But after that I went off to work and we got a baby-sitter. She came from the country and had to live with us. So in this fifteen-meter room lived me, my mother, my husband, our two children, and the baby-sitter—six people. All in this one room—can you imagine? We had a communal kitchen. There was another woman who lived in the other room of the apartment.

Our baby-sitter slept in the kitchen because there wasn't even room for another bed in the room we had. So that's how we lived. A lot of people lived like that, not just us. My son was born in April 1962, and in September we got our own apartment. It was not a nice apartment—a *Khrushchovka.* It had two rooms, the first a little bigger, the second smaller. The city had been destroyed, hit harder than many other cities. The apartment was just like this one we live in now, just the same. It was a new apartment, and the plumbing worked.

We kept a sitter for Michael until he went to kindergarten. We had many baby-sitters because it was hard to get a good baby-sitter.

Fear of Leading a Jewish Life

It was impossible to observe any Jewish life. We were always afraid that our neighbors or coworkers would find out. We didn't follow the traditions or celebrate the holidays. We couldn't raise our children with it. And we didn't tell them they were Jews until people started saying it on the street or in school. But they understood that it was better not to say anything about this to anyone. No Jews could. In Russia it just wasn't possible. They trampled on Jewish culture and traditions.

My Father Is Rehabilitated

After Stalin died, they started to unearth all the crimes he committed. So in 1957 I received a notice that my father's arrest was for nothing and he was guilty of no crime and was thereby rehabilitated. My mother suffered so much. I have this letter with me.

We knew emigrating wasn't possible at that time. In the early 1960s my husband's family, which is large, couldn't all leave Russia together. They had many problems.

We could read certain books when Gorbachev came in, such writers as Vasily Grossman or Solzhenitsyn. The only book of his that was published in the Soviet Union was *One Day in the Life of Ivan Denisovich. Samizdat* was available only in Moscow and Leningrad; we didn't have that kind of thing. We could only read those things when Gorbachev came in with *perestroika* and *glasnost* and democracy. And that was a big game itself. There were better books, though, than Solzhenitsyn's—*Heavy Sand, Children of the Arbat,* by Anatoly Rybakov.

We could discuss these things only in our house, in a circle of friends. But we could not say what we thought in public, at work. Only at home. Our circle was Jewish people, but at work, we were friendly with other people too. We could not be unfriendly or not help each other.

My husband says Jews always worked hard because there was just that kind of situation. Jews assimilated in Russia and made a very large contribution to Russian culture—music, painting, science, with their minds, hearts, talent, good will, and for them Russia became a homeland. Maybe even more than for Russians. Jews made this large contribution to Russian culture, but I say, no one ever valued this. My husband says that they did in some measure. We both agree that they gave awards, but rarely.

We were not members of the Communist party. We could not have been if we wanted to. For Jews that was very difficult, but we never wanted it anyway. No one in our family was ever in it.

The Effects of Chernobyl on Our Baby Granddaughter

Our son left Minsk with his wife and daughter, though they didn't have a sponsor here. Their little girl was born the year after Chernobyl, in 1987. She was born healthy, but before they brought her to America she was sick. She had stomach problems, eye problems. Her stomach was always digesting improperly. The doctors said they would keep her to feed her, but there was nothing to eat. Three months before the departure, she hadn't gained a single gram, and she was already ten months old. Anything you gave her, she threw right up—fruits, vegetables. Probably everything was covered with radiation, and it just made her sick. She was a weak child. When they got her to Vienna and to a doctor, only then she started to get better. They fed her baby foods, things without radiation, and she started to get well right away.

Chernobyl made Michael want to come to this country. The year his daughter was born there was nothing to eat. Everything was poisoned all over. He was an accountant but didn't have work. So he was sent on business into areas near the Chernobyl accident site. The accident was in 1986, and they left in 1988.

When Michael and Alla left Russia with the baby to go to America, I understood that I couldn't live that way anymore—without my son, my granddaughter, with everything becoming horrible. After Chernobyl the ecology was ruined.

Waves of emigration had already started. Gorbachev permitted everyone to leave. We joined that wave. At work I had to let them know I was leaving. There were some difficult moments, but at least people who were leaving were treated a little better than previous groups. Before, a person who wanted to leave was subjected to meetings, cross-examination, and so forth. My son went through that. But by the time we left there weren't problems like that. My son left in 1987, and we in 1989.

The Blank Line on the Emigration Form

It's interesting that when I tried to emigrate from the Soviet Union, I was supposed to fill out a form on which there was a line, "If your parents are living, where are they? If they have died, then in what year and where are they buried?" And I couldn't fill out this line, because I basically never knew my father, never knew where and when he died, or where he was buried. They shot him maybe, who knows.

Since 1936, when he was taken away, we didn't know anything about him. So I didn't fill out this line, because I didn't have this information about him. So they didn't want to accept my documents and process my exit from Russia. I was forced to turn to the head of OVIR and write him a long, detailed letter about why I don't know anything about my father and why I didn't fill out this line on the form.

Also, when I was leaving Russia, I had trouble, because on my documents my father's name was Michael, and I had a letter saying his name was Moishe. They asked me, "What does this mean?" I told them that when I was younger I could not tell the truth.

We arrived in Chicago April 4, 1990.

Remembering the Well-trampled Path

I lived a very hard life in Russia. The land is beautiful; the regime is awful; it's a bunch of thieves. They destroyed the lives of generations of people. Of course, we couldn't realize in Russia our dreams, our capabilities, our interests, our inclinations. We were always held within some kind of boundaries. Two steps to the side were not possible. We went along the notorious, well-trampled path. Of course, we reconciled ourselves to this fate; we never knew any kind of freedom. We always felt rage, everyone did, rage for the Communist party, rage that because we were Jewish things were denied us. I would say we lived a horrible life in Russia, horrible. My husband says he lived a very interesting and full life. Even though things worked against him, he still had a good life. He just loved his work. Russia is a beautiful country, beautiful land. He could travel and paint. But it has to be said that for all this he didn't receive any salary. He earned money from commissions, from various things, but aside from that, you could say he was a free artist.

It's Not a Shameful Thing to Be Jewish

Of course, my children weren't raised as Jews in Russia, but I hope that they will give their children training in Jewish culture and traditions, that they won't be ashamed to be Jewish. It's not a shameful thing to be Jewish. In Russia it *was* a shameful thing. Everyone was afraid and hid it. But I want the children to study what they want, to live according to their principles and desires, and that no one stops them from doing what they want with their lives.

My daughter's son had his *brit* when they arrived here. My grandson was eight years old. They went to Mount Sinai Hospital. They couldn't do that in Russia. They weren't raised as Jews in Russia. They didn't know anything about it, but here, where it's possible, they want to become acquainted with Jewish culture and rituals, and I think that their children will be raised completely differently. They've got what we couldn't give our children in Russia.

Izrail Radunsky, age 25, Minsk.

Izrail and Nella in front of one of his paintings, Chicago, 1992. Photo © 1992 by Bruce Mondschain. All rights reserved.

Беларуская
Совецкая Соцыялістычная Рэспубліка

Белорусская
Советская Социалистическая Республика

ВЯРХОЎНЫ СУД   ВЕРХОВНЫЙ СУД

гор. Минск, БССР

В/№ и дата   12 сентября   195 7г.   № 5-10

С П Р А В К А:

Дело по обвинению РУБИНШТЕЙНА Моисея Мироновича,
1904 года рождения пересмотрено Верховным судом БССР
16 августа 1957г.

Постановление Особого Совещания от 22 июля
1936 года в отношении РУБИНШТЕЙНА Моисея Мироновича
отменено и дело производством прекращено за недока-
занностью обвинения.

И.О.ПРЕДСЕДАТЕЛЯ
ВЕРХОВНОГО СУДА БССР   /К. АБУШКЕВИЧ/

BYELORUSSIA SOVIET SOCIALIST REPUBLIC
SUPREME COURT

Minsk, USSR

September 12, 1957, #5-10

N O T I F I C A T I O N

The case which charges Rubinshteyn, Moysey Mironovich, born in
1904, was reconsidered by the Supreme Court of Byelorussia on
August 16, 1957.

The resolution of the Special Conference of July 22, 1936
regarding Rubinshteyn, Moysey Mironovich is canceled and the case
dismissed because of insufficient evidence to prove his guilt.

Seal

Chairman of the Supreme Court
of Byelorussia

Signature
K. Abushkevich

Letter of Rehabilitation of Moishe Moronovich Rubenshtein, Nella's father, dated September
12, 1957, 21 years after he disappeared.

IZRAIL RADUNSKY
Portrait of the Artist in Search of a Landscape

Though attuned to the woods and waterways of his native Byelorussia, Izrail Radunsky surrendered to the pressures of family members yearning to escape the land going sour around them. A commercial artist employed by the state to create posters for theater, opera, and other cultural events, Izrail sought out isolated places for the work he created on his own—landscapes: abandoned barns, empty farmhouses, fields of grain, the silver frozen Volga, the Baltic Sea, places where the wind could blow unobstructed. But Chernobyl was poisoning the air and land even as the government was assuring the populace that all was well.

Soon after their son Michael, his wife Alla, and their daughter Rita emigrated to Chicago, the rest of the Radunsky clan did the same—Izrail and Nella, their daughter Luba Lishnevsky, her husband Yuri, and son Paul, arriving in April 1990.

Less than a year and a half later, Nella and Izrail Radunsky reside in a Near North high rise with a Lakeside Place address evocative of lakeshore vistas and lifestyles of the rich and famous. The reality, however, is a Chicago Housing Authority vertical melting pot of ethnicity surrounded by the chipped edges of poverty. On a hot, windless summer evening, chairs crowd the concrete entry terrace where Soviet emigrés, mostly women, draw a breath and gossip in their native tongue. A double amputee in her sixties or seventies, fixed like a Buddha in her wheelchair, is a vocal part of the group that pauses only briefly to exchange greetings with the genial artist escorting guests inside. An Indian or Pakistani couple also enter the building as a young black couple take their baby out for a stroll. In the locked vestibule, an amiable black security guard screens comings and goings. Izrail nods cheerfully to all.

The elevator jammed with passengers takes us to the Radunsky apartment where Nella and daughter Luba, who serves as interpreter, are waiting.

The apartment, clean and cheerful, showcases Izrail's work. One piece, an assemblage, depicts Gorbachev's lithographic image, political posters and the Red flag juxtaposed with real objects: a pair of woven willow slippers once worn by peasants and an empty wooden spoon. "These are the results of perestroika— nothing to eat," he comments. The work seems to ask, Who is this hero?

One remarkable canvas is a wide, dreamlike rendering of wild horses, the foreground in oranges and greens beneath a yellow sky. A boy is beckoning to the mythic creatures. By contrast, the theatrical posters are stylized in decorative bold motifs and colors. The portraits in oil are realistic; the landscapes, impressionistic.

As did the French Impressionists a century ago, Izrail prefers the plein air method of working. He observes ruefully, "The air in Chicago isn't like the air

in France." He needn't state that it's unlike that of Byelorussia. Luba under-
scores her father's dilemma. "He lives in Russia anyway, but he's here and he
wants to work."

Despite no avowed bitterness, Izrail alludes to an incident in 1979 that
impacted a major exhibition of his work. When the citizens of Minsk were
celebrating the October Revolution during a period of anti-Zionist fervor,
authorities confiscated posters in the city center advertising his show because
of his given name.

My Own World

I was born in Minsk, Byelorussia, July 29, 1929, the oldest of four children. As a
child I was interested in people, in everything. At school I was always drawing.
When a math teacher would talk to me, I'd be thinking and imagining things. I
built my own world and didn't think much about classes. I very much loved to
read. I drew caricatures of the teachers. I wasn't a very good student. They would
call my parents to school.

My father was at first a worker at a factory, then after the Revolution he
became an office worker, a director in a rest sanatorium. My father sang well and
danced well. But best of all, he was a hard worker. He was a party member. I don't
know why, because I wasn't. After his promotion, we lived not only in Minsk but
also some other places in Byelorussia. And before the Second World War we
lived in the Caucasus, in Sochi, Russia.

My parents and grandparents spoke Yiddish, and so did I. But when we lived in
Russia, we didn't speak Yiddish. When I was a little boy, we celebrated Jewish holidays, but later the Soviet government didn't allow it. We were Jewish in our souls.

Why We Survived the War

Right up until the war our family, my parents, brothers, and sisters, lived in Sochi,
Russia, and that's why we were evacuated to Novosibirsk. I was twelve when the
Germans came to Minsk, and Mama and my brother and my sister were evacuated to Novosibirsk. My father worked in the military hospital. We were there
until 1945. I went to school with other Jews. In Russia there was an organization
that helped the families of people on the front. More than seventy of our relatives
were killed, because during the war the Germans killed all the Jews in Minsk.
After the war some Jews returned to Minsk, but those who remained during the
war had been killed.

A Jewish Artist?

I studied five years in Minsk and then six years in Moscow. It was very difficult
to get into an art college in Byelorussia if you were Jewish. The artists' institute

didn't admit me because the director of the institute said, "What will we do with him as a Jew?" Since they didn't let me study in Minsk, I tried Moscow. In Moscow it was difficult too, but I passed the tests and was admitted. Maybe it was easier because they liked my pictures; I was a talented kid.

Remembrance of a Jewish Past

I was interested in Jewish culture, so I read and learned a lot about it. Sometimes Jewish actors were in Minsk, and all the Jewish people would come and there would be tears. In 1948 the Jewish theater was closed, and after that very seldom could people listen to Jewish singers and language. Nothing was left.

During the Stalin years there was some food in the store because people were afraid of Stalin and therefore worked. But he spoiled the Revolution. He was a very cruel person. In 1927 my wife's father was persecuted by Stalin. Her father was a member of the Communist party, worked at a plant, and was one of the best people. At that time many people were persecuted. My wife doesn't know why he was killed. They came to the house, took him, and that was it.

A Memorable May Day

In 1955 in Minsk at a May Day demonstration I met my wife. She was a beautiful girl, and still is! She had a lot of boyfriends. We had a civil ceremony; though we wanted to keep up the traditions, we couldn't.

A Philosophy of Art

Art is intuition. It's impossible to say—God. I love humor, and my feelings and soul are in my pictures. Artists are truth-tellers. An artist is distinguished by how he feels the subtleties of all this, not by what he can "photograph." An artist's work differs from that of a photographer in that he doesn't merely record something on paper but has his own style. If an artist has his own language, his own style, he will be recognizable. Van Gogh, Gauguin, Lautrec, Seurat, Monet have their own language, and they are recognizable, so an artist should be recognizable even by any one work even though the subject matter of individual paintings might be different.

The Secret of How to Create a Work of Art

The time it takes to paint it, plus my whole life—that's my secret of how long it takes. I find a "long place"; I have to go through a lot to find it. That all goes into the time of painting, do you understand? Then I paint. Later, I might paint half a day in my studio and return. I wouldn't say that I paint quickly. Maybe three, five hours. The most important thing is to find harmony and the poetic side of what you're painting—harmony, the rhythm, the music. It's Dostoevskian.

My subjects include the Baltic Sea, the countryside. My landscapes are drama, the music of Bach or Chopin. I like Van Gogh, French impressionists, Monet, Renoir, Toulouse-Lautrec, Cézanne. In Byelorussia I was a Russian artist with a Jewish heart.

My Career as an Artist Employed by the State

I was a member of the artists' union and worked as a graphic designer for publishers that took special orders for posters.

I did theater posters, ballet, festivals, concerts, all possible kinds of cultural events. They are contemporary, modern, for the theater. There are many theaters in Russia; every theater orders posters. It's not the world you imagine. After Stalin died there was culture.

Posters are difficult work, but I enjoyed it. I tried lots of variations, did a lot of things. I usually worked on something for a month or more. They didn't even want me to leave because I did such a good job. Before I came here I gave the state museum 230 examples of the work I'd done my whole life.

I loved the land, the beauty of nature, so I combined different kinds of jobs in order to do these things. This was for my soul; the other was to earn money. I had personal exhibits. Some envied me that I could describe the Russian landscape; they envied Jews. By bus, by train, I traveled around the whole country. I would get commissions and go to paint things. During vacations I would go to the country. I painted my own things all the time, on vacations and not on vacations.

My work is now in the Russian Museum. People bought things from my exhibits. Some of my works are in museums in Minsk and in Moscow. I am represented in private collections and in the Byelorussian Art Museum. I took part in poster competitions. And I received prizes twelve times. I was a member of a number of different professional organizations—the National Union of Artists, the National Art Fund of Byelorussia, the Russian Union of Artists, and on a jury in Minsk.

The political views were always the view of the Communist party. You had to do socialist realism; other views were forbidden. Otherwise you couldn't find work. It became easier to work after *perestroika* and *glasnost* began.

The Russian government helped artists, but it wanted artists to fulfill state orders. The government ordered things and then supported artists. But artists' work in general had to reflect the politics.

Anti-Jewish Politics: My Exhibit Posters Are Banned

In 1953 when I graduated from the Minsk Art College I worked on my own things. I didn't look for any work. I worked well, so work found me. But they didn't let me forget I was Jewish. Administrators, the cultural ministry oppressed me. I was a good person, and people who know me related to me well. But the cultural ministry, the artists' union always oppressed me. For Russian artists it was easier to get a new commission, a job, to go anywhere he wants. When the job was done, the artists' union would accept his job, but for me, all the time I felt that I was Jewish.

In 1979 I had a personal exhibition and big posters with my name, Izrail Radunsky, on them in the center of the city. It was the anniversary of the October Revolution. There was a square where there was a demonstration, and the administration removed these posters with my name on them. I was fifty years old.

The Winds of Chernobyl

I didn't feel a change around me after the Chernobyl accident. It takes time. But now we know that there are more and more sick children in Byelorussia and the Ukraine. The biology and ecology have been ruined. The government said everything was OK and not to worry. Only after about three years did they start to get people out of these areas. We didn't know all the truth about this.

The only reason I decided to leave was because my son left. It's really the only reason.

I want to say that in general, to be an artist is great happiness, and no matter where a person is an artist, he'll find things to gravitate toward. It's happiness even if the artist doesn't have money. Here I have freedom, but I don't have commissions; no one knows me here. What kind of freedom is that?

It's always painful for artists. The artist always absorbs the difficulties of the place where he's located. But any way, any where, to be an artist is happiness.

PART II

THE GLASNOST VISA

6

TWO GENERATIONS
OF HEROIC REFUSENIKS

THE REZNIKOV FAMILY

WHEN GENNADY AND Sulamith Reznikov decided to risk everything to emigrate, they placed themselves and their three sons in a special limbo. Once the government refused to give them permission to leave, they had to survive on a critically reduced income and plan every step they took, from dealing with hostile authorities to helping Sergey and Vladimir skirt the military draft.

Every step had a purpose, every step, within legal parameters, and every step, legally substantiated. Each member of the family, even Michael, the youngest, took a public role in protesting a system intractable on the issue of human rights. The Reznikovs were visited by senators, congressman, and representatives of organizations trying to further the cause of human rights.

Although their future daughter-in-law, Marina, was not a refusenik, she too was drawn to activities that asserted her Jewish identity. She and Sergey met in Moscow at the first Jewish cafe.

GENNADY REZNIKOV
Grief Doesn't Need Exaggeration

Describing how he lived from infancy until marriage in the teeming apartment on Moscow's Arbat Street, Gennady Reznikov speaks without visible emotion. Lack of privacy and low living standards were too common from his perspective to be worthy of complaint. But remembering how, despite a gold medal in science, he was set up to fail an oral exam to enter the university, he relives the anguish.

He wanted to use his fine mind in work that would challenge him, but was turned down from employment at the Institute of Engines. Stoically he describes his painful ordeal not only as a Jew but as a man well qualified to find a job in a city where jobs were plentiful, who saw others before and after him being hired, while he was told there was nothing for him.

He eventually found a low-level aviation plant opening that required an educated man. His hard work led to a better position at the Institute of Engines and the chance to earn a Ph.D. in energy conversion. Finally, his expertise in the new field of fuel cells helped him chip away slowly at anti-Semitic obstacles so that he attained the elite post of laboratory chief at a research institute— until his refusenik activities began.

Most of the rest of his story can be gleaned from Sulamith, his wife of over thirty years, or his sons Sergey and Vladimir. Sergey, twenty-five, and Vladimir, twenty, at the time of the interviews, shared their refusenik experiences. Even Michael, now eleven, marched in protests with his mother, wearing a placard that read, "Nine years old and nine years a refusenik."

At first Gennady postponed the follow-up interview because his work testing fuel conversion systems, the same kind of work he did in Moscow, drains almost all his time and energy. Then months after the first interview, a telephone conversation revealed that for him it was just too painful to remember the past. The testimony of the rest of the family leaves no doubt of his candor.

The Reznikov family of five had been "in refusal" for a decade by the time the family emigrated in 1989.

My Roots

My mother gave to the world four sons. One died when he was four. I was the third son. My older brother was born in 1929, I in 1937, and my younger brother in 1950. So, I was born in Moscow, April 16, 1937. My parents are Lev Reznikov and Sophia Lubinson Reznikov. He was born in Yunechah in the Ukraine in 1904, and my mother in Orsha in Byelorussia in 1906 or 1907.

Growing up in Yunechah, the Ukraine, my father went to *heder* and learned Hebrew, Yiddish, and Jewish history and Torah and so on. I don't know exactly how many years he attended *heder*. He knew Russian, but at home they spoke Yiddish. So he talked Yiddish with my grandmother, only Yiddish.

My father's father was a middle-level worker at a mill. He was a Jewish person in a small *shtetl*. My grandfather had four children, and he was able to make a living for his whole family, so my grandmother was a housewife.

My mother's parents had both died by the time she was six, her mother of cancer, when she was just three or four. She had two brothers and three sisters, all older, and they raised her.

When my mother's sisters got married and their husbands went to Moscow, they took my mother with them. She had little schooling, attended Russian school for seven or eight years. She didn't know Hebrew. In Moscow her sisters' husbands introduced her to my father, and they got married in 1928.

Communal Living in an Apartment on Arbat Street

We lived on Arbat Street and occupied a room in a very huge communal apartment that consisted of eight rooms. In each room lived one family. And each family had three, four, even five people! So, there were about forty people in one apartment. It was awful!

We lived in one room. We shared a kitchen and bathroom with the other families. It was a real problem because everyone went to work at the same time. There were two toilets and one bathroom for forty people. So every time someone was in the toilet it was a problem for the other people. And always people were standing in the corridor knocking on the bathroom door. This was a true communal apartment.

My father was an ardent Communist. He did not complain about this kind of life for our family. First of all, he didn't have any choice and he saw that everybody around him lived in the same conditions, except for high-ranking party bosses. He didn't have rank, any rank. When he was twenty, he was an active young Communist, a member of *Komsomol*. He believed the Soviet regime would help Jews to get equal rights and to become equal with all other nations. Communist slogans were so attractive. They promised to make all people equal, to give them all rights and chances to be happy.

Misconceptions about Living Conditions in Russia

I will try to describe my understanding of the misconceptions of how we lived, because I have met a lot of American people who do not understand. They always look at the troubles from the outside, and, as a rule, the problems are sensationalized. But they were real troubles; they don't need exaggeration. Because, you see, real grief, real tragedy doesn't need exaggeration. When you see people are dying, then there's no place for exclamations and so on. It's a real tragedy. As a rule, all newspapers, all reporters always try to find hot spots to sensationalize events. It's the same picture in this case, I guess. It's really difficult to find appropriate words to describe the situation in order to help understanding.

For a child growing up in these conditions, this was normal. Knocking on the bathroom door was normal. I was not hurt by all these conditions because it was my normal everyday life. I got used to it; I did not know anything else. That's why I could not imagine anything else. I *could* imagine that it could be different, but that would be some kind of dream, not real life.

My Older Brother Dares to Speak Openly

First of all, let's remember the time we're talking about. It was the Stalinist era. That's why nobody was *so* brave as to speak aloud of political concerns. If a wife and a husband spoke about something, they spoke privately, so that nobody—*nobody*—else could hear. But I did hear. The first person to speak openly about political problems was my elder brother Yefim. He was eight years older than I. And he read a lot of books. He was sharp enough to understand that this life was awful and that we lived in abnormal conditions. He spoke loudly in our room in this communal apartment. And my parents were so afraid of his speeches that they tried to shut him up. I was, as all other children, caught up in all these new ideas and began to compare official propaganda with real life, and I found a lot of discrepancies. Yefim was the first person who taught me to analyze and understand life. I'm very grateful to him.

Yefim died in 1979, the same year I applied for emigration. He was fifty. He had a second heart attack, the first having come ten years before that.

When he was twenty, he belonged to a group of young students. I don't think they had a name, but they met in the Lenin Library and discussed books and political events and so on. They didn't have any specific goal. They were young and free; they all were at a very dangerous age, around twenty. Some of them were arrested and taken to the militia station. In Russia, secret police are always secretive. So everybody was arrested by the militia, and behind them was the KGB.

Yefim was taken to the militia station and interrogated. He was very frightened, afraid he could be kept there. But fortunately, they let him go after several hours, though he was interrogated two or three times. They didn't have any proof that he was an active part of this group. This was in 1949, long before Jewish discussions. As a rule, in all of these groups, Jews played a role. So if something happened, you could be sure that Jews were always involved. Because in Russia Jews were very active—like yeast.

Stalin Closes Down the Synagogues

Our sense of being Jewish was very slight. My grandmother, my father's mother, observed all Jewish traditions. She was the only one of my grandparents I knew. She went to synagogue every Saturday until, along with all Moscow synagogues, it was closed in 1948. That day she returned from the synagogue in tears because it was the first time she couldn't pray! It was horrible, because it was the beginning of all the troubles with the so-called cosmopolitism in Russia. Later came the trial of the so-called doctors-murderers, "murderers in white." All these bloody things began in 1948. Also, all Jewish activity was being persecuted. Jewish theater was closed, simply everything Jewish. Then the anti-Jewish campaign began to grow.

My grandmother knew when Hanukkah and Passover came, and she observed all of the traditions. We had matzah. It was very difficult, because you could buy matzah only at the Moscow Central Synagogue, only right before Passover. There were long lines, but she bought it. And I really admired her—how strong she was. She was very old and very weak, and she spoke Russian with difficulty because Yiddish was her first language. But she was wonderful, and for Hanukkah she made *latkes*. She was the only one who kept up the traditions except my uncle who made the same thing, but nobody else did, and that's why we didn't know what Pesach, Hanukkah, Yom Kippur, or all the other holidays meant. I knew about the traditions and history only after I began to think about them much later, when I got married.

But the next generation, my father and mother, tried to assimilate. They tried to become Russians. It was really a dangerous time to speak Yiddish in the street. I did not know Yiddish. My grandmother spoke with my father, but my elder brother tried to prevent that because he was afraid that I would speak Yiddish in the street and that it would be dangerous for me. I realized then what it meant to be a Jew. I was eleven years old. It was dangerous to be Jewish and very unpleasant because all my so-called friends teased me—*zhid*.

Russian Like Everybody Else

My parents felt themselves to be Russian like everybody else. But they were wrong because all Soviet propaganda—news, radio—tried to persuade people that Jews were so bad, that Jews betrayed the Russian people—all bad qualities characterized Jewish people. You might read in the newspapers and magazines stories about bad Jewish people, people with typical Jewish names. Nobody wrote that someone was Jewish, but they wrote *Isaak*, *Solomon*, and other Jewish names such as Abramovich. It was an anti-Jewish campaign. You see, average people like my parents couldn't understand; they too believed all the newspapers. They also blamed these people, because the propaganda was not about Jewish people but was specifically about *bad* people. So they, with all other Russians, said that those bad people did bad things.

Now I will try to explain some double thinking of my parents. As you know, double thinking was the common way of thinking in the USSR. My parents wanted to be like all other people, like Russian people. They wanted to be indistinguishable from everyone else. It was the safe way to survive, the easiest way. The Soviet regime liked people who were like all the rest and hated and persecuted those who tried to develop their individual features.

But at the same time when my parents would hear about somebody's marriage, their first question was if he (she) was Jewish. That was very important for them. That is why since my childhood I had known that I must marry a Jewish girl. So my parents tried to assimilate, but something in their mentality was strongly Jewish. They did not want to deny that they were Jewish.

Ordinary Versus Official Anti-Semitism

In our apartment people's attitudes were mixed. Some were anti-Semites, and they treated us differently. Some were normal people. There are anti-Semites who treat you badly in everyday life, at home. But when anti-Semitism becomes officially sanctioned by the government, you have a bad time. Jews were fired from their jobs. This was the late forties and early fifties, 1948 to 1953, even 1954. So those six years were terrible, awful.

My father lost his job. He was an accountant. He played with numbers. He had rows and columns, like math exercises. From central planning he would get these figures and then divide them according to some kind of distribution system. Things were shipped based on his numbers. He never saw the goods—only numbers. It was very simple work because he knew all the figures and would just repeat them each time. There was no job satisfaction, and the salary was low. After he lost this job, he found the same kind of work at another place because his friend hired him. You see, in Russia we could live only because we had very good relationships with people. People got very low salaries everywhere. In the US you could have one person who does a certain kind of job, but in Russia on this job there might be ten to twenty people. One person could leave and the work would go on. No one was essential. Every boss knew he could hire maybe five or ten additional people, because it was the state system. There was a lot of waste.

My mother was a *prodavschitsa*, a salesclerk or shop assistant. She didn't enjoy her work. She cut and weighed the food—sausage, even bread—and collected the money. She worked at the counter, but sometimes she sorted the vegetables and took care of the produce section, too. Because she worked in a food store we had enough to eat; we got additional food.

I Try To Enter Military School To Help the Family

We had a very low standard of living. We never had enough money from one payday to the next. That's why at age fifteen I decided to join military school, because they promised to provide a uniform and food. I was trying to help my family because we didn't have enough money to live. But I soon understood that I couldn't join because I was a Jew! When I was seventeen I graduated from school. I was ranked number one in my school. I had a gold medal for straight fives. I could not bring this medal with me to the US. My very good friends brought it here for me. It is for excellence in the sciences.

I Knew My Real Place

I tried to enter Moscow University and failed, not because my knowledge was poor but because I was a Jew. I was excused from exams because of straight fives, but I had to have a so-called interview with someone at this university, and I failed this interview. It wasn't a big disappointment. I was already prepared for that. I knew my real place in this life. That's why I understood that all my preconceptions were right. So then I entered the Moscow Automobile and Road Construction Institute. It was a second-rate institute. And in five years I graduated from it with all A's—no B's—all honors. But I couldn't get a good job because I was Jewish—the same situation. Nevertheless, I always tried to find a place that corresponded with my knowledge, my mind.

I was very strong in all subjects in school but especially math and chemistry. I'm able to do any kind of research or scientific work, and that's why I tried to find this kind of work. But it was impossible, and only because of my Jewishness. They couldn't tell by my name—Reznikov isn't a Jewish name. It's a mixed name. There are Jewish people and non-Jewish people with this name. But everything was finished when I showed my passport or even before, because I would have filled out the *anketa* [form] where item number five was nationality, and I had to write *Evrey*.

It was an odd story because a lot of people were needed in industry, and there were a lot of vacancies. There were long lines in front of personnel departments. And I waited in these lines, and everybody before me and after me was hired, but only I was not. I heard a lot of explanations—maybe my education doesn't exactly correspond to this place, or they don't have positions, but people after me in line got jobs at this place. I know about all these troubles not from somebody else, but I felt them inside my own skin.

In Russia to apply for a job you can go to the personnel department of a company and talk. So you have an opportunity to have an interview at any place, with no limitation. That's why every day I had a lot of interviews. Every day. Eight hours a day for a whole month I was interviewed and interviewed and interviewed. And all the people who were interviewed before and after me got offers.

I found one place, the Institute of Engines, where they needed me. The chief of the engineering department offered me a job. But the next day when I brought my papers to the personnel department, I was told there were no vacancies. After that I found a job at an aviation plant as an engineer because—it was very strange—there was a department at this plant where only low-educated people worked, exclusively women. They needed an educated person to supervise, but nobody applied for the job because the salary was very low. I agreed to work for a low salary and went on to make a big success at this plant.

After nine months the chief of that engineering department of the Institute of Engines told me that the chief of the personnel department had left for another job and that the new man could not refuse me because he did not have enough power, and maybe I would try again for the position.

But now I had a job, and they didn't want to permit me to leave because I was a very good worker! Nevertheless, I left and I began to work in the Engine Research Institute where I began to study fuel cells, an absolutely new field. Nobody knew about fuel cells. I began to study, to learn the literature and so on. In nine months another organization, the National Research and Scientific Institute of Power Sources, tried to organize a laboratory for research on power cells. There were no specialists in the field at that time, but I was almost a specialist in that area by then. And they invited me to work with them. Again the personnel department didn't want to let me join this institute. And again when the chief of the personnel department was on leave, my boss arranged this matter.

I Was Like a Tank

Again and again, I had to prove my right to be at this place. I would spend additional energy, health, time, and efforts and so on. But I was lucky that in 1962 I got a position as an engineer in this institute, and I began to work in this very new field of fuel cells.

I was a very hard worker, so I was told that I would be promoted very soon. But all my promotions were very small, and I was just behind all my colleagues. We were very young and ambitious, and we were working in a very new field. Several of us were—I can't say talented—but we were a little higher than the average, and we were hard workers. Maybe five or six of us were very good together, and all of them got promotions. I was always the last to be promoted, and it was only because of my Jewishness. I can't say that I never got promotions because I eventually became chief of a lab—the highest level for a Jew.

I was in charge of a laboratory of thirty-two people, with two Ph.D.'s in addition to me. Before I got this position, I completed my Ph.D. But it's a rather long story because my chief and some other people tried to stop me. They kept trying to make me slow down. But I was like a tank—persistent, consistent, and a very hard worker. I got my Ph.D. in energy conversion in 1971.

A Good Reason to Celebrate the October Revolution

Sulamith and I met when we celebrated the day of the October Revolution—it's a great festival! I met her in 1956. In Russia we have three official holidays, May 1, the October Revolution, and New Year's. I was at a party with some of my friends from the institute. The hostess of our party was a student at the printing technology institute. Sulamith was with a group that had been at another party, but it was late and the parents had come home, and the group had to go elsewhere. They all came to the flat and joined our party when it was really late. She was beautiful, with red hair like the real Sulamith of the Bible!

She was a student at the Moscow Institute of Printing Technology. The same as any other Jew, she could not enter the university. And she was very clever and brilliant, but nevertheless she could not do very well with her studies. She was a good engineer, so she got a mechanical engineering degree. Her parents helped her—in Russian we call it *blat*. They helped her to get a job as a low-level engineer. She didn't like this work, but she too could not get a promotion because she was Jewish. So we fell in love, and then we married in 1958, just before my graduation.

SULAMITH SHTERNBERG REZNIKOV
Courage to Stand for Freedom

While many refuseniks chose passive resistance, Sulamith, whose temperament corresponds with her fiery red hair, plunged publicly into the fight for freedom. She is fiercely proud of her three sons, Sergey, Vladimir, and Michael, who stood beside their parents in the struggle. Among her greatest fears was their inevitable army service, deemed by Russian as well as Jewish parents a worse fate than prison.

Sulamith's sense of justice reaches wider than her personal circle. Two stories that could not be included here indicate her sensitivity to any kind of bigotry.

The first arose in the refusenik group itself. The KGB forced a refusenik in Dnepropetrovsk to recant publicly. A poet, he had been imprisoned for his activities in a town where foreign journalists were not allowed; authorities could thus abuse human rights without attracting attention. The KGB had thrown his Russian wife in a mental hospital, where she received the full barrage of "therapies." To save her, he met KGB terms. Though no one was hurt by his forced disavowal, he was shunned by many refuseniks.

The second story goes back to the anti-Semitism that arose in World War II. Sulamith recounted the experience of a family member who was wounded on the frozen battlefield and lay overnight, groaning for help. Ignored by medics who knew he was Jewish, he was eventually carried back to a hospital but died after his ordeal.

Sulamith was active in the Jewish refusenik community from 1984 to 1989 as a leader of the Jewish Women for Emigration and Survival in Refusal, which was formed at the end of 1987. On more than one occasion she was arrested for demonstrating in public. Once she was searched unsuccessfully for the slogan she concealed. It was ingeniously written on cotton fabric.

Today, following her own personal struggle to reach freedom, she would like to dedicate her talents to assisting immigrants.

Early Recollections

My parents were both born in Dunaevtsa, but their families moved to Odessa, which is where my parents met and married. I was born in 1937 in Moscow where they later worked. My mother was a chemical engineer, working with the galvanizing of metals. My father started in airplane construction. His work was secret, so he did not talk much about it. In 1942, during the war, my father had to become a member of the Communist party because of his job.

What's in a Name

My father gave me the name Sulamith. When I was a girl the children insulted me because of it. Once I wanted to change my name. I asked my parents why they gave me such a strange name. My father said, "I thought, she doesn't have a motherland, a language, a tradition, or a history; she doesn't have anything Jewish. Let her have at least a Hebrew name." And they named me Sulamith.

I don't remember any Jewish tradition in our home. We did not celebrate holidays or keep kosher. They did not know about it. But they gave me a feeling about it. I knew I was a Jew from the time I was born. I don't know how they did it, but they made me proud of being a Jew. They always said, "Jews are very honorable. They're very smart. They're famous." They gave me that feeling.

I was four years old when the Second World War began. My mother worked then at a military plant, and my father at a military aviation plant. When the war began they could not leave Moscow. I left the city for Gorky with my father's mother, sister, and her daughter.

We lived there awhile and then we went to Chelyabinsk in the Ural Mountains. Then my mother came to the Urals, and I lived there with my mother. My father could not visit because they relocated his plant from Moscow to Irkutsk to be away from the bombing. And then in 1943 he moved with his plant back to Moscow.

School Days

The first day I was in the first grade, September 1944, I remember it like today! There was a big room with desks, little tables. At this time schools were separated for girls and boys. Stalin wanted it to be like in ancient times before the Revolution.

On the first day the teacher asked everybody, "What is your nationality?" Because my last name was Shternberg, I was usually last on the list. The teacher asked each girl to stand up and answer. And all the girls stood up, and each girl said, "Russian." I sat in my place and thought, "What will I say when it is my turn?" *Everybody was Russian!* It was my turn; I stood; she looked at me. I couldn't force myself to say it. I looked at her, and I said, "What should I say? Russian?" I could not pronounce "Jew."

"No," she answered, "you are a Jew." The whole class—everybody turned. When I recall it even now, I cannot suppress tears. I was so small. I couldn't pronounce that I was a Jew.

"Stalin Is a Bandit!"

There was a period when Jews lost their jobs. My mother and father both became unemployed around 1947. By 1948 they had found work but with difficulty. My father had to change his profession. My mother found a job in hers, but she interviewed for a long time before she found it. Her profession is very specialized, and she was good at it. Before she retired she was chief of a big department, the third highest in command in this plant. My father finally found work in Moscow, but he had to change professions. He worked with *systema upravleniya, automatika.* I remember him sitting at the desk studying and learning new subjects. He became a senior engineer, the head of a big group of engineers.

My father never discussed Stalinism with me. Maybe he did not want his daughter to have double thinking, but he knew how things were and he hated it. When I was little—this was during Stalin's era—*every* time he took a bath or shower, when he thought nobody could hear him, he said, "Lenin is a bandit! Stalin is a bandit!"

They Deny Me My Gold Medal

When I was in high school in ninth and tenth grades, the last grades, my teacher was anti-Semitic. We had many teachers, some anti-Semitic, some not. But my main teacher was. She arranged it so I didn't receive a medal. It was 1954, and my parents were afraid to do anything about it. They knew it was not fair. They said they knew I was a good girl, that even without the medal I could enter the institute, and so I did.

I was in the *Komsomol* when I was younger. Everybody was in it! It was strange if someone was not. When my children were at school, I said, "No! You cannot!" But it was strange, too, even for them.

At the institute we discussed politics but only between our friends. I started reading certain kinds of things: books, but especially *samizdat*, which began after 1956 when Khrushchev spoke for the first time about Stalinism and repression. Khrushchev began in a very small way what Gorbachev did in a big way later.

I read so many books! Among them Solzhenitsyn, Mandelstam, and Greenberg. We read foreign writers, such as Orwell—*Animal Farm* and *1984*—and many others. I read *A Day in the Life of Ivan Denisovich*. It was available only at the time it was published. But after that Solzhenitsyn was "bad." You couldn't find that book. They stopped publishing it.

An Accidental Meeting on the Holiday

Gennady and I were students at different institutes when we met. My friend's birthday was November 4, and she celebrated it November 7, on the anniversary of the Revolution. We were with her family, but it became late and we had to leave. But I could not go home because transportation stopped in Moscow at 1:00 A.M., and it was probably a little bit later than that. A few of us students went to another girl's place. It was far, but there was another party for the holiday, so we walked there. Coincidentally, my husband was at the other party, and we were introduced to each other.

We met in 1956, and we got married in 1958. By then we had finished the fourth year. We were at different institutes and finished our studies the following year. At first we lived with my parents because they had two small rooms. They lived in one room, and we lived in another. It was small, but at that time in Moscow it was *such* great wealth to have your own room. My husband left his family and lived with me. Later we moved in with his parents, and then they received an apartment and moved, so one of Gennady's brothers moved in with us. Our room had two windows. We hired workers to build a wall dividing the big room into two rooms; we had our room and so did his brother.

When my first son was born, my husband said, "This place will be very bad and noisy, and nobody will be able to help you. You should live with your parents."

So, from the hospital I went with my son to my parents, and my husband lived in our room and visited us on weekends. My mother helped me with Sergey though she worked. My father worked but helped me too. He loved his grandson as only a grandfather can love, and this love was mutual. Meanwhile, Gennady did not waste time. He wrote a scientific book and received money for it. We borrowed more money and bought our own cooperative apartment! Sergey was two years old in 1967 when we moved into our new apartment. One year later I went back to work.

"We Don't Need You"

Usually in Russia the mothers work. They take children to day-care, to kindergarten. The father alone cannot support a family. We no longer had a cheap state apartment and had to pay much money every month, but my parents helped us. I went back to work for many reasons. I didn't want to be only a baby-sitter, a housewife. And we needed money too!

Because I was Jewish, I couldn't find a job at once. I had studied in the Institute of Printing, but I never worked in this area. In answer to a request, the institute from which I graduated assigned ten student engineers, including me and two other Jewish students, to a research institute. When I came there, they said, "No, we don't need you." They took only seven, though they needed ten. They did not take the three Jewish engineers.

After that I was allowed to look for a job on my own. This was not easy either. According to a huge list of different specialties, they needed engineers in my field, mechanical engineering, but when I went to a plant, they said, "No, we don't need you. Go there. They will take you." After a while, I could no longer bear to hear "No" again. So my father asked friends. One friend arranged for me to be admitted into the firm where she worked. My job turned out to be chemical engineering, not printing engineering! When Sergey was born, I had stopped working. When I had to find a job three years later, it was in mechanical engineering for the medical industry, because again my father asked a friend who asked a friend.

When Vladimir was born I kept my job and worked there until Michael was born. My supervisor was a Jewish man and a very good person who let me work part-time.

If I'd Had a Choice

When I was working at the Mechanical Design Bureau for Medical Industry, I drafted big blueprints of equipment. For example, my last project was a machine that cut the frame for eyeglasses. Sometimes I thought about doing something different. I had chosen this specialty because I had only fives at school, and I thought I ought to be an engineer because this was a hard but good career. But it was a mistake because I love children. I could have worked with children. And I love history. When I was a schoolgirl I studied English and was, maybe, the best in my class. But nobody said, "Go into history, go into English! Don't be an engineer!" My parents said, "You have to have a specialty." Engineering was a good specialty at that time in Russia. Besides, anti-Semitism made it harder to enter an institute where you study history and English.

Three Children

It is unusual for someone of our generation in Russia to have more than two children. Among our friends, we were the only family with three children. That was because I love children! I would have had more than three if I could have. When my first son was born, I said to my husband, "Let's have more." He said, "No, I cannot support more!" After my father whom I so loved died suddenly, I cried all the time. Then my husband decided that I ought to have a new baby. And I had a son, born five years after Sergey. He was named for my father—Vladimir.

For Russia, two is enough. People would say, "Oh, you have two children!" In Moscow, most people have only one child.

When I became pregnant with Michael, the doctor said, "You're pregnant. I want you to have an abortion." I said no. He was surprised and said, "At forty-one you want to have a baby?" And I said, "Yes. Even at fifty years I will have a baby! I love children." He thought I was crazy, but I felt myself young. They worried a little bit, but I had a good delivery. Michael was born in 1979.

We Become Refuseniks

Then we decided to emigrate. Everything made us decide this! As we thought about it, we discussed it. Many people left the country, including our friends; each family had to make this decision for themselves.

In 1979 when we applied to emigrate the first time, my husband worked in an institute. He had some authority, so we knew we might receive refusal on the grounds of secrecy. The work was very important, but in Russia, everything is secret! We applied nevertheless. If we did not apply, *we* would be the ones keeping ourselves in Russia. We wanted to apply, to say, "We want to emigrate. We don't want to live here."

Before we applied, my husband quit his job. It was amazing for his colleagues because he had a very high position—chief of the laboratory. He found a job without any secrecy, and we applied.

It was the beginning of 1981. We were waiting, and there was no answer. They didn't give us an answer for many months. At last there was a meeting of the Communist party, and I wrote to this meeting to complain that I hadn't received an answer. They immediately sent me a refusal!

My Concerns about Israel

I wanted to go to America from the beginning, and when we first applied, we were going to go to America. My sons didn't think about it then, but during the years of refusal they began to study Hebrew, to study Jewish traditions, Jewish history, and they and my husband decided to go to Israel. One of our friends said, "I'm very glad that you received refusal. If you had not, you would go to America. Now you will go to Israel!" At the beginning of 1988 we decided to go to America. There were many reasons. First of all, I was afraid. I was afraid because there are many Arab countries, and Israel is a small country. The other reason was because I had such a strong feeling for Israel. I knew if I were to go to Israel I would fight politically. I feel that Israel should be just for Jews, that because of the conflict between Jews and Arabs, there can't be peace on this land. And I don't like hot weather! Also, because of my vision problems, I have trouble seeing Hebrew letters. When I opened a Hebrew book, I knew I couldn't learn Hebrew *ever!* I said, "No, we will go to America."

Life "in Refusal"

We were called refuseniks, but we did not sit back and wait—we fought. It was a rule, I could apply only twice a year. So, every six months we applied again. We wrote letters to OVIR. Every six months we applied, and nothing changed. We wanted to emigrate, and nothing changed. They said, "No, you have security problems—secrecy."

When you applied to OVIR, it was required that you bring a document that showed where you work, that you don't have debts, and that it is known that you want to emigrate to Israel. At work they did not want to give this document to me. I struggled with the director and supervisor. In the end they had to give me the document because it's against the rules not to.

A supervisor can be criticized for employing people who want to emigrate. Then he might say, "Quit your job. After that, we'll give you this paper for OVIR." They absolutely refused to give me that paper at first. They wanted to force me to quit working. If I had gone to another job, if I could have *found* another job, they would have asked me, "Why did you stop working at your last place?" Because everybody in Russia has a special "Labor Book" that lists all your jobs—when you begin, when you stop.

When Michael was born, I had stopped working, we had already applied, and my husband's salary at the new job was reduced. He was not laid off, but it was lucky they needed him. He had changed his profession to get this new job. He had taught himself to become a computer programmer. Now we had three children instead of two, and his salary was reduced. So he took on extra jobs. He became a physics tutor. Students came to our house several times a week. He translated from English to Russian and edited scientific articles published in special magazines. Moreover, we sold many things—our piano, my sheepskin coat, and some of our books. We had a good library with many books. We were able to obtain *samizdat* books. We read them at home then gave them to other people; others did the same for us. We also listened to "Voice of America."

The Refusenik List

Our women's group would meet and say it was necessary to make a list of refuseniks. But it was only discussion. When I joined, I said, "If we need to make a list, I can find some names. When I call them, I will ask them if they know other refuseniks." Soon I had many names, addresses, telephone numbers, and I called and asked for others. I typed the list with my two fingers because even though I had a typewriter, I'm not a typist. I called other cities, and they sent me a list from Leningrad and other places.

First of all, I asked people, "Do you want to be on this list?" Some of them said yes, they wanted to, because they were willing to struggle and try to push authority to let them go. Some said, "Yes, we are refuseniks, but just now we cannot go, because of circumstances." For example, one woman said, "I will wait until my daughter graduates institute." Some of them said, "No, we are afraid." Some of them might say, "My son is in the Soviet army. I must be quiet now or he will have troubles in the army." After the son came back home, she would go on the list. I had a list of people who were willing and ready to struggle, to take any risk.

Approximately 400 refuseniks were in Moscow, Leningrad, and several other cities. It was not a complete list because nobody gave us the information. Certainly OVIR did not!

I called long-distance to Leningrad, Odessa, Kiev, Minsk, Kharkov, Penza, Gorky, Talinn, Riga, Vilnius. Some people from Irkutsk called me after they saw our ad in a *samizdat* magazine about Jewish life: "Now there is a list of refuseniks. If you want to be on this list, call Sulamith Reznikov and Tatiana Rosenberg."

I was really working full-time at home. Our phone was busy all day long. I paid the long-distance bills; somebody had to do it. I didn't talk long. Of the people I talked with I would say more than half of them have left already. I am told there are 400 new refuseniks on the list. Most of those on my list have received permission and emigrated. Because they struggled, I think, and bothered the authorities.

There is a group of refuseniks however, called "poor relatives," people who cannot get permission from their relatives to emigrate. In order to emigrate, it is necessary to receive permission from your parents, if alive; or if you were divorced with a kid, you need permission from the former spouse.

After several years in refusal, beginning around 1984, we began to receive visitors from America and England. We gave these visitors names of other refuseniks, phone numbers and addresses. And they give these names and ours to other visitors to Moscow. Sometimes these people were congressmen and senators. Usually they were tourists. My husband kept a big copy book where he wrote the names. Some people from the Council on Soviet Jewry visited the refusenik community in 1988, our last year there.

The Foreign Visitors

The visitors from America and England would come and talk; they gave us moral support. Sometimes they would bring a gift, and that was material support. A tape recorder I could sell, for example. But the main thing was we knew that we were not alone in our struggle, we had support from the outside. If, for example, my husband or I or someone else was arrested, I could call America, and everybody would know about it. When we went to demonstrations, it was not a pleasant deal. But we invited foreign correspondents so in other countries they would know about it. We felt that we had many friends in America and England. They supported our spirit to struggle, to wish, to wait.

Although there were many refuseniks, until our women's group organized the list of refuseniks, there was no way of reaching a Jewish community. We created a kind of information center, and I could assign people to call so that everyone was informed about demonstrations or visits to the Communist party about requirements. Some people in other cities did not have phones; I wrote them letters to find out about their situation, and they wrote me back.

After I had typed the list many times, somebody found computers, and other people put the list on computers. Then I did not need to type it with two fingers! It was necessary to do several copies. When President Reagan came to meet with Gorbachev, we gave this list to different American representatives, to congressmen, and to aides of Secretary of State George Schultz, who was concerned about human rights. We had a meeting with the State Department aide and gave him our list. I think Reagan had the refusenik list at his first meeting with Gorbachev.

Demonstrations

Sometimes we informed people in other cities about demonstrations in Moscow so they could take part. Years ago it was dangerous; you could be sent to prison. But times changed after the meeting of Gorbachev and Reagan in America, in December 1987. There was a big demonstration in Washington, on December 6, maybe 200,000 people, and on the same day there was a demonstration in Moscow.

From this time there were many demonstrations. The militia was always around. Sometimes they did nothing, just watched. Sometimes they arrested people and took them on a bus and drove them to headquarters. They forced them to write why they were at the demonstration and wanted to know where their poster was. On December 6, the militia did not arrest people, because there were many, many foreign correspondents. Again, they didn't arrest anyone in January 1988, when the big delegation of human rights representatives of the Helsinki Committee was in Moscow watching the demonstration.

I Am Arrested

I was arrested several times. When Reagan came and we had demonstrations, we were not arrested. During one of his visits, we had a demonstration of only women and children, June 1, Children's Defense Day. Michael participated, and we demonstrated near OVIR. His slogan was, "Nine years old and nine years a refusenik." On that day the militia brought buses but did not take us. We were only women and children, and there were many foreign news correspondents watching.

Once I was brought to the militia. They charged me ten rubles for illegal demonstrating. I said, "It's not fair!" They searched for my slogan, but nobody could find it because I hid it under my clothes. Usually they took everybody's slogans and tore them up. They searched me and searched my purse without success.

One slogan was "Human Rights from Paper to Life." In Russia nobody had human rights. In questions of emigration, there was no law about leaving the country. Without any law everybody in authority could do whatever they wanted.

Sometimes when we were at demonstrations, people came and asked us, "Why are you standing here? What do you want?" Some of them didn't like Jews; some of them were interested; some of them were angry. I remember one woman said, "Why do you want to leave?!" I asked her, "Do you like Jews?" That stopped her. "That's why we want to leave this country," I said. Another woman once said to me, "You Jews—you don't work. You only eat our bread." I said, "Yes. Let us go! Let us leave! We don't want to eat your bread! We don't want to live here! We want only to leave!" She didn't know what to say!

Some refuseniks did not go to demonstrations because they were afraid. I was afraid, but we had to do it! I can't say we were in "danger." Fear, yes. We tried to do everything openly, so everybody would know about it. I was most afraid for my children. Sometimes militiamen might beat people they arrested. They might kick and punch. I wasn't afraid that I would be beaten because I'm a woman. I was afraid for my husband and sons, because they are men.

A Forbidden Rite—Circumcision

After my children and husband began to study the Torah, tradition, Jewish history, they made the decision to prove themselves Jewish; they decided on circumcision. They did not have this done when they were born because it was very dangerous to do in Moscow. It was forbidden, and the KGB threatened people who did it with arrest.

Some religious refusenik friends took us to people who knew a doctor that did it underground—a surgeon employed in a hospital, a refusenik. Everybody called him only by his first name because of the risk.

We met in our apartment. Several people from the synagogue were present. We used our dining table as a surgical table because it was wide and long. We put a big tablecloth on it. The doctor brought his instruments, everything. We closed the outer door and did not open it again because of the danger. It was not just an operation as in a hospital. Afterward they said several *brahot*, and we had a *l'haim.* It was made with tradition and religion. It occurred twice in our house. My husband was circumcised in 1983 and my sons Sergey and Vladimir, one year later.

As usual when this doctor did it in somebody's apartment, many people came to be circumcised; the first time people came from Leningrad, Batumi, Moscow, and Yerevan, the capital of Armenia.

When Gennady had his circumcision, it was actually scheduled to be in the apartment of our refusenik friend whose eight-year-old son had some medical problems and was to be circumcised too. Their apartment was far away from ours. We had to take public transportation to get there. Everybody had arrived including the doctor and the old men from the synagogue, when suddenly some foreign people came to visit the family. Because of the foreign visitors, the militia or KGB might have interrupted.

Gennady called me and said, "We're coming to our apartment. Prepare something quickly!" The boy's father stayed to talk with the visitors while the boy and his mother and everyone else came in a taxi to our apartment. The operation was then performed.

The Army—Worse Than Prison

But, of all our concerns, I was afraid that my sons would be conscripted into the army. It's not like the American army. For Sergey and Vladimir, the army would be worse than prison. Some people prefer to send sons to prison than to send them to army. Because in the army they might be killed.

I worked with a Jewish woman whose son was killed in the army. He was standing and somebody shot him—not during battle or anything. My friend who is absolutely Russian had two sons. The elder who was in the army was killed this past summer, in 1990. The army is dangerous for Jew or non-Jew. And we were refuseniks! It was more dangerous, because after they were in the army, we would receive another refusal on the grounds of secrecy!

In early September, Sergey decided to contest our refusal. One early October day I was at home. I received a call from OVIR and the woman said, "Did you receive refusal?" I said yes. She did not say, "You have permission." But I knew it meant permission. I immediately said, "Can my husband stop working?" She said, "Yes." And I understood.

I called my husband and told him we received permission. He had wanted to stop working because of all the responsibility he had in the refusenik community. After I called, he stopped working immediately! Then I called Sergey and told him the news, and he began to cry! He was so glad because we waited so long to emigrate, and it was so sudden.

It took much time to receive the papers, the visas from OVIR. Then it took time to buy tickets. I could buy tickets only for the end of January 1989. And we arrived here May 11, 1989. We came the usual way through Vienna and Italy and waited there for papers from the American authorities.

We Learn American People Are Not Mean

The rabbi of the synagogue in Oak Park and the congregation helped us very much. People who leave Russia can't bring much, only suitcases. We didn't have anything. We brought only some family pictures. But people from the congregation gave us old furniture, dishes, pans.

Everything here surprised me. I like the people. Chicago people are friendly. Bus drivers, train drivers, they open the doors. People in Russia—never! There you run to the bus. The driver sees you and shuts the door and goes!

We had been told that in America people are mean to each other, that Chicago is a very bad city, many factories, no trees, that there are many industrial plants in residential areas! Instead we found many trees and parks.

Some people say Soviet Jews come just to be part of America. Once in Russia we discussed this question with a friend of ours. He said he wanted to go only to Israel and that most people who go to America want to assimilate because of the big pressures Jews experienced in Russia. I think some of them feel that way, but nevertheless, I feel that many people come because they feel they can be Jewish in America.

SERGEY REZNIKOV
A Double Life

Sergey chronicles the double life and double thinking required of a second-generation refusenik trying to succeed in the USSR though planning in secret for a future outside. The Reznikovs lived a decade with suitcases packed and ready to go on first notice.

Recalling years of misery as the class scapegoat, Sergey describes his transformation, coached by a Russian friend, from victim into victor. He made sure his brother Vladimir benefited from his early humiliations.

In the last years of the decade "in refusal," he theorized about the dilemma of meeting the woman in his future before leaving Russia; that event materialized. After a storm of paperwork and calls to officials, in the summer of 1990 he succeeded in bringing Marina to the U.S. for a visit. They were married in September 1990. There was no certainty, however, that she could acquire a permanent visa.

My Mother Corrects Me for Calling Someone a Bad Name

I was born in Moscow in 1965. My earliest memories go back to the time when I lived with my parents and maternal grandparents in their communal apartment in the center of Moscow.

Postcard with Gennady Reznikov pictured. Circulated by an American support group with directions to mail to the General Secretary, Mikhail Gorbachev. The family was refused permission to leave until 1988, ten years after they first applied.

Photograph of the first meeting of the Second Generation Refusenik group, April 1987. Formed of children of people who had been refused for secrecy reasons. Some of these young people applied on their own at the age of 18 and then were refused on the grounds of "hereditary" secrecy. Most of these young people are no longer in Russia. Sergey Reznikov is second from left in front standing row (in plaid shirt). About six months after the meeting, Eugene Kremen, second from right in front standing row (in dark sweater) disappeared with his entire family. Efforts to locate Eugene in Russia, USA, or Israel have been unsuccessful.

Photograph of participants in a hunger strike sponsored by a group of women activists and held March 6–8, 1988, on the occasion of International Women's Day. The participants divided into small groups and each stayed for three days at the apartment of one of the group. (Left to right) Back row: Faina Semenova, San Francisco; Anna Sofman, Dallas; Natalia Reznikov (no relation to Sulamith), New York City; Natalia Cherniak, Boston. Front row: ? Belostotsky, San Francisco; Anna Stambler, Hartford; Eugenia Feldstein, Chicago; Sulamith Reznikov, Chicago. (Woman in left foreground is not identified.)

Московский городской Совет
народных депутатов
ИСПОЛНИТЕЛЬНЫЙ КОМИТЕТ
ГЛАВНОЕ УПРАВЛЕНИЕ
ВНУТРЕННИХ ДЕЛ
УВИР
Колпачный пер, 10
Москва, К-6, ул. Петровка, 38
Телефон 200-84-27
/9 04.88г.   № 15/ 133
На № _____ от _____

Гражданину Резникову Г.Л.
проживающему по адресу:
117485 Москва, ул.Бутлерова, 10, кв. 258

В связи с ходатайством о выезде
в Израиль на постоянное жит-во

     В выезде в Израиль на постоянное жительство Вам и Вашей
семье отказано в связи с осведомленностью в государственных секретах.

Начальник УВИР   С.И. Алпатов

Тип. ХОЗУ ГУВД МГИ, 1986 г., з. 418—100 000

Refusal Notice   A historic achievement for the Reznikovs. After eight and a half years of refusal, this is the first documentary evidence. They considered this document a form of victory for their cause. (Translation: You and your family are refused to go to Israel for permanent residence in connection with your possession of state secrets.) Form is dated April 19, 1988. Gennady Reznikov had resigned the "secrecy" position over nine years before.

The Reznikov family take a moment to pose in front of their recently purchased suburban home. From left: Vladimir, Michael, Gennady, and Sulamith. (Sergey and Marina were unable to participate.) Photo © 1992 by Bruce Mondschain. All rights reserved.

I became aware that I was Jewish when I was in kindergarten and kids were mocking and teasing one another. I was participating in all of this, but I didn't know what it meant. When my mom heard me telling someone, "You are a dirty *zhid!*" she was astonished. At home she explained to me that I should never ever call anyone by this name because we are Jews ourselves, and this is a dirty word that is used against us.

For a long time I could not quite understand that we were different from other people. Because indeed we weren't different; we were the same. We didn't observe any traditions. We didn't observe Jewish holidays. The only thing that distinguished us from the rest of the population was the fifth line in our internal passports.

At that time I had no Jewish friends. At least, I cannot recall any. I knew that I was Jewish. I knew that I had to hide this fact in order not to be beaten up.

The Class Scapegoat

The kids were not particularly anti-Semitic. They just needed an excuse. I played the role of class scapegoat for several years. My achievement in sports was extremely poor. I was weak, and I could not defend myself. I preferred reading to playing football [soccer] outdoors. My father urged me to train, to become stronger, to do push-ups. My mom tried to defend me by going to school and talking to teachers, to try meeting the parents so the hooligans would be punished.

I was the scapegoat in my class from first grade on. In ninth grade I got extremely tired of all of this. I had a Russian friend who used to say to me, "I like you despite the fact that you are Jewish." He was very strong and had trained in martial arts, wrestling, karate, everything. I persuaded him to bring me to his karate class. He trained me personally every day for maybe half a year. We would get up early at 6:00 and go to the school yard where no one would see, and he would teach me karate. After I picked up some of it, he brought me to his karate class, and I trained there for about a year. Then once I was again challenged and fought back successfully; it was a kind of a miracle. A real scoop! The talk was, "That guy struck Reznikov, and Reznikov struck back and knocked him out!"

The last year in that school, people knew that I was able to stand up for myself. At that time I was very proud. I came home with bruises, but I showed one of my old enemies who had tormented me for many years that I could strike back.

Maybe my poor performance showed my brother, Vladimir, the negative model to avoid. He's a very strong person and, from a very young age, decided he must defend himself. He trained and trained. When he asked me for something, I would tell him, "I'll give it to you if you do fifty push-ups right now," and he would fall on his knuckles and do them. I encouraged him, and he grew up to be strong, much stronger than I. We used to argue when we were younger, but it's very dangerous for me to argue with him now.

I Learn to Think Strategically

When I was in high school and everyone else joined *Komsomol*, I would not. At first this was a practical consideration, because when one applies to OVIR for an exit visa, one has to leave *Komsomol*. Then you must announce the reason—that you intend to go to Israel. So if we applied for emigration, all the people around me would know that we were applying. This is what we tried desperately to avoid. We did manage it, somehow.

When you are young, they make *Komsomol* membership sound like a privilege. But when time passes and they discover that you did not try to join *Komsomol*, they try to drag you in. They want to report to the regional *Komsomol* committee that 100 percent of the students are members.

In school I was interested in chemistry. I did pretty well. I was winner of the city Olympiads in chemistry for high school students. Because I really wanted to study chemistry at Moscow State University, I prepared for the entrance exam and in 1982 applied there first. I was sixteen and had just graduated from high school. Usually people graduate at seventeen. Most children start first grade at the age of seven, but at six I could read, write, and do basic arithmetic, so I was admitted a year earlier.

Acceptance to the University or the Army

When I applied to Moscow State University, we had already been refused visas. I was well aware that now my chances for acceptance into the university were low, and I had to design back-up plans. This was possible because the exams at Moscow State University are given in July, and the entrance exams to the other institutes are given in August. If you fail at the university, you still have a chance to be admitted the same year to some other institute. This is crucial, not just a question of prestige or profession. It is a matter of avoiding the Soviet army.

The army itself, even in peacetime, was a bad place for anyone, but especially for Jews. They are discriminated against and humiliated. To avoid the army my parents rushed to enroll me in school early. People are drafted into the army at age eighteen. Since I graduated at sixteen, I had two years to try for a higher education. Even if I failed to be admitted to an institute or university the first year after graduation, I still had a second chance. Only if I failed a second time would I be drafted. All of this was consciously designed by my parents.

Before I applied to the MSU Department of Chemistry, I had been told that this department was the most liberal in the whole university and, as a Jew, I had a chance of being admitted there. I couldn't even dream of being admitted to a humanities school. There were just a few departments where admission for a Jew was possible at all. I trained hard for a year and a half before the exam.

The average time for an oral exam is ten to fifteen minutes. I managed to get a very anti-Semitic professor who gave me an exam in physics that lasted for more than two hours. I was given questions clearly out of the range of the school program. I even managed to answer them, but nevertheless, he gave me the lowest grade he could.

I went to appeal this grade, and they told me, "Listen young man, you still have a chance. This is not the lowest grade possible. You can still compete, so go on and. . . ." They then stated that I exhibited bad manners by making this appeal and that if I didn't stop, they would transform my grade to the lowest, so I would be out of the competition right away.

I had trained hard for a year and a half before the exam. Nevertheless, I failed because of this grade in physics, and the university didn't accept me. I performed probably better than I've performed since. I was absolutely at the top of my form. Recently I discovered this professor's name in one Western publication where he's described as one of the leading activists of the *Pamyat* organization.

When I was admitted to another institute, I was the captain of that institute's team in physics, and we made it to the Moscow City Olympiad in physics among undergraduate students. We won the second place among nonmajoring undergraduates. So I believe I knew physics pretty well at that time for the level I was required to exhibit on this test!

In 1982 I entered the Moscow Institute of Oil and Gas Engineering, one of the well-known refuges for refused Jewish students. Unofficially, people know that the forty institutes and universities in Moscow are divided into several clear categories. There are several institutes where no Jews can ever be accepted. Jews know that and don't even try. And there are some institutes where Jews can be admitted if they perform extremely well or have some connections, some protection, and Moscow State University is one. There are also several institutes where everyone knew the policy was fair; Jews flooded these institutes.

In my institute program in mathematics, Jews were about 70 percent or 80 percent of every group. There were groups where just two people out of twenty would be non-Jewish. In order not to disturb the authorities, the average number of Jews in this institute as a whole was kept to a reasonable level, 3 or 4 percent.

I received a standard Soviet degree, which is probably closer to a master's. It amounts to four-and-a-half years of instruction after completion of high school, and then half a year of independent work on a thesis. After I completed the thesis, in which I tried to optimize a work schedule for a large factory, I received my degree and worked for a year. At the time, I was very much interested in my thesis topic. I realized that I would have nothing better to do in the Soviet Union in case we were to stay, so I was prepared to embrace it, and I did.

I had many Jewish friends, but few of them knew we intended to emigrate, that I was a refusenik, that I read *samizdat* books, or that I met with other refuseniks. My refusenik friends and I met privately, and if we were sure that no one could hear us, we would discuss something really important to us such as politics and refusals.

The Empty Barrel Makes More Noise

Life went on—on two different levels. On the public level it was normal, as usual, but I tried not to participate in political debates with my friends because, as I used to say, the empty barrel makes more noise. I knew I was not an empty barrel.

In 1980 the Olympic Games were in Moscow. The authorities were afraid of unauthorized contact of Soviet citizens with foreigners. They demanded that people who could leave the capital do so. In particular, they demanded that all schoolchildren be taken away from Moscow at the time of these Olympic games. We had no *dacha*, but our friend, a prominent refusenik, did. She invited us there to spend the two summer months. Her place was like a refusenik club because people would come and go and discuss all these matters. In many ways being a refusenik was very exciting. Even now I must confess that I miss some of the spice of that life.

From 1986 to 1988 was probably the most intense portion of our refusenik life. My mother became one of the activists of a women's group in 1987. We knew a lot of active people, but we didn't take an active stand until 1987 when I graduated from the institute. We were afraid that if we surfaced in the refusenik movement, I could be expelled from the institute and drafted into the army. So as soon as I returned from military camp, as soon as I was sure of getting the military rank, we changed our way of life.

The Sacred Duty of Each Soviet Citizen

I attended military camp with other students from the institute. To understand Soviet life, it is necessary to understand the role of the army in that society. The Soviet constitution says that army service is the sacred duty of each Soviet citizen. The law states that only males between the ages of eighteen and twenty-eight are subject to draft. The draft is for two years in the army or for three years in the navy, and every young man can be drafted.

In practice, they draft almost everybody. The only possible way to avoid it is to be either a mental patient or literally crippled. Also, full-time students had the right to defer the draft until graduation.

First, in most technical institutes there is an obligatory military training program, which all male students must attend. This program leads to officer's rank. If you are admitted to an institute, at graduation you will be given a diploma equivalent to an American B.A. or M.A., and you will also be given a military rank in the army reserves. I attained the rank of Soviet lieutenant in the reserves.

Second, the Soviet army needs privates much more than officers, and if you *don't* have an officer's rank, you can be *sure* that you will be drafted as soon as you turn eighteen. If you manage to defer the draft until graduation and you do get your rank, there are different odds as to whether you will be drafted or not.

Third, being Jewish is a strike against becoming an officer. When privates are drafted, no one cares what their ethnic origin is, because Jewish or Russian private make no difference. But they clearly try to avoid having Jewish officers in the army. A Jewish boy who gets through institute and obtains a rank can be almost certain he will *not* be drafted.

Statistics show that maybe one out of ten institute graduates must go on to serve for two years. Because there are so many Russian graduates, if you are Jewish, it is virtually impossible that you will go. Although I never had a guarantee, as a Jewish officer I was almost sure that I would not have to serve.

I was in military camp for a month; it was part of my basic program. The happiest moment of my life was when I crossed through the gate of the military camp, as we were coming out. We were all singing, dancing, and chanting.

The Circumcision Conspiracy

While I was at the institute, my father decided to be circumcised. There was really a great deal of conspiracy involved. They avoided using the exact words on the telephone and used a kind of code. It was also dangerous for the *mohel*, the ritual surgeon.

About a year later, my brother and I decided that we wanted to be circumcised too. In April 1984, the day after our circumcisions, I had military training at the institute; I had to march in uniform. It was pretty painful the first day. I managed to get through so no one suspected that there was anything wrong with me.

The Name of Stalin Was Erased

I was not raised in the tradition of communism though it was around me. I was taught not to let it in. It is as if you are swimming in mud and covered with it. Once you are home you take a hot shower, and you are clean. It was the same with this Soviet ideology. While not opposing it openly in school, with friends, or in public places, I always knew, from maybe the fifth grade, when I was ten, that this was all propaganda, lies and nonsense.

When schoolchildren are admitted to the Young Pioneer organization in third grade, they are usually told the story of Pavlik Morozov, a story that presumably happened in some Russian village. A Young Pioneer, Pavlik Morozov caught his father, a *kulak* [prosperous peasant], trying to hide grain from the authorities. Pavlik reported him, and his father was arrested. Then Pavlik became a great hero; the whole village praised him; local authorities shook his hand. But his relatives plotted against him and killed him in the forest. So he is a great martyr.

His picture and the story of his martyrdom were held up as the ideal for Young Pioneers. When I came home I told my parents the great story of Pavlik Morozov. They didn't tell me right out but helped me arrive at the conclusion that his heroism consisted of reporting his own father! This example was one of the first holes in my Communist ideology. By the time we decided to emigrate, clearly I was no longer swayed by it.

In school they taught about Lenin and the Soviet heroes, but not Stalin. The name of Stalin was erased completely; there was no mention of him either good or bad, as if he had never existed. We knew the name Lenin, and the next name was Brezhnev. That was it.

My Other Education

Judaism was something new for me. First of all, it didn't come to me in one day but seven years, a period of gradual development. I started by reading books. The first book I read on the subject was Herman Wouk's *This Is My God.* It was a translation from English, an American book, where he explains the very basics of Judaism to laymen.

Also, we had a relatively good teacher who tried his best to read and educate himself. When he explained something to us, it wasn't just the reading from the Torah or *Tanakh,* but he tried to read commentaries and discuss things with us, and we gladly participated. We met once a week at someone's apartment for about two years. It was very dangerous for our teacher to do this and also dangerous for us, but his risk was much higher. He was also a refusenik.

Before the group dissolved in 1986, we had one frightening incident. One of our students told someone that she attended, and somehow this information leaked to the authorities, and our *moreh* was visited by the KGB. They warned him to stop, but he was courageous. We continued. We were, of course, a little afraid and a little shaky each time we gathered, but there was also some excitement about that. We knew we participated in some risky business.

The Lenin Library Was Our Stage

I took part in demonstrations and was detained once for three hours with other demonstrators. It was difficult to estimate the number of people detained because people were forced into different buses and driven to different police stations. In our station there was a group of about twelve or thirteen people. So I can estimate that the total number of people participating in the demonstration was between thirty and forty. In 1988, for almost half a year, weekly demonstrations took place in Moscow. On Thursday afternoons, people would gather on the stairs of the Lenin Library in central Moscow, the biggest Soviet library. It was chosen as the stage for the weekly refusenik demonstration.

The militia would wait with their buses, and people were sometimes beaten, sometimes not. People were thrown into buses and taken away for interrogation to the police department. We felt that because the world was aware of what was going on, we weren't likely to be put in a dungeon or jail. Our best shield, our best support was the attention of the West.

Mother's Refusenik Activities

When it became clear that refusenik activity was not immediately punishable, several refusenik groups and unions emerged. One of these women's groups was led by Judith Ratner, who later, got permission to emigrate. This was immediately after my mom joined the group, so she attended the first meeting of the group maybe a week or two before Judith Ratner received permission.

Soon the group started to meet at our apartment. My mother was given the group's records and proceedings. So, in the beginning her role was more like that of a bookkeeper, then she took a more active stand.

For several months, maybe half a year, she was very involved with the compilation of refusenik lists. I remember our family had to do dishes, wipe the floors, and cook our dinner because Mom was too busy speaking on the phone, typing, and correcting records.

Father's Activities in the Movement

I believe my father was well-known in this refusenik community, especially in the last years. He was in the initiative group of the Moscow Symposium. A group of refusenik scientists organized a symposium on the problems of secrecy refusal, late in 1987.

My father had written a paper for the symposium, he analyzed the publications about refuseniks in the Soviet newspapers, and he tried to read between the lines. He also worked on the organizing committee and edited submitted papers. Some people brought articles to the symposium that were too sharp and biting. They had to be made less sharp and not so openly directed against the government. Other people were just the opposite, not specific enough about matters that concerned them.

I was at the symposium as a sort of security person, one of the young people guarding the doors. If the militia came, we would have to warn the people inside. I met the now-famous Peter Arnett who became the foreign correspondent in Baghdad; he was then in the Moscow bureau of CNN, and I met him several times. He came with his camera people. I also answered telephone calls. Several important figures such as Senator Edward Kennedy called from abroad and spoke with refuseniks. It was a big event.

This symposium lasted for three days. There were several sections. There were about thirty reports prepared for this symposium. It took several months to prepare, to select the papers, to select the speakers, to organize the meeting place, and to get in touch with foreign correspondents.

My dad also participated in work teams of refuseniks like the Legal Seminar. It was a group of refuseniks who organized to study the legal aspects of refusal. They tried to prove and document the fact that they were held illegally, that it is against the Soviet law to deny visas on the ground of secrecy.

The Second Generation Refuseniks

Until 1987, our main concerns were not to reveal that we were refuseniks to anyone who was not a refusenik himself. In April 1987, there was an idea to organize a so-called second generation of refuseniks. We were children of refuseniks, sometimes of very long-term refusenik families. We gathered and organized in order to consolidate our efforts to get out and to attract attention to our situation from the West. Most of my last year and a half in the Soviet Union was spent in this activity with the second-generation refuseniks.

These activities continued until the departure of most of those who participated. I know that letters I signed appeared twice in the *London Times*, but of course I was not the only one who signed them. And we were monitored, which was very important. I had a support group in London. A girl from the group called me every week, once a week, just to make sure that I am alive and not in jail, that everything's fine. This was clearly designed for those who were tapping our telephone, so they would know that I am monitored and if they arrest me, they would not get off easily.

They knew I was not afraid of speaking out, naming names, and that I was giving her all the local news—like the fact that some vandals broke tombstones in the Jewish cemetery, or some people got new refusals, or this person was humiliated by OVIR officials, news of this sort. We were all determined to make ourselves as much of an irritant to the authorities as possible so that we put them in the position of having to decide either to put us in jail, to arrest us, or to give us permission to go.

Our Appeal to the West

We had grown up in refusal. We compiled an appeal to Western organizations and support groups. I spoke before groups of visitors as both a member of my family and as a second-generation refusenik. We didn't have formal leaders and formal distribution of responsibilities. We called ourselves the "Second Generation of Refusal Movement," just as if we were a crowd of people running together in the same direction.

The youngest in the second-generation activity were probably sixteen, and the oldest were perhaps thirty-five. We invited refuseniks to participate. We had maybe sixty people on the list, and maybe twenty-five of them participated actively. Maybe ten of them gave their time to doing things like writing letters or preparing speeches, and I was among them.

This was our statement: "Until everybody who is willing to emigrate can do it, this is not enough. We would like now to draw attention to the situation of second-generation refuseniks, the children of long-term refuseniks. We claim that our situation is even worse than the situation of refuseniks in general, because in addition to the common refusenik problems, we have unique problems of our own."

In my case, I explained, my family was refused permission to leave because my father had security clearance ten years ago, and ten years ago it expired. Now, I'm more than eighteen years old. I'm an adult according to Soviet law, and I want to apply by myself. I apply for emigration to OVIR, and OVIR does not accept my papers. They say, "We cannot break up your families. Our task is to reunify." They say they cannot accept my separate application because I am part of a family. That is the first obstacle. The second obstacle was genetic refusal, so-called hereditary refusal. If they accept my papers, they refuse me on the secrecy grounds. *I* had no secrecy, no access to anything, no clearance, no classified job. But still they say you are refused because of secrecy.

I applied alone, separately from the rest of the family. I was refused, of course, because of this secrecy consideration. And I demanded that they give me details. Whose secrecy is this? Is this my own secrecy or my father's secrecy? They sent me this letter: "Your application is refused because of security considerations." That's it.

The Categories of *Samizdat* Literature

Samizdat literature falls into several distinct categories. One is Jewish traditional and religious literature. These are translations of canonical texts and commentaries to them and books for beginners and literature like *Megillat of Esther*, the story of Esther, or the Passover *Haggadah*. The second category would be the pure dissident *samizdat*. It focused on the tragedy of Russia and the Soviet Union, especially during Stalin's time.

Before the truth about the labor camps and extermination was published in the era of *glasnost*, all was documented and available in books that were distributed secretly, books like *Gulag Archipelago* by Solzhenitsyn and other books of the same type, personal accounts of people who went through all of these horrors, analysis of the history of politics, and historical books on how Stalin rose to power. Clearly, the heritage of Stalin was a point of fixation of this dissident movement. I regard it as an extremely clever step by Gorbachev that he made all this public. He let the steam out, and that reduced the pressure greatly because it was almost half of what they wanted to say—the truth about the past.

There were also books about the current situation and the *Chronicle of Current Events*. Roy Medvedev was a historian who wrote about the past. He wrote about Stalin, about Khrushchev. But the *Chronicle* was done by Sakharov and his friends. It was an account of the current violations of human rights and other events in the Soviet Union. There was also literature, the art that was banned in the Soviet Union. This way we read many books like Pasternak's *Doctor Zhivago* and *1984* by Orwell. Also, *samizdat* provided the work of Soviet writers who emigrated and thus were prohibited for a long time from being published in the Soviet Union. The officials were not so much afraid of the contents as of the name of the author.

At the Synagogue I Meet a Young Woman

I met Marina just two months before we received permission to leave. Her family was in Moscow, but they were not part of the refusenik network. Marina was at the synagogue with a group of her friends. I knew one of her friends who was very active at that time in Jewish culture and worked as a waitress in the first Jewish cafe in Moscow. She took Marina along, and that's how we met.

Maybe it was what you would call love at first sight. I am not sure. Probably. Psychologically, meeting her right at that time made it a bit difficult for me to leave right away but, for the rest of my family, I felt I had to leave.

In October 1988, we were first telephoned and told that we would get permission soon. In three weeks we got the postcard from OVIR notifying us that permission was given. For a month I tried to quit my job. They didn't let me go. I had graduated a year before, and, according to the Soviet regulations, I had to work at the same place for three years. Education is free, but in return, you are a slave of the state for three years. They don't say anything about emigration. They say that for three years you have no right to change your job. But I told them that I'm not going to change my job. I'm changing my country!

Our family left Moscow for Vienna on January 22, 1989. One of my first tasks when I got here was to bring Marina for a visit to America. She and I were married four months ago, here in America in a suburban synagogue. It was impossible for her parents to be there, but there were a lot of people. It was difficult to obtain Soviet permission for Marina to leave and American permission to enter this country.

MARINA PAPERINA REZNIKOV
A Hopeful Start

Marina and Sergey had planned her visit to Chicago before Sergey left Moscow in January 1990, but marriage was an uncertainty. When Marina with her fine, dark features was first interviewed, one year after their good-byes, she was on a visitor's visa. The couple were concerned enough about the future to wish to keep her identity anonymous, though they were indeed radiant newly-weds. Their marriage, performed in an Oak Park synagogue, was the first Jewish wedding ceremony she had beheld. Meanwhile, they didn't want to create a public stir because there was no assurance that the State Department would grant her a permanent visa. Despite the gravity of the situation, in their threadbare studio apartment above a beauty parlor, there was a transforming spirit of hope for the future.

Marina's observations of the Jewish cultural and educational resurgence in Moscow indicate that it not only attracted many young people like herself but that it was conducted less furtively under the malevolent gaze of the KGB. Until she left, however, whether she was at work, in the food market, or on public transportation, she felt the sting of bred-in-the-bone bigotry.

In 1988, Marina received a degree from the Moscow Institute for Building Construction after concentrating on architecture as well as engineering. Her education, like Sergey's, was largely determined by what institutes would accept Jewish students. Today, while Sergey pursues an academic program, Marina works at the Jewish Federation of Chicago and dreams of furthering her own education. Meanwhile, she has received a permanent visa from the State Department and has been able to sponsor the immigration of her parents and brother, now reunited with her in Chicago.

A Glimpse of the Family Tree

I was born in Moscow in 1966. My mother, Svetlana, is from Moscow, and my father, Leonid, is from Leningrad. In 1964, when they married, my father came to Moscow. We had an apartment not far from the center of the city. There was a quiet and calm place nearby, one of the great vast parks of Moscow, Sokolniki. Ours was a private apartment. When I was little my parents, my little brother and I lived in another apartment with two bedrooms. We later swapped this for our last one, which had three bedrooms, so we could live with our grandmom.

My father is an engineer technologist in the building materials industry, working with the use of lime and gypsum. He studied and began working in Leningrad and moved to Moscow when my parents got married in 1964, there continuing to work in the same kind of job.

My mother taught music. She studied at the Moscow Central Music School at Gnesin Music Institute, then in Music College, and in the Gnesin Music Institute in Moscow. She taught in a school, plus she had a few students that she taught in the apartment.

It was my mother's mother who lived with us. Her maiden name was Rosa Mazirova. My granddad's name was Pavel. He changed it from a Jewish name because it was dangerous to keep it. The last job he had was in the design and construction of the Moscow metro. Granddad worked very hard and was rarely at home.

I never knew my father's father because he was wounded at the very beginning of the war and died. His name was Mark Paperin. My grandma now lives in Leningrad. Her maiden name was Basya Mirkina. She was born in 1904; she's eighty-seven. She has a second husband, and they live together in Leningrad. He's eighty-seven too. My grandma was a very popular singer in Leningrad. She sang classical songs, romances, lyrical pieces. When she returned to Leningrad after the Second World War, she became a teacher.

My family always managed when it came to food and economics. We all worked—my mother, father, brother, and I—the last two years. In Russia we had "ordering of goods." At your job you could buy foodstuffs. There were dairy foods and hot dogs, sausages, sometimes meat, cheese. Sometimes there were vegetables too because our organization had a contract with a few stores, and they sent us food.

School Days: I Was Unique in the Class

I started school when I was seven. The school was near my apartment. In school, when I was very young, I think a few teachers acted with obvious unpleasantness, but the rest hid it, so I was lucky. I was the only Jewish person in our class. There was a boy who was half Jewish, but they considered him Russian. Since kindergarten I have had one Russian friend; we lived in the same building until I left the Soviet Union. We attended different schools, and we couldn't see each other often. Now we correspond, but seldom. My closest girlfriend was my cousin who is still in Moscow.

When I was young, I remember that in class the teacher kept a registration book and would record our grades in it. Most of the information about us was in these books, which were supposed to be confidential. On the last page, one column was nationality. And only I was Jewish. Sometimes the teacher forgot about taking the book when she left the room, and then the students would open the last page and say, "Look, look, a Jew, one Jew!"

I Decide to Become *More* Jewish

My family really did not observe any Jewish holidays at home. Very rarely did we buy matzah because it wasn't approved. I was at the institute when I decided to become more Jewish. There were five groups in our department that attended the lectures together. We had many Jewish people in our group, and we kept together. At that time many of my friends became very religious. My parents were afraid that I might "fly out" of college because of my interest and aspirations to be Jewish. This was during my first year of college, in 1984. It was still scary to participate in Jewish events then.

I applied at an institute in Moscow where there was less competition and because there they'll accept Jews. It's a very big institute, maybe 1,000 students. I passed the four entrance exams very well. I studied architecture, building construction details for residential and industrial buildings. At first I didn't like it, but in the second and third years I liked it and fell in love with it. I was almost an architect! I graduated in 1988.

A Rebirth of Jewish Culture

For me, things changed after *perestroika*. I became interested in Jewish culture, and I went to a few Jewish organizations. This was in August 1988, after my graduation from the institute; I was twenty-two. There were the Moscow Jewish Cultural and Educational Society and the Moscow Society for Friendship and Cultural Relations with Israel. Both organizations, like many others springing up at that time, were directed at waking up the Jewish people from fear—despite the rise of anti-Semitism—to "shake" them, open their eyes to freedom, to help them discover the facets of Jewish culture, history, Jewish origins.

The Moscow Jewish Cultural and Educational Society was located in the private apartment of Yuri Sokol, one of its organizers. There were two rooms and a kitchen in his apartment, and he lived in the kitchen. He gave both of the rooms to our society. The library was in one of the rooms, an exhibition dedicated to the Holocaust in the other one. And even in the hall there was an exhibition about Jewish heroes of the Soviet Union during World War II. In the library were many books about Jewish culture and history, in Russian, English, Hebrew, French, and other languages. Also there were lecture series on Judaica. We invited many interesting people to give lectures: Americans, Canadians, Australians, Israelis, and, of course, Russians. We had a few groups for Hebrew and English studies. Teachers were volunteers. I gathered a group of young people together and organized activities, mixers, and put on evening teas, and several evenings a week we watched videos of interesting films about Jews during World War II.

We organized musical performances and invited Jewish people to take part in them. Many well-known musicians came and took part in competitions. Toward the middle of 1990 the Moscow Jewish Cultural and Educational Society had 1,500 members and guests.

The second group, the Moscow Society for Friendship and Cultural Relations with Israel, met at the apartments of a few members. Members of the society arranged meetings with representatives of the Israeli Consulate in Moscow. Because Israel had no official embassy in the USSR, it had an office in the Dutch Embassy. Many Israelis came to the Soviet Union as visitors, and came to the society to tell us about Israel, their life. We wanted to know more about the country that was called in the words of the Soviet press "the country of Zionism" and "the enemy of the Soviet Union." We wanted to find out as much as possible about the Promised Land about which we had dreamed and that was based on notions formed by secretly reading books such as *Exodus* by Leon Uris and *Glorious Brothers* by Howard Fast.

Many books, Israeli publications in Russian, Hebrew, English, were in the library. There were books about aspects of life in Israel—about *kibbutzim*, education, industry, people, celebrations, cultural and political life. A few groups from our society went to *kibbutzim* to work there, study Hebrew, and go on many excursions in Israel. We organized slide shows and videos to educate Jews about Israel and lent them tape recorders with popular Israeli singers.

Both societies arranged trips to the Vyalki, the place not far from Moscow to celebrate the Jewish holidays in the early fall and spring. We usually took the train, and we would take up three cars. We would hear a lecture about the story and origin of the celebration, dance, sing songs, meet with new people, play at sports. The first time I went to celebrate, it was *Sukkot*, and the "feds" with their scowling faces looked us over and followed us. But we were having a good time, and this didn't stop us, although it was unpleasant to feel their piercing gaze.

At Work: No Place for Lofty Ideas

The institute assigned me to a small building construction group with thirty-eight people. I redrew sketches from other people's sketches and did calculations, but whatever I did, my boss recalculated. I didn't have any kind of interest in my work because I saw that nobody needed my work. There was no chance to have lofty thoughts. My boss corrected every last thing I did, so what was my work for? I would do things right, and she would correct everything.

It's a tradition in the Soviet Union to send the urban employees, like engineers, to do agricultural work like digging and pulling weeds. But where I worked, my boss sent *only* me to an agricultural work farm.

A lot of the research institutes sent their employees to the collective farm from a day to a month in the summer and in the fall. Most of the people who were sent were Jewish. I was the only Jewish person in my department. Most of my friends went to the collective farm. These were foolish jobs because the people who supervised us did not give us gloves and instruments to work with. We did it all by hand. It was crazy! Our hands hurt.

So my friends and I weren't really treated very well by our bosses. But not only that: in a store, clerks would try to sell us the worst vegetables and fruit. They would choose them especially for us. I could not argue with them. People standing in line would say what they thought about me or my Jewish face. In public places, on public transport, in stores, people would scorn you, put you down, and from this they seemed to get enormous satisfaction.

My Parents Oppose Emigration

I thought about leaving Russia when I started at the institute. But my parents said, "No, no, no, never!" I think I wanted to go to Israel, maybe America, I didn't know. A lot of my friends from the institute were interested in leaving too. They left before me. That spurred me on. When I graduated from the institute, I had decided for sure that I should leave. Sergey and I had already met by then.

When I started to attend synagogue, beginning with Rosh Hashanah in 1988, I went very often, on Saturdays and every Jewish celebration. Many people came together near the synagogue to talk and sing songs and dance. When I began going to synagogue, my brother was in the army, but after he returned, we went together.

I felt that almost all strata of society hated me because I'm Jewish. I didn't want to live in a country where from time immemorial Jews have been scorned and hated. I wanted to feel myself a full member of society, but how could that be possible if in school you were teased by being called "Jew"; if at the institute you wanted to enter, the grades on your entrance exams were lowered and your friends, also Jews, were prevented from getting in? Because of the fifth line on your passport—"Jew"—you were rejected for a job. Either they found fault with the most unexpected trivialities or openly, right to your face, informed you that for Jews all positions were closed.

It seemed all the state policies were directed toward destroying everything in you that is human. Jews who studied in institutes and simply walked around the synagogue during a Jewish holiday were kicked out of the institute for an "amoral act." This happened to my cousin and several of my friends at the institute.

How can one live in a country where a sense of freedom has been blocked since childhood by the purposeful so-called upbringing of a patriot of the homeland? This was a country where people fighting for freedom were considered insane and were sent away, either to labor camps or prisons. For these and many other reasons, I wanted to move to a different place. I made this decision before I met Sergey.

I Meet Sergey

We met in Moscow, near the synagogue. My friend worked at a Jewish cafe in Moscow, the first Jewish cafe. Many people went there. Sergey and his friend were in this cafe, and she was their waitress. They talked together and liked each other and decided to meet later. She asked me to come with her, and she introduced Sergey to me; that is how we met. Sergey's friend lives in Boston now, and he's married. My friend lives with her husband in Toronto, Canada. I knew Sergey only about five months before he left on January 21, 1989.

I really did not know when I first came here if Sergey and I were going to be married. A lot of time had passed, and he could have changed his mind. The first time we looked at each other, we realized what had happened. We decided to get married!

We were married at the Oak Park synagogue. It was a big party, about sixty people, many of them American. They made me feel very welcome. I had never seen a wedding in synagogue. I saw and I participated in it! I was stunned by it all. Sergey broke the wine glass. Sergey's parents had the food catered for the wedding, and everything was delicious.

Chernobyl

We knew about Chernobyl not right when it happened, but some days later. It was a calamity, a frightful blow for the whole country. I had studied a little nuclear physics, so I was able to imagine what occurred. I was really upset because I also understood that the USSR was not ready for this catastrophe. There was silence in the press about the extent of the explosion and its consequences. After a year many books and articles came out, analyzing the Chernobyl disaster and the causes of the meltdown. They described the heroic attitude of the people there, who really didn't know the air that surrounded them was fatal.

This misfortune illustrates that the government and ruling elite didn't care about members of society, about people who work at nuclear power plants. It was one of the factors that helped me reach the final decision to leave the Soviet Union.

We were worried about things like food. Most food came from Byelorussia and the Ukraine. Food supplies were affected, maybe not to the extent as in Chernobyl itself but from nearby as well. People had no Geiger counters to measure nuclear radiation in the soil, ground, air. Collective farmers had continued to harvest. It is not their fault, because they knew nothing. But other people knew too much, and they kept silent. I thought it must be shouted as loudly as possible, "Stop! Don't do this!"

I Am a Russian-Jewish-American

Now I'm taking a clerical course at the Business Career Institute of Jewish Vocational Service. I take courses in typing, accounting, computer software, business writing. We have English lessons. Right now I work one day a week at the Jewish Federation. I am planning to be admitted to a university in computer science. I really want to go to the University of Chicago. It is one of the best universities in America. Otherwise, I will try the University of Illinois or Northwestern. I think I can pass out of a lot of subjects I've already had.

I like the University of Chicago area where we live now. The university's buildings are like castles with towers, belfries, fountains, with many entrances with arches. I find Chicago amazing architecturally, so many different styles in one area.

Being Jewish is important to me. I want to feel Jewish, but I think it's difficult. I have many Russian roots because I grew up there. I do feel Russian because of the culture. I feel myself Russian when there's an occasion to be proud of something in Russian culture. I feel myself a Jew when I celebrate Jewish holidays and when the Jewish people in Israel or in any other part of the world are in danger. I feel myself American when there are troubles among Americans. It is very difficult to explain.

VLADIMIR REZNIKOV
Determined Faith

Unlike the others we interviewed, Vladimir was introduced to us on a visit to the library of the Spertus College of Judaica where he was employed part-time as a cataloger while a student at the University of Illinois in Chicago. Because of his interest and willingness to participate in the Oral History Project, he persuaded the rest of the Reznikov family to do the same.

A Positive Outlook on My Jewishness

It never occurred to me to be ashamed or to regret being a Jew. I think I developed this positive outlook because of my parents, who, from the beginning, when I began to deal with the fact that I was Jewish, would explain things to me or would give me books to read. One was by Howard Fast, about the Maccabees, *Glorious Brothers.* It was historical fiction based on the Maccabee stories. I read other books like the Bible, and the Israeli-Russian journals like *Israel Today.* This was exciting for me because it was forbidden to have these things.

I think these forbidden books usually would come to us through other people who got them from somewhere, but I think that initially they were brought by some visitors from abroad. I was ten when I started reading these things. I remember exactly because that was the summer of 1980 when I was in the house of some people who had all this literature; I began reading it and was very interested. It was probably the beginning of self-enlightenment and interest.

I remember when I was eight or nine, my parents were discussing the question of leaving Russia for America or for Israel. But it probably didn't have any political context. First I think I was more interested in Jewishness, and I had become acquainted with Jewish traditions rather than with political ideas.

I Become Politically Aware

As for political ideas, I think first I began speaking politically when our house was visited by some foreigners, people from the West, who came to visit us because we were refuseniks. I recall that we were put into refusal in 1979 when I was nine, and our first visitors were in 1983. American institutions or organizations had these lists of refuseniks and people who needed help. They finally got our name on these lists, and we were called by phone or notified somehow, and my parents met with them.

Once we became refuseniks, my parents changed their jobs. Actually, my mother gave birth to my younger brother, Michael, who is now almost twelve. He was born in February 1979, and we got refused in October 1979. After that my mother wouldn't work. She chose not to work and probably wouldn't have been able to if she did want to, so she knew that it was a dead end. Before refusal, my father decided not to take the path of a dissident but rather that of someone who *thinks* otherwise. He was an engineer in engineering chemistry, and in 1977, two years before we applied for a visa to leave Russia, he quit his earlier job because of the secrecy matters.

Help from the West

I think we survived during this time because a big chunk of aid came from the foreign visitors: from Europe, from the States, and, though rarely, from Israel. There were also people from the refusenik community helping us because they would get similar material aid from the same source. Once in awhile we would get some presents that would support us. It could be clothing, for example; we might get a coat that had the value of three months' or more salary.

Though I knew that we were deprived, my really great parents brought me up in a way that I would be happy with whatever I had. So I knew that I didn't have things, but I never felt uncomfortable because of it. I always was satisfied with what I had. We weren't hungry, and we had a roof over our heads. And we were warm enough in the winter, definitely. Thank God!

I don't remember any Jewish holidays being celebrated when I was younger. I believe that none of them were celebrated up until probably 1983 when I was bar mitzvahed and my father became acquainted with some religious leaders of the Jewish community in Moscow. After that we celebrated some of the holidays, like Passover, Purim, Yom Kippur, but they were not strictly observed according to Jewish tradition. We knew that they were holidays, and we would have dinner, or we would have some friends or American or European guests who led the seder or the Purim dinner.

My "Bar Mitzvah"

I didn't have a bar mitzvah in strictly religious terms. I didn't go to the synagogue. I knew that I had "bar mitzvah twins" in London and in Pennsylvania and a couple more places around the world, who prayed in my name when they were bar mitzvahed, but I didn't go to the synagogue or have any religious ceremony. I did not read from the Torah, though I definitely saw a Torah in Russia. When I was thirteen, I believe, I saw one from a long distance. By the age of thirteen I read in Russian a translation the Christian Bible. Later on I saw a Torah, and I even read some of it, not before an altar, but just for myself.

When I was fourteen I was very interested in Hebrew, and I found people in Moscow who were studying Hebrew. I tried to attend a couple of courses, but somehow my connection with them was lost, and the only thing that I had in my hands was a book of Hebrew, which I actually started to teach myself. Later on my parents, my father in particular, and my brother became interested in Hebrew, and we got a teacher. By that time I already knew Hebrew enough not to have to attend these classes.

Friendship and Faith

We definitely all supported each other somehow. I think that being in refusal all these years, we learned what it meant to have good friends, to have people who think alike and who have the same hopes and the same faith, who will help each other.

I think by now maybe 95 percent of these people have emigrated to Israel and the United States. But back then it was not the case. People whom I knew began emigrating in 1986–87; by 1990 almost all of them had left Russia.

Being Jewish gave me a sense of responsibility, that I couldn't do something that other people might, like steal, or something else that clearly was forbidden by the Torah, if I knew about it. In Russia children knew there was a state law, but they didn't know there was Christian law. They would steal or do something else if they wanted to. For example, I would walk with my friends from grade school, and they would go into a store and want to steal some buns or something else, just to do it, because it was very easy to steal from the store. I wouldn't do that. I had this moral idea even though I didn't think of whether my friends were Jewish or non-Jewish in particular at that time. I just knew that I was Jewish and I would not do it.

Under Surveillance

I don't think my family was aware of being watched by the secret police, but my father would often say that we didn't do anything against the law. Even though they felt they were being watched or overheard, I don't think my father worried about what he was saying. By expressing unusual or nonconformist ideas we were not breaking the law, and we were not doing anything against the system.

When I was in high school, there were people who were questioned about this and that. It was a math school and very good; there were many Jewish students. The principal was very afraid that the authorities didn't like this school because of its Jewish population. It would be a disaster for us if officials found some reason to dissolve it. There was some dissidence there and the principal was trying to halt it. She wanted to prevent the school from actual disaster, so she tried to eliminate people or ideas that were nonconformist. She expelled a couple of people because of their Zionist or religious activity. She expelled a couple of my friends. She even wanted to expel me, but I quickly decided that it was better not to talk about Jewishness or other matters concerning religious or social matters. Study at school was for studying. So I stopped. But there was a time when they wanted to expel me for participating in a Purim celebration. I think she did these things with the great idea of preserving the school from destruction from above.

This was a pretty good school, and I didn't want to lose my place in it. The standards of education were very high. To get into this school, one had to pass three or four rounds of exams. I took the exams when I was fifteen. So I was there three years and completed the course of study. After that I went to the Institute of Railway Engineering, and my course of study was applied math and software engineering.

The History Books Become Obsolete

With *glasnost* came many changes that caused difficulty from the teachers' point of view. There was a big change when it came to the teaching of ideological subjects such as history or political science. These teachers would be very confused. They didn't know what to teach or how to teach Marxism. Sometimes we would have some materials in our textbooks canceled as wrong or old-fashioned.

For example, in 1936, under Stalin's purges, the Communist party adopted a new constitution. In our constitution of devout socialism it was written that the Soviet country and the Soviet economy had come to the point where they had already achieved the Communist basics from which we could build communism. All this was rubbish! Usually we would learn that in these years from 1932 to 1936 there were great achievements at all levels of industry and agriculture, and after they finished with this constitution, everybody in the Soviet Union was utterly happy and utterly satisfied.

With the start of *perestroika* in 1986, we began to read published materials about the purges, so we knew about the thirties. We knew about the famine of 1932 when millions of people died. We knew about the concentration camps and about the real cost of industrializing the country in ten years. This transformation was, by all standards, Soviet and non-Soviet, a miracle. The production grew like 500 percent in ten years or something.

But we knew that all this was achieved by the death from exhaustion of slave laborers who did all the construction. And we knew the real facts about the constitution that proclaimed freedom, liberty, and equality of rights. When we came to this chapter about the achievement, the good works, and the constitution, we would just skip it. Because what was written in the book was a waste of time, the teacher didn't know what to discuss.

Even more than just skipping a chapter, on the final exams they skipped questions regarding the Soviet period of history, from 1917, the time of the Bolshevik Revolution, until 1970 or even 1980. We would answer questions only about czarist Russia or everything that occurred before the Bolshevik Revolution. We were lucky because we had less material to study.

I definitely knew of people being released from prisons or being brought back from exile. I was very well acquainted with the son of Joseph Begun. My parents were very good friends with the Slepaks, and other people who had family members in exile and in prisons, so we knew about the release of most of these people.

The Chernobyl Cloud

I think I learned about Chernobyl when the news was published or when I heard the rumor that a Swedish radio station was panicking that the Chernobyl cloud was over Sweden. We learned about Chernobyl several days after the explosion. They didn't say anything, probably because of May Day, which is a national holiday in Russia.

We found out what happened much later. The first day when it was reported there was an item in the back of the newspaper that said that one of the reactors in Chernobyl blew up. There wasn't a big fuss about it. So we supposed that it might be a big disaster, but it wasn't presented in a way that one would know. I don't remember when I really understood about it. That came later. The central authorities began reporting on it more and more, and afterward we would have the different stories in newspapers and journals about people. These appeared later on, after Western pressure. Not the same day.

There really wasn't any kind of an emotional reaction in Moscow, not that I know of. There were jokes about it, about two-headed people, that sort of thing. Because Moscow is far from Chernobyl, you never perceived it as a real danger.

Regrets and Resolutions

I only regret we could not take more people with us. There were people I left behind, people who definitely do have a chance of coming here. They are not on the list, they have not yet applied, but they are going to. And there are many of them. I have many very good friends, whom I miss more than anything else.

I don't have any nostalgia over the country itself. I miss that I can't walk the streets of Moscow or whatever, but for me that's not as important as my friends.

Here I have hope for the future. I have the freedom to choose something and do it, even if I'm not sure that I'm doing the right thing. I have a sense of purposefulness and freedom to travel wherever I want.

I'm not sure about my intellectual aspirations, but I am sure about my career. In Russia there was always a dead end, some point where you stopped going anywhere. A case in point: Our friend who left Russia in 1972 came to visit us here at Thanksgiving. He had just gone back there for the first time, eighteen years after he had left. He saw his old friends and found that they were in the same place, doing the same thing, getting the same money and in almost the same situation as before. The only change was that they had children who were already taller than he was.

I have considered doing some computer and mathematical work, but now I'm thinking of doing more in business or international relations. That's absolutely different from what I could do in Russia.

What has been important in my life so far is the support of my parents. In every stage of my life, my parents helped in educating or enlightening me.

As for my history, I believe we shouldn't judge others too harshly or even by the same standards, whether it's Russia or the situation here. My story is absolutely different from someone else's story. We shouldn't say everything in Russia was bad or everything here is good. There were good things there that are bad here and vice versa.

7

UNCOMMON ENDOWMENTS

THE M. FAMILY

ARCHITECTS MILA AND Victor M. and their son Larry represent the kind of family any enlightened society would wish to count as its own. They are intellectually aware, proud, and striving. Because she had a Christian father and Jewish mother, Mila's internal passport was stamped "Russian." Victor, the son of Jewish parents, held one stamped *"Evrey."* They are raising their son in the Jewish tradition. Nature and nurture combine in Larry to form a young man uncommonly endowed to meet the future.

MILA M.
A Life in Two Worlds

Mila could easily be the heroine of a neo-Tolstoyan novel, with her exquisite sensitivity, courage, and spirited elegance. Had she chosen to be a Communist party functionary, she might have risen to enjoy the perks inherent in the corrupt system she abhorred, but she believed stubbornly in merit and talent as the proper criteria for reward.

An architect who planned symposia for the Society of Moscow Architects, she aspired to excellence in a milieu where government dictated ideas and party hacks aborted promising new programs.

From tales imparted by both sides of her family, Mila learned as a child the chronicles of loss, political imprisonment, death, or marginal survival of her ancestors. A love of Russian culture was their commonality. It sustained them through the birth pangs of the Revolution and the brutal decades afterward. Mila's passion for aesthetics is her birthright.

The apartment that Mila, her husband Victor, and son Larry occupy in Chicago is furnished austerely but with an eye for contemporary design. Had the life of a fashion model appealed to her Mila might have easily attained it. Her fine bearing and willowy grace transmute jeans and a sweater into designer wear.

She recalls her history in terms of family legend, Soviet politics, dreams and work. The bittersweet separation from parents, brother, school chums, and the culture that nurtured her was her trade-off for freedom. She relates her candid history anonymously to protect family members still in Russia.

Early Childhood

I was born in 1954, in Obuchovo, a little town about twenty-five miles outside of Moscow. I have a brother who is five years younger than I who is still in Russia. I spent my earliest months in one of the houses on Moscow's central streets. This house will always be one of my favorite memories. An apartment on the fifth floor belonged to relatives who adopted my mother after the tragic loss of her parents. It is now my uncle's home. Mother grew up there and remained even after marriage, but when I was born my father insisted we move to our own place. That's why I grew up outside of Moscow.

My uncle's house was always hospitable, and he kept its door open to me. My uncle's wonderful library was where I spent many favorite hours. He never had his own children and treated me as if I were his own. I spent my student years there. It was not only convenient to the school of architecture, I also had use of everything that I wanted, including the library and my own room. My uncle is a very educated person and made a great contribution to my upbringing. I carry the bitter memory of the last time I was in his house and said good-bye to everything. Who knows when I'll return?

Stalin's Terror and My Grandparents' Deaths

My mother was born in 1929 in Moscow. Her father was a well-known lawyer; her mother taught ballet. They moved to Kiev because of my grandfather's promotion. He was responsible for resolving some important political and economic questions of the developing republic.

That's why he was one of the first people murdered during Stalin's Terror. He was arrested and disappeared. The first arrests under Stalin began in 1932–33, but the Big Terror began in 1937. My grandfather was a political person but not on a high level, neither a big politician nor a member of the Communist party. He was a labor activist, and there were a lot of people like that, especially after the Revolution. I really don't know whether he had Communist ideas or not or, like many others, was just deceived. They were all young and idealistic and tried to follow the ideas of Marx and Lenin—everybody was going to save the country and make it better. He used to travel to major cities in southern Russia doing propaganda of some sort. Later, he became a paid organizer of the Communist party; I really don't know what happened. Maybe he changed his point of view. It is a dark spot in our family history, and I do not know the details.

My mother would never discuss any of this with us. She was six or seven years old when this happened. Her mother, my grandmother, was in her twenties, and what happened overwhelmed her. After the tragedy and terrible loss she suffered, she developed a fear of the unknown and of death. She ultimately committed suicide. My mother stayed with relatives in Kharkov, a Ukrainian city. She was sent from family to family. Though she was treated very kindly, she still felt like an outsider. She never talked much about this; she is a very discreet person.

When she reached her twelfth birthday, she went back to Moscow to my uncle's family. She graduated from art school in Moscow in 1950 and had started to work in an art studio before she met my father. In order to find a job, she had to leave Moscow after graduation. The graduates from Moscow would be assigned to smaller cities. Of course, people would prefer to stay in Moscow because of the higher living standard there. It is really different to live in the provinces. In spite of her move, my mother has stayed an authentic Muscovite.

My Proud Paternal Ancestry

The other side of the family had a kind of legendary past. My father was born in Obuchovo in 1927, the same place I was born. He was a very good teller of family stories. One of them is about an ancestor who did a great service to a dignitary and acquired favor with him. He was given a title and some property. His son was one of the heroes in the war with the French army in 1812. My great-grandfather was a manager for one of the Russian tycoons who owned textile factories. My great-grandfather bought land there and a few retail stores.

The family had been quite rich before the Revolution and in Obuchovo were associated with a textile factory. Although the factory did not belong to my father's grandfather, he worked closely with the owner as the manager, and so he had a nice house. They were very proud, and he was strong and relatively wealthy.

When the Revolution broke out, it changed so many destinies, brought so many tragedies. I don't know how my grandfather could survive the Red Terror. Thousands, millions of people were killed in the civil war. Those who were not killed died from hunger. These times were truly a medieval dark terror.

The Revolution changed my grandfather's life. He was a very smart man, and he predicted that this terror would be for a long time. That is why he gave away everything he had—his house, property, money, and belongings. The factory was given to the new government, and the family became very, very poor.

My father was one of five children and the only boy. My grandmother sold the last of her jewelry to buy food for the family in the great famine of 1930. Although they survived, it was dreadful just worrying about food for your children, my grandmother told me. Our family's mainstay was devotion to Russian culture, history, and art. From childhood my father dreamed of being an artist. He studied world-famous art traditions.

My Father "Defects"

In 1941 when my father was fourteen years old, World War II began. At the very start he was sent to the western outskirts of Moscow to build the fortifications against Hitler's tanks. The fact that unarmed children and old people couldn't be a really effective force against such an army was not considered by Russian authorities who gave the orders. After a week of working in the rain in a desolate area, my father realized the absurdity and danger and with his friend escaped at night on foot. It took them a few days, but when he returned home, he found out that all those who remained near the lines had been surrounded by Germans and captured. It was certain that they had perished. Unarmed, how could they stand up against tanks?

That night two officers came to the house to arrest my father. They threatened to shoot him as a German spy, accusing him of giving away important war secrets. My grandmother started to fight, cry, kiss their boots. It may have helped. They left the house. My father knew a year later he would be drafted anyway, so he left home and went to Leningrad to join the navy.

Under Stalin everything was very strictly regimented. During his years in the navy, my father had a few confrontations with the authorities and came close to being arrested. He was very young and didn't always cover up his feelings. Father left the service because of injuries and contusions.

My Parents Meet and Marry

My parents met in 1952 when he was on a family vacation. A year later they were married. My father had to support the family while completing his education at an engineering school of Moscow, so he went to work in the textile factory.

From childhood he dreamed of being an artist, a painter. All my childhood I was provided with paintings and drawings that were copies he made of the greatest artists. He preferred Dutch artists and only Russian artists who were classical in form. It was tough living with him in my youth because of the difference in our tastes! But, of course, I respected him.

After a few failed attempts to attain an art education scholarship, my father graduated from college and became an engineer. Everything that he touched worked well. He was very skilled technically and invented a few machines that actually helped workers in the factory environment. Studies showed that in textile factories there were chemical and other dangers for workers. So he invented a special ventilation system. He also tried to invent a machine that would go to the moon. He was not crazy but very talented and imaginative. Probably it was his creative outlet. But he continued to draw and taught me to draw. All my childhood I remember how he drew!

My mother had formal training in textile design and worked at the same factory with a group of sixteen other artists. She designed ornamental carpets. She always decorated the apartment, and Father built the furniture by himself.

An Early Lesson: The World Has Two Faces

My father told us about the crimes of the Stalin era. He felt a responsibility to do this. We were taught to keep silent about what we thought and what we knew, to be careful in the way we communicated with different people. I always knew the two faces of the world, and had proof of their existence many times. Since childhood I've believed only in the honor of my family and the dignity of my parents. I'm thankful for everything they did for me, for their understanding.

During childhood, because my mother was Jewish and my father Christian, they followed Christian traditions by celebrating some Russian Christian holidays, but that was all. My mother didn't even mention the word *Jewish* on my records. I took my father's lineage, so being Jewish did not affect me as a child. I know that for some people it was a real problem. My husband was lucky that it was not a problem for him either.

Career and Marriage

I went to public school in Obuchovo and trained to be an artist. When I decided to go to architectural school, my parents supported me in this. I was very happy in architectural school. I worked at my studies, which came quickly to me, partly because of some previous knowledge of architecture.

I was married when I was very young, and in that regard I was stupid. We were students at the architectural school when we met and married. Larry's natural father was half-Jewish. This was not something I considered when I married him, it was just a coincidence. He was an architect; after five years we were divorced.

I met Victor after I graduated from the Moscow Institute of Architecture in 1981. We were soon married, and I was looking for a new and more interesting job. With my master's degree I began working at the State Company for Housing and the Institute of Soviet Architecture in Moscow, which is like your American Institute of Architects here.

In my work there, I noticed incongruities. It was clear that the privileged and educated had more money and opportunity than others. For example, our members were often invited to go abroad, to take tours, to make contact with other people in other countries. I observed how these people worked together and how they interacted.

In my work, architectural ideas and theories were developed in a kind of think tank. But these ideas were controlled at the creative level by Soviet thinking. If they thought they would benefit more from something else, the party people could publicly cancel projects—in front of everyone. I was committed to the society, but the air seemed full of black lies. I could not respect these people.

Of course, I often thought of leaving Russia, of going to America; when I was young it was always a kind of dream. I would draw pictures of America; I even had dreams about it. But, my childhood dreams of America were sort of filed away because I was so busy with husband, study, and family. It was not until there was a shift in the political situation that these dreams again became important to me.

A Working Mother

In Russia, you have to stand in long lines for food and other stupid things. A lot of time is just wasted. I worked eight hours a day. After school, sometimes my son would spend time with his friends and more often he was just at home. When he was born we lived in student housing, and they had a day-care for the infants. There were about twenty babies to one nurse and an assistant. They didn't worry about changing every child's diaper and things like that. I didn't worry too much about this because I was very busy and studying a lot, and this was just the way to do things. Luckily, Larry turned out well.

I would go to the store usually every other day, after work or classes, to buy food. Sometimes I would get milk at lunchtime and take it home and then sometimes go to another store before going back to work. Sometimes there is a little deceit at the office to leave to do this.

Sometimes I would go to the cooperative food store at night after work, and sometimes Victor or my mother would do it. That's why I could sometimes work late. To arrange shopping in our free time like this was tricky to do. Women have much more to do over there than men. Here there is no trouble getting food, just too many choices.

I did very well there, but felt I had to sell my soul to sell my programs that I believed were good. I developed the ideas for symposia at the Institute of Soviet Architecture. I invited experts in the specific areas to come and make presentations. I think becoming disillusioned was just a slow process. I felt that my ideas, my creativity, all went into one big void and that Russia had a real ideological problem. No matter how good an idea was, things could always be canceled by someone farther up the political chain. This I found very frustrating. I felt it was a stupid system.

I feel that I am Russian; I'm sorry about that. I felt very comfortable as a Russian. When I felt *un*comfortable it was with the people who lied and who did not appreciate the work of others. Then I was not only troubled, I was disgusted. It was not from the point of being Jewish but just as a Russian.

I was the one in the house who first said, "Let's fly," but we had discussed it often. Though my husband was concerned about his parents who were staying, I convinced him it was time to go. My parents actually were ready to leave with us.

I was nervous. In March we filed the emigration forms, and on June 28, OVIR called me. Immediately we started preparing for this great step in our life. We had nothing valuable to sell or to save, nothing we could take with us. We sold some of our art books and mostly presented them to our friends as gifts. When it came to buying our plane tickets, we did not have enough money. Our parents helped a little, we had saved a little, and I sold my very good coat. It was fine Canadian leather and very difficult to get in Russia.

We had some furniture left, but soon we were ready to go. I had friends, connections, to get tickets because there were long lines even two years ago. We decided to go in September. Some friends saw us off, but not many.

Expectations and Reality

To discuss our expectations and what we actually met here is not simple because life is very complicated. I met things here that I could not imagine. Some people call it culture shock or just a new lifestyle. I would say we made a great step, and it demanded that we review everything that we had learned and known before. We had to revise some of the ideas that we had about America.

It doesn't mean that it was worse than we expected; I would say it is even better in some respects because we were lucky. We found jobs, and this is not easy for most people who come here. That is what I think is most important.

Even after a year at my job, my American experiences provide difficulties, problems with the language, and adjusting to life here. My own ambitions seem to cause problems because I wish to be treated like a professional, as I was in Russia. I know my capabilities could be wasted here. I also know my skills can be expanded, and this I do, but it is a real struggle.

When I first came here we decided Victor would apply for an architectural job and I would just do design and space planning because it is much easier to find this kind of work.

When I started in this office, oh my God, that was so bitter! Nobody trusted me. What was my experience in Russia, what did it actually mean? Without the English language nobody could believe the kind of education I had in Russia. The first weeks were just close to being the death of me from the tension, from trying to understand what people were saying! Particularly in the English language, you know, slang, even your ordinary language, is difficult, not at all like radio news. People spoke quickly; they didn't pay attention to whether I knew the language or not. Some kind people tried to do it nicely, but people less kind took no time. But this is my problem, I know that, I don't blame them. I should have prepared better. I only took German in Russia, and so I had very little time to take some private classes in English before emigration. So I decided after a few months' experience in my office that I would put all the time and energy I had into private lessons in English. I went to the most expensive and one of the best language schools—the Berlitz School. It helped me a lot, particularly in conversation, in reading, in vocabulary and understanding what others say. It also helped with pronunciation. Right now, the tension is gone, and I am doing better.

I try to do a good job. It is very complicated to communicate in a new language without being able to express myself as I could in Russian. When we came here we met an architect who told us, "Guys, you are beginning a new life in a professional field in Chicago, and it will go very slowly. It will be very difficult for you, and it will seem impossibly slow at first."

This is true, but my previous experience helped me so much, and I feel comfortable working here. Here they are very pragmatic; they know some specific catalogs and what they were taught, but very often they are not able to handle the pencil, the brush, to do the actual artwork. They are very often just not sharp; it is very encouraging to me. I think we were taught to be more creative than here.

Our Son's Education and New Life

We sent Larry to the Jewish Day School, but we are actually disappointed in the level of education. We thought he would get a more serious education there, more control, more discipline. I think the Jewish schools are better than any others here. He is in seventh grade, and we do not know what our plans will be for him. Right now he is getting a scholarship so that we can afford the day school, but otherwise he would have to go to a public school. It is a dilemma, because he is doing all right there. Even though he was well educated in Russia, he did not have any early Jewish education. He tries to adjust in his own way.

In Russia, they teach the same subjects in seventh grade as they do here but much differently, more seriously and in greater depth. They study literature but also write compositions. Here it is a kind of play, and students don't try. Work is not even assigned. Maybe we talk too much about our way, but schools are better in Moscow. We would prefer to send him to a private high school, but it is too expensive.

He hasn't brought home the school discussions about Jewish culture and *kashrut* [dietary laws], because he knows that I am so busy and involved with work. We were not really involved with these observances from our childhood, and for us it seems weird, a different way of life. We think about this, we think about the differences in spiritual thinking and in the customs. Of course, he has asked me not to buy ham and similar things, and I do what he asks.

I hope that he will get a good education; I think human beings who understand this world, who have more knowledge, expand this world with their intelligence. I think it is important that we keep him reading, and I hope he never knows problems and difficulties like we had in Russia. I want to bring him up with the expectation of doing good for people, to have good taste in everything, in his surroundings, his life, and to be close to his roots.

I hope he creates a new life with good friends, because he left very good close friends in Russia. One of them was the grandchild of a very famous composer, and they were so smart, so good. These children arranged very interesting activities on their own. I think he misses them very much, and he tries to keep this to himself, inside himself.

Comparison and Contrast

In comparison with other Russians, I had a good position, a good life, a good salary, and people were envious of me—and the work I did.

I never tried to collect objects, and I guess I just felt so much freedom facing the new future in America. I was prepared for this emotionally, physically, and it didn't bother me that I didn't have valuable things to bring with me.

It is true that the things around us now, we didn't have in Russia. I mean, the stereo system, some appliances in my kitchen, but they don't mean much to us. Of course, we know we can go and buy stereo systems, a new TV and new coat and stuff like this, but the most important thing is the way I feel inside myself. I feel free, I feel an interest in my life, in my future. Even if I meet difficulties again, I have a curiosity about life, and it helps me. My previous life just happened; it is over. I feel enthusiastic in spite of many, many difficulties, psychological difficulties, language difficulties and things like that. I see everything as a new beginning.

How We've Changed in America

We recently saw friends who were visiting from the Soviet Union. My friend is half-Jewish. She hasn't decided yet if she would like to emigrate. It was then I realized how much we've changed since we've been here. This let me have a new look at people and their values and their lives. The thing is, if people have a problem, like buying shoes, or a piece of meat for their children, they have problems, but this is not as serious as a "root" problem. Because, it seems to me, I have root problems. Tomorrow I might be fired. My friend doesn't have to worry about her job. She will have a job. The little stuff is very important for her, but not for me. That is why our values don't intersect with each other. They are on different planes. For her it is very difficult to understand our problems because we have all this stuff, objects that they don't have in Russia.

She came here to look around and compare with Russia. There are a lot of things that she compares to what she *knows* from life in Kiev. She always compares her life with that of her relatives in Washington. She criticizes how they save money, how they spend money, how they live, and tries to find their mistakes. She criticizes everything because she misunderstands why they do what they do. Like all Russians, she just insists you have to do it *this* way. It is a particularly Russian attitude to try to convince others that their way is wrong.

Discovering Jewish Rites of Passage

I never attended a Jewish wedding, *brit*, or funeral. I didn't know even one experience like this. Our son's circumcision was the first, and after that we attended one in our friend's family.

Our son's circumcision was absolutely a starting point for him. After he came back from summer camp, he told us he wanted to do it. He asked us and we decided to do it, no problem. We were not upset when it was being done. It was done in the hospital, but we asked the synagogue to help us, the FREE Synagogue on California Avenue. They provided everything, the *mohel* and all, and they paid for it.

Perhaps we didn't put a great meaning on this. I saw the difference in our friend's family because this has always been part of their life. The boy was born, and they did this to be involved in the spirit of something. I felt a sympathy for this little child and his mother. It was solemn because many friends got together and celebrated this event. I felt that it meant something to all of them.

I would like to discover our relationship to the Jewish community. We moved into a Jewish community. We came here and people were very kind to us, including our neighbors and people around us. They kept trying to help, to give advice, but they did not push. I like this very much. I don't feel that I am really involved in serious religious procedures and rituals. Maybe it is too late for this, for me, I don't know. But it is really interesting to see that contemporary life includes even strange aspects of the community. Like the Jewish Orthodox, for example. You see people have a right to be what they want to be and to live the way they want to live, and nobody cares. It is phenomenal! I think it is great. It is, I would say, the strongest feeling I have about the Jewish community here. It has the right to exist, and I can see it! It is the freedom of choice. I don't feel that I would follow their examples, probably not. In fact, we met a few young religious Jewish families here. They invited us over for their Friday night, and we spent a few times in their houses and apartments. It was fun, and we recognized some of the Jewish foods we had eaten in Russia, foods like stuffed fish, and it was great!

In Russia, ethnic food was Asian food, the Middle Asian food. There was not much Jewish ethnic food. Matzah was very hard to get, but most good synagogues let people buy it. Maybe I was fifteen when I first tasted matzah. But it was not something special.

For Victor, I think it was important that I was Jewish. For me, all my life I spent in a circle of Jewish people, Jewish friends in architectural school. It was just natural to be among Jews. Nobody paid attention that it said "Russian" on my passport. Russians accepted me as a Jew, and Jews accepted me as a Russian!

But I didn't live comfortably in both worlds because I hated the regimentation. It is terrible. To be against the idea of government handing down rules about how people should think—I would say that this applies to all people in Russia, not only Jews. I think that all the people I knew felt this way, that it is not just a Jewish perception.

Every Effort and Energy for the Dream

Step by step we are building our new life. Day by day we become more Americanized. We are lucky to create our professional careers as well. It was not easy to start from the beginning to prove our professional competence. Every day is a struggle. But I know if I want something and put forth every effort and energy, one day I'll reach my goal. I dream of interesting professional careers for myself and my husband, a good education for my son, good friends in my house, and being together with my parents. And I'm happy to know I'm OK; I'm on my way to having it. I thank my lucky stars.

VICTOR M.
Blueprint for a Fresh Start

Victor is quick to let you know that his life was not affected by the stamp on his internal passport. He wishes to separate himself from the Russian Jews who were persecuted by the state. Had the term cosmopolitan *not been tainted by its use against the Jewish national minority in the late forties and fifties, Victor might be so described.*

Not only can he theorize adeptly about cultural differences, he and Mila share a certain, urbane courtesy and would mingle easily with the elite of any civilized society. His fine features and open manner coupled with his superior education undoubtedly insulated him within Moscow's intellectual milieu from the discrimination that arose where Jews were an identifiable population. He wants to make clear, there was no such thing as a "Jewish community," because there were no communities in Moscow.

His parents were physicians who raised him to love Russian culture, a love that impelled a career in architecture. As a young architect he rose in the Soviet system: he successfully designed housing for the masses; he had a book on interior arrangement published; he won several architectural awards for standardized housing designs. But his real reward could not be ignored, rationalized, or defended. It was the duty to repeat endlessly designs that worked before. After thirteen years he knew his future would remain standardized.

Born the year Stalin died, he recalls hearing political discussions in his teens, when people had begun to feel safer within a trusted circle. He is concerned that anti-Semitism is rising, and he believes (like some of his peers) that the activities of Soviet immigrants here may be scrutinized by KGB spies reporting back to Moscow. Because both his and Mila's parents are still there, he asked that family names not be revealed.

More than any other aspect of adjusting here, the responsibility for providing for oneself and one's family is the most overwhelming. At thirty-seven he worries about employment security, the cost of educating a child, and how to support his parents—if he can afford to send for them. Weighed in the context of American freedom/responsibility versus Soviet repression/security, the latter at moments perilously tips the scales. Nonetheless, Victor denies any regret.

Victor and Mila were married in 1981, seven years before they emigrated. Before leaving Russia, Victor adopted Larry, Mila's son from a previous marriage. So apparent is the affinity, you would assume they were father and son by birth had they not informed you otherwise. One of their favorite activities is debate. The two concur, however, that the Soviet educational system has a competitive edge. While the Soviet workplace boxed in many talented people like Victor, he is testing the hypothesis that Soviet educational methods are superior to American.

Despite the diverse changes confronting him here, Victor is curious to learn more about his ethnic background. No longer afraid of association with the Jewish victim stereotype, his emotional guard slipping, he explains why at this time in this place when he reads about the Korean community or the African-American community, he readily identifies himself with his own, the Jewish community.

No Ethnic Communities in Moscow

I grew up in the city of Moscow. We lived in an area of many different kinds of families. There was no area in Moscow set aside for people of different backgrounds. They were all mixed, with no division or any nationalistic area at all. There was no such thing as an "ethnic community" in Moscow. It is only in America that we have seen this.

In our family, I was an only child. My father and mother are retired doctors. My mother was a gynecologist, and my father specialized in infectious diseases. He worked at the Ministry of Health as an administrator for many years.

It is not possible say how our standard of living compared to our neighbors because we did not live in an area with a certain income. There may be fine, highly educated people and right next door would be very poor people.

Our life, in comparison with our surroundings in Russia, was good. When I was living with my parents, we had a nice, big apartment with three rooms in a big building. It was something like the apartment we live in here in Chicago. But this was rare in Moscow. Usually people there live in tiny apartments. Almost everyone in Moscow lives in high-rise apartments; there is practically no such thing as individual houses in Moscow.

When I was about fourteen or fifteen years old, I remember that both my parents were working, but I remember more about school than about my home. In Russia, unlike here, children can stay at school after their classes are over, until it is time for their parents to come home from work. I guess this is similar to what you call day-care. Other than that, it was much like public school here.

I graduated from a very good specialized English school. I started studying English when I was in the second form [second grade] when I was about eight years old. But I was very slow in English. We studied the language four or five days a week, about forty-five minutes per class.

I don't remember any special holidays or events. My parents were very busy and worked very hard. Their salaries were not very good but good enough according to Soviet standards.

I was supposed to help out around the apartment, but I guess I was a bit lazy. The house was empty all day, and it was very small, so there was not much to do. My mother prepared the meals. She would stop on the way home to pick up the food for the evening meal. This was very common in Russia.

Jewish Only on the Register

We did not really have a Jewish life in our home. But they don't let you forget that you are Jewish. On your passport it is written that you are a Jew, not Russian or Georgian, but Jew. My classmates in school knew that I was Jewish. There was a register book at school where everything was listed: name, address, nationality, parents, all stuff relating to the student. Of all the people in my class, I was the only one who was a Jew.

I didn't feel too bad about this. No one made a big issue of it. There are a lot of Jewish jokes in Russia. You know, Jews themselves like to make these jokes. But there was nothing seriously wrong in my childhood about my being a Jew.

My grandparents spoke Yiddish. They were around when I was very little, and sometimes they spoke Yiddish together. They were much closer to the Jewish life before the Revolution. Both my grandfathers and both my grandmothers had good Jewish backgrounds, maybe not religious really, but they were brought up in Jewish neighborhoods in the Ukraine.

In my home, we did not celebrate any Jewish holidays. The tradition was lost after the Revolution, especially in the big cities. It existed maybe in Kiev, maybe in Odessa, but not in Moscow. There were very few religious Jewish families in the city. After the Revolution, some of the Jews tried to forget their Jewish background because there was a feeling that there were no missionaries any-more, just culture. Everybody was different, but there were no educational or opportunity differences from one person to another. This was a very strong feeling in the country, especially among educated Jews.

Some of the first political discussions I became aware of were when I was about thirteen or fourteen years of age. I remember people all around were criticizing communism, the way of life, and the politics. This was after Stalin's death when people felt it was safe to make these criticisms in your own house, among your own friends.

My parents had mostly Jewish friends. The Jews did have some common complaints that were different from the non-Jews because of discrimination they experienced. To some extent, their opportunities were limited. My father definitely felt he had been held back in his field because he was a Jew. In general, Jews were not allowed to hold certain official positions.

How and when this all began in Russia, I do not know. But then it began to be a common state policy against Jews. Neither of my parents had friends who were arrested or anything like that. But there were a lot of victims of Stalin in the older generation, that of their parents. I knew some of them.

I do remember one thing about the Doctor's Plot back in 1952. My father had graduated from the institute, what you call a university here, in 1953. He was sent to work at a very prestigious research institute in Moscow to gain a Ph.D., but then he was not admitted. He was good enough, one of the best, but he had to practice in a village. We can say it was discrimination; it was not really a tragic situation, but he was disappointed. He was qualified, but he was turned away. Of course, he was not the only one who was not admitted. Both Jews and other Russians could be turned away. It is true, there was a policy of obligatory service to the country after graduation, but exceptions were made for outstanding students. It was unfair and a case of anti-Semitism. That is what I think.

Career Blueprint

At a very young age I decided that I wanted to be an architect. My parents were pleased with this decision. I have some talent in drawing, and in Russia architecture is a very well-established profession. I applied and was accepted into the School of Architecture. Of course, the government paid for my education. This was one of the best things in Russia.

I received my master's degree at the Moscow School of Architecture and then went to work at the State Company for Housing, and while I was working I also did my research and dissertation for my Ph.D. This is a common practice.

My dissertation was on the architectural aspects of housing, different technical devices that make things work better. It has always been difficult in the Soviet Union to get housing completed quickly and efficiently to meet the total need. The policy in the Soviet Union is to build typical or standardized housing because it is cheaper to build once the mechanical problems have been solved.

I was interested in all kinds of buildings, and I had many different projects. This was what I worked at for thirteen years. It became boring. It seemed that I would be doing the same thing over and over. Not that everything was boring; I managed to do some interesting things. I had fun with some small projects, but it is difficult to stay at the same point for years and years.

Mila and I were married in 1981. She and I had different work situations. I had a very good career and some recognition. I was involved in some very interesting projects. I built a series of small, modest houses, and then I participated in several competitions and won several awards.

I had a book published on residential interiors. It was written for average people. They could learn how to arrange furniture, how to choose color for an apartment, what choices there are in furniture, how to put together a kitchen, and similar matters.

The government was trying to encourage people to live better, with more comfortable things. Of course, in America you hear that Russians are all so poor. This is not necessarily true, at least in Moscow. The standard of living for educated people in Moscow is kind of high. People are more interested in culture and do not watch so much television. They are interested in literature. Actually, they do not have the opportunity to buy cars and houses, but they spend more time in cultural pursuits.

To Emigrate or Not to Emigrate

Although our life in Russia was going smoothly, my wife and I decided in 1988 that we would like to leave the Soviet Union. Some of my relatives had already left Russia, my cousin the first. Some friends had begun to leave in the seventies. But, after school I finished my postgraduate course, and had a very good job.

I did not experience anti-Semitism, though my father did. You know, there was a certain Moscow circle. (Now everything is changed, by the way. I am speaking about the time after my institute studies, after I finished at the School of Architecture.) In certain circles of architectural institutions and offices and studios, there was no special problem of anti-Semitism. Sometimes the suffering that Jews went through, or are going through, in Russia, is a little bit exaggerated. I am not comparing it with the times now. All this *Pamyat* and fascist stuff is disgusting, a very terrible thing. But when I was young, after the institute, there was no such environment that you could say was unbearable for Jews. I don't think so; at least I didn't experience it.

Those I knew who had emigrated went to the United States, but a close friend of my parents went to Israel. Friends my age mostly went to the United States. My wife was also very interested in making a change. The only problem was my parents. Don't forget, I have no brothers or sisters. I had been seriously thinking of emigrating for many years, since my best friend left in 1979 or 1980. But at that time it was so difficult to decide.

We had no problems when we made application to leave in March of 1988. No problems at all. We got clearance for the States in June of 1988. Things were moving very quickly then. My parents were pleased with our decision. At their age, they felt making such a change themselves would have been very difficult. Yet they did not try to do this when they were younger. I would like for them to join us here, and they will apply. When they will apply depends on our decision. The applications will be in Washington late this year.

It is wrong to say the Russians don't want us to leave. They are likely to say, "Go to your Israel." Shortly before I left I was invited for a sort of private conversation with one of the local high-ranking authorities. It is not that they invited me because they really *wanted* to convince me to stay. Somebody told them that they must try to persuade people into not leaving, so they tried to convince them, particularly the well-educated young people, not to go. I have an architectural degree, and this is a very highly educated level. But now they are letting all Jews go. They said they didn't want us to leave simply because this is the official policy.

I don't know why the general concern over emigration. I think they are concerned about the political base of Russia when so many people are leaving. If you are an official, you are under the obligation to give the official party policy on the one hand, but on the other, you want some things yourself. So they didn't even try very hard to convince me not to leave Russia. But it was a policy! They were obliged to do so.

We arranged and paid for our own transportation here, and we arrived in November of '88. It took us several months to arrange everything, and we came through Austria and Italy, where we stayed two-and-a-half months. It was great. I worked there as a tour guide. I could use my knowledge of architecture in Rome and Venice. We stayed in Ladispoli, a little place near Rome where many Russians live.

A New Cityscape

It is difficult to describe our life here in America. Everything is new and difficult. There is some feeling that we should learn more about our Jewish background, but not merely from a religious aspect. Our son wants to learn more, to do more. It is interesting to see a Jewish community and to find out about Jewish organizations.

My relatives here in Chicago who have been here for eight years sponsored us so that we could come here. We liked Chicago because it is a big city, and we came here also because we were a bit afraid of New York. As yet we are not very close to a specific community here. Also, architecture here in Chicago is very good, and we felt it might be easier to find jobs here.

In Italy and Austria we got a lot of help from the Joint Distribution Committee. Our way of life in Russia was very different; we did not have any money. We sold what we had. What we earned there went toward necessities, not for a car or things like that.

When we arrived in Chicago, the Jewish Family Service paid for our apartment, gave us money for food, gave us job contacts, and medical insurance for a certain period of time, which was very good. The Family Service helped us with counseling and guidance about schools. The supervisor we dealt with was very good. She was Russian and had been here about fifteen years; she was excellent.

When we came to Chicago we stayed at my relative's house for three weeks. My relative had applied through the Jewish Family Service here, so he referred me there. Also we went through HIAS, because they had contacted and interviewed him to see if he was willing or able to be a sponsor.

Now I am working for a large architectural firm. My first job was with a medium-sized firm. We started working in March. Our son was able to start school right away. He had studied for two years in the special English school in Moscow. He had a comparatively easy time at school; he had close friends that he knew. He also makes friends easily and is much more secure than others. At first he went to a public school, but then we received a scholarship for a Jewish school. But we feel there is less education for him here than there was in the same grade in Moscow. He is now in the seventh grade, and in Moscow the seventh grade is very serious—physics, chemistry—very technical, and very serious in literature. There is also lots of competition in sports in Russia.

A New Concern: Persecution

What I miss most about Russia is my parents. In Russia there is a difference between Russian, Jewish, or Georgian. In the U.S. we are all Russians. If I had Jewish friends still in Russia, I would be concerned about them. We were not concerned about ourselves when we were there, but now we are amazed at how quickly things have changed. *Glasnost* has been good in many ways, but Jews are having a more difficult time. I hope that our parents are not in any danger. I don't think that they would allow actions against Jews in Moscow. The population in Moscow is well educated, and I don't think there is a large following there for this movement. I hope not, but things are completely different since we are here.

Pamyat is a concern, but I don't think they have real support. But still, people are so afraid of everything, they are so full of anger against the government, against the system. They want to find someone to accuse of historical faults and the Jews are obvious, because some of them were the first, most important Communists. Of course, they were subsequently thrown out of the party completely and also the high ranks of government. As a rule they were allowed to be engaged only in science or industry but not in official activities. But still, as it has been for centuries everywhere, Jews are obvious scapegoats in Russia.

It is not right to say that all Russians hate Jews. It is the same anti-Semitism that is everywhere else. For hundreds of years there have been many Jews in the Soviet Union, so anti-Semitism is higher there than it would be in China where there are no Jews.

Perspective on Freedom

Certainly we have changed, and changed a lot. We have changed in our attitudes toward life, in our perspective, in our responsibility for ourselves. I feel this responsibility for our family and for our future much more strongly here than in Russia. The situation is tougher, and though we are really much better off than in Russia and we enjoy this life, I am aware that tomorrow I could lose my job, or I should be saving money for my retirement or for my kid to go to college, a problem that we didn't have in Russia. We want it to be a good institution. Now we can't even afford to think about paying for a good education with our own money. All this I call responsibilities.

I am praying my parents will come here in a year or two. They will begin a new life here and will have no money, no savings, and so I will be responsible for them, more so than I would be in Russia. Lots of things like that are on my mind.

I am not saying that I have regrets. On the contrary, I say that maybe this is real life that we are dealing with here. You know, in Russia, maybe you are more sure of your future. But what future is there? It is very little money, life completely under the yoke of politics—that is the future that we had there. But some of the things in Russia we did like better. The problem of education is solved much better in Russia than it is here, I think. Maybe I will change my mind. But the free education is a very good advantage, a crucial advantage that Russia has. That may be the only thing that I can say I regret in the United States.

Belonging to a Certain Community

With regard to Judaism, the environment in the United States makes me understand that here there is clearly a certain group of people that I should know and should understand and feel myself a part of, though I am not religious. And certainly I feel myself more Jewish than I felt in the USSR. Because of discrimination or persecution or unfair attitudes, I felt it was a negative experience to be a Jew. Here, I have a positive experience of being a Jew, of belonging to a certain community, and I enjoy that!

When I read in the newspaper here about the Korean community, Black community, another kind of national community, I feel that I have my *own* community. This is my own Jewish community, of the Jewish population of the United States. I did not feel that in Russia. In Russia, I simply had a stamp in my passport that I was a Jew, and that is why I was not the same as any others.

LARRY M.
I Could Be a Senator

In 1988 when Larry and his parents left Russia and almost everything he loved, he was twelve. They explained that his life would be better, that he would have more opportunity. But, unlike his parents who had become disillusioned with serious ruptures in the structure of Soviet life, Larry loved his surroundings and interesting friends. Like his parents, he had been largely untouched by the anti-Semitism all too familiar to other Soviet Jewish immigrants.

Throughout Larry's boyhood his grandfather had entertained him with stirring tales of his adventures at sea while serving in the Soviet navy. Larry's uncle introduced him to fishing escapades. At school classmates elevated snowball fights to epic battles between European "parties" and debated issues that demanded real knowledge. Because Larry was well steeped in world literature, favorite books are not only vividly remembered, they helped shape his dreams for the future. In the interim, opportunity for Larry today means freedom to choose.

The first Jewish rite of passage he attended in this country was his own brit. *After a dynamic experience at a Jewish summer camp outside Chicago, he took his own leap of faith by deciding to undergo what his American friends experienced in the first week of life. At the age of twelve Larry consciously affirmed his Jewish identity through the ancient covenant of circumcision.*

His identity has been tempered by circumstances of both nature and nurture. His natural father (who is half-Jewish) lives in Russia. Victor has adopted him. A shared love of learning and extraordinary mutual respect mark the relationship between Victor and Larry. They debate politics, history, personal conduct, and, of course, what it means to be Jewish in America.

Both parents help formulate his plans for education, a serious theme woven into family life. Mutual trust also permits Victor to accompany Larry on forays into more advanced mathematics, to recommend books, and to share ideas. In the years he has been father to him, Victor has helped Larry identify his emerging sense of self. Despite the enormous changes in their lives, despite nostalgia about friends and family still there and scenes of Moscow, the boy envisions clearly what he would like to do as a man.

As his powers of intellect and moral certitude mature, Larry can survey the panorama of his future and pronounce confidently, "If I want to, I can be a senator."

Earliest Memories

I remember a long corridor, and I was always playing there. I had a lot of toys in a huge box. I was always playing with my toys in that corridor.

I also remember going to the hospital. I don't remember why, but I remember I went with my teddy bear, and it was a little teddy bear. I was five years old.

My grandmother, my mother's mother, took care of me most of the time, but in the beginning it was my father's mother.

My grandmother told me a lot of fairy tales. My grandfather, my mother's father, told me other stories, like about what happened after the war and things like that. He told me about sailing into Leningrad, about how he was a sailor during the Siege of Leningrad. He told me a lot of stories, some of them really strange, some of them really interesting, about his ship, trying to reach Leningrad when the river was frozen. They had to hit the ice with the ship, and the ice would pile up and pile up until they could not move anymore. Then they had to call a special ship that could go through the ice easier and have it show them the way.

He told me stories about shipwrecks, what kind of engines they had, how the cannon and the machine guns worked, things like that. Maybe because of that I know how some things work a little better than other kids who were my friends in Russia, and much better than most of my friends in America. Here, not a lot of kids are interested in that stuff.

Snowballs and Strategies

Also, we had more games than here. I do not think it was a very mature thing to do, but we would fight in "parties" with snowballs, and we would have strategies against each other. I was a leader of one of the parties because I could not stand anybody standing over me!

We had team names—ours was the English Party, and our teacher was called the "English Queen." We also had a "German Queen" and a "French Queen" in our school. There were other people involved, so we were fighting with them and plotting against them. The whole thing was fun!

My friends and I started to get serious about the future in third grade. We talked about getting a job, who we wanted to be, what we were going to do with our life. They started teaching us history in the fourth grade. In third grade I wanted to be a doctor. This was even before I knew my father's parents. They are both doctors, but my great-grandfather of my real father was a doctor and was killed by Stalin. I think he had some views—I don't remember what—he had some views on things that were not liked by Stalin.

The Matzah Was Dry

I'm not sure I remember exactly when I realized I was Jewish. I knew it for a while before the time we left Russia. I think my mother told me about it. I wasn't *very* little, but I had a little sense, anyway.

I remember one Jewish holiday being observed. I was still in kindergarten, probably five or six years old. My mother and I and some others went to a synagogue, and I was sitting on the person's shoulders looking around. I was not really "in" the synagogue; the doors were open and everybody was outside looking in. I didn't know what it was all about. Maybe it was Simhat Torah.

There were many Jews in my class. Some of my friends were Jewish; it was about even. I was not treated any differently because I was Jewish—no, absolutely not. I never had any bad experiences because I was Jewish. There was absolutely no difference. I felt that being Jewish was normal.

I remember eating some food considered to be traditionally Jewish like matzah. I had matzah about two days after I went to that synagogue for Simhat Torah.

Some people talk about gefilte fish as a Jewish food. I don't like it. I ate it in Russia. I had eaten strudel, but I didn't know it was Jewish food. Food like *hamantaschen*, those little triangles—I never had those in Moscow, only here. The matzah tasted dry; it was very dry. We did not put anything on it; we ate it plain.

I've never been to a Jewish wedding or circumcision in Russia. I was circumcised here. It was not frightening, and it was not really painful.

From There to Here and It's OK

When I learned we were coming to the United States, at first I didn't really feel it would be any fun. I mean, we had TV there, so there was nothing special about that. And I really did not take it very seriously. Then, when we actually left, I was very upset for a few minutes. Then I started to get over it, and now we are here and it's OK.

Probably I was upset about leaving my friends and my family, mostly my grandfather. I just finished writing some letters to them.

The last thing that we studied over there that I remember was algebraic equations. This was in the sixth grade. They were not really hard. What I am studying now, with my dad, is much harder. My dad is just giving me some problems to work. It really helps me.

Household Politics

I wasn't part of the discussion my parents had on politics, at least not very often. I remember Dad and I used to argue, usually about history, not politics. We were talking about the German invasion of Russia and how the Germans were able to conquer so much land and how Hitler came to power, and something about Lenin, and that he was Jewish, and how smart he was. And things like that.

My mom was always on the "right" side. She was very "right," not "left" like a Communist; she was as right as anybody could be! She was much more conservative. My father, I think, keeps his opinions to himself, which I like. He is not stubborn and doesn't stay with one idea. I think that is not wrong because you have to see all of the visible situation, which I don't do, for example, in the Israeli situation. We talk often about that. You have to see both sides of the question, and I see only one. And then my dad always shows me the other side. So, it is very, very nice of my dad, and very smart to see both sides, not just stick with the one side that he is on.

Fishing Russian Style

In Russia I liked to go fishing. I used to go fishing at a lake with my uncle. This was my mother's brother, Sergei. It was against the law when we did it. You see, there is a way you can catch fish for nothing, with just a stick. So what we would do was get a stick and on the string put a lot of hooks so a lot of fish would get caught on one string. Some people would get a lot of fish with dynamite or with a net, but we didn't do that.

When my uncle's friends were over there, they did not catch anything at all. We started with a normal fishing pole, and we got five fish!

The biggest change for me was leaving my family and my friends. In Russia, it was much more interesting to talk with them, the friends my age. We talked about different things, more mature things, from politics to things like mathematics or sometimes history. Here, all they do is play games. OK, I can live with that. But most of them, I know, are really not interested in learning anything.

Most of the people I have met, which is not really a lot of people, but most of them were people who were not very interesting to talk to. They did not have enough knowledge. You see, it is great to argue, to know a lot, and the friends I knew in Russia were interesting to talk to and argue with because they knew really, really a lot and because they could give you good arguments.

Literature and Life

We did much more reading there. The most significant book I read was probably *The Three Musketeers*. I also read some books on Russian history. I have read Pushkin, Gogol, and other Russian authors. Also *Ivanhoe, Tom Sawyer*, and Soviet authors, too. It was absolutely normal. The books were usually simple to read. Sometimes it would be difficult to concentrate on a subject because sometimes the passages were long and things like that, but still it was very, very interesting. It was probably the most interesting thing I did in Russia.

Books were in the original version, no difference. The best thing I think that I have read here in English was *The Hobbit* and *The Lord of the Rings*. A friend of my mom gave me a list of books, good American books, science fiction and others I might be interested in. I read much more for fun. That is also why I read in Russia. Because, you know, when you read, it just seems different—part fun, part education.

Most of the books that you get education from are not books on mathematics. You don't really read those books too often. I read one. It was called *Elementary Algebra*, for example, and it had exercises that I had to do. I cannot say that it was a very interesting text, you know, but most of the books that I read are for education and for fun. For example, when we argue with my father about different things, even about my bird catching, I bring examples from books. I learn a lot of things from books.

Resolving Conflicts

Because I go to Jewish day school, I have more Jewish friends, but I still have other non-Jewish friends, too. I feel very comfortable with both.

I don't think there's any kind of conflict between the very religious education we get in the day school and the fact that our home life is not religious. Not really, just sometimes some of my teachers start talking to me about having a lot of non-Jewish friends. You know, that is the part I do not like about that school. Because that does not mean anything. There are some Jews who are worse than some Gentiles, and there is no problem about that.

A teacher told me my good friend, a Russian, was using drugs because he lives in a neighborhood where a lot of people do drugs. That is not fair, because she was judging, she was looking in his locker, and she was bugging him for the school year. I don't think this is the right way to come to a situation. He is Jewish, and he comes to Hillel Torah. He told me they even were talking with him about it. Kids in the neighborhood had approached him with drugs. Of course, he is a very smart person, one of the smartest Russian kids I know of in America, and he was smart enough to say no.

Soviet Teenage Drug Use

In Moscow there were not really people who would approach kids and try to sell them drugs. Some teenagers would organize themselves, but they would not sell drugs, not that I know of. They would get together to inhale glue, for example. Drugs cost a lot of money, so they would use stuff like that instead.

There were two reasons for doing it. First, they tried to prove themselves, the same way people everywhere try to prove themselves. They wanted to prove to themselves that they can do something that is "cool." The other reason is that most of the people who use drugs are very weak people, who cannot hold themselves together and say, "This is really not cool."

Being Jewish, the Essentials

I find the dietary laws they teach at school very difficult, because most of my life, so far, I have lived without those laws. It is pretty hard to go and change now.

Actually, I could live without a Jewish day school without being upset. Of course, I might be upset leaving my friends that I have there. I'm used to that kind of change. I've changed seven schools in my life.

I am not really a religious person. I don't think that I have to be religious to be Jewish. Some people say you do, but I really do not agree with that. Because it is not really a religion; it is a group of people who live in a certain area and have certain traditions. Religion is only part of those traditions. Probably, living in Israel is one of them. But that is not absolutely necessary because it changed thousands of years ago. I might like to visit Israel, but I think it is too dangerous a place to live in. Well, it is not because I'm scared of getting shot at; that doesn't happen very often.

There are nonreligious ways to be Jewish: being nice to other people, but that is the main thing about Judaism. There is one main concept, and all of religion is about it. And the concept is that you should do unto other people the way you want people to do unto you. And this is a concept that should be in every single religion, and I think that this is the concept that a Jew must follow.

I might want to belong to a synagogue, but I wouldn't be excited about it. I think that the Orthodox is the real, true religion. And Reform or Conservative are just the easy way to do it. So I think that if you are going to follow anything, you should follow the Orthodox, and if you don't follow the Orthodox rules, you shouldn't go for Conservative or Reform. To me they are really like not believing in the religion.

The Map of My Future

If I were going to draw a map of my future life, one of the things I would put on that map is sailboats, after medical school, then a house on a lake or on the ocean. Then I could go fishing again as I did in Russia.

To go to medical school, I am going to have to get a very good education. I haven't thought about where I'll go to high school; I don't know a lot of high schools yet. I'm more likely to go to public high school, I think. But I hope that after I finish that school I will be able to go to a good college.

I had studied English in the Soviet Union from the second grade. First we spent one hour a day, and then in third grade, it was ninety minutes. I don't think my language and vocabulary developed good enough because I want to have an English accent. A real British accent, not American. I could probably develop that if I went to England!

I have really wanted to go to England, from the time I read *Ivanhoe*. If I could, I would like to go to England, both before and after I go to medical school! If I had my choice of any place to live in the whole world, the country I would want to live in is England. I like it; it is ancient; there is a lot of sailing, British accents, nice food, nice people, and the Beatles. I first learned about the Beatles in fourth grade; my dad told me about them. I have heard their music, and I have one disk of theirs in Russia, a regular phonograph record, not a compact disk.

I used to take voice lessons in school. I sing, but I don't study voice anymore. I would like to play guitar. I will try to find a school for this.

What Is Important to Me?

There are two things that I think are really very important to me. They are freedom and liberty and, of course, the opportunity to do what I want. I mean in the law. I mean, I could be a senator—I could be anything I want, actually!

My friends and my family come first. After that, nature, like the little animals, the environment. Some birds—I haven't seen birds here like the Russian sparrow; to me they seem different here. The Russian sparrows are little, and they are kind of playful, and they are much more interesting to watch.

I miss a place about forty-three kilometers from Moscow. There is a small forest, and it is filled with mushrooms and flowers and berries, and the light and shadows give you a very good look on how nature really should be. I would like to go back to Russia. Yes, definitely. I think I might go back in about two years. Not with my family, just to see my friends. I feel empty without them.

I think that some of my relatives or friends there will come here. Yes, I think so. Sooner or later.

8

A QUEST FOR BELIEF

ALEX AND RITA BLINSTEIN

ALEX AND RITA Blinstein had each begun a private spiritual journey before they met. His quest took him into the rarified air of the mountains while he explored an underground culture of literature, philosophy, music, and poetry. Hers began when she discovered the forbidden religion of another faith that opened her mind to the weaknesses of Communist ideology and its attendant spiritual vacuum. Their meeting, when she was twenty-one and he was twenty-seven, and subsequent marriage was the beginning of a commitment to provide their children with a new set of old values.

ALEX BLINSTEIN
To Find a Balance

At the age of twenty-two Alex Blinstein was a champion collegiate boxer of the USSR. He had been able to enter the Odessa Institute of Food Technology because of a coach who brought talented athletes to the institute. These athletes were able to travel to other cities and republics where matches were held. Later, Alex earned a master's degree in engineering and landed a good position in management.

Alex, born in Odessa in 1950, grew up with a love of literature, philosophy, and music; in light of his family circumstances, his attainments were astonishing. His father had been incapacitated by mental illness; his mother lacked formal education and was barely able to provide food and shelter for the family. Their living conditions were horrendous by any standard.

The opportunity he had to travel to athletic competitions gave him the chance to observe and meet people from other walks of life. After his boxing career he developed an interest in mountain climbing and met a circle of people who were interested in other systems of thought and who were critical of the political system he had just taken for granted. These conversations fostered not only new friendships but brought to light a new world of literature and culture, including books that were forbidden and tapes of poets who had been executed.

Alex became a manager for the Institute of Food Technology and traveled to sites where new plants were scheduled for construction, to lay the foundation for various developmental phases. These included research and planning for land use, water and energy resources, interdepartmental permits and general coordination of the on-site engineering.

He met his future wife Rita when he began working for the institute. At the time she was engaged to be married to someone else, but during some moment of doubt in the relationship, she and Alex decided their future.

By the time the Blinsteins were able to emigrate, they had two children. Alex had to settle for a lesser career in this country, but he remains concerned about the balance one must maintain between materialistic enticements and other values. It is not unusual for Alex to carry a book with him by a favorite writer such as Vladimir Nabokov.

Early Survival

We lived in the worst of conditions, unbelievably the worst, in a basement without any utilities except water. We built a fire for cooking. Until 1966, we didn't have a gas stove, and I had the duty of preparing coal or wood for winter. My mother received a very small salary, and we worked hard to survive on this.

I have few memories of my father because, after 1955, he was hospitalized. What I remember most about him is his kindness, that's all. Before he was sick he never spoke about his war injuries or the battles he was in, and later it was impossible to speak with him about things like that. I remember that during the war he was wounded in the leg by a piece of shrapnel. He was badly wounded, and his nervous system was affected for years after he returned from the war. His health grew worse and worse every day.

My mother worked as a janitor in the medical clinic. She had no sort of formal education. She could read but not write. Before the Revolution, Jews who lived in the *Mestechko*, the Pale of Settlement, except for the fortunate few who managed to get to the towns, did not receive any kind of education. Although many people believe that the Revolution opened the doors for all Jews to receive an education in the USSR, the fact is that after the Revolution, people could not attend school, college, or university, unless they grew up in families that owned no property. Some Jews had a little property, not much, but enough to bar them from school.

There were some Jews on a higher, intellectual level who were in the uppermost circle of Russian culture, such as writers, but this was rare. Unfortunately, my mother didn't belong to this circle. Such matters are, of course, the work of fate. We can't choose or change. We can only live.

I grew up in a wet basement. The walls were always dripping. My father's relatives didn't help with anything, but Mother's brother did what he could: sometimes with money, sometimes with coal in the winter, because coal was not easily gotten.

From the 1950s to the beginning of the sixties, it was easier to get food than now, thanks to Khrushchev's reforms, and by comparison things were not bad. Sometimes we had enough food, but not all the time. In the summer, our supper would be fresh tomatoes. My mother often tried to put some away to save for later, because I had the habit of eating and not being able to stop! I was also fond of sugar cubes and could eat a whole box at once. Sometimes we had chicken, usually on a big holiday—New Year's, the First of May, the Seventh of November. My mother would also try to make gefilte fish and other Jewish dishes. She had the utensils and would grind up the fish, but we had no refrigerator, so my mother usually put all the food under the window ledge to keep it cool so it wouldn't spoil. We lived near an open market, a bazaar, and she sometimes would get fresh food there.

A Poor Start in School

It is strange, but I began to read at a very young age. Although there were no books in my house my interest developed and later I acquired some books of my own.

In the Russian school system, the first four years you are taught by one teacher who instructs in all the subjects. I had very bad luck with a teacher who was an anti-Semite. She punished me every day. I would stand in the back of the room until three, four, even five o'clock. Every week she would call for my mother. In Russia the best possible mark is five. From the ages of seven to eleven, I had only ones or twos.

When I entered the fifth class, my luck changed and I had a very intelligent literature and language teacher. He was Jewish, and he gave me a lot of help and really saved me. Only after four years of school did my mother realize what had been happening. At the end of the first quarter she finally received a letter from the board saying, "Your son is a very good student."

I Take Up Boxing

I took up boxing in 1963 when I was thirteen years old. In Odessa it was very popular. In Russia at this time sports were one way to enter an institute, that is, if you had some potential. Because they needed athletes, they would make sure you received good coaching and, along with this, the chance to become a student. Without sports it would have been impossible for me to enter the institute.

Athletics was an alternate way for Jews to go to the institute, to receive an education. The standard way is to be very talented. But besides talent, you still need something more. You could say that what you need to succeed is "talent plus connections." I would say that no less than 15 percent of the population of Odessa was Jewish; it was one of the most Jewish towns in the USSR. And yet every institute has 2 percent or 3 percent Jews. In this 2 percent are people who have connections.

Boxing was my major sport. I was the student boxing champion of the USSR in 1972, when I was twenty-two. This was my last title, before I finished the institute. It was no small achievement! I competed with students throughout the USSR.

Work and Alternative Opportunities for Education

I didn't go to the institute the way people usually do after eight grades. As a rule, students would start ninth grade and complete an education comparable to high school in America, but I had to go to work after the eighth grade. I was fifteen when I started in a factory that built heavy metal parts and machines. It was on the factory floor where I had my first major encounter with anti-Semitism because I worked among some very low-level people. Some of them had been in prison. The difficulties and problems I had came mostly from the fact that factory work wasn't my field. I never liked the machines or the noise. It resembled assembly line work except there was no line; in Russia, only the largest factories have actual assembly lines. We had teams that competed against each other.

I worked with people who were entirely Russian and ranged in age from twenty to sixty. I was the baby. I made some mistakes because of my inexperience with the machines. More seriously, I had no experience with psychology, with people, with getting along, and like most young people I wanted to act older. Sometimes I provoked them. There were some anti-Semitic reactions, but I may have provoked them by acting a little too smart.

Sometimes we went out together and drank vodka. First thing they taught me was to drink vodka, and you couldn't refuse because if you refused, you provoked them further. "You don't like us!" And so I drank with them. I was a good student in this case. But, systematically, they still let me know that I was a Jew.

After two years I changed jobs. I didn't like the factory work so I went to work at the seaport. I joined a different sports club, which gave me the opportunity to work in the seaport. Though it was less money, it was also less work, and I received good training and had a lot of free time.

In that job, we did a relief map of the port. We went out in boats and dropped lines, using a depth finder to make measurements of the port and to map it. It was a more interesting job than my old one. I did not experience any anti-Semitism there.

When I worked at the seaport, I continued my education in the evening courses. At the beginning of the sixties, this was a very good way for Jews to get an education. A lot of Jews went to work first after high school graduation. I was able to receive a good education this way, because the teacher was very good. Twenty people may have registered, but the average number of students attending was about six. If I had really wanted to, I could have a received a very good education. But unfortunately I was too young, and also I had to train rigorously for the club, so I didn't attend regularly. Though I didn't have particular success in the evening school, I hoped that I could use the background for continuing my education. For Jews, this wasn't enough, because we had to prepare twice as well as the others. I didn't do that, because I was young. We weren't a typical family.

My mother, because she was so busy and tired, let me run my own life. We shared visiting my father in the hospital. One week I went, the other she went. For fifteen years, maybe from first grade, I began to visit him without her. He talked with me, but his condition was very changeable and hard to treat. They called it schizophrenia, but this is not the right word; he had some kind of mental illness. It came on in 1955, when he was thirty-five years old.

A Helpful Coach

How I got into the Institute of Food Technology was an adventure. This institute had a very influential coach who was more a sports manager. He invited some of my friends and me to this institute. I had some difficulty at first because I was Jewish, and I was not well prepared. These two factors were too much for one person. The next year I also received an invitation from an institute in Kiev, but the manager at the food technology institute helped me, and I became a student there.

I started school and got my boxing training in different clubs; we had a lot of training out of doors, in another town, with the Soviet team. The institute had its own gymnasium, but the manager arranged boxing tours. In 1966 I began to travel to all kinds of towns. What I had learned on the street by the age of sixteen was different from the rules of the ring. But I always used my head. Some athletes are very strong, some have quick reactions, but I used strategy. This was my trademark in sports. In the street, unfortunately, my strategy was completely unhealthy!

Eventually I Understood

I traveled to many towns in the USSR: Moscow, Kiev, Leningrad, Riga, Talinn, Krasnoyarsk, almost everywhere, but I did not get a better idea of life in the Soviet because of my travels. We grew up in a certain system, and this system was designed to keep us confined from birth. My understanding about the socialist system came to me very late. Only maybe in 1974, after reading some new books and meeting some new people, I acquired some new ideas. My first friend who went from Russia to America in 1972 left during what some people call the first wave of emigration. I didn't understand why anyone would want to emigrate though my friend, a talented mathematician who could not get into Moscow University, told me that eventually I would understand.

In Tashkent I met some interesting people, most of whom are now in Israel. One of them years later became my sponsor when I arrived in Chicago. People who know a lot about the Soviet socialist system never speak with you openly because this is very dangerous, and any Soviet person could call the KGB.

The Rarified Atmosphere of the Mountains

Within a month a series of major changes occurred. I graduated institute, and then went to vacation for a month at a climbing camp and was able to spend two more months working there.

At this point I changed my sport. I seriously took up mountain climbing. Boxing wasn't enough for me. I had become a champion and then turned to something entirely different. For five years I spent time working in the mountains. Once I met some very interesting people from Leningrad, very intellectual people. From our meeting in the mountains and our friendship they began to share their knowledge about books, about people. This was the beginning.

I came to the mountain camp with a group of students, and after this we were invited to the tour camp. This is a little different because in the mountain climbing camp there are only climbers, but in the tour camp there are usually people who are not only climbing but walking and enjoying nature. In this camp there were a lot of instructors and tourists from different towns, like Leningrad.

By then I understood that there was something wrong, but I was not sure *what* was wrong. And these people who had more life experience and knowledge about the political system, they first opened my mind about this, and from this moment I began to have a deeper interest in the Soviet system. I began to read books that usually are hard to find. It was sort of risky because a lot of people received prison sentences for having these books.

I was twenty-four and felt old enough to be doing this, because usually people understand the system sooner. Though maybe it's good when you don't understand exactly what's happening in the country where you live because then you won't get too upset about what a crazy system it is.

Unfortunately, there was another side to this work at the mountain camp. This was a republic of two nations—Kabardins and Bulkartsy. In certain places there were Kabardins who did not have good relations with the people surrounding them. Stalin had captured many nations after World War II and relocated them from one region to another. The Bulkartsy had been captured and taken to another place, and only many years later could they come back; they hate all Russians. And in this atmosphere it's very difficult to survive. I decided it was better to go home and try to use my diploma. But that summer in the camp played a big role in my understanding.

In Russia good books are always popular and everyone tries to get them, so I couldn't always find certain books in the stores. But after this, I began to read Solzhenitsyn, *First Circle*, and philosophy, Nietzsche, Freud. I read memoirs by some of the original members about growing up in the Communist party from the beginning of the century to 1930. It was very interesting because it was the first inside information about the party I had read and a very moving book.

I Was a Hiring Risk

After that summer I returned to Odessa. For a long time I couldn't find a job, because in Odessa at this time a lot of Jews were leaving for America and Israel. Whenever a Jew left for Israel or America from their department, the bosses of factories or any kind of organization would get a hard time from the bureau of the Communist party. It was very difficult to find a job, not exactly because I was Jewish, but because they were afraid that if they took me I would leave in a few months.

It took me six months to find a job, but eventually I found a very good one and worked there twelve years. It was a large design institute where I was able to learn a lot from highly educated people. Maybe 60 percent of the employees in this design institute were Jewish, a typical situation in a town like Odessa. There would be a lot of Jews in a design institute because Jews usually desire a profession, as opposed to factory work. A lot of them are here now and have found good jobs. A lot of my coworkers listened to the Voice of America and Radio Liberty.

My background was right for this institute. I was assigned to a department that needed a young man without a family who could move around to any town. Eventually they took me and I was able to rise in salary and position. I was in one of the high positions at this institute when I left Odessa.

My wife worked at the same place for fourteen years. She came after high school and studied in the evening program. I came after institute because I had the opportunity to attend day classes.

The Tashkent Connection

After working there for a half-year, while on a business trip to Tashkent I met a group of people who became my very close friends. One of them, Yefim Godler, became my sponsor. He was known as an activist or dissident. After he came here he learned his friend, the poet Irina Ratushinskaya, had been imprisoned. He organized a committee to help liberate her and four or five years argued on her behalf with President Reagan and British Prime Minister Margaret Thatcher.

My Work and Travel

I worked in a department responsible for the building of factories. When a firm was planning to build something, a lot of agreements had to be made with governmental departments. On my trips I would learn about trains, water, canals, energy, power supply, then I would bring all the information to my institute. After engineers designed something, they needed plan maps of different kinds, a series of agreements, and hundreds of inspections in order to actually build the facility. Because the engineers were based in Odessa and the factory was elsewhere, new information had to be brought back and discussed. This took years, while they built this plant. For twelve years, I spent one month in Odessa and the next month in another place. I was constantly in planes, trains, and hotels.

I was still living with my mother in the same basement, almost until I got married. Around the time Rita and I became engaged my mother received an apartment. She had waited for this apartment twenty-five or thirty years. Before our marriage, Rita came to help my mother get ready to move. She saw to it that my mother took only some clothes, because everything else was so bad that there was nothing to take. This was in 1978, three months before our marriage. Afterward we lived two or three years with my mother.

We Knew Instantly

When I first met Rita, she was engaged to be married. I knew her supervisor and told her of my interest, but she said that Rita was engaged. So I turned away. But after half a year, there was some institute party at a discotheque. I remember the date was February 27, because on that date we decided the whole question. I wasn't often at work because I traveled so much—I guess I just saw something in her that I liked. We had had some conversations maybe four months before this party but not serious ones. In Russian this is called *perekur*.

Rita was friendly and open. I appreciate this kind of human openness and altruism. We were dancing, and that evening I had to take the train to another town. We had fallen in love in one evening. We both knew it, and there was no explanation.

I had some ideas about emigration before we were married, when my very good friend, who now lives in Montreal, influenced me. I was at an anniversary party of the climbing club. It was a big concert of some Russian bard, who wrote the music and accompanied himself while he sang. I remember a big turnover of my feelings when I was listening to the concert with all the people I spent time with in the mountains. It was the atmosphere. This was about climbing, about friendship, about love; they were not political songs. In 1979, I was married, and we began preparing some documents. Exactly at this moment emigration was stopped for almost ten years. Only at the end of 1987 and beginning of 1988 could people again emigrate.

Chernobyl

Odessa was far from Chernobyl but not far enough for safety. I was afraid for our kids. Just on the day of the disaster we were outside in the country with our friends. It was a very sunny day and unusually warm. I later remembered the day, and became concerned, but you always try to be hopeful when things are bad. The distance between Chernobyl and Odessa is maybe 300 to 400 miles.

The explosion occurred at the start of *glasnost*. Every month the information changed. In the beginning they said one thing, next another. This was the problem with *glasnost*. We worried not about the environment at first but about surviving. Because when *glasnost* began, anti-Semitism showed its face officially.

Glasnost and *Pamyat*

First of all, *glasnost* was also the beginning of *Pamyat*. The greatest source of *Pamyat* was probably the Russian Union of Writers. In the USSR art has unions. It was Stalin's idea, knowing the influence of art, to have the arts under his control.

In 1930 all the writers, actors, painters, and other artists formed unions. The Soviet Union of Writers come from different republics; there was the Armenian Union, the Ukrainian, and so on. The Russian became the most anti-Semitic and two magazines, *Molodaya Gvardia* [Young Guard] and *Nash Sovremennik* [Our Contemporary], began publishing anti-Semitic material. At that moment I realized that *glasnost* was taking strange turns. There were not only anti-Semitic statements, but novels, big novels. Vasily Belov, whom I very much appreciated before, wrote one of the first.

Last year we read about a 1988 or 1989 meeting of Jewish writers where a group of *Pamyat* people broke in and attacked them. Then, a very remarkable man, Aleksandr Mann, was killed. He was an ecumenical priest of Jewish origin who had been trying to eliminate barriers between different beliefs in Christianity and between Christianity and Judaism too. He published books abroad, before *glasnost*, and the KGB had been after him for some time. He was a spiritual father to Solzhenitsyn and many people in the intelligentsia.

They killed him ritualistically, in a very old Russian style—with an axe. He was fifty-two and was very popular. He had begun to lecture on TV about Christianity. I think it was not only *Pamyat*, but the KGB and the party, who work together. In Russia nothing could happen without their involvement. (Trotsky was killed similarly.) Mann didn't die immediately but got to his house and died in the arms of his wife. I've read a lot about him in the *Chicago Tribune* and the best Russian newspapers, *New Russian Word* from New York and *Russian Mind* from Paris. A lot of famous people have asked Gorbachev about an investigation, but there was none. Since then two or three people have been killed who published independent newspapers.

Our Journey Here

We had good luck in our travels here. In Vienna we had an unbelievable place. I don't know why, but we lived in the center of the city in a very old family hotel. They made a museum of this family home. We invited our friends to see it. There were old rooms and old furniture; it was unbelievable. It's a wonderful memory.

In America I can only be disappointed with myself. I don't have enough professional skills. My skills were very specific; I never prepared to come here, and I can't use my skills here at all. Unfortunately, I'm over forty with two kids, and it's not easy to change one's profession. I could take classes, but it is too late for a major change. This is not even a disappointment.

Rita is working as a designer. I'm working as a lab technician. It doesn't challenge my abilities, but I'm glad I can work and bring home a salary.

Family Pressures in the U.S.

A thousand books have been written about marriage and how it works. I am beginning to think that marriage is something unexplainable; it's like faith. You either believe in it or not. For Jews, I think that the family survives for the kids. If there's some conflict, everyone works around it and then forgets about it. But I feel kids are the most important thing in life. If you lose them, you have nothing more. It's a more difficult life with them, but it gives you more satisfaction.

For the future, it is most important to find some balance in this life. We must choose what should come first: education or a house, this job or that, to give more time to the kids and spend family time together, or find some better way to support them and raise them in America.

People aren't so open in America. On the surface they are very open, but it's not easy to be close and understanding. There are so many ways to spend money and time, you can become neurotic trying to decide what to choose. I want to find a balance between material life and other life. I think it's a problem in American life, materialism going deeper and deeper into the human being. People are surrounded with bigger and more, every day a new thing.

So far, my children are going to a religious school. They are getting a Conservative rather than an Orthodox education. We have had some problems at school, the prejudice of some American kids toward Russian kids. They would say, "You came here because you don't have money." My kids told them, "We *do* pay money." So there's a little prejudice here too. It's interesting, because these are children whose grandpa and grandma came from Russia.

From Russia I miss my youth, but I can't bring it back here *or* there! We all lose our youth. When I lived in Odessa, every day I would come down the same street where I grew up. There was my school, and my friends were nearby. Nabokov explains that to some it seems that we lose our fatherland, but really we have only one fatherland, and that's our childhood.

Wedding picture of Alex and Rita Blinstein, Odessa, September 8, 1978. Maid of honor, Yelena Mirochnik, now in United States; best man, Mike Gill, now in Israel.

Passover 1991, at home. Anna, then 10, teaching her parents how to conduct a Seder using a Haggada translated into Russian. From left: son Simon, Rita's mother and father, Anna, unknown, and Rita. Alex was photographer.

Rita and Alex strolling down a street in their suburban neighborhood. Photo ©
1992 by Bruce Mondschain. All rights reserved.

RITA MASIS BLINSTEIN
There Was an Emptiness

Rita grew up with a sense that something was profoundly missing in her world. She had enjoyed a quiet childhood in Odessa; she had friends, outside interests, a decent job, and a storybook romance with the man she married. An engineer in refrigeration technology, she had earned an M.A. despite anti-Semitic impediments even at technical institutes. At work she was popular, and she and Alex had two fine healthy children. She was convinced, however, of the void in her life, when her two-year-old son spoke his first word. It was "Lenin." This small milestone made it apparent that from birth to death, the icon of godlessness brooded over her and her family.

Rita's story includes the account of how a friend's mother was driven to madness and an early death by KGB persecution, part of the accretion of evidence against life in the Soviet Union.

In 1979, when the young couple first contemplated emigrating, Rita's grandfather, an ardent Communist, assured her that he would allow her to leave Russia, only over his dead body. The opportunity to leave had been brief, and almost a decade passed before they could try again.

Now that the family is settled in Chicago, Rita and Alex maintain an open house for relatives, friends, and particularly recent immigrants who need a hand getting settled. They were happy to sponsor Rita's parents, her sister and her family, as well as Alex's mother. Meanwhile, the sense of emptiness diminishes as the children, Anna and Simon, take their place in a society that allows them to study and observe the faith denied their parents and their parents' parents.

An Exceptionally Quiet Household

When I was growing up, six of us lived in a three-room apartment: my parents, my mother's parents, my older sister, and I. My parents lived in the middle of the apartment, and everybody had to go through this room to get to the kitchen or to go outside. My sister and I shared a room until I finished high school and she went to the university. And my grandmother and grandfather had another one.

Because of my grandmother's illness, I had a quiet childhood—no noise, no kids, no birthday parties, no visitors. Somebody was always with her, my mother or my grandfather had to be there to help her. I had birthday parties at a friend's house, and I would always visit my friends at someone else's apartment.

My mother worked close to our house so she could walk to her job and come back during lunchtime. It took about fifteen or twenty minutes to walk, so after her job she very quickly could come home. My grandfather didn't work at that time, so he was usually home and could take care of the kids, house, and cooking.

When I knew him, my grandfather's occupation was being a Communist! He was a member of the Communist party, and he really believed in it. He had worked in some position at the seaport administration. Our family's first apartment had been built for seamen by the seaport administration. We could walk to the beach and swim, but the Black Sea is dangerous, not like Lake Michigan. There anything can happen. There is a lifeguard, but only the best swimmers could swim there. I was ten or twelve years old before I was allowed to go there without an adult, and only on crowded summer weekends.

I don't remember that my parents ever told me I was Jewish, but I remember how I learned. I was five years old, and it was just after we moved to our new apartment. I was playing with my friend Tanya in the front yard when another girl came along. I remember her particular words. She asked Tanya, who's a natural Russian, not Jewish, "Why are you playing with this girl? She's a Jew!" And my friend said, "Why not?" Neither of us knew what it meant. But I remember that I paid attention to what she said. What was wrong? Why shouldn't my friend play with me? My friend was angry and upset.

Later, in our school years, my sister was tormented and beaten more than once by some boys who called her *zhidovka*, and for a while my father had to meet her at school and take her home so she wouldn't be bothered.

Grandfather's Hero Was Lenin

Grandfather often talked about being a Communist, and when I was a child I found some of those old stories interesting. But I grew up fast, and when I was fifteen or sixteen, I didn't believe in it. My grandfather's hero was Lenin. We didn't talk about Stalin because by the sixties we had learned everything about Stalin, mostly by the second year after his death. Khrushchev opened the door, and everything was discovered. So Stalin wasn't a hero in *my* childhood.

But grandfather's opinion about Lenin was like a wall, and nobody could destroy that. He was not only a very strong-willed person, he was also the owner of the apartment, and my father didn't argue with him because we lived in such close quarters. There was a lot of strain in that household, but my sister and I didn't know because my parents were quiet and happy as a couple; they were trying to keep peace in the family.

Family History

My father's side of the family was killed in the Second World War—all of them. They lived in a little village near Odessa, an hour away by bus. There were 100 of these small villages full of Jewish families. During the Second World War Odessa was occupied by Nazis, and they killed all the Jews who couldn't get out. Some of them like my mother-in-law went to Tashkent. She was there the whole four years of the war. After the war she was left alone because almost her whole family had been killed—her father, mother, and sister with her little daughter, two of her brothers, and others.

My father and his older brother, who is still in Odessa, survived, but only because he was away up north in the navy. His younger sister was an army medical nurse. The youngest brother, about sixteen, was killed along with his parents. I saw his picture. His smile was unbelievable. All the people from all the villages were shot and killed in just a few hours. Nobody knows where they are buried.

My mother graduated technical school as an economist. When they got married, she had only a high school education, and my father urged her to do continue her studies. My father finished at another technical institute just before the war and then in the war was an officer. He finished the university in June, 1941. So he took part in the war and a lot of battles, and he earned some certificate of recognition. He finished his duty at Bucharest, Rumania, in 1945, the end of the war. Afterward he came back and married my mother in 1950. In 1951 my older sister was born.

After my mother graduated, she worked as the account administrator of a big shoe store. My father was an inspector in the food industry after he finished his education in food processing. So he was food storage inspector, inspecting any kind of food that came to Odessa by sea, air, train. He was famous in his field. He could have gone for his Ph.D., but that would have taken a few years, and he would have had to live in Moscow. He decided not to do it and continued to work in the food industry until he retired.

Politics in the Sixties

I knew what happened in Czechoslovakia when the Russian troops went in because soldiers were transported at night from Odessa. We were told it was because Czechoslovakia was a special district where problems were under the supervision of troops from the Ukraine. That was part of their job. They also brought the dead soldiers back at night so nobody would see them.

The KGB was busy with people who stood out in any way from others. I'll never forget the tragic story of my classmate's mother. The mother's problems began during the Brezhnev era. She was well educated, a musician, who had finished the conservatory, and she worked at the local radio station.

Her former husband, an officer in the Soviet army, was stationed in Moscow while her son was in the Soviet army as well. The KGB noticed that this woman was arranging broadcast of recordings of music or poetry by some Jewish artists. It was not 1 percent political, but they were Jewish, and the woman had a Jewish mother.

Her neighbors began to torment her. She occupied a little room in a big communal apartment. They had just one kitchen for all of them and played cruel jokes on her, such as tampering with her food so she couldn't eat it. Fifteen years have passed and I'm still upset about that. I was one of the few people she could trust. I was seventeen, attending the institute and working, but she lived close to my job in downtown Odessa and a few times a week I would came to her apartment to spend a little time with her. I was afraid for her life. She explained everything to me, clearly, and I knew it couldn't be false, because I knew the KGB could do anything they wanted to, especially to people who couldn't fight back.

She lost her job and couldn't find another because everybody knew what had happened. The city housing authority didn't give her the permit required to live in the apartment, and she was unable to get even a small room, so she became homeless: no job, no money, no one to help her. She wasn't strong enough for a war with the KGB.

She didn't ask me for money, but usually I would bring something to eat like sausage, bread, butter, cakes, mineral water, but she couldn't even eat, she was so nervous. She lived a couple of years in shock, afraid even to go to the kitchen to make tea.

At last she went to Moscow to the Moscow Party Congress to try to get help. At that time I was in the Crimea where her son was stationed in the army, and I met him there. He knew what was going on but couldn't do anything until his officer granted him a few days to go to Moscow. Meanwhile, she had been put into a psychiatric hospital. They put her there, as they did the dissidents, and they medicated her. After a few days her son was able to take her home. After that experience she lived only a few months longer. When I saw her just before her death, it was unbelievable; she was mentally shattered. She was not even forty years old.

They had cut off all her hair; when I saw her I couldn't recognize her. She didn't recognize me or even her son because of the medication. She didn't do anything wrong. She was just trying to help the Jewish young people to play music, to publish their poetry.

The Quota Was Zero

After high school, I went to an institute that students normally attend for five years, something between college and university. Because I was in the evening division and had a full-time job, it took me six years, attending classes three times a week. I did it this way not because my family couldn't afford to send me to school but because I was a Jew. I had finished the special math high school with very good grades, but I couldn't even try to enroll at the university. My dream was to go into architecture. My sister had finished this course, but in the structural division. The director of the institute said to my father, "I'll give you some good advice. Put your daughter in any other institute but this, because she couldn't start here if she were an Einstein—because she's Jewish, that's all."

At this institute the Jewish quota was zero in 1974. My class in the special math school had about thirty-five kids, and 80 percent were Jewish. So almost all of them went on to higher education at Odessa University in the computer programming division, which was not a wide field, and only this area was possible. But I didn't feel math was my field.

From Hand to Hand

My father decided to enroll me in the institute of refrigeration technology because he knew that it offered a high level of technical education, and I could find a job. To assure my entrance he paid 1,000 rubles to the director, from hand to hand. And for what? After five years at the special math school I had very good grades. I had already taken many of the subjects, so I only needed to study the technical ones. So why did he have to pay money? So that I would be allowed to take the test and answer the questions, the same as everybody else. So that I would not get an automatic failure. Actually, I passed all the tests with A's.

They didn't have enough people in the evening division because not many people wish to work full-time and study at the same time. In Russia they usually plan the number of people who can attend. If there are more than that number, they have a competition. In my division there were empty seats in the classroom. Even so, my father had to pay. I guess I was one of the best students because I helped everybody. I knew almost all of the subjects like drafting, and I could help everyone do the homework and pass the tests.

I Become a Manager

During the day I was a drafter where about 200 people worked. It was a special design institute of the food-processing industry, and my particular job was to build plants for processing baby food. There we had canned food for the wintertime, such as soups, vegetables and fruits, milk with fruit and yogurt. Almost everything was made from fruits and vegetables. Very little meat was used because of the problem in processing meat.

I worked as a drafter for six years on the automated control systems, which is similar to my field in America. After I finished institute studies and received my engineering degree, I worked as an engineer of refrigeration systems. I prepared the drawings and estimates required for the safe refrigerated storage of products produced in summer that were to be distributed six to eight months later. In each room temperatures varied for different foods; each room had different cooling equipment. Sometimes I went into the field to help the people who were building the plants, to solve problems and make sketches for them. In the last couple of years I was a middle-level engineer. Even though I was young, I had spent almost fifteen years in Russia working. I had the experience, but I didn't like being manager. I didn't know how to say, "That's wrong, you need to fix it" or "You're lazy."

What Is Love?

Alex and I worked at the same company. We met when I was twenty-one and had a boyfriend I was going to marry. After I met Alex, in one day I knew. I said no to my boyfriend and yes to Alex. My daughter always asks me, "Mommy, how do you know what love is?" And I say, "You can't be told, but you can feel it. If it comes, you will recognize it. So that is love, and it comes from God."

We worked in a medium-sized company. It was 200 people so it was close, like a family. And I had worked there five or six years by then and everyone knew me. I was seventeen when I started. So at first everyone was my "baby-sitter"; I grew up there. Alex worked in a different division, as a manager who organized the documents our company needed to build a new plant. To coordinate the paper-work is the hardest job, because in Russia most organizations don't know what they are doing even though they are spending money and time.

Alex was an unusual guy because he loved music and poetry and sports. And he was absolutely romantic. He didn't think like everybody else in Russia. He had gone all over the country as an athlete, and afterward he traveled for his work. He could see how people live, what they believe. He loved to talk to people and discover what kind of life they had led.

Alex was interested in me before I knew it. His feelings were so strong that at our first real meeting, the first time we spoke, he just said, "I love you and would like you to be my wife." And I said, "I would like to also." That's all. It was just one moment like a shock. I mean, if you put two fingers in a socket, you would feel the same reaction—like a fire.

The Start of Our New Life Together

We didn't have a wedding as such. Everybody came to my house, then to the government office that was just across the street, a thirty-minute ceremony. The next day we took our tourist bags and for two weeks went to the Crimea where we had a close friend. We spent a little time in the mountains because Alex was a mountain climber.

At first we lived with my mother-in-law in a new apartment in a new district, for which she had waited for almost thirty years. Fortunately she had a son and was able to get a two-room apartment. If she had a daughter she would get just one. This way, we occupied one room and she had the other.

When we had been married for two years, I was worried about Alex's mountain climbing. I told him, "You need to decide which is more important because mountains are very dangerous." I had just finished institute and already was pregnant. After Anna was born I moved to my mother's apartment in downtown Odessa. My mother had three big, separate rooms; the place was bigger and pretty close to my job, so I was able to walk to work. I had a part-time job, from one to five in the afternoon, and the first part of the day I took care of Anna. Then my father would come to help out.

Sometimes my grandmother's sister who was so kind would help. She was the baby-sitter for everyone in her family of nine kids, typical of Jewish families in her day. She was the oldest and had never had a family of her own. Like a lot of old people in Russia, she had a hard life. Though she was almost eighty, she still did housework and childcare.

Grandpa's Opposition: "Not Until I Die"

We tried to leave in 1979, but the best time to leave was 1978. My grandfather said, however, "Never, not until I die." And that was the truth. Six years later he died. But unfortunately at that time we couldn't get out because the government policy had changed. Although we had an invitation, the Russian government was closing the doors. They literally closed OVIR offices, so there was just one office in the whole city.

There were thousands and thousands of people who spent the night in line to apply to emigrate. We had to mark numbers on our hands to keep everyone in order. A few people organized the line, but they couldn't stay all day because they worked. Everyone got a number, and there was a list of the numbers and the names of the people who were standing in this line. At that time we understood that it was impossible to get out of the country because of the number of people. The last person who left Odessa in 1979 was my supervisor.

The Soap Bubble of Anti-Semitism

I don't remember one particular reason for leaving. I can't say something happened and we decided. Our whole life was impossible. I didn't have too much pressure in school, but my husband couldn't finish high school, just evening high school while he worked. After that he had started the institute in the evening division for years, but he couldn't find a job because he was Jewish, even with a master's degree when everybody needed people like him. He would answer an ad, but as soon as he showed his passport, they would say, "We don't need anyone now." Anti-Semitism was like a soap bubble. We were inside. So that was absolutely clear. It was our life. We knew about it from birth. Nobody was surprised when it happened to him or her because that was the usual case. That was the foundation of our wanting to leave.

My husband had read so much literature and poetry and listened to heretic tapes of people who already left, people who had written the best observations of Soviet life. All his friends had left, but we had just been married and didn't know when emigration would again be possible. So we couldn't plan anything.

A New Set of Considerations

When I came to Chicago I still loved architecture and thought of going to the Interior Design Institute, but I decided that my kids' attendance at Jewish school was more important. Even with scholarships it costs $300 each month. I decided to give them their education first and after that, we'll see.

I work as an electrical designer at a company that employs 3,000 people. It is involved with power station plants—nuclear, water, or others, but primarily nuclear. We do work all over Illinois and in other countries, such as China and Indonesia. They have three different levels of electrical work. Mine is in the middle between drafting and engineering. The company prepares all kinds of drawings for their clients at power plants.

The Void

Communism made animals of people because it removed God and didn't put anything in God's place. The Communist authorities could not fill the place that God occupied. They were trying to do this but they couldn't, so it was an empty space. An empty space cannot remain empty. I believe that was one of the important reasons why people in Russia were made crazy, were made like animals. Because they grew up without God. They grew up without the rules of humanity, the rules of democracy that all over the world people know.

Perhaps it's amusing, but my son's first word was "Lenin." Not "mommy," not "dad," not "Anna," not "sun," not "grass." He was two years old. It was during the October Revolution celebration, and pictures of Lenin and red flags were all over the city. Anna, who was six, said, "Look out the window, how many Lenins there are!" And Simon said, "Lenin!" And I thought, my gosh, we need to get out, no matter how. That's unbelievable, a little baby, two years old, just starting to talk, and that's what he says. But Anna had already told me she believed in God. She had a very good mind already. For her it wasn't a matter of what kind of religion. She had some feeling. She didn't think of what God it must be or what kind of tradition to keep.

Jewish tradition unfortunately is not really inside of us. Mostly it's outside. I wasn't atheistic at all, my whole life. Even though I got an A in atheistic philosophy, I knew it was a lie. Unfortunately for the KGB, they couldn't reach inside your mind. You could believe what you wished as long as you didn't tell anybody.

I first learned about God by reading about the Christian religion, because the Jewish religion was impossible to find anywhere. You could get the Bible underground. Some people I knew had the Bible at home, as part of the culture. We also had a little Bible, for traveling. My friends from Leningrad had one illustrated with very famous pictures by a French painter.

My daughter's first religious experience was after she started to read. She might spend twelve, fourteen hours a day reading. So she started to read the Bible. It was written in the old Russian language, not in the modern language and was a little bit harder. But she could read some of the famous passages of the New Testament. She read about Jesus Christ because he was a famous person, and she believed what she read, that he was somebody who was born 2,000 years ago and did perfect things for all people. About the same time she started kindergarten. One day she said to me, "Mommy, I believe in God, but it's secret information. Don't tell anybody about it. It's just for you. Because I know that if somebody else knew about it, it would be very dangerous for my family."

When we look at ourselves here, we are Russian and not Jews, because we speak the Russian language. For us, to be Jews here means to acquire some part of the religion. I have a few American friends who still keep the tradition, and they invite us to Jewish celebrations such as Rosh Hashanah or Hanukkah and Shabbat. We didn't know anything about Shabbat before.

When we came here, one of my first reactions was to get my kids into Jewish school. That's what I did. Recently my husband asked me what we're going to decide—to buy a place in the suburbs or send the children to Jewish school. We couldn't afford both. I said, "We've already decided. We want them to know about the traditions and give them some understanding about God." So, we will try to give them a Jewish education because it is important.

9

CONTEMPORARY COMMENTS

IGOR AND TATYANA FERTELMEYSTER

IF MUSCOVITES IGOR and Tatyana admit to differences of opinion, clearly their diversities offer each fresh insights, like the breezes that fan Odessa from the Black Sea, which itself figures into the background of each of their stories. Perhaps they sometimes imagine Lake Michigan is the sea at Odessa, only the sky is brighter and breezes smell much sweeter.

IGOR FERTELMEYSTER
No Oxygen at All

For Igor Fertelmeyster, the Soviet Union was stifling. In Moscow, when sense-less regulations were imposed in his workplace, he dared to make his objections known. No doubt his uncommon sense of humor allowed him to do so with impunity. Igor is self-possessed and at ease being interviewed. His obvious intelligence and quick wit heighten the appealing impression he makes.

His comparison of the culture he left to the one he adopted is objective and refreshing. He trims the extraneous and tweaks authority. The same irreverent approach also describes his relationships with family members. He tells us that his maternal grandfather emigrated briefly to Palestine with an older brother,

231

but, being idealistic about communism, he returned. Until this forebear's death, he and young Igor debated their ideological differences. Igor sums up the ironic twist of fate with characteristic good humor.

Beginnings

My wife, Tatyana, has a phrase she likes to use when she talks about me with her friends. She very often says, "You know the people from Odessa, they're different!" Actually, I wasn't born in Odessa, so it is sort of a joke on both of us. I was born in Moscow on June 22, 1956, the anniversary of the beginning of the Second World War.

When my parents met for the first time, my father was a sailor, and he lived in Odessa. My mother was on vacation from her job in Krasnodar and was visiting with relatives who lived in Odessa. By chance, her relatives lived directly above my father and grandmother. My parents were both very attractive people, and they discovered each other quickly. Maybe the sea air in Odessa helped. My mother's summer holiday was not a very long one, but they made time to see each other often and were married about a year later. They didn't tell me anything about how I was born!

When they were first married, they lived in Krasnodar where my mother was sent after graduating from the Institute of Engineering. This was because it is the law in Russia that after you receive your degree you must go to work in some place that is chosen for you. When I graduated, practically all the people who lived in Moscow stayed in Moscow. But when my mother graduated from the institute, not one of her group stayed in Moscow. To get educated people to live in all parts of the Soviet Union, the government, in its wisdom, made the job decision for all graduating students.

From Yiddish to Ukrainian

I knew only my grandmother because my grandfather was arrested in 1937, when my father was seven years old. My grandmother later received a paper that said he had died in 1943, but he probably died earlier. Since my grandfather was only an accounting clerk, he was probably arrested because he was a Jew. They told my grandmother that he had belonged to certain organizations and that was why he was arrested. This was Stalin's crazy idea. I only knew a few things about this because I think parents try to protect their children from bad things. In Russia they did this not only for the children but for their own security.

Even after the famous Twentieth Congress of the Communist Party when Khrushchev spoke about Stalin and what he had done, your political history was marked on any application form. They would ask if somebody from your family was "repressed," arrested or something like that. Also, they asked if you or your relatives had spent any time in occupied territory. Every person who lived in occupied territory in World War II was considered not a hero but a criminal. Those people who were freed from the concentration camps in Germany came back to Russia and then were sent to concentration camps in Russia. They were considered traitors because they were caught!

It was a very difficult life for my grandmother, and when she got old she often cried. She mostly cried about her husband; they had only lived together, maybe, eight years in all. My grandmother did not marry again, so all her life was spent in Odessa raising her children.

When I was very young, everyone in Odessa seemed to speak Yiddish. When I grew up, about half of the people in Odessa spoke Ukrainian. So, it was probably easier for my grandmother to remember the Jewish traditions and try to observe them because Odessa was such a Jewish city when she was younger. In Moscow, although there was not much contact with other Jews, both of my mother's parents spoke Yiddish.

I remember a little of my great-grandparents from both sides of my family. I remember that my father's grandfather had a business where they made cooking oil and that after the Revolution he lost everything. When I saw him, he was very, very old and very kind to me.

My grandfather on my mother's side was born in Minsk, and when he was twenty years old, he went with his older brother to Palestine. His brother stayed in Palestine, and my grandfather came back to Russia because he was a Communist and he believed in their ideals. Maybe if he had changed his ideas at the right time, I would have been born in the right place!

My mother's grandfather believed in all the Communist ideals and plans for the country. My parents were not members of the Communist party. But, when I grew up, I knew they understood the situation of the country and were not happy with all the Communist rules and regulations. But my grandfather? He believed until his death, and he argued with me when I criticized the rules of the country. It was difficult to change his mind. When someone tells you that your country's system is wrong, it means that all your life was wrong!

Education, Soviet Style

I didn't start reading early—I was probably about eight years old—but I have never really stopped since. I remember that when I came home from school I would read until about six o'clock when my parents came back from work. Reading was my love from the time I learned how! I read now, also, maybe too much!

Before I went to a specialized school in math and physics, it seemed I changed schools almost every year. First, I went to one school, but then we changed our apartment, and I was in a new development. Then they built another school that was closer to our building, and so I went to that school. I stayed in one school from fourth grade to eighth grade, and then I went to a specialized school. At an early age I discovered that I liked mathematics, physics, and that branch of the sciences, so I enjoyed mathematics school.

When I graduated, I tried to go to the university but I failed, probably because I was Jewish. I applied and had exams, but I didn't pass. After graduating from my mathematics school, it was impossible to get a D on a math exam! One problem was so difficult that I didn't know anyone who could solve it. It seemed impossible. So then I tried to enter the Machine Building Institute and passed all the exams very easily. There is no problem for Jews in going to technical institutes because there is no real demand for places at these institutes.

I have to explain the situation because it may be difficult for you to understand. If your father was a doctor or lawyer, you can't attend the same kind of school as he did. You might have connections that would help you to enter. In America, you pay money and you go to the university. You pay? You stay. In Russia, everything is free, so the faculty chooses who can study at any particular university, and because it is free it is *their* choice, not yours. So, most of the Jews study in technical areas like machine building or civil engineering. You must be special to go to Moscow University; not many Jews get to go there!

I am not sure, but I suppose there is a special percentage of Jews allowed to study at the university, and this percentage is probably less now than it was under the czar, when it was 5 per cent. It is difficult not only for Jews but also for people from the Caucasus—Georgia, Armenia—to pass the entrance exams for the medical institute in Moscow or for Moscow University.

Being Jewish in Russia

It is hard to say when I realized that I was Jewish. When you are little you just accept the way of life in your family. You don't know what makes you different. My parents did not know anything about Judaica or Jewish history. Our family celebrated some things, but not Jewish holidays, just the usual government holidays and family events. We celebrated anniversaries, weddings, things like that. For a birthday it was typical to eat, eat, eat, and it was perhaps more fun there than here in America, because you could eat anything you wanted. In Russia there is a special preparation for a birthday, and people tried to get something unusual to eat for the celebration.

There is another meaning to being Jewish in Russia. In America the term covers people who belong to the Jewish religion, even if there are a lot of assimilated Jews here who do not think they are still Jews. In Russia, we have a special mark on our documents with this name, *Evrey*, as our nationality. Even in first grade this was marked on all our documents. So, somebody probably told me about it, and probably in a less than nice way.

Work and Love: Why I Paid My Dues To *Komsomol*

When you finish the institute either as a full-time or part-time student, you cannot choose between positions that are available; they *put* you in a job at the age of twenty-two. I was first in my group, so I could choose among many positions, but I was advised to go to one place, a machine-building plant.

I really loved that place because of the people. It is very important where you go to work for the first time; you need to be with people who can help you to learn more in your field. I also met Tatyana, my wife, while I was working there, in the headquarters of the *Komsomol* organization in our plant. It was very funny. I finally understood why I was paying dues to the *Komsomol!*

Komsomol, the Communist Youth Organization, has active branches in schools, the Soviet equivalent of American high schools, and usually everybody belongs. When you get a job, your dues go up. There are special newspapers that feature articles about *Komsomol* activities and the work that *Komsomol* members do. I had written such an article about a project that our group was working on, and Tatyana was a journalist at a newspaper that printed these articles. Since it was a technical article, she went to the plant to talk to the people involved in the project.

My friend and I went to the office, and I think he may have done most of the explaining. I never expected to meet someone like Tatyana. She was very attractive and so interested in learning about things. She said that she was taking our phone numbers in case she had any more questions. We took her phone number, supposedly for the same reason.

We were married in two months! After two weeks of knowing each other—and I was out of the city at another plant for one week of this time—we began to live together. Tatyana had a one-room apartment, and so I joined her there. This is *not* the usual circumstance in Russia.

We went on our honeymoon before the wedding because I decided to change my job, and I had some vacation time. Tatyana was attending evening classes at the university, and she had exams, so she had a vacation from her work to take the exams. We spent that time as our honeymoon.

We were married in the usual state wedding palace ceremony. It was very official. I participated in three weddings in one year: our own, the wedding of Tatyana's witnesses, and the wedding of my brother. All the ceremonies were just the same, and I was laughing under the surface. There is a special text that the representative of the Soviet government pronounces for the bride and groom, and she goes through it without any emotion! Three times in one year really made it seem funny to me. Of course, it was an important step for each of us, but not very inspiring!

We had two wedding receptions because we didn't have enough room to invite all the friends and relatives. So, we had one party for relatives, and then in a week we had another party for friends. At the parties, we drank vodka and danced a little, but there was not much room. Sometimes people have the reception at a restaurant. We did not; it was too expensive for us. When we got married, we were living very well for Russians. My salary was equal to $158 a month.

When I met Tatyana I did not know that she was Jewish. I think it was important to my family that she was Jewish because in Russia, especially, there are a lot of problems with intermarriage. In the Soviet Union there are some Jewish/non-Jewish marriages, but probably not as many as there are intermarriages between different nationalities within the Soviet. Even before marriage, Jews understand that they might have trouble with their parents-in-law. Most young people marry and then share an apartment with the parents of one of them. It is a closeness that does not leave much room for adjustment. It is worse in the Jewish/non-Jewish marriages because it is very difficult for Jews to receive any promotions and difficult for them to find good jobs. So a wife understands very quickly that her husband never gets promoted because he is a Jew. Then she may start to complain, "Why did I marry you when I could have chosen another man and not have these problems?"

Divorce is as common in Russia as here, but maybe the reasons are different there. I think the main reason for divorce in the Soviet Union is that everyone has to live with his parents. The second reason for divorce is drinking. You cannot imagine how much a Russian can drink. I could drink a pint of vodka at a time, and I saw one guy drink a liter of vodka and work after that!

Actually, my philosophy about marriage changed because I was so much older than is usual for a first marriage in Russia. I think that marrying quickly is the only way to do it when you are twenty-six years old. Otherwise you see that this woman has this bad side and another woman has that bad side, and you know you will never find someone perfect. And I know I am not perfect, either!

Nightmares about *Pogroms*

A year after our marriage, many young Jewish people had begun to leave Russia or to apply to leave. When my cousin started the process to leave Russia I didn't think he was doing the right thing. I changed my mind when my daughter was born because I began to have nightmares about *pogroms*. I knew that it was possible for them to happen in Russia and did not want to be there if it happened again. I spent five years arguing with Tatyana about this.

It was impossible to leave Russia then, and later Tatyana picked the right time to leave, 1987. We made this decision when visiting friends who had received permission to leave. There was another couple with them, and they asked my friends to offer them an invitation to Israel; I just asked if they would do the same for us. We waited three months to get the invitation and five months to get permission to go. All in all, it was very easy.

One can read about *pogroms* in Russia, but it seemed as if they were only possible before the Revolution. But it really came through to me that they were still possible. When we left, we did so mainly because we had a child. Even now,

I can't say that it is better for me in America than in Russia because I had a good job, a decent apartment, and, the most important thing, in coming here I lost my friends and the circle I was used to living in. How can I say it? When you live in America, you begin to forget about all the difficulties you encountered in Russia and remember fondly all the things you left there. But I don't feel bad that I left.

Why Not Israel?

I don't think that we really considered going to Israel when we were in Russia; the main thing was leaving Russia! There is no big difference between countries outside of Russia. There *is* a big difference between Russia and the other countries in the world. Also, we really didn't have anybody we knew in Israel. Some friends of our relatives are there, but they were not close to us. Here, in Chicago, I had a cousin, and we were close when he lived in Russia.

So much is different from what we thought it would be. Some things we could never have begun to imagine. Our trip here was the usual journey. We spent twenty days in Austria; it was very beautiful. I had been in East Germany and in Bulgaria on job assignments, but Austria was better! I didn't connect these reactions with freedom, but more with the different stores, the things, and mostly the food that was available. You cannot even buy apples in Russia!

It is hard to explain the difficulties in Russia. Everything that is easy in America is difficult in Russia. There are shortages of food, clothing, apartments—of everything and anything. Now it is even worse than it was when we left. I read in one letter that there is nothing on the shelves there, and what little there is becomes less and less. The most difficult thing is the insecurity. You don't know what will happen the next day, and it is possible that *everything* you can imagine, or can't imagine, will happen. This applies to all Russians, not just Jews.

When applying to leave Russia, everybody knows exactly what to do because he knows a lot of other people who are going to leave, and others who have already left. Also, everyone receives a set of instructions on how to prepare for leaving. It is about ten pages long and provides the names and addresses of all the organizations you need to contact. There is a list of all the papers you need to fill out, with specific advice on how to make the process easier.

In times prior to our trip, most people went from Moscow to Vienna, then to Italy, and finally to the United States. But when we arrived in Italy, we found out about America's refusing entry. It had been very easy to get into the United States. The interview at the American Embassy with the INS [Immigration and Naturalization Service] used to be rather informal. Then, just when we arrived in Italy, America changed its rules, and people began to get refused by America.

We lived in a townhouse with another family. Two of the families we knew got permission to go to the United States, and other Russians left Italy day after day. But a third family got refused; they spent four months in Italy. In the beginning I couldn't believe it. I thought that America could not refuse anybody. America had been very generous to Russian immigrants.

In the first eight cases, I could see some reason for their refusal. Then people began to be refused without any obvious reason. Sometimes refusal was justified, but only in a few instances. Only now have all the people who were in Italy with us arrived in the States. The last family spent more than a year there. Before we left Russia, we had only considered going to the United States. In Italy we had time to consider that maybe if we were refused by America, we might go to Israel.

The View from Here

We thought it would be easier for us to adjust in a country where we knew someone. Because there are different rules, both major and minor ones, and people behave differently from what we were accustomed to, we needed some- one to give us advice, and we were really good pupils. I followed all my cousin's advice when we first arrived! Now, I don't. He told me where I needed to apply for social security, how to write my resumé, how to open a checking account in a bank. The language was also difficult. I remember how scared I was when I went to apply for social security. Everything was so strange for me, I walked along the street, and it was really scary. Now I am at home.

As for being a Jew in Russia, mainly it means that you feel different. No, not that *you* feel different, but that other people *make* you feel different. A lot of Jews find out that they are Jewish when they first go to school. Then other people, teachers or other students, tell them something that is not polite. There are a lot of cases where teachers belong to a Russian nationalistic organization, *Pamyat.* I read an article about one school in Leningrad where all the teachers, including the principal of the school, pushed all 300 Jewish children out of school. I don't remember what was unusual about this school, but it is very common with the specialized schools for there to be more Jewish students than in the regular schools. Jewish parents want their children to be educated in many different fields.

When I grew up, all companies or groups seemed to be formed mostly along nationalistic principles. Most close friendships seem to be too. A lot of my friends were Jewish, not because they were the best people for me but because, if I knew somebody was a Jew, that made me feel a different way toward him and be closer to him. I also had Russian friends, and it seemed that at some point we just couldn't understand each other. Between Jews there were fewer points of misunderstanding.

Maybe for people who try to hide their Jewishness, it was more difficult to live in the Soviet Union because they had to think all the time that they couldn't show that they were Jews. For example, you could not mention the maiden name of your mother, because that would show you were Jewish. It was simpler for me because I never tried to hide that I was a Jew. I really didn't have a lot of difficulties connected with my Jewishness.

My parents and my brother are still in Russia. My mother has visited since we have been here. She didn't like America when she was here, but now that she is back in Russia, *now* she likes America! But my family's coming here mostly depends on my father. When we were going to leave, he wouldn't even speak with me. Now he has completely changed his mind about emigration. But it will be very difficult for him to give up his job. He is a manager, and he deals with a lot of people. People like him, and he lives for his job. So, to lose his job would be to lose practically the most important part of his life. When he retires, it would not make a big difference for him whether he is in Russia or here. It will still be difficult for him because at his age it is very difficult to learn a new language.

Pamyat—The Name Means Memory

I am concerned about their still being in Russia. One worries about everything one can imagine and even things one cannot imagine. On a Russian TV program before we left, they announced that the *Pamyat* organization was going to make *pogroms* on the fifth of May. I could believe it. Another time there were slogans out on the street that there would be Jewish *pogroms* on the 1000th anniversary of Christianity in Russia. They were going to celebrate in this way. Nothing actually happened, but people were afraid. There were slogans all over the countryside and articles in the newspapers saying that the KGB did not let it happen.

Anti-Semitism in Russia has become more open. I used to speak with the guys in *Pamyat;* they were just stupid, but that group can be really dangerous. *Pamyat* means memory. *Pamyat* members say that Russian nature is spoiled, that Russian culture has been destroyed, and that it is not right for the Russian government to sell all our natural resources to the West. What they say is logical except they blame Jews for everything.

Their slogans make a lot of people feel that they want to make changes in the right direction. I saw people who came to Moscow from faraway places to speak with the men from *Pamyat.* Russian people are used to thinking all those who are blamed for anything in the newspaper are actually good guys. Russian newspapers wrote that Solzhenitsyn was bad, that Sakharov was bad. Now everybody knows that they were not bad. So, *Pamyat* is still called bad, and there are plenty who think this really means they are good.

I never met the leaders of this organization. I only read interviews in Russian-American newspapers. But, the members on the lower level are very pushy. They don't want to listen to any arguments. For example, I saw an incident when some man called a member of *Pamyat* an anti-Semite, and the *Pamyat* member tried to grab him and bring him to the police because he called him a bad name. *Pamyat* never says that it has anything against Jews, only against Zionists. But all the Zionists have already left Russia. *Pamyat* usually speaks against Zionists and Masons, but they really don't know who these people are. They say the Masons are a conspiracy organization. There *were* Masons in Russia, but I am sure there are very few now.

The Oxygen Supply

It is really strange for me to hear that the American government has made a law about clean air and that Chicago is one of the worst places in America. The air in Chicago, compared with Moscow, is perfume! I think there are some places in Moscow where there is *no* oxygen at all!

There are only rats and cats on the streets in Russia. One of our biggest surprises here was when we had only just arrived, and we saw squirrels! We have them in Russia, but in special parks, not on the street.

TATYANA FERTELMEYSTER
Questions without Answers

Tatyana is a journalist; she wants to learn the facts of what is happening around her, and then to share this knowledge with others. Because of her mastery of Russian, her "lack" of fluency in English is irritating to her, but her vitality and communication skills would make her understood in any language. Her narrative reflects her vivacity, along with the range of information she has amassed.

Her experience while on maternity leave as a freelancer for a magazine, answering letters from distraught mothers, tells more than book-length socio-economic treatises might about the failure of the great Marxian experiment.

During the first interview, Tatyana was planning to visit her parents in Israel. In the subsequent interview, she shared her family experiences there. Ever the professional, she would like to write a book about Russian-Jewish immigration from personal experiences as well as from working with newly arrived immigrants through the Jewish Family Service.

A Good Start

I was born in Moscow on April 8, 1959. My parents lived in a common apartment with a few other families. Later, we lived in an apartment building that was like a big village! Moscow is a big city, and if you live in an apartment building, you usually don't even know the names of your neighbors.

Our parents took a lot of interest in our building, and they built a very good yard. It was an important part of my childhood because we could be out of our apartment and away from our families. We could play and have a good social life, and our parents could be alone together.

Igor's parents' wedding day, Odessa, 1954.
Standing: Leonid Fertelmeyster and Galina
Feller. Seated: Tsilya and Izrail Feller.

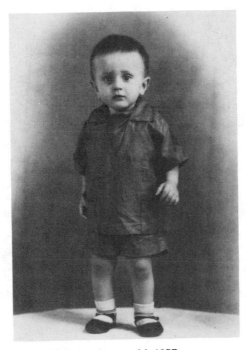

Igor in Odessa, 1 year old, 1957.

Tatyana, 3, left, and Galina, 5, right, 1962, with
grandmother Basya Brestina (their mother's
mother) who backpacked with her siblings out
of the Pale.

Tatyana and Igor in America, 1992. Photo © 1992 by Bruce Mondschain. All rights reserved.

My Grandmother Backpacks Out of the Pale

My grandmother was the oldest child, and she had four siblings. They lived in the Pale. After her mother died, her father decided to remarry, but the children disliked his new wife. My grandmother took all the siblings away from the family home with packs on their backs. They planned to beg for food if necessary. I think that all of them grew up to be well educated. Other than my grandmother, I only knew her sister. The three brothers were killed in the Second World War.

Jews could not get an education when they lived in the Pale. One good thing that the Soviet Revolution gave Jews was the opportunity to go to big cities to attend colleges and universities. I think that this is how my great-uncles got their education. They left the Pale when the Revolution opened doors for them. Later those doors were again closed for Jews, but there was some period when education and change was possible.

I also know something about my mother's parents. Her grandfather was a shoemaker, and he moved his large family to Argentina because of the situation in the Ukraine. The poor situation, for instance, was lack of food, and was connected with *pogroms*. He brought them back after a few years.

My grandmother died when I was about twenty. She was the usual sort of representative of her generation because she believed strongly in the Soviet Union. She was a member of the Communist party. It was difficult to argue with her, but we did argue because when I was sixteen, during the late seventies, the situation in the country was awful. People worked hard but had nothing, and the stores were empty. My mother worked as a journalist and saw a lot of what life was like in different parts of the country. When we tried to say anything to my grandmother about conditions, she would get angry. But, at the end of her life she began to change a bit and to understand that something was wrong with the system that had been her whole life, despite the terrible situations it had caused. She died in 1981.

Purges: Stalin's "Cleaning" Process

In the mid-thirties, my grandmother was near arrest. Stalin imprisoned many members of his party, during the purges. It was a regular process: "Today we 'clean' this office, tomorrow we 'clean' that office."

Some commission would come to each office, plant, school, anywhere, and each member of the Communist party had to explain himself: What did he do? Where was he before the Revolution? Who were his parents? And so on. You could be out of the party because your father had a small business. Even if you decided not to side with your father when the Revolution came, even if you were a great activist in the Revolution, the most important thing for them at this moment was that your father had a private business. This was a very good time for unscrupulous people because they could replace those they accused, become supervisors, and take places in the party, which they did often.

My grandmother was saved from a very unpleasant situation when it was her editorial office's turn to be "cleaned." There was a large meeting where everybody had to stand up and say, "I am guilty" and so on. When she was on the stage giving her speech, there was a panic in the auditorium because they saw blood. Because of the nervous pressure, she suffered a sudden uterine hemorrhage and had to be hospitalized immediately. By the time she was back at work, it was the next office's turn, so they forgot about her, and she was saved from being purged.

Once a newspaper article saved my father's mother. She was a professor and lecturer. One day she was to give a lecture about a particular writer. The morning before the lecture, she opened up the main newspaper and read that he was an enemy of the people! She called the university and said that she was very sick and could not come! That was the situation in the country. There were twenty years of constant fear, the life of two generations, the life of one and the beginning of life for another.

"Be Afraid . . . Be Very Careful"

Our parents warned us to be afraid, to be very careful when we opened our mouths. Everyone was so warned. For Jewish people, the worst period was at the end of Stalin's life, in the 1950s, when there was the case of the Jewish doctors, the Doctor's Plot trial. Earlier, there was a period of particular torment for Georgians and Tartars, as well as for Russians, Ukrainians, Byelorussians, whoever you were. Most of all Stalin was afraid of the old Bolsheviks, because they knew him not as a big leader but on their same level. These people, members of my grandmother's generation, people between seventeen and twenty-five during the Revolution, were the main population of his prisons at that time.

My grandfather was from the Ukraine originally. The beginning of the Soviet state, in the 1920s, was a pretty good time for the country and for the Jewish people. A lot of Jewish people had participated in the Revolution, and one of their motivations was to change their lives so they could have an education and become many different kinds of professionals.

At the beginning, nobody could stop them and really a lot of Jews were in good universities and had good jobs. The difficulty for Jews in education began again in the 1950s. Now, it is one of the slogans of the *Pamyat* organization that the Jews had all the positions—because they really could do it then.

My grandfather was a very well-educated person, but in the 1950s, he left his job and couldn't find anything else. He thought he might have to become a shoemaker like his father. Some friend of his gave him work, but I'm not sure what kind. My mother was thirty-eight and in Moscow University; her specialty was the Russian language. She graduated at the beginning of the fifties, and at that time, state anti-Semitism began to explode like a mushroom, so she couldn't find a job, either.

My Father Loved the Sea

My father left his family when he was pretty young. He wanted to be a sailor. He was Ukrainian; his home was on the Black Sea. The war began when he was seventeen, and he was evacuated with his family to Siberia. People from the Ukraine and other parts of Russia were moved to the Urals, Siberia, and Uzbekistan during the evacuation of civilians from the western part of Russia.

My father lived in Siberia with his mother until he was eighteen, when he could join the army. That was his dream. When he went to the medical commission, however, they found that he had a heart defect. Then he asked his friend to go for the physical in his place at to another commission office. His friend passed the medical exam under my father's name. My father worked in some military school and took courses, and he became a lieutenant of artillery. His participation in the war did not last long because he was a lieutenant, and a lieutenant's service at the front was usually very short. My father was saved from the front lines because of what happened when he left the underground shelter once with one of his army friends. His friend whom he loved was killed, and my father was injured. He lost an eye, was hospitalized, and then couldn't stay in the army anymore. Instead, he became a student at the university.

This was possible because he had just come from the army. He came from a Ukrainian school, and his Russian was awful. When he read for the exam, some professor came and asked, "Who did this?" It was that bad! My father said, "I did it!" Well, he was in full uniform with all his medals, so they said, "Do you have any friends here?" "Yes," he said. "Let your friend sit here and correct all your mistakes," they said. So, my father became a student in the geography department of Moscow University.

As a result of all this, he became an oceanologist. He worked with the sea, as he had always wanted. He was very happy, but due to heart disease, his active life was over when he was forty-nine. He is still alive, but he is mostly disabled. They wanted him to have surgery and they ran some tests, but the tests were traumatic. He was paralyzed afterward and could not talk. Later he was able to talk, but he could not use his hands.

My mother and father moved to Israel in January 1990. I am going to visit them this October. I haven't seen my parents since we left Russia in October of 1988, almost two years ago.

My Mother Wept When Stalin Died

My mother was a student at Moscow University. She and all her friends were members of the Communist party; all of them believed in the party. When Stalin died, she was sitting in her room crying, when a neighbor came and told her, "Yes, you should cry. But I will cry because he didn't die a long time ago!" This old woman had been a prisoner and knew about Stalin's crimes.

When Stalin died, it was like the end of an era for my mother. She didn't understand all the bad things Stalin had done. She hadn't seen the neighbors inform in order to put another neighbor into prison. Sometimes it is impossible for someone to think that another human being can be put into prison without any cause. When people did see someone taken away, they thought he had to be guilty. Only when *you* were taken did you begin to think that it was a mistake. Even when they were taken prisoner, some people thought, "I'm here because of a mistake." It was difficult for them to understand that *all* of them were there because of the system.

Why Jews Embraced Communism

All my grandparents and parents were Communists. There was nothing in my life that was religious, that was Jewish. I don't think that this was because they were Communists. For my grandmother, it was important to take her siblings away from the life they had in the Pale and to go to some city to get an education, to have a new kind of life. It was the same for my grandfather who, although he was the son of a very poor shoemaker, managed to become a professor, an editor, a very educated person. It was important to them to make their life different from that of their parents. I think that is why my grandparents assimilated so actively into the Russian population, in the Ukraine, in the army. I grew up thinking that there was no difference between the nationalities, religions, etc. I had friends who were Russian, Jewish, Armenian, and Georgian. Even today I do not think that it is important what nationality and religion people are. What is important is what kind of person you are.

As far as experiencing anti-Semitism when I was growing up, certainly I did. I don't know why or how it happened, but most of my close friends were Jews. Maybe there is something in common between us. All my good friends were successful; they were journalists, which is not an easy position for Jews to obtain. Some of them were engineers like my husband, and all of them were educated. My husband did not get the education he had wanted, but he did have one. He had a diploma; he had a profession; he could work.

At Five Kopeks a Line, a Journalist

My mother did not give me any special advice. The only thing I remember is that once, when I was in school, I wrote something sad for my literature lesson that she read and said, "I'm sure this girl will never be a journalist." For her it was probably a great surprise that I became a journalist and a really *good* one.

When I graduated school, I was crazy about math; I thought I would become a mathematician or a computer programmer. I passed the exams and entered an institute in Moscow that was pretty much open for Jews. There are a lot of Jewish students, and they usually go to the technical schools, like engineering schools, not universities. I stayed at this institute one semester, and that was enough for me. No more math!

My mother told me that there was only one thing to be done; if I left the institute that day, the next day I had to work. I took a job as a messenger for *Pravda*. I worked in the part of the editorial office where the newspaper is typeset. I learned a lot from this process and decided to apply to the journalism department at Moscow University. I was accepted into the evening classes, and I became a journalist, to my own satisfaction.

It was difficult to find a job, but I found one at a newspaper that we called a "junior" newspaper because young people in Moscow found work there and because the salaries were so low. For more than a year I worked without any salary. I was paid only for articles I wrote. This system was used because it was for young people and not like a *Pravda*. Each line printed in the newspaper paid me five kopeks—not much!

A lot of journalists began on this newspaper, but after a year, a year and a half, all of them tried to find other jobs. For Jewish people it was more difficult to find a position, so they worked for this paper. The publishers recognized this. About 80 percent of our editorial office was Jewish. Now, all of them who stayed in Moscow have very good jobs. Now it is easier for Jews to find a position.

After working without salary for more than a year I got a very good salary of sixty-five rubles a month. I had a very good life, an absolutely free life. I began there when I was twenty, and I still lived with my parents. Then I got married; I met my husband through my newspaper.

Finding the Facts and a Husband

Because I wrote about economic problems, I needed to do articles every day. Sometimes it was impossible to leave my office, and then I had to take information from two phones and hear my typewriter go like a machine! I told my supervisor that it was enough, I could not work that way any more, and I had to talk with "real people." He said, "Go ahead, find something interesting."

At one plant in Moscow there was a branch of *Komsomol*, the Communist Youth Organization, for fourteen- to twenty-eight-year-olds. Everybody joined *Komsomol*, and joining was not any more difficult for Jews. It was sort of a special case if someone was *not* a member. Each organization, each plant, had its own *Komsomol* committee. I came to this committee because of my newspaper; its name was *Moscovsky Komsomoletz*, which means a member of the Moscow chapter of the *Komsomol* organization.

I went to the committee to ask for more information on an article one of the workers had written about his project at the plant. They tried to explain it to me, but you have to be an expert in the engineering field to make it clear to someone who is not. I told them that I couldn't understand what they meant and to let somebody from the team explain it to me.

So, two guys came—one was my future husband! That is how we found each other. I was twenty-two, then. We started living together two weeks after our first date! My parents didn't have time to say anything. In two months, we were married officially. My oldest daughter was born September 2, almost exactly nine months after we first met.

For Six Years We Disagreed

Igor tried to push me for about six years to leave Russia, from the beginning of our marriage. I said no, I couldn't do it because if we had brought our papers to OVIR, the organization that gives you permission to leave, I would have immediately lost my job. And how could I live without my job?

During those six years Igor and I had some disagreements but not really fights. He was not demanding because he could see that everybody we knew, who asked for permission to leave, was refused. We also considered my mother's situation. Because of my father's illness, she was the wage earner for the family. I knew that if I brought in an exit application, *she* would lose her job the next day. She would have nothing, and she would not be able to support the family. I also thought about Igor's father, who was a big chief in his business and who might also have lost his job if we had applied three or four years ago.

When *perestroika* began, they said, "Everything is new; we will rebuild." I saw a lot of new words but not a new reality. Nevertheless, I changed my mind. First of all, I had my two kids to consider. I realized that my family was the most important thing for me, more important than my journalism or any other ambitions. I knew that I could be refused and lose my job, but I needed to do this for my family.

Actually, nothing happened when we applied because the times had really changed. What pushed me to make a decision was the job I was doing at that time. I was at home with Eugene, who was a small baby. In Russia you could stay at home with your newborn child for a year and a half and receive thirty-five rubles a month.

I Got Letters

When Eugene was born, they changed the rule and you could stay home up to two years. The last half-year was without any pay. I took a job with a magazine named *Family and School*. They needed somebody who could answer letters for them. The magazine received a lot of mail from mothers all over the country. Reading this mail was what pushed me to make the decision to emigrate. Every day I read letters from mothers, around 90 percent of whom were mothers with many children, for whom there are some special rules in Russia.

The history of these rules is that, at the end of the war, because a lot of men were killed, the government tried to encourage women to have more children. In some places, if you have three or more children you can go to special stores. In other places, it is four or more children. In Middle Asia, it is five or more because in Uzbekistan and the other republics, it is very popular to have many kids. If you have less than five there, you cannot go to the special stores. If you have more children, you can have an apartment and you can have more food. In the regular store you can stay in line a long time and still find nothing.

The letters I read were something like, "I have three kids, and in my district you must have four or more if you want to buy meat and milk in a special store. What shall I do with my three kids? What is your advice? I don't have time to stand in line three hours to buy two pounds of meat." Another letter read, "I just delivered my fourth child, so according to rules we have in our area, now I can apply for a washer, but only two mothers can get washers during one year. I will be fifty-fifth in this line, so I will get a washer when my newborn baby is twenty-eight."

The more I read these letters, the more I wanted to answer them. But the more I read, the more I understood that it was impossible for people to make changes for the better within this system. The system was like a wall, and you could kill yourself fighting against this wall and still change nothing in the life of your children.

I understood, then, that I had to create a better future for my children. If I could not change the system I lived in (and I was absolutely sure that I could not), I had to take them away.

The final point that changed my mind was that Igor's friend, who was refused for eight years, finally got permission to leave. So I saw that it was real, that it was possible. We gave them our names, and they arranged an invitation from Israel for us. To be invited was the *only* official way to leave the country.

Abortion in Russia

Although there is some contraception, it is legal and very common to have an abortion. The pill is not popular at all. When the pill was first produced, somewhere in the world, the Soviet press wrote that it was awful, and people were afraid to take it. As a result, you can only sometimes buy packets of the pill. But now, I have heard that you cannot even buy aspirin! There is a major shortage of condoms, which is a big problem, especially now with AIDS. If you don't have any contraceptives, the only kind of contraception is abortion.

Some authorities felt that if abortion were easy, it would not be good for the country. In many hospitals in Russia, even in Moscow, it was impossible to get any painkiller during an abortion—maybe only for a lot of money. For many people it was the only way to deal with their situation. Not everybody is ready to raise five children. It is difficult to do in America and impossible in Russia!

Exposé or Inference

I tried to change the system as a journalist, but it was impossible. Once I went to a small factory and talked to the director who told me they made fabric and that the main problem was that they had nothing with which to clean the air. Women, a large part of the workers, worked in this dirty air.

When I brought this material to my supervisor, who was a very good man, also a Jew, he said, "I'm sorry, we cannot write about this." I accepted this because my mother taught me it's your right to write whatever you want, and it is the editors' right to put into the newspaper whatever they want.

I think that good Russian journalism is more interesting than American. It is more like literature. It is a special art, and nobody knows this art in America because you can say openly everything you think. There is a special skill to writing in such a way that they can put it in a Russian newspaper. You cannot come right out and say things; you have to let people infer.

"AIDS Is a Capitalist Word"

We began hearing about AIDS in Russia maybe two years before we left, 1986, 1985. *Pravda* did not have articles about it. I don't remember where it was first discussed, maybe on TV or the radio. They said that it was an English or capitalist word and that it was a homosexual problem, and since the Soviet Union doesn't have homosexuals or drug addicts, AIDS would not be a problem there.

When cases of AIDS began to occur, they wrote in the newspaper that they had five cases, and four of them were foreign citizens. They said it was possible because they didn't check foreign students and foreign workers and that Russia got AIDS from foreign countries. The first Soviet person who got it worked somewhere in Africa, and he had some homosexual contacts while there. What is really dangerous in Russia is that you can get it not only from sexual contact but also from medical equipment because they use this equipment many times without sterilization.

There is now IV drug usage in Russia, and they are beginning to write about it. When I grew up, I was absolutely sure that we didn't have persecution, that we didn't have drug users, that we didn't have this or that. My mother, for example, told us she was sure that there was no tuberculosis in Russia. Then she herself got it after the war, and she was put in a special hospital or sanitarium where she met a lot of people with the same disease.

My New Career

I work for Jewish Family Service, with the resettlement of new families. Now I write out papers, and papers, and papers. Filling out forms is awful. I write them in English and hope nobody will ever read them. But I would like to write a book someday about America, about how I see it.

PART III

ALBUM LEAVES FROM OTHER JOURNEYS

THE SHVARTSMANS OF KIEV
Wandering in Search of Work

Mikhail Shvartsman, civil engineer, retired
Born 1920, Akkerman, Rumania

I was born in a well-to-do family. When I was one year old my family moved to Bolgrad, which was a center of Bulgarian colonialism at that time. In a city of 25,000, my grandfather was the head of a community of 1,500 Jews. At city hall all of the minority groups had a representative. There was no anti-Semitism between the Bulgarians, Greeks, Jews, and other nationalities. There were many Bulgarian, German, Albanian, Moldavian, Caucasian, and Ukrainian colonies in south Bessarabia, between the rivers Danube, Prutt, and Dniester. There were even a few Jewish agricultural colonies grouped around this "New Jerusalem" which, until 1940, was a capitalist country.

From 1933 we sensed what was happening in Germany. On June 28, 1940, after [the Molotov-Ribbentrop] pact with fascist Germany, Russians took a big chunk of Rumania named Bessarabia. Our town was suddenly occupied by the Soviet Army and I was not permitted to leave. Because my father had been financially successful, the Russian government put him on a departure list for Siberia. He fell under a great deal of pressure which hastened his death at the age of 52, in December 1940. I was not allowed to leave Bolgrad. My mother had never worked outside the home all those years and needed my help.

After my father died, I worked as a road repair technician. The work was not physically hard. Since Bessarabia was now part of the Soviet Union, I was sent into the Red Army at the western border where my engineering skills in road building and tunnel construction were needed.

When the war started on June 22, 1941, I was eight miles away from the border. A great many people were killed right away because the artillery and bombing were so heavy. I managed to get away from this hell and in July moved to Odessa, the Ukraine, and worked on fortifications there. In August, when the German army came toward Odessa, we were moved by sea to the Northern Caucasus, the port of Novorossijsk. By October 1941, I was assigned to a special engineering battalion of Army #56, the one battalion for this whole army that worked strictly with mines. The majority of people from this battalion in time were killed because of danger and unsafe conditions.

I worked in this special battalion building temporary bridges after the others were destroyed. We didn't have enough food, we were cold, standing in water in freezing weather. We lived in trenches, used hay for warmth and wore all our clothes to keep warm; we went without bathing. There were kitchens on wheels. If they could get to us at the front lines, we could get a cup of hot soup. Otherwise we ate frozen bread.

During this period the fascists tried to "burn" anti-Semitism into the Russian army. Before going into the attack, German bombers would drop flyers that said in Russian, "Kill the Jews." I am sure that Russian deserters were in those planes with the Germans.

After the war the anti-Semites used to say, "You fought your war in Central Asia where everybody had been evacuated. You were defending Tashkent instead of really fighting."

At that time the population of the whole Soviet Union was 178 million. Statistics say that before the war there were 2.4 million Jews registered in Russia, about half of them women. Four hundred thousand of them were actually in provinces from Poland, Rumania, and the Baltic which were occupied in the first days of the war. Most of the Jews who remained in these territories were killed in concentration camps.

In the war 500,000 Jews fought at the front; 200,000 were lost. Three hundred thousand survived.

The remaining Jews were only 1.12 percent of the population, but the highest military honor, Hero of the Soviet Union, was earned by 11,000 soldiers and officers, 137 of whom were Jewish. They were about 2 percent of those who received the medal, almost double the proportion of Jews in the population.

Four Jewish people implemented decisive improvements in war technology in 1943. General Vannikov was a minister who designed new weapons for the army. Isaac Zaltsman produced new T-34 tanks. New kinds of planes were produced by Rubinchik. General Jacob Grigorich Krazer saved Stalingrad. Until the Battle of Stalingrad, the Russians had been retreating and the Germans advancing. After that the situation started reversing.

In 1942, I went to Stalingrad. I was an assistant commander of the technical and engineering forces. I carried weapons and participated in the battle. In January 1943 I suffered a contusion when a mine exploded, and three of my comrades died. I was ten feet from the explosion, standing in a crater made by a previous explosion. It was a miracle I survived. Then, from almost freezing, I got pneumonia. I spent four months in a mobile hospital headed by a Dr. Voronov, who happened to be Jewish. There I received blood transfusions. After the pneumonia, I developed tuberculosis.

When I improved, the medical committee decided I could not return to the front. It was now April of 1943. I was sent to Baku, the capital of Azerbaijan, to Georgia, then to Duschanbe, capital of Tadjekistan in Middle Asia, where I was working in a weapons factory by the Amudarya (Wild Water) River at the Afghan-Uzbek border. On the opposite side of the river was a 50,000 person army of Tartars, waiting to recover their territory from the Soviets. Nationalists wanted Hitler to win to get their land back. During the day we worked in the weapons factory; at night we guarded the border to prevent people from invading. There were individual incidents but no open war. These incidents were never reported.

Though the war was winding down, we were building new factories—probably because of concern about Japan, since Germany was no longer a threat—five identical factories there at the same time in Chodshejli, Turkmenistan.

I met Lyuba, my future wife, in 1944 when I was a senior engineer and she a staff engineer. We were married in 1945 after the war.

On May 5, 1945, we knew the war was over. The treaty with Germany was signed on May 9. For all the poor, hungry, suffering people, it was joyful.

At the end of the war they wanted to assign experts to rebuild the cities and factories. In 1945 I was sent to the border town called Kiliya, on the Danube River near Rumania, to rebuild a grain-processing factory. Everything had been destroyed during the war when the Germans retreated. As supervisor of this reconstruction I had control over all the materials, including the grain, wood, metal, and other supplies. While I was in charge of the construction site, Lyuba was in charge of an engineering planning department.

There were people who worked for the KGB who wanted to get hold of some of these supplies for their personal use. When I wouldn't cooperate by giving them what they wanted, they began to make trouble for me.

A cousin of mine was sent by Stalin to a labor camp in Siberia (and remained there a total of fifteen years) for "undermining the Soviet system," for Trotskyism. At that time if you had a relative in prison for political dissension, you could lose your job and perhaps be sent to prison also.

The year 1945 produced a tremendous grain harvest. The government insisted that people quickly build those huge grain-processing factories and fill them with grain before the grain spoiled. The KGB pressured people to work overtime so they were working twenty-four hours a day.

Because of inefficiency in delivering construction materials, the mood of the construction work became unbearable. We got everything we needed only with great difficulty and supplies often came late. Under normal circumstances the construction would have taken two years, but we were ordered to finish in eight months, and, on top of this, the weather was not the greatest. Because we didn't have enough stone and construction materials to build the foundation, we took apart an old fortress near the Danube River for materials. Under tremendous pressure, the people I worked with built a temporary wooden bridge to the Danube River because time didn't allow us to build something more substantial. I tried my best because we desperately needed it to move grain from the factories to ships.

One of the supports of the wooden bridge was broken one night by a large truck loaded with grain. The KGB blamed me. They said I was like my cousin, that I did it on purpose. I was threatened with prison, but my former supervisor, who was in charge of a huge construction site in Kiev, went through high channels to clear my name.

In 1951, both of us wanted to enroll in courses which prepare engineers for the coal industry. But Jews were not permitted. We brought all our papers in and wanted to take the exams but were not allowed to do so. At the last minute, after we had gone to the highest officials, we finally got permission to take the exams—but in one day! All six exams in one day!

Because we graduated with honors, we had the right to choose where we were to go. We were given several choices. Three of them were very far north—by the glacial ocean in Siberia—and one was in Asia. We decided to go to Asia simply because we didn't have winter clothes. So we found ourselves near the Chinese border. There I became the chief engineer of coal mine construction. After two years, we moved to Tashkent, the largest city in Central Asia. There was a huge amount of construction going on there.

My mother lived in Kiev with our older daughter. We missed each other so much. Our daughter Svetlana was ten years old when we returned. If all of us had moved to the places where we worked in Asia, we would have lost our apartment and when we came back we would have had no place to live.

We returned to Kiev but regretted it because we were faced with serious anti-Semitism left over from World War II. We were not treated like other citizens; people avoided us. We had not been treated that way in Asia. But, in Kiev they needed me; they needed my skills. All told, I worked with grain processing factories for twenty-seven years as a technical leader for the Republican Unification project, which had construction sites all over the Ukraine but was based in Kiev. Lyuba, at the Kiev Project Institute, was in charge of a big construction bureau.

I would have liked to go back to Tashkent. Conditions for Jews were better there. I just wanted to work where the nationality on your passport wouldn't be so important.

Lyuba Boruchova Braker, civil engineer, retired
Born 1920, Korosten, the Ukraine

Some time in 1933, in the middle of the night somebody burst through the door and started searching the house and looking through everything. It was the secret police. They were looking for gold and jewelry and money. We had no gold in the house because at that time my parents always reinvested everything into the business. After they turned over the factory, they really didn't have anything, and they had sold a lot of things to be able to eat. The police didn't find anything, but they arrested my father anyway. He was in jail for six weeks, and then my mother decided to buy some jewelry, hide it in the ground somewhere, and then invite the secret police in and say, "I'm sorry. This is where I hid it and you can take it now." After she did this, my father was allowed to go. It was such nonsense. Over a period of years it happened several times, that someone would burst into the house looking for things, but that was the only time my mother did something like buying and hiding jewelry. They had too many debts to do that again. The secret police thought that *bourgeois* people were hiding money even though they had turned in factories and other property. Property was confiscated so everybody would be on an equal basis, nobody would be richer or poorer.

There were about 40,000 people in Korosten, and maybe 80 percent of them were Jewish. Korosten was close to Kiev, about seventy miles away. After my father turned the factory over to the state, he stayed on as a technical advisor.

But we saw that father could be arrested again by the secret police. So, in 1937 my parents left the house, left everything, and went to Dnepropetrovsk. They did this in secret. Nobody knew that they had left but I stayed behind because I was studying in school. I lived in our house with my older sister. My sister was working. My middle sister was in the English department of a college in Dnepropetrovsk. In 1938 my parents decided to sell the house. My mother came and sold it in one day. She just signed the papers over to the buyer. My older sister and I stayed at a neighbor's house until I graduated and then we moved to Dnepropetrovsk and joined the family. That's where I went to the institute. Dnepropetrovsk was a big city, but it had few Jews.

When I started at the institute it was the first time I had been in a Russian school, so courses were taught in Russian. I knew Russian very well, but the terminology of certain subjects like mathematics and physics I knew in Yiddish and that was a little harder, but I was a very good student.

On June 22, 1941, the radio announced that the war had started, and after about two weeks bombs began dropping. Those who stayed behind were not seen again. They were the people who died in places like Babi Yar and Kuznetsov. It was thought that since Dnepropetrovsk was far from the border the Germans would never get there, so, not only did we not leave right away, but we had relatives from other cities who came and stayed with us until we thought it was time to leave. We left in August, just a couple of days before the Germans entered the city.

We took only necessities like clothes with us and traveled by cattle train. We thought that the Germans would be stopped right away and wouldn't get very far so we didn't think of going further than the countryside. We thought that would be plenty far. We went to Pilonovo, a small village, a railroad stop, in the countryside between Stalingrad and Moscow. We stayed there until July 1942. Many people had gone to the front, so the village needed people. There, my parents and I worked on a collective farm gathering vegetables. My middle sister taught at the school, and my older sister was a bookkeeper. There wasn't much to eat, but we didn't starve.

In July of 1942, the bombs started dropping. All of a sudden there would be a huge number of planes, all directed on this small railway station. The sky turned black, and everything was just wiped out. After two days, whoever survived just left. We had to walk because the railroad was bombed out. We set off toward the next railroad stop, north to Kamyshin. We then took a train to Central Asia to Turkmenia. Some trains were blown up completely. A lot of people perished, but our train got through. We arrived two month later in October.

Though we experienced bombing in Kuybyshev, a city on the Volga, when we got to Central Asia it was safe. We went to that city because we had a cousin there. But pretty much we were there with strangers. Our parents stayed there until 1943, when Dnepropetrovsk was liberated. I moved around until the end of the war so I could keep working.

I went to Chodshejli as a civil engineer, and that is where Mikhail and I met. We worked in the same place. He was a senior engineer and I was one of his staff engineers. We were married in Chodshejli in 1945. I had a small apartment and that's where we had the wedding. It was very modest. I couldn't even buy a new dress. There was nothing in the stores for sale but there were a lot of men's ties. I bought thirteen ties and made a little dress out of them. I was very thin. I opened the ties and made a skirt from them, and from the linings I made a blouse. It was handwork that I did in the evenings after work.

Svetlana, my first child, was born in 1946. By then we had moved back to the Ukraine to Kiliya. She was born in the hospital. After the war there was no electricity in the hospital, so for light they used a kerosene lamp. A midwife helped me, an older woman who was very nice. I worked until the last day of my pregnancy and went to the hospital in the morning. The baby was healthy. She was a big girl, almost nine pounds. I had been very active so the delivery was not too bad. I stayed in the hospital for six days. After the delivery I stayed home for one month. We were living with my mother-in-law then, and she helped.

In Kiliya I was a staff engineer, doing construction planning, a lot of paperwork. This was the project of rebuilding the grain storage elevators that Mikhail supervised. In 1947 we moved to Ismail, and in 1949 we moved to Kiev. Until 1951 I continued to work in the building of grain elevators.

In December, 1955, Mikhail and I were transferred to Tashkent and we remained there until June 1956. Natasha was born there. They had electricity and a doctor there for the delivery. It wasn't a bad experience even though it was ten years later. Well, I wasn't eighteen anymore—I was thirty-five. I went there in the evening and had my daughter in the morning.

Birth control was not available in those years. I became pregnant four times between the two births and had abortions. My sisters also had a lot of abortions. Abortion was against the law, but in different cities the law was enforced differently. In Kiev I went to a hospital. Doctors performed the abortions, which were worse than labor. You gave the doctor some money and you got better service. (Sometimes you paid a little more and then it became legal!) There were years that you couldn't go to the hospital no matter how much you paid—until 1952 I think—and you did it at home. If it was done in the house, then you just paid whoever did it there. Now they have some methods of birth control, not the pill, but the IUD [intrauterine device]. Sometimes condoms were available, but they were not advertised.

Since 1988, starting with Gorbachev's reforms, we could attend synagogue— the only one in Kiev. Although it was watched, matzah was sold there and classes opened for the young children. During Jewish holidays there were lots of people who wanted to attend, but it couldn't accommodate everybody. Many times we tried to get in but were unable to. We would just stand there outside. Only religious activities were going on, nothing political.

We thought about leaving the Soviet Union for a long time but didn't try to do so, because people who tried lost their jobs. The worst part of life in the USSR was that we were deprived of normal conditions, normal human conditions people live in, just because we were Jews.

THE BERSUTSKY/ETINGEN FAMILY
A Life of Limitations

Izrail Bersutsky, economist, retired
Born 1929, Kotujany, Moldavia

My village of 6,000 people was near Kishinev. About 1,000 Jews resided here. My father had a small business selling fur pelts that he bought from trappers. I was the oldest child and had one brother and two sisters.

My father conducted business from our house and made a good living until 1940, when we became part of the Soviet Union and Soviet troops occupied this territory. All private businesses were stopped. The Jewish schools and synagogues were closed. My father was employed at the same work after that, but it was no longer his business.

In 1941, the war broke out and the Germans invaded. My father was sent to Siberia to a "work front" on a construction project. All the able-bodied Jewish men were sent away, but the Moldavian men were allowed to remain.

My mother took us as far as the River Dnestr in Moldavia with all the other Jewish people who remained after the men left. A ghetto camp was created there. Only five families from this ghetto escaped to Uzbekistan. My mother's relatives remained in the ghetto, her sister, her father, and all the others. We never heard from them again.

Most of the people were killed when the German soldiers bombarded the place. They would fly over the camp and drop bombs, if they saw people or a train. A few families survived the ghetto, but from the concentration camps, nobody came back. The bombing was horrible. I saw how they killed people. Parts of bodies, hands and legs, were spread all over. After that, food was very scarce. Once in two days we had meals, a cup of cereal and something to drink. On the train, we were given soup and bread every other day. After we reached Uzbekistan it took a month to get food regularly. We had no money and only the clothes we wore.

For three years we lived in Shorechan, a small village, and in the town of Fergana for two more years. My mother and I worked, but my brother and sisters were too small. We were given 400 grams of brown bread a day for each person by the authorities. I worked eighteen hours a day on a farm gathering cotton and also grain. My earnings were two pounds of grain a day. When possible, my mother traded this grain for milk and vegetables.

Although we were in the South, winters still were cold, the temperature falling to 35 degrees Fahrenheit. We lived in a one room hut made of *glina* [clay] without furnishings, electricity, or water. It had a roof, and there was one very small window; during the day for light we opened the door; at night it was dark inside. We carried water from the river, but it was polluted. We slept on hay spread over a dirt floor.

While my mother and I picked cotton, the younger children took care of themselves. Summer was very hot, and when we got a cut, we got an infection. The fertilizer we used was very bad for the lungs. Once the children were older they too went to work, even if they were sick, or they would not receive any bread! They had only bread. In summer it was better because we could gather berries. At harvest time they dispensed a soup that wasn't very good, and the workers would stand in line for it. It was offered only when they harvested, to the father of the family, for two months in the year. In my family only I had a cup of soup. Because of lack of food and medicine, people were dying every day.

After the war ended, my father joined us in 1946 from Siberia. He was working in a military chemical plant, but he was not well after his work in Siberia. In Uzbekistan it was very hot, and everybody from our family had tropical malaria. Father was the sickest.

When we returned to Kotujany we found our house had been used by German soldiers as a stable for their horses. We had to clean it up and rebuild it as best we could. Out of a thousand Jewish people only 100 survived. The synagogues and *heders* remained closed. I worked in a produce warehouse and went to night school. As the eldest son, I became the main support of the family.

I graduated from night school when I was twenty-two and moved to Kishinev. There at thirty, I graduated from technical college and worked as a manager in a small government-owned food market. I went on to earn a master's degree in economics. Although I was a trained economist, as a Jew I could not get work in this field. Instead I worked in a small college, the Cooperative Technicum, teaching food processing. In 1961, I married Frida Braunshtein, an electrical engineer, when I was thirty-three and she was twenty-six.

In 1973 when I first applied to emigrate, I was refused. The Soviet government required that Jews who wanted to emigrate had to pay for their education—6,000 rubles per diploma, 12,000 for my wife and me! We decided to wait until times were better to reapply. The next opportunity came in 1980, and I was again refused and had to give up my teaching job. I found work in a food warehouse.

The only thing I miss about Russia is that my wife, Frida, is not here with me. She died September 7, 1989, three weeks after we arrived in the United States.

Greta Bersutsky Etingen, computer programmer
Born 1962, Kishinev, Moldavia
When I was a child my mother spent a lot of time with me, and I think everything I know is because of her. At the age of seven I started school; I also went to a special school for music and studied the piano for seven years.

At school I had problems in fifth grade, when I was about ten years old. In Russia, your father's first name is used as your middle name. It was the time of the Yom Kippur War in Israel, and the Russians hated Israel, so when Russian girls and boys heard my father's name, Izrail, they laughed. The teacher laughed also and tried to get everybody to say my middle name, because it embarrassed me. The two or three other Jewish children in the class were teased this way too, so we stuck together.

My mother celebrated the Jewish holidays at home as best she could—Passover, Shavuot, Purim, Rosh Hashanah. On Yom Kippur we stayed home and fasted. I was never in a synagogue in Russia. It was hard to observe Jewish holidays, but when we could we stayed home from work or school.

I graduated public school in 1979 and entered the mechanical institute in Kishinev. I didn't graduate until 1986 because after we had applied for a visa, they would not accept me there until 1981. There was a limit on the number of Jews they took, but it was the *only* one that would accept Jewish students, even though Kishinev had a university and seven institutes. There were about 8,000 students in the institute; maybe 500 were Jews.

In Russia, Jewish people knew that they would be treated differently. They gave us different tests; our homework had more problems that were harder to solve. But it was not all bad, I think, because we *could* do this work. I graduated in 1986 and worked in a mechanical plant as a drafting designer. This is what I would like to do here, but because we didn't use computers for drafting design in Russia, I have to go to school to acquire the skill.

I met Alex in Kishinev. He came there after his institute training to work in Kishinev, and then we met each other! He came to the engineering institute from Leningrad. His friend was my friend's brother, and they introduced us. We were married in 1986, the year I graduated.

My family always had a very bad apartment; it was only one room. The kitchen was without windows and like a closet. The bathroom was very bad, no bath, only a shower. My parents and I all lived in the same room. After Alex and I got married, we had a smaller room for the two of us. Bela was born in 1987. When she was nine months old, we applied at OVIR; in 1988 we received permission to leave. I then sold our piano and everything we had or gave things away. We flew from Moscow to Vienna and were there two weeks. It was nice there, but my mother was already very sick. We went on to Rome for about a month and then came here.

Alex works as a machinist for a company involved with military aircraft. In Russia he was a manufacturing engineer, working with tool and die and machinery parts. I work part time at McDonald's. We have had much help from Jewish organizations. Right now, they are trying to find jobs for us, for me and for Alex. From Russia, all I miss is my friends.

THE GEKHTER FAMILY
The Tragedy of Our Parents

Lydia Halip Gekhter, dentist, retired
Born 1922, Chirnigov district, the Ukraine

Mother didn't work. Father was a boss of the trade department of the secret police. Before the Revolution he was a civil servant. I knew that my father's mother was Jewish, so I considered myself Jewish. We had matzah, but we didn't celebrate Jewish holidays. My childhood was at the time when people were eliminated for being Jewish.

We had everything. My childhood was very good. We rented a brick house with two big rooms, a big kitchen, a porch, all this for four people. There was a big garden and running water from a pump in the back yard. Our neighbors were wealthy Russians, cultured people, professors who rented the house to us. I didn't know any anti-Semitism.

I met Raphael, my future husband, in the hospital in Frunze, Kazakhstan, during World War II, where I was working as a nurse after being evacuated there. He had bad wounds in his head and leg. His family was from Minsk, and he was very handsome. He had been at the front, serving as a lieutenant in the tank division and was wounded trying to cross the Dnieper River at the time the regiment was surrounded. Germans pushed and kicked him and left him alone to die. In fact, his parents received a letter that he died during the attack.

Later my husband served as a military doctor in Siberia near the Manchurian border, and I was a dentist. He was sent there on military orders, not as a punishment. Although while there I did not feel different because I was Jewish, when we came back from Lake Baikal, after eighteen years, my husband didn't receive a promotion because he was a Jew.

Vladimir Gekhter, engineer/tool and die maker
Born 1952, Minsk, Byelorussia

We lived in Siberia fifteen years. It was very hard to live there. I was there from the age of two until I was sixteen years old. When one is very young, the world is wonderful. I thought that I was the happiest child in the world because in child-care and in school every day I was told I was—because I had been born in the Soviet Union. But, on the other hand, my friends knew I was Jewish.

When I told my parents about the boys calling me a Jew, my father told me to be proud because there were many famous Jewish people. But this was little help to me because I was surrounded by friends who were different from me. Even if

I were the best in the class or in any activity, I would still hear behind my back "Jew." I had very good Russian friends who understood that it wasn't fair, but what could they do? I can't say that all Russians are anti-Semitic. There are a lot of good people in Russia.

My father wanted me to grow up with other Jews. That's why he wanted to bring me to Minsk. He dreamed about this his whole life. It was a great gift to me because I had thought I was the only one on the planet who was Jewish, and there I found Jewish friends. After we came to Minsk, my father got his illness. He worked for a couple of months. In Siberia there was a shortage of dentists, so my mother had no problem working there. When she came to Minsk, she couldn't find work as a dentist and found work as a nurse.

When I was growing up, I wanted to be a doctor like my father. Many of his friends who were teachers in the medical institute told me, "Vladimir, don't even try to go to the medical institute. Now what they look at is not your knowledge but your nationality." There wasn't much competition for engineering because of the low position and salary, but the Jewish quota for medical school used to be 2 percent. I don't know any recent Jewish medical school graduates.

That is the tragedy of our parents. On the one hand, my father knew that Jews were the objects of under-the-table jokes. On the other hand, he really believed in communism and loved Stalin. He told me, "When I went to attack in World War II, to fight, I cried, 'For Stalin, for the Communist party!'"

I was invited to the Academy of Sciences to work, but in Russia it was all paperwork and approval, all procedure. I had to fill out the papers and get approval from my Communist bureau, but I couldn't get the papers and go ahead because I couldn't get access to some equipment in the academy. As a result I couldn't finish my work because I couldn't get equipment, special adjustments, fixtures or official books. I left this job because I felt like a small child beaten by a very cruel man.

I was asked to build a plant on a *kolkhoz* and spent years working on it. I found, fixed, and installed equipment. It's not like in America where you call and get equipment tomorrow. In Russia you fight for every machine, for all materials. I believe I was a very good manager because my plant had made 2 or 3 million net profit. Everybody worked for their salary.

I had some power, made decisions, and developed new products myself. I also developed connections between sales, development, and production. After I had all the connections, they tried to push me out because I had too much power. I decided then that this country, the Soviet Union, will never change, except maybe after a civil war.

I didn't want my kids to have the same feelings I had while growing up. I wanted them to feel equal. My father told me, "You should always reach for higher goals, because anyone can reach the low and middle." Although I listened and had high goals, I didn't realize my dream of a higher of education, or attain my goals. Today I still have high goals. From the Soviet Union I brought my family, my occupation, and my knowledge. I brought shoes, shirts, and ninety dollars in my pocket for everybody.

It's my opinion Russia is not a good place for Jewish people to live. It's bad for everybody. But for Jews? They are very afraid. It's more dangerous for them.

Anna Gomon Gekhter, accountant
Born 1954, Bobruisk, Byelorussia

We moved to Kirov in the republic of Russia when I was small, and I grew up there. I remember it as a middle-sized town. We were the only Jews. If there were other Jewish families, I didn't know them. We moved there because my father was in the military service and he was sent there to serve.

Living in this small town was very difficult. Before and after the Revolution, it was a place where people were sent as a punishment. But, after the Soviets came, it was a place of military service. I know it was a place of punishment, because it was cold there. It's near the Ural mountains. Some famous writers and revolutionaries were sent there. All her life my mother hated this place. They were there more than twenty years.

There were no labor-saving devices there. I helped by washing the dishes and cleaning the floor, everything by hand! My younger brother did nothing. My mother made me feed my brother and cook for him too, but I don't think I did it very well. Everything I made for him he put down the toilet.

When my father, who was a member of the Communist party, quit the army, there were no political discussions. It wasn't acceptable at that time to discuss such matters, but later on, I heard that he did not choose to quit. He was forced out during Khrushchev's time when it was the policy to get rid of Jewish officers. After World War II, there were a lot of Jewish officers who stayed in the army.

After his army service, my father became an accountant at a big department of the same plant where he later became assistant manager. I have one memory about these days. My mother was angry at him because he was never home on time, and she thought that he preferred to be at work. She was so angry she went to his office to speak to him. Maybe he was working so hard because he was afraid. At that time he did not have the proper education for this job.

I was always afraid of something being said to me because I was Jewish. I knew I was silly. It was just me. Even now sometimes I feel a little pressured at work when people say something about Jews. I feel timid, but I have not suffered very much from this. That's what is strange! I am afraid of what might happen. There have been a few little things, but you can't always live without incidents. For example, when I graduated from institute I was sent to Minsk to work. The manager of the department acted as if she did not want me. She told me I'd have to go to a collective farm to pick potatoes and that I would have to travel on business trips. But my son was a one-year-old, and I couldn't do it. I went to the manager of this organization and explained about the baby. He was kind and found me a different place. So it was just a little incident.

Everybody did collective farming, but they didn't have the right to send a woman with a little child. Everyone went, even mothers. This is duty! Every fall we went and stayed for one week, then returned at harvest time.

I can't understand why my mother didn't leave with us. She is a doctor and suffered so much because of being Jewish. Often she heard *Evreyka* or *zhidovka*. Sometimes patients would even say, "Go to Israel and treat people there." I believe she stayed because of her mother. My grandmother is religious and follows Jewish traditions. She would never leave Russia; she doesn't want to abandon the graves of her husband and children.

ALEXANDER AND IRINA UMAN
1984: Under the Eye of Big Brother

Alexander Uman, electrical engineer
Born 1948, Kiev, the Ukraine

It happened that I had been invited to a party in Kirovgrad in the Ukraine, where I was working for a month and living in a hotel. At the time I was working as a field engineer and not paid much. It was in 1984 and we were just talking, politics and everything else. A Jewish gentlemen who I knew enough to go out with on occasion had invited me to the party. There I met someone that I now know worked for the KGB.

As I learned later, this man reported to the KGB that I had said something suspicious and that I had borrowed some dollars from someone. At that time, during the Andropov regime, in 1984, the Korean jumbo jet liner had been shot down. After a month, people from Kiev wrote to me and told me that some gentlemen from the KGB approached them and asked about me and told them to write down evidence about me. Some of the evidence came from people from where I worked, people who were not high-minded, who were drinkers, and who did not like me too well anyway. They were afraid of the KGB, and the KGB forced them to write and give evidence.

They spoke to everybody around me in such a way that it seemed I was of questionable character. About a year after that, I was "invited" to KGB headquarters for an interview. This time two officers took me to their office and asked me questions for about five or six hours. My wife knew about it and was very worried. They showed me all these papers, and they told me, "Here, these go back a year and another year before that." They accused of me of this and that and wanted me to sign papers that were "evidence" about a period when I was in a certain area.

At this time they didn't allow Jewish people to learn Hebrew. They were very strange about foreign languages, and they were opposed to Jewish culture and thought. They were looking for Hebrew teachers, and this is the way they did it. They were asking me about the Jewish man I knew in Kirovgrad. They tried to frighten me into giving evidence. They said they were going to put me into prison, but I said that I could not tell them anything. I said that the man in Kirovgrad was a nice person, that we had gone to the theater and had mutual cultural interests, and that was all. But they pressured and pressured me, and the next thing they said was, "If you don't sign, we will tell everyone at your workplace that whoever put this in writing should appear at a meeting and give evidence against you."

There wasn't any question of treason in the accusation. But if they held such a meeting, I probably would not be able to survive at my job. I thought the meeting would not be that bad, although I never had such an experience before in my life. To me it seemed stupid. And after all this, it was only a threat.

I think they really did not intend to send me to prison and only wanted to put pressure on me and frighten me. At the end they said that I could go, but if something else ever came out, this was the last time that they could let me off. But I wasn't sure, because they could tell me one thing and my friends something else.

My neighbor, in my flat, had told them everything about me. He said that I listened to the Voice of America on the radio, and I did. He had been a captain in the Soviet army, but after that, he was sent to prison for taking bribes from soldiers who wanted to stay in Kiev.

Irina Chervonsky Uman, electrical engineer
Born 1957, Kiev, the Ukraine

I wanted to be a teacher. But it was impossible. I couldn't study at the teachers' college. Almost no Jews could become teachers. So I forgot about it and went to Moscow and took a course in college in communications. They teach engineering for communication—for the mail, automation for the mail service, sorters, and so on. I was there five years. Although I lived in Kiev and took correspondence courses, twice a year I had exams in Moscow. After school I worked as an electrical drafter, designer, and then engineer in the same company. I became an electrical engineer after the five years.

It was a very big engineering company. Many Jewish people worked there. My boss was Jewish and my friends—I had many, many friends. I liked working there. I worked fifteen years in the same place. I had a break when I was pregnant and took two years off then. When we got married we lived in our own place; it was bad, a small room, but our own. When we had the baby we still lived there. We shared the kitchen. Two other families cooked with me. We had many, many problems. There were two other families, which meant three women in the kitchen. I had good relations with them, but they didn't like each other. It was difficult. They weren't Jewish. They were Ukrainians, and we could hear when they spoke with other people about the Jews. After four years we got a new apartment. We had applied just after we were married and waited seven years. We were very lucky! Some people wait twenty years. We moved in 1986 to the new apartment in the new area. It was a good apartment. It was far from our old place. It was very mixed. I didn't know Jewish people there. We still worked. I had a very comfortable feeling about my job and when I came home, I was with my family. I heard what people say about Jews, but it didn't affect me. We lived far from relatives, but we met each other once a week. My friends came to my apartment, usually, and we went to theirs.

The only time I felt bad about anti-Semitism was when I couldn't go to college. I tried three times in two years. It was not a good time.

We decided to leave Russia in 1979, a year after we got married. So we applied. By then emigration was closed. We didn't lose our jobs or anything. I wasn't a boss, I was just a drafter. I had some uncomfortable disputes with my boss, but that was it. He asked me why I want to leave the country.

When Alex was investigated by the KGB I had a terrible feeling. We didn't tell our parents or friends about this. We spoke about it only with each other. It was a terrible time.

STAN AND ELEANOR KHAZAN
They Told Us All Was Well

Stan Khazan, electrical engineer/designer
Born 1953, Romny, the Ukraine

I was born in a little Ukrainian city, Romny, and lived there for one year and then our family moved to Lvov, a big town. I lived for a long time in Lvov. In Romny, we lived in one apartment with my grandfather and grandmother and my mother's sister. We were all in two rooms. I remember the apartment because they are still living in it. We used to visit my grandparents every year after we moved.

It is difficult to talk about the neighborhood where we lived in Lvov. We lived in a four-story building with many apartments on a floor. The children I played with were mostly non-Jews. In Russia my name was Slava. It is a Polish or Ukrainian name but not Jewish. I was not the only Slava on our street, and when they wanted to call me or one of the others, I was "Slava-yid." I had only one Jewish friend, and he was a little older.

My friends were mostly Ukrainian, Polish, and a few Russian. The Jewish families were scattered and did not live close together. This gave me very mixed feelings. Mostly I felt comfortable with my friends, but I remember, and my mother remembers, when I once said, "Mother, I don't want to be a Jew."

Sometimes I had problems. I remember an instance when I was alone and all my companions threw stones at me. I did not understand why nobody helped me.

On political holidays we would have a day off. We would meet with relatives and talk together. Not really a celebration. Russian families often discussed politics. My parents criticized the government regime, but when I was younger I disagreed with them. I said this was not a good idea because if the government made mistakes, it is the fault of the times. I believed in the system, but they did not. This is the way Russian education works. "Communist ideas are the best ideas in the world. Capitalism is the worst thing for people." The whole party line.

In college, we had competitive exams before we could become a student at the university, and there was a quota for Jewish students. This was illegal because the law said that all nationalities should be equal. In my town, Lvov, it may have been worse than in other Ukrainian towns because of more anti-Semitism. I know that in Lvov it was something special when a Jew entered medical college or the university. Before World War II, the population of Lvov was approximately one-third Jewish. After the war there were still many Jews there, but when the Jews were allowed to emigrate, a large number left. When I was a child, I remember there was a place in Lvov where you could meet with other Jews. Now the only place left in Lvov where Jews can meet is in the Jewish cemetery.

Eleonor Khazan, computer programmer
Born 1959, Kiev, the Ukraine

At the time of the Chernobyl explosion, our daughter Julia was four years old. It happened on Friday night, April 26, 1986, but we didn't know anything until Monday, when some people at work knew and told us. Stan didn't believe it. He felt that if it really happened, somebody would inform us. There was nothing in the papers or on television. It was almost the first of May, a work holiday.

People whose work was related to nuclear physics understood that it was dangerous. I couldn't understand because it was not my field. They advised people who lived in the city to leave and to drink milk with iodine. The second day after Chernobyl, our friends' relatives called them from America and asked, "Are you still alive? Get away from Kiev!" and gave them real information. They said don't drink the water, just use mineral water. Then my parents' friends sent us a long letter with instructions on what to do. They knew that our government would not tell us.

Some people thought because of the tragedy the government would cancel the celebration. Everybody said that we should close the doors and windows, not do anything outside. The outside air was very dangerous, especially for children. But our government decided to hold this demonstration to show people that nothing happened, and we had to go to a bicycle competition. I don't think any of the parents wanted their children to participate in this demonstration, but school teachers pressured the children. And it worked. Because people do believe what the government says. You know, if the government says we should do it, then maybe it is not so dangerous.

On May 5, after four days of holiday, we saw the news in the paper. Usually we had a two-day holiday, but it fell on a weekend. It was really good weather, and people had picnics outside in the forest. And then, on the fifth of May we came to work, and my coworkers were really upset because friends of theirs who worked in nuclear physics said that some people drove their children to other cities to stay with their grandparents or others. I panicked. Stan did not have a work phone, so I just called my mother and said I was going to the train station to buy some tickets.

I didn't even say anything to my boss. I didn't think about my job. On my way to the train station I worried about the future. When I arrived there was a really huge line, and everybody talked about the same thing—Chernobyl. That the only ones who got to leave the city were the children of officials who left before the fifth of May! They sent their children away the twenty-sixth of April.

In the line everybody talked about what he or she knew. I told them what I knew, what my experience was. And we just had to analyze the information the best we could.

That evening they began to tell to us on radio and on television not to worry. "We are working on this problem. We will take care of it."

We had only one place to go, to Stan's parents, to Lvov. It wasn't a good place to go, but it was better than Kiev. My parents did not go, just my grandmother, Julia, and I. Grandmother stayed with Julia, and I returned to work. Kiev was like a dead city. I never knew how awful the feeling was when you don't see any children.

Every institute had devices to measure the radiation, Geiger counters, and civil defense nuclear experts, but they didn't give us any information about the radiation level.

Of course, people in Kiev were angry, and the more intelligent people were the angriest. Many people who don't know anything at all about nuclear radiation were not as concerned. Our government was saying all is well, don't panic, don't believe what other people tell you. But educated people knew. You can't see nuclear radiation; you can't touch it. Still, what could we do? We could only go to the library and take out a book on physics or nuclear energy, to try to analyze the situation ourselves.

And then the heads of the companies would not give the mothers a day off or vacation time. We had a schedule for the year. You couldn't just call up and say that you were sick. You needed a doctor's signature as proof. But if I were to ask, the doctor would say, "No, you are not sick."

People were very angry. Especially since government officials, to prevent panic, said don't permit the women to leave the city with children, though their children had already left Kiev. At this moment I said, if everybody *could* leave the country, nobody would stay here. Not because they were afraid of radiation but because people realized no one cared about them. But if they don't care about me, or my children, don't prevent *me* from caring for myself and my family!

At home in their Chicago apartment in 1992, Mikhail Shvartsman and
Lyuba Braker proudly display photos that depict their personal history
beginning with their marriage in 1945. Photo © 1992 by Bruce
Mondschain. All rights reserved.

Greta Etingen on her weekly visit to bring groceries to her father, Izrail
Bersutsky. Photo © 1992 by Bruce Mondschain. All rights reserved.

The Gekhter family enjoys a breath of fresh air: Vladimir, his mother Lydia, and wife Anna. Vladimir and Anna have just acquired a home in the suburbs. Photo © 1992 by Bruce Mondschain. All rights reserved.

On a brisk day, the Uman family pauses in front of a fresh produce stand in West Rogers Park. From left: Vladimir, Alexander, Igor, and Irina. Photo © 1992 by Bruce Mondschain. All rights reserved.

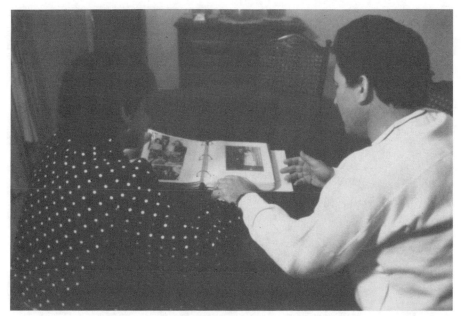

Betya and Boris "Gilman" take a moment to reminisce with the family photo album. They are still reluctant to reveal their identity. Photo © 1992 by Bruce Mondschain. All rights reserved.

Lena and Serge Goryunov take a quick break to plan their day's activities. Photo © 1992 by Bruce Mondschain. All rights reserved.

Daniel Danilov, Shamail's father, standing far right, with Red Army comrades during World War II. Picture taken in Baku, Azerbaijan. Daniel fought for Berlin and was later wounded in Czechoslovakia and invalided home.

Chelmnitsky farm, in the Ukraine. Pictured from left: Yelena's cousin Victor, her mother Svetlana, Yelena, sister Nadzhezda, and cousin Alla, circa 1959.

Yelena and Shamail (Sasha) signing marriage document while official observes, April 21, 1981. The wedding celebration was a few days later.

GEORG AND ANYA PAVEL
A Place of No Return

Georg Pavel (pseudonym), Ph.D., heat and mass transfer/metallurgist

Born 1946, Minsk, Byelorussia

My father grew up in a family of nine children. He had begun working, but then World War II began. He had finished some course of study, but never graduated from an institute; he was a salesman. By the second year of the war, he was in military service. My mother was at school in the Leningrad Academy of Biology and Psychology when the war broke out. She spent all of World War II there. She survived the blockade though she told me she buried a lot of friends and gave virtually her last piece of bread to help bury them.

My mother told me that before the war, Leningrad had huge stocks of food, of clothes. Then one day, all the stocks were burned. Huge stocks! She guessed it was done at Stalin's orders. Stalin hated the city because Leningrad never supported him; Stalin's enemy, Kirov, was from Leningrad. Leningrad is known for its intellectualism.

Of course, Russia can really make things a mess. They sent workers and farmers into that city to live and work, and in a few years they lowered its cultural level. To me it seems that Stalin had planned it. Actually, even now, the cultural level of Minsk, Leningrad, and Moscow is down from before the war.

My grandparents from my father's side were both killed in World War II. I know that the Nazis killed my father's brother in a place called Chojniki. After the war when my father made inquiries about his brother he realized he had been killed only about a mile from where my father was fighting at the time.

My father didn't like to talk about the war. He was stationed near Leningrad and conditions were terrible. They didn't know where the Germans were or where the other Russians were. It was confusing, and many officers died. He was probably a lieutenant then but became a captain after the war. He said he spent a lot of time in the snow, and all around him was death.

My father had a lot of war medals for Leningrad and he valued these medals more than others. They are not like the modern medals that Brezhnev and the others gave out. But the Russians gave little recognition to the contribution of Jews in the armed forces during the war.

I was the *only* Jewish kid in the class. When I was eleven or twelve, one day in front of the class my teacher decided to analyze words with the syllable *zhid* in them. The class started to laugh at me. So, I stuck my neighbor with a pen! This was before ballpoint pens, and the pen had a sharp point! My father had to come to school and talk with the teacher. After that, the other boy realized that I was fighting for something important to me. When we were grown up at the institute we still had a good relationship. He realized that I was tough and that I wouldn't accept any stuff like that.

During the Khrushchev years, I once went to a Jewish concert at the synagogue in Minsk, and the KGB took pictures of me with my grandfather. I was between seventeen and nineteen years old. They kept these pictures and because of them I was not permitted to enter the post-graduate course at the Byelorussian Polytechnical Institute from which I graduated. However I was able to continue at the Institute of Heat and Mass Transfer, thanks to Aleksey Lykoff, the director there.

Lykoff was a very old, intelligent man who was not anti-Semitic. He had finished in the old Russian educational system before the Revolution and knew French. He said, "I don't care about nationality." Of course, he was pressured by other people around him. I was lucky to have the head of the institute accept me for post-graduate work. I was honored that this famous man would invite me to discuss scientific problems with him. He really encouraged me.

I did my thesis and research in a very interesting field. It was on the Reiner effect. Max Reiner is an Israeli professor, who discovered a very particular aspect of the behavior of air. I read his research in published articles and I knew that he was a professor at the Haifa Technological Institute in Israel. After I received the Ph.D., I just continued research in this field. Mr. Lykoff believed it was a very worthwhile field of research.

Lykoff wished to become president of the Byelorussian Academy of Scientists. He was famous, he had medals from the Paris Academy and the London Academy. Many scientists, even in Chicago, know Lykoff's name and work.

But he was not given this position! They gave it to someone nobody knew at all, a man who hated Lykoff. Because Lykoff could not get money for research, the pressures on him were terrible. Then he had two heart attacks and died at age sixty-three from a third. At the time of his death, his wife decided not to bury him in Minsk but in Moscow. Because he had been so great to me, I left work and went to Moscow for his funeral; we drove all night to get there.

After Lykoff died, I was forced by the laboratory chief to leave the institute. Once they pressured me out of the institute, I applied for permission to leave Russia. We applied to leave Russia in February 1978. We "stood in line" almost one year just to turn in our documents. Our son was not yet one year old. My work documents were stamped that I was going to leave Russia and Minsk for Israel. We were able to turn in our documents in November and were refused in December; we were given no reason. They treated us like animals. We sent letters asking for the reason we could not leave Russia. We had meetings with the hierarchy of OVIR, but no one spoke with us. It was if we were dogs.

At OVIR we went into a huge room with no place for us to sit. They did not say anything. I stood; my wife stood. I said I would like to leave Russia because I had relatives in Israel. They ignored me and kept asking, "Why do you want to leave Russia?" I was afraid to say anything because you could be put in jail if they didn't like what you said. But, I hadn't been careful enough. I failed myself. I had told someone that it was an error when Russia sent troops to Afghanistan. I was just talking with a couple of guys around me. In Russia you never know what will be reported. Then they refused me. It was my mistake; I wasn't careful.

My wife lost her job when we first applied for permission. For two years she was not able to work except to do some designs, drawings, schematics, or things like that. I worked at different places. I drew some projects for students, translated some articles from English. Sometimes I worked in different shops to repair things, radios, small appliances. Then, about a year after refusal I found a very small position with a very low salary as a design engineer and started to work again. Almost to the last day I kept two jobs in order to feed my family. My wife could not even find a job after the refusal. Only in the last years when *perestroika* started, she found work as a salesclerk. My mother helped us out with food and other things.

Before we were refused, we lived in a one-bedroom apartment on the first floor of a five-floor apartment building with four apartments on each floor. Each apartment was allowed a small compartment in the basement for storing potatoes and other vegetables. In the spring a terrible smell would come into our apartment from this stuff. Because of it our son was ill and crying all the time.

In 1984, we exchanged apartments for our son's health. There were advertisements in the newspaper for exchanging apartments. We found one by a widower with two adult sons. Since the sons had married and left his apartment, he wanted to move. At that time our friends had just gone to the United States and sent us a postal money order. So we went to his apartment and we paid him money for it. It was a slightly better apartment, about the same size as the other. Then I was able to see that my son had physical therapy, and he started feeling better.

A couple of times there was a fire near our apartment and I was concerned for my family. I didn't know if we were the target or not.

We had lived there about one or two years when I had a terrible confrontation with my daughter's teacher. He discussed her in front of the class! Again it concerned a Jewish activity, a Jewish concert, which she had attended with me. He said things like, "Just remember what she did, everybody." He said, "Start with first grade."

In Russia they kept an eye on you all your life, from when you first started school, everything went on your record. The fact that I had stabbed another child with a pen was on my record. It was even on my daughter's record! My children's records were blemished because of what I had done as a child. And because they were Jews, too, they would be held back. I felt that during the last year anti-Semitism in Minsk had gotten quite terrible, the worst since 1964, since what I experienced at technical school.

When I applied to leave Russia, there was a three-hour open meeting and they told me that if it were 1937, they would have killed me. There was a large round table, with people sitting around at it and standing. It made me feel horrible. I was sweating, but I kept myself cool and collected, to try to be more wise than these people. To show that I was strong, not to break. I spoke softly. They shouted,

"You are like Sakharov! Everybody around you is wrong but you are never wrong!" Sakharov was being slandered in all the papers at this time.

There were about forty people in the auditorium. I had to go to this meeting because otherwise they would have just thrown me out. I was the only Jew on this professional committee. I had to keep my job; I had to feed my children. They shouted at me openly. I just said that it was not 1937, the time of the purges under Stalin. I told them I was not going to cross the border like a spy; I would like to leave Russia openly. What I had done was according to the law.

Afterward, at the order of the director, I had to leave my position and take a lower one. So I quit my job.

We left Russia in November of 1988. I remember the day exactly. We had applied six different times in the hope that we would get permission and leave Russia as soon as possible. We got permission on the tenth of November, and on November 22, we left Russia. We left our furniture, everything, to my wife's sister, to relatives, friends. When the door opened, we just grabbed our children and left.

We had plane tickets departing from Moscow. We went by train to Moscow and from Moscow to Vienna by jet. We wanted to leave as soon as possible, so we went through customs during the night.

When we set out, we didn't know what the circumstances would be, so we packed some grain, rice, honey, and sugar, "just in case." In customs, they made a total mess of it all. They tried to find a second bottom in my shoes! They tore them apart. They even broke apart all my chess pieces. The chess pieces! They checked for three hours; we were standing all the time. These customs examinations took place in one big room with a big table, and everybody could watch.

It is a mistake for Americans to believe that anything changed with Gorbachev. He is anti-Semitic; in Russia you must be in order to be in the government. Gorbachev is not very strong. Russia has a huge army, a huge police force, a huge KGB. They spend money for the military so that everybody can stay in their positions of privilege.

I believe, first, that the army and the police will be against Gorbachev, because they want to keep the strong order there before. Second of all, Gorbachev is afraid to make changes. Even if he would like to make changes, he is afraid to. You never can tell on which side changes will fall in Russia. I don't think Gorbachev is any different than any other party heads. He is just interested in getting money from the West. The economy of the country is simply in terrible shape.

I read an interesting novel, *Life and Fate*, by Vasily Grossman. This history was not published for twenty years. It was about Jewish people during World War II. About how Jewish scientific people were repressed in Stalin's time and confined in camps.

Grossman wrote that anti-Semitism existed in all countries from the time of Rome, but that in Russia there was government anti-Semitism. Officially they denounced it, but they seemed to encourage the national uprisings where people were killing each other. I have a deep feeling in my soul that they caused it purposely, because then people didn't think about their own plight.

We came in January 1989 to the United States. I know that I will never go back to Russia. Not even for a visit. In Russia I was afraid for my children. I was afraid they might make up something about us and that our lives might be in danger. After they refused us, I never felt safe in Russia.

Anya Pavel (pseudonym), engineer/computer programmer
Born 1955, Minsk, Byelorussia

My mother became one of the leading doctors in Minsk after she established a small women's department for expectant mothers with heart problems. My aunt, my mother's sister, is also a doctor. They were really devoted to each other and graduated from medical school together.

My father was a construction engineer and the chief of a huge building company. In Russia for a Jewish man to have such a position was not easy. It really showed the respect he had earned. He was a very energetic man.

Before they could marry, my father dated my mother seven years. She lived in Gomel, and he lived in Minsk. Every weekend he would go from Minsk to Gomel. My grandmother didn't permit her to marry him, because her family had a little higher level of education than his family.

My mother's father was a doctor who graduated from St. Petersburg University, now Leningrad University. My grandmother was a chemistry teacher. They had a very high level of education for those times before World War II.

My father lost his parents and sister in the Minsk ghetto during World War II. When the fascists came to Minsk, the first thing they did was to round up the Jewish people in a ghetto they set up and then kill most of them.

My father had two brothers and a sister. The men all served in World War II. His sister was only sixteen. She was with his parents and uncles and aunts, all of whom lived in Minsk. My father had a plan to help them escape to the forest, and went back to Minsk to get them. One hour before he arrived, they were all killed.

There are things in our family that are hard to explain. On both sides of our family nobody had red hair, except my father's little sister. When he spoke of the past, he told me about it. Our daughter, who was named for her, is now the only one in the family with red hair.

My mother also had a story of hardship. In 1937 it was a disastrous time, not only for Jewish people but for many educated people. Stalin either sent them to special concentration camps or they were arrested and put in prison. My mother's father was arrested, without any explanation. My grandmother had to live alone with the four children. It was such a hard time that she died when she was only forty-seven years old, while my grandfather was still in prison.

My mother was the oldest in their family. Her sister and two brothers lived with her. They were allowed to send him only one small food package once a month. Then suddenly, they stopped hearing about him, and for five or six years they didn't know where he was. After ten years Grandfather was released from prison. He had two heart attacks there and was very sick when he came home.

I remember my grandfather because when he died I was almost eleven. He lived with us but never spoke with his grandchildren about prison. Sometimes they closed the door and he spoke with my mother and her brothers about it. We never learned why he was released, any more than why he was arrested.

My father went to Jewish school before World War II. He knew Yiddish really well. My mother didn't speak any, but she understood. Sometimes when they wanted to hide something from us, my father spoke Yiddish and my mother answered in Russian. We understood everything! When I was maybe three or four years old, my father would say, "We're speaking Chinese."

My father was a man of action. I never saw him sitting and watching television, never. He was involved in doing all kinds of business. But there was one special undertaking I will never forget. For a long time the Byelorussian government ignored the petition of the Jews of Minsk to put up a monument to the people killed in the ghetto. Finally the authorities told them, "OK, you can do it, but only with your money and your skills. We won't give you any help."

My father took charge. He created a committee and raised money. I was lucky, because I grew up with this background. Many people of different cities and places in Byelorussia came to our home with donations. If someone could bring only ten rubles, it was OK. If he could bring 10,000 rubles, it was OK too. In a special book, my father kept track of every person who donated to the fund. My uncles and aunts, even we children were involved in this. We put down every person who called who wanted to donate.

We raised the money, and they created a monument. It was small but beautiful. The people had been killed in a dry riverbed. The committee put the monument in the very place where the Minsk ghetto had been. It was really exciting for us, not only for my parents, but for all Jewish people present that day.

This monument was made from a special kind of stone, and beautiful words were carved on it. It became a tradition to come to this monument on Victory Day in Russia; at nine o'clock there would be a meeting and special events. There were always a lot of flowers. When I used to go with my father, there was only Jewish music. My parents always looked forward to that day. I thought that it was the most important holiday in their life. When people in Russia celebrated the Seventh of October and the First of May, my father said that those weren't holidays for us. "We have only one holiday—the Ninth of May." Because we couldn't celebrate Passover, Yom Kippur, or Rosh Hashanah, there were only one or two days when we could hear Jewish songs and music.

When my husband and I became a father and mother, we went every May 9 to this monument. By that time there was no Jewish music, only Russian songs. Still, this day is one I remember as a really great holiday, a holiday for all Russian people, the day that the Russians memorialize World War II.

After the war, my father was arrested and imprisoned for almost two years. Though it was before I was born, it's an important part of our family history. I remember it as if I were there. It was terrible because one day my father just didn't come home. Nobody understood why and it was never explained to him. He never had a trial. This was around the time of the Doctors' Plot. My mother had a dreadful time.

She was working as a doctor, and she told me, "Can you imagine that people stayed away because I was Jewish and I might kill or poison them?" It was the official attitude in Russia. All the newspapers said that Jewish doctors wanted to kill Russian people, to kill Stalin. For almost three years it was a terrible time for doctors. My mother couldn't work.

The Doctors' Plot trial was in 1952. My father was in prison from 1951 to 1953. It was a critical time for my parents. Of course, this was all before I was born. My aunt and uncle were in China because my uncle was a military officer. So my mother was without her sister, and *my* sister was then almost nine years old and grandfather was sick. My aunt sent her salary from China every month to help my mother. Somehow they kept up their spirits and managed to get through.

My parents read books that could not be published, *samizdat*, typed manuscripts. In Russia the author Kuznetsov was the first to write about the fate of Jewish people in World War II, about people outside of Kiev. And Yevgeny Yevtushenko wrote some really wonderful poetry about it. It was forbidden to print it too. My parents kept it at home. It was called *Babi Yar*. They were so excited about it. I remember my father decided to write letters to Yevtushenko to thank him for this poem.

When I was in the ninth grade, in the last months of my mother's life, I spoke to her in the hospital of my dream about being a doctor. And my mother told me, "You can't do it because it's impossible now for a Jew in Russia to enter medical school. You shouldn't dream about it. You should go to a technical college."

That was the only way for Jewish children, because technical colleges have only written exams. All the other universities have oral exams. When you have oral exams, they know you are Jewish. Written exams are taken anonymously. This is the reason why almost every Jewish person coming from Russia is an engineer or computer scientist.

This is also the reason why you don't hear anything about Jewish lawyers. Because to be a lawyer you have to graduate from the university, for which there is an oral exam. When I was in school I went to a two-year premedical program and graduated. The whole time my mom would say to me, "I know it's your dream but you should forget about it."

So I went to the polytechnical institute. It was boring for me, but I didn't have any other choice. I endured it; it came to me easily, but I hated it.

Our family had a three-room apartment; one bedroom for my parents, one for me, and a library that was a reading room with a bedroom area. It was a cozy apartment that we rented from the government. Once the government gives you an apartment, you can live there as long you want.

My family had lived in this apartment since right after I was born. They moved there when I was two months old. It was the first time in their life they could live with just me and my sister. Right after my parents died strangers came into my apartment and rummaged through my rooms. The man who wanted to take it had been our neighbor for ten years. He knew my father and shook his hand every morning. As soon as my father died, he decided to kick me out! Nobody looked me in the eye. One bigwig wanted to have our apartment and to him it didn't matter what I or my relatives thought. My teacher was so upset after this that she came to this man and said, "How can you do it?" He told her it was none of her business. Every day they called us, pressuring us to get out.

We decided to make some kind of compromise with the Soviet government. At this time my sister had been living in the apartment of her mother-in-law, who had just died. My sister went to one of the Soviet offices and said they could take her apartment and that she would move into mine. It was the only one way to keep our apartment.

Georg had a serious problem at his job—not with the work but with some of the people. He hoped that he could accomplish something; he had a lot of ideas. Once he came to his boss and said, "I've invented something." "Why?" his boss said, "I didn't ask you to!"

We explained our feelings and frustrations to our closest friends. We read articles and books, including a lot of Jewish books. We thought about government lies and a system in which people were afraid to speak honestly. And we understood that these people were accurately describing life in Russia.

Sometimes I felt that not only couldn't we *say* certain things, we could not even *think* about them because almost all people were two people. One person was outside and another person was inside. When I started to work I realized I hated my job and how angry I was with my country because I couldn't go to medical school.

When my daughter was born, I went to the hospital, my mother's hospital, where everybody knew me from childhood. By Russian standards I had excellent care, but not by American standards. There were seven women in one room, which was not clean. I lost a lot of blood because no one was in the recovery room. My aunt knew many doctors and made calls so I got the help I needed.

There were some problems after our daughter's birth. For almost one year her legs had to be in casts. But with the help of my aunt and my husband, I could manage and I didn't interrupt my studies. I delivered my baby on the seventh of December, and on the second of January I was in the institute! I took the test!

When we got a negative answer to our request for an exit permit, the next ten years of our lives became impossible. I lost my job. Georg lost his job. Our son was two months old when we got refusenik status, so now we had two children. We couldn't feed them. We couldn't pay for anything. It was a terrible life. I tried to find a job, but I couldn't because each time I applied for something the personnel department would call OVIR and OVIR would tell them, "She wants to leave Russia." I was without a job for two years. Finally, a former classmate helped me find a job.

Around the time the first Jewish families from Minsk started to emigrate to America or Israel, an incident occurred in the Jewish section of the cemetery. One day I came there to put flowers on my parents' graves and found the monument destroyed. There had been a picture of my mother and father. It was broken with a huge stone. It was terrible. When I came home I was in shock. I thought, "Never do I want to be in this country—never."

Not only my parents' monument but a lot around them were broken. It was terrible to look at. There was nothing left. In my life, it was the first time I was aware of vandalism in the Jewish cemetery. Maybe in my parents' lives it was not.

YURI B.
An Unseeable Future

Yuri B. (pseudonym), engineer, machine-building company
Born 1954, Minsk, Byelorussia
At the start of the Second World War, my mother came to Satanov, her birthplace, and urged her family to move to safety in the East, to Chabarovsk, where she was a medical student. Within two weeks of the start of the war, the Germans were already near Kiev. Her father disregarded her advice and told her that Germans had come to the same place in the previous war. They never killed Jewish people and had permitted them to stay in their homes. My mother could not persuade him and had to leave. Several years after the war she came back just to find out what happened to her parents. I was six years old, and I remember we met a woman who told us everyone in the Jewish village died.

This village was near the old Russian-Polish border. After 1939 the border moved to Poland because there was an agreement between Germany and Russia that part of Ukrainian Poland and Byelorussian Poland would be ruled by Russia. There is a river near this place that was the border, and under the river was a tunnel that had not been completed.

Shortly after the war started in 1941, before the Germans came, people from a neighboring village came to the village of Satanov with guns and took all the Jewish people and made them enter this tunnel. They sealed the opening with large stones and the entire village was buried alive—men, women, and children, maybe 200 people. All the belongings and the materials of the homes were taken away. Nothing was left. A typical Ukrainian hut had a dirt floor and was built of bricks made of dried grass and mud, too low for a person inside to stand. Materials from Jewish homes were used to improve Ukrainian huts. After the war no one was punished for the crime. I saw what was left of the village, and my mother told me about it. Eight of her family died this way.

My father's mother survived the war. Father had two sisters and his parents. On the second day of the war, my father went to the army. His family tried to leave Barisov, but his father turned back because he became separated from his wife and daughters at the railroad station. He thought they might have gone home, so he turned back to find them. They weren't there and by the time he got back to the station, the train was gone. He couldn't get transportation after that and remained in the town and died there. Nobody knows how.

My wife's uncle who lived in Minsk told one joke at a celebration during Stalin's time. There was a cake decorated with a drawing of the Kremlin. He said, while cutting the cake, "Now we'll cut out the Kremlin." Someone who was at this party wrote a letter to the KGB, and her uncle was arrested and died in prison. People who live here can't understand how this could be.

In 1986 the Chernobyl accident occurred. It is only 320 kilometers from Minsk. We learned about Chernobyl from Swiss radio a week after it happened. It was before the May Day celebration, and everybody went to the demonstration. After that we learned we could not use the food. In the newspapers they wrote that onions should not be eaten because the bulb, which is underground, absorbs a lot of radiation. But if I can't eat an onion, how can I eat a cucumber or any other kind of vegetable? It made no sense, but that's the typical Russian way. Then someone wrote an article that said we shouldn't eat the food, but the article was censored so we could read only part of it. But where were we going to get other food? It was difficult to buy any food in Russia, let alone without radiation exposure. When we were on vacation, we met a woman who worked in the medical department that checks water and soil pollution. She told us that everyone who worked there signed an agreement that they would never tell about the radiation levels of Minsk and other towns.

Now in Minsk, the situation is the same as it was in Chicago in 1920. I saw the movie, *The Godfather,* about crime in Chicago, about Mafia people who killed for money. If you opened a business you had to pay them. This problem is now in Russia because more freedom is the policy. The police are weak now. There is no law against taking money from someone else. It's difficult to sue in this situation. You can read in Russian newspapers about criminal practices. People come to any place where a business has opened, now that small businesses are allowed in Russia, and demand the owner pay them every month. If they won't pay, they will break their equipment. And who will give them back their money? In Russia, they can't insure their property.

The criminal stands on firm ground. A boxer who is thirty-five years old, for example, who doesn't have any other kind of training, could come and demand money from me. These people wouldn't protect me from any other group that might come after me. It's easy to make money this way. Such things can happen because for the first time the situation in Russia is not tight enough.

It's difficult to understand how a country as rich as Russia, with so much land and mineral resources, forests, vast territories, two oceans, and a lot of seas, could be so poor. It could be the richest in the world, but it's one of the poorest. What has done it? Only the wrong system.

I had a good job and a second business as an entertainer at weddings and parties. My wife and I had a car, a good house, a dacha, things that were only the dream of most Russian people, but I understood all this was nothing because I couldn't solve the problems. I could see no future for my son.

BORIS AND BETYA GILMAN
Terrible Truths

Boris Gilman (pseudonym), mechanical engineer
Born 1947, Tashkent, Uzbekistan

I remember everything about my childhood in Tashkent. Maybe because my grandfather raised me and taught me so much. He lived with my mother, his youngest daughter, when he was a very old man. After World War II he was in his seventies. When he died in 1952, I was only five but I remember this night as clearly as I see you today.

My grandfather's name had been Abraham Gorchov, but before the Revolution he changed it to Gorokhov, the Russian pronunciation. In those years Jewish people were not allowed to work or live outside of the boundary of Jewish settlement called the Pale. In order to work in Kiev, he had to change his name.

My grandparents had come to Tashkent during World War II from a village in Byelorussia. They were very religious and we kept a kosher home especially for my grandfather. He had special dishes, utensils, and even another special set for Passover. He spoke very poor Russian to me; no Yiddish was allowed at home. This was in reaction to political events in 1946 or 1947, when Stalin and his government killed all the cultural leaders of the Jewish people.

We had eight or ten big rooms, but there were no indoor conveniences such as running water. If we needed drinking water we had to walk about a mile toward the river where there was a spring with a faucet from which we could take water. We used to carry two pails at a time on our shoulders; we could drink this water without boiling it. For other purposes, we had a channel in our street that collected rainwater which would have to be boiled for drinking purposes. In Uzbekistan everyone used this kind of water, but there were a lot of diseases like dysentery and typhus.

In the Ukraine before the Revolution, my grandfather and his four brothers had a family business in the lumber industry. He was a lumber specialist who could tell by looking at a tree how many feet of board of a certain size could come from it. He had several people who worked with him to chop down the trees. The timber was floated down the river to another town where the wood was then milled.

Before the Revolution, Grandfather was not poor, but certainly not wealthy.

He had twelve children to support. After the Revolution he became very poor. The state took over his business. They lived in a small village and my grandmother opened a little store, as did many other Jews. My grandfather was "without rights" because he owned a business. Because he kept the business, my mother could not continue her education past the fourth grade. Around 1927, when my mother was ten or so, she decided to move to another village to study, a matter she never told us about before we left the country.

She lived with some other relatives but her mother or father would come about once a week to bring her food or other things she might need. She was mostly on her own. Because of this decision, she finished four or five grades of *gymnaziya*, but her older sisters never received an education.

After 1929 my grandfather became part of a collective farm. In 1933 when there was widespread famine in Russia, he could ask for a piece of bread from the public storehouse because he worked on a state collective farm. A lot of people, not only in Russia but in the Ukraine, died because of the lack of bread. On this farm no one died of starvation.

In 1933, at age fifteen my mother moved to Ivanovo-Voznesensk, a city near Moscow. One of her sisters lived there as a student, so first my mother worked some time on the farm and then took a certificate to Ivanovo to be permitted to study there. She studied five years in a technical college and then went to work in Tashkent. Before World War II, she had moved back to Byelorussia because her parents had grown old and were living alone.

In the 1940s, after the Germans invaded Russia, my mother returned to Tashkent. In 1943 she worked as a railroad engineer. She was a captain, because the railroad people were considered like an army. She had a uniform with epaulets. Meanwhile, my grandparents had escaped from the village in the Ukraine to Tashkent. After the war they stayed there with all the children in the family. My grandparents bought a little house. This was the house of my youth.

In Tashkent, there were about 2 million people, many of them Russian, maybe 40 percent were Uzbek, and maybe 2 or 3 percent were Jews. Right after the war there were a lot of Jews there, including Sephardic Jews who moved there from Buhkara and Andizhan. Many people moved to Asia from Russia and the Ukraine. I believe Stalin instigated this population movement for the purpose of having them settle in the new Russian territories. He moved Jews and others around to mingle with different populations. As a result, Russian people began to live in Uzbekistan, Lithuania, Kazakhstan, Moldavia, in various republics. Now, as a result, Gorbachev can say, "I cannot divide the USSR, because Russian people live in every republic."

Anti-Jewish thinking began to resurface between 1947 to 1953; the Nazis left behind the message that the Jews were responsible for everything that went bad in the Soviet Union.

When I was twenty years old, when I would meet a girl, I would say nothing about my Jewish nationality. If she asked me, I might answer, but maybe not.

With other Asian people I did not mention it. Because we all studied in the same school, from being with these people, I knew that Jews were considered "bad."

In 1947, there had been a Jewish Anti-Fascist Committee that helped the Jews in Europe. Mikhoels, a Russian Jew, a Soviet actor and theater producer in Moscow, was on this committee. He was known all over. America helped this committee with food for Jews in the Soviet Union. This committee received assistance from the Joint Distribution Committee. Mikhoels was killed in 1947, and this was a signal for the killing of all Jews. Many intellectuals were killed then. The Doctors' Plot in 1953 was the climax of this period. Between 1947 and 1953 all the newspapers were full of these stories about the guilt of the Jews and the crime of cosmopolitanism.

My parents met in 1946, were married and then went to the Far East where my father was assigned as an officer. First, in 1946, he was sent to Pogranichnyy, on the Chinese border. It was a bad place, and by 1947 there were several camps there for Japanese prisoners, soldiers, and officers. He was a doctor for these internment camps.

Although my parents went to the Far East together, my mother was an officer in the railway corps and could not get the release from the railroad to join him. The place where my father lived was not far from Vladivostok, so for several years my parents were married but lived separately.

You can understand the situation of the country after the war only if you could see the horror. At that time many women were without husbands and could find *no* husbands. Few men were around. I think my parents knew each other only about seven days when they got married. They lived together for a short time after those years apart but in 1950 they separated. They were divorced after about four years.

In Russia, if someone divorces, they must send 25 percent of their salary to help care for the children. If they do not, they could be convicted and forced to pay. My father also sent gifts for me and when I could read and write, he sent me letters. When I was seventeen, every year he would take me for a vacation. Several times he came to Tashkent to see me. At seventeen, I met my half-brothers. One had just been born; the other was twelve years old. I also met my future wife that year.

Until 1970, my father was an officer in the Soviet Army. He had been assigned to the Far East in 1953, and there was a huge camp designated by Stalin and his government as a place of exile for all the Jews in Russia. My father knew the place.

But my father attained a rank between major and colonel and was the chief of a large hospital in Vilnius. I think he believed what he was told about the system because there was no reason to question anything. By 1970 he had good pay from the army, a personal car and driver, a big apartment (for Russia), and was living in a good city. It had taken maybe twenty years for him to reach this rank after the war, but they took it away after only two weeks. In the Russian army officers who had lived many years in Khamchatka or Sakhalin as he had, usually could change their assignment to Europe. But some general needed this position for another person; so my father had to retire from the army.

When my father first told me about Stalin's plan for the Jews, I didn't really believe him. He had become a Communist in 1943 during World War II, but changed his views after the war. Maybe I believed this was just one isolated event in seventy years in the Soviet Union. I didn't want to leave the USSR with him.

Betya Gilman (pseudonym), obstetrician and gynecologist
Born 1954, Chernovtsky, the Ukraine

Chernovtsy is not far from the Rumanian border. Before I started school, for two or three years, I was in a small class taught by a Jewish woman born in Chernovtsy, who had studied in *gymnaziya*, and was trained as a kindergarten teacher. There were three, sometimes four children, sometimes just two of us. She taught us how to read and a little bit of math and even German. The class was run on a private basis and not really allowed by law.

People who were born in Chernovtsy were well educated because the city was previously part of Austria-Hungary. Then it was part of Romania before it was incorporated into the Soviet Union in 1940.

Our grandmothers, my husband's and mine, were sisters, which means that we are second cousins. Even though Grandmother spoke Yiddish to us, I can't speak it now but I understand every word. I cannot say that my grandmother was very religious but she knew all the traditions, all the Jewish holidays. We knew Passover, Purim, and Rosh Hashanah, and when it was possible, we had a home celebration. It was very difficult, but we were able to get matzah for Passover. A group of Jewish people made the matzah underground and sold it to other Jews.

Jewish children were a little bit ashamed of being Jewish. Chernovtsy was a very Jewish city, and half of the kids in my grade were Jews. In Russia, I could not tell people what went on at our home. My father was born in a different society, not a socialist society, and his mind was very nonsocialist, unlike that of my mother. When they got married, my mother got used to his direction of thinking, and my grandmother could understand my father since she herself was a bit of a capitalist. All my father's thoughts were directed to earning money for his family to live well. But this thinking was not allowed; this way of living was against the law. Therefore, we were raised not to tell anybody what was going on at home.

Then, in 1961 when I was six or seven, my father's brother was arrested because he had some gold coins at home. He was in prison for seven years. My husband's father paid money so that he wouldn't have to go to Siberia, and he was in prison in the Ukraine.

I was afraid; for all my childhood I was afraid of the authorities and maybe it was because my grandmother told me, "Don't tell anybody about anything." We lived near the town police headquarters. I had to pass it on the way to school and I would cross to the other side of the street because I was afraid.

When Khrushchev was dismissed and Brezhnev took his place, I can't remember that anything changed in my family. My uncle was still in prison and everybody was afraid. Nobody ever believed that after Stalin anything would be different. My parents knew that Stalin killed a lot of people. When my uncle came home from prison in 1968, he talked about his experience. He had been in prison seven years but he came home a sick, old man.

In our city there was a university and a medical institute and nothing more. My father didn't want me to study anywhere else in the country, so at seventeen I went to the medical institute and studied there for six years. I started at Chernovtsy, and then graduated in Tashkent. It was an unwritten law to accept maybe two Jewish people in the whole graduating class. It was different for different towns, but Chernovtsy was a Jewish town, so only 1 percent, not more, was accepted.

In 1974, there was a big trial about corruption, with maybe twenty people from the Ukraine being tried. Two of the people who were arrested were the directors of the medical schools in the Ukraine. Many of these officials illegally took money, which was a big source of their income. They testified that it was an unwritten law that every year before the admission tests for medical school, they got calls from the heads of the cities saying, "This year you can accept just two or three Jews to your medical school, so you'll have to decide whom to accept."

My father was arrested and put in prison in 1974 at the time of this trial. He was in prison because he wanted my sister to study near home and had given money to transfer her from one city to another city. A lot of people were involved. During the trial, only my mother could visit him. She was allowed to see him from a small room with a pane of glass between them. She could speak to him only through the telephone. He couldn't really tell her anything because people were watching and listening, and he was not allowed to write to her before the trial. There was such a law: he could not communicate with the family.

He was in prison six months before the trial, from April to September, and he could not write any letters. The trial lasted one month. He was sentenced to spend seven years in prison. He died after serving one month of the sentence. He died of a heart attack in prison after spending seven months there. He was just fifty-three. After my father died, I didn't believe in anything that was going on in Russia.

I first met Boris when I was ten and he was seventeen. His father is my mother's cousin. We met when he and his father went to visit Grandmother, and I was visiting at the same time. When I was sixteen, he decided he would wait for me. We were married in 1974, when I was nineteen.

My family left in 1979 for Israel. The biggest problem was that once they applied to emigrate, they were no longer allowed to work. They had to spend any money they had on living expenses. It was a six- or seven-month wait for a reply. They had to sell all their possessions.

This was before Gorbachev showed us all the "dirty laundry" of our country. Then we saw what other countries had. It opened my eyes; I understood what this country would face.

In 1985 I insisted that our family apply to emigrate. It was just when Gorbachev took power, and everybody talked about joining their families. We applied, and three months later we were refused permission to leave. Then I went to the head of OVIR to ask why. I said that I had my mother and my sister there, Boris's father and brother there—everybody from my family was in Israel!

He said, "When your parents left this country, they left their citizenship! They knew that they were leaving family here, but they left their citizenship! Therefore, they are not your parents anymore! Your sister is not your sister and your mother is not your mother because they are not Soviet citizens! And you cannot join them because our policy says that we cannot allow you to go to an enemy country, Israel!" He was the head of the Republic Immigration Bureau in Uzbekistan. At that time, we could only apply to go to Israel.

After they refused us in 1985, we had to change our jobs and we decided *not* to try to leave any more. From 1986 to 1988, I worked at a hospital in Tashkent as a gynecologist. Tashkent was a very big city like Chicago, if we had been in the Ukraine, I never could have found another job. Boris was a supervisor of a design department for textile machines. We could just live on our salaries.

For a while, Boris wanted to join the Communist party because it would have helped his career. His mother was such a strong believer in the Communist society that it seemed the normal thing to do. I said, "You can choose me or the Communist party and your career! Your main career is our family."

When the newspapers published the truth about the corrupt system in Russia, Boris became very ill and went to the hospital. He was so discouraged because he had believed in the system all the time, and everything was false. Russia was a country with no past and no future. Boris became very depressed. I tried to treat him myself for three months, but nothing helped. He was in the hospital for a month. The day he was discharged from the hospital, I called my mom in Israel and I told her we were leaving the country.

I didn't have anyone left in the Soviet Union, so I decided I had to leave. Anywhere and anyhow, just to leave the country! I don't lie about it, I miss nothing from Russia.

The last thing that happened when we left the Soviet Union is that the customs officer wouldn't let me take my wedding ring because he said it was too big. It was just plain gold, but it was heavy.

I wanted to leave Russia when my family left. I would have been happy to go to Israel with my mother. But Boris's mother didn't want to go where his father was. She came with us and didn't have anybody anywhere else. She was born in 1917, the year of the Revolution, and was raised together with the country. She was an engineer but very poor and had spent all her money on us. She helped us to raise our children, and we had all lived together in her house. So we would not go to Israel because she didn't want to go there.

LENA GORYUNOV
There Are Miracles

Lena Goryunov, engineer, agricultural research
Born 1954, Kiev, the Ukraine
My grandmother spoke Yiddish, and my parents knew enough to speak it when they didn't want the kids to understand. There was a time when I saw that to be Jewish was shameful, because when my grandmother began to speak Yiddish on the street, my mother stopped her. She was afraid.

My mother grew up in a religious household. Her grandfather was a very religious man. In his *shtetl* he was the one who took care of selling the matzah. It was a family legend that he could not refuse matzah to anyone who needed it on Pesach. He would sell what he could and leave just enough for his family. My great-grandmother would say, "So-and-so needs matzah and cannot afford to buy it," and my great-grandfather would say, "OK, give him some." Then another and another would ask, and he could not refuse. But my grandmother noticed that the amount of matzah was the same as when they began selling it. It was a miracle!

At the time of the Second World War both my grandmothers and their children were evacuated. A lot of people were evacuated at that time. This was a very difficult time for all Soviet people because all the supplies, factories, and other resources had been destroyed. A lot of people died on the battlefield, and just about all the Jewish people of Kiev were killed nearby at Babi Yar. It was a major tragedy.

Many people, not just Jews, know about Babi Yar because at the time the government didn't want to admit that in this place so many Jewish people were killed. Many people asked them to build a memorial there for future generations. They refused and instead put up a rock with a sign that said that during the Second World War Jews and a lot of Soviet people and members of the Communist party were killed there. But this is a special place where mostly Jewish people were killed. On that occasion many Russians, writers, poets, Ukrainians, and other intelligent people were gathered there. They read poems and spoke very warm words, but the government did not allow it as a memorial. The police did not allow people to go there and place flowers.

Fortunately, my parents and grandparents had relocated from Kiev and most survived. After the war, when my mother and grandmother returned to Kiev, my grandfather had been killed. Grandmother had to raise her four children alone. My mother was seventeen, so at that time she worked and at other times she took classes at the institute.

My father and his mother returned after the war and found their place was now occupied by others who did not want to allow my grandmother to move back. Some relatives allowed them to stay with them for a while. These relatives of my father were neighbors of relatives of my mother, and so they met each other. Later, while my father was still a student, they were married.

When my brother was born in 1947, just after the war, there was nothing to eat; it was a very hard time in the life of most Soviet people. My mother told me he was born prematurely and was very weak. He could not walk on his own until he was about seven years old. In 1954, when I was born, clinics and hospitals were (and still are) in terrible condition. Antiseptic conditions were very bad. My mom got an infection and almost died. I was ill with scurvy. She wrote a letter to my dad to ask my grandmother to raise my older brother Uri, and my dad to raise me.

When I was four months old, the doctors allowed us to leave the hospital and come back home. It had been necessary to feed my mother better food and vegetables. In order to get good food for his wife and children, my father was forced to stop his classes and find a second and third job, so he never had a chance to finish his education.

When I was growing up, I remember that after classmates abused me and called me "Kike," I told my mother I didn't want to be a such a thing. She explained that "Kike" is a very dirty word that means Jew. She said, "I am a Jew, and your grandmother is a Jew, and your father is a Jew. Are we dirt?" So, I learned I was to study hard and get the highest marks because I was Jewish. This was my first lesson. The next time they called me these names I defended myself. I actually bit one boy.

My mother told me about Jewish customs, but we did not actually observe them. I knew that we had Pesach, and we were supposed to eat matzah. My mother prepared very delicious dishes, but we did not know anything about why we ate them.

When Serge and I were students, we decided to go to the synagogue. While he was there, his mother got a call saying, "If you don't want your son to be dismissed from the institute, tell him never to go there again."

When we decided to emigrate, I was working as a research engineer and he was working as a computer programmer in construction. We were dismissed from our jobs. I was working in the civil engineering institute, and I was dismissed from all my classes. For half a year we couldn't find any job. We sold all our books and our carpet and tape recorder. I worked as a baby-sitter, and Serge had some students that he tutored to prepare for their examinations. His students and the children I baby-sat for were Jewish.

When we told our parents ten years ago that we wanted to leave Russia, they were so scared. They gave us a bit of a hard time. But now, his mother and my parents feel guilty and are glad we made the decision.

After seven or eight months, I found a job with a very low salary, but I was very happy to find it. A month or so later, Serge found a job.

When Eugene was born I stayed at home for three-and-a-half years. We kept our apartment, and Serge kept his students. In the Soviet Union, the rent, electricity, and gas charges are very low. Food took almost all our salary.

We had no information except the Voice of America, but we could tune it in only in the middle of the night when we were sure no one else could hear. Many people including our friends also listened to it, but no one tried to discuss it. You could be put in prison for this.

Russia is a fine place to live for two weeks; Moscow, Kiev, and Leningrad are fine cities for sightseeing; it is a good place to visit but not a good place to live. There is really nothing on the shelf. Sometimes there is no salt, no sugar, no tea, no coffee. We have received letters from friends, saying they are out of this or that. To be of real help we would have to buy out Dominick's [a Chicago grocery chain] because we have so many friends still there. Because of the lack of everything, people in Russia are very angry and they are looking for a victim, a scapegoat to blame.

Our friends there are afraid to be too clear in their letters because nobody can be sure who might read the letter before we do. Before I send a letter back, I check every word because I do not want to make trouble for my friends.

We came to America March 14, 1989, after leaving Russia in December 1988. The hardest thing when we arrived was the language. We had studied English in Russia and could read, but we could not understand it here; it became just noise.

We have been in America more than one year now, and sometimes we cannot remember how we arrived. Our first impressions are confused. I remember that when our plane landed, everyone started to applaud. After that I don't remember anything, except there were all kinds of officials and excitement.

A people without roots is not a good thing. It is important to us that our son understand his Jewish background because our culture, our Jewish history, was stolen from us, and we want Eugene to be proud that he is Jewish, the way others are proud they are Armenian, or Russian. It is important that he knows that if you are a good and intelligent person, it is more important than anything else.

We now do the blessings on Shabbat, and we had a seder. Not a real seder because our parents didn't know how to do it. Serge's mother cried at the seder table because she had never had this before. Now our son can teach us how to do it, and Serge's mother knows Jewish songs, and she likes to sing them. We have a lot of Russian neighbors who are our friends now. Serge's mother lives with us, and my parents live five blocks from here.

Not long ago we were strolling in our neighborhood with our friends, and some children were playing. We realized that they were singing songs in Hebrew, and when we looked, they were our sons!

SHAMAIL AND YELENA DANILOV
Singular Internal Passports

Shamail Danilov, engineer
Born 1953, Baku, Azerbaijan
In Baku maybe a fifth of the population was Jewish. Now many are emigrating because the situation is so difficult. There are various nationalities, but there are

two different kinds of Jews—Ashkenazi and Mountain Jew. For this reason there are two synagogues. I'm a Mountain Jew.

Maybe they call us that because our ancestors lived in the mountains once. Our Jewish language differs from Yiddish. It is like Farsi. There are no Hebrew words at all. One of my grandmothers was Iranian. The difference between, say, a Moscow Jew and me is basically, in Moscow and in the Ukraine live European Jews, Ashkenazi. Many Mountain Jews like me live in Central Asia—Samarkand, also in Uzbekistan. They're called Bukharski Jews. There's a city there, Bukhara, an ancient city. They have a Bukhar language.

In principle, Baku is an international city. There were many Russians, Jews, Armenians, and Georgians. Now, of course, there are nationalistic problems between Armenians and Azerbaijanis. It's a horrible situation; many Armenians have been killed or chased out of the city.

During the Second World War my father fought for a long time and was an invalid of the war. He got to Berlin and served somewhere in Czechoslovakia. He told various stories about how hard it was to fight, that often there wasn't anything to eat, that there would only be something to drink, vodka or liquor, for the officers.

As Mountain Jews we celebrated bar mitzvah, only for boys. Mine was at home. My father was a religious man who knew all the rituals and read Hebrew. I brought the Torah to the United States with me, although I can't read it.

After I graduated from the institute as an engineer, I was assigned to Surgut, in Siberia, to work for three years. It was a quite a change from Baku! I had to get all new heavy clothes, otherwise I would have frozen! The average temperature there is 45 below Celsius in the winter. Very cold. Baku is very warm; in winter, snow usually falls for maybe a week, and then it quickly melts.

I worked in the *taiga*, a kind of forest indigenous to Siberia, at an oil transport station you could get to only by helicopter. About 150 people lived and worked there. Three large oil-transporting pipes run through Siberia. At this station were three huge pumps that sent the oil farther. Because Siberia is very large and the route very long, you had to push the oil farther and farther. Because the winter is very cold there and the viscosity of the oil changes, the oil had to be heated. I was the boss of twenty-six people who worked with the oil-heating system.

After work we went to a club where they showed movies and had dances. We sang songs, talked. And there was hunting for wild game. I hunted mostly birds.

Yelena and I met and married in Baku. We had a civil ceremony at ZAGS because a marriage in a synagogue is not considered a legal one. We had a big party afterward. In the South we usually have big celebrations after weddings. Usually the men's and women's celebration are separate, but we had just one. We had around 200 people, a lot of relatives, especially cousins from my side. You have to invite everybody.

We didn't decide right away to leave Baku. The situation in the country was worsening. Things at work were more difficult, and it was more and more difficult to raise a family. With the economic situation, recently it's become practically impossible.

Yelena Chernolutzkaya Danilov, store department manager
Born 1954, Baku, Azerbaijan

My father grew up in the Ukraine, where his relatives all lived, in a village near Khmel'nitskiy. Every summer of my childhood we would visit. We would stay there practically the whole summer, and then we would return to Baku. This was a beautiful time.

My mother and her mother were born in Baku. Only the relatives from my dad's side came from the Ukraine. I do not think that these two cultures were very different, except for the language. My father knew Ukrainian, but at home we never spoke it. I would hear it when we traveled to his relatives, and they conversed, but I didn't take it in.

My father went to Baku to do his mandatory military service. Now in the USSR men have to serve two years, but during that time, after the war, he had to serve for seven years. There he met my mother; they married, and he stayed.

There was never any religious observance in our household. Only my great-grandmother was religious. But that didn't affect us children. That was somehow her own personal matter. She went to church, but she never forced us to go. Maybe because of the government policy, in school there wasn't anything. We never really had any religion in our family. Only on holidays my grandmother would celebrate somehow—bake a *kulich* [a traditional Russian Easter cake] for Easter and bring some to us. Of course we enjoyed it, but it didn't seem like a religious celebration. As far as anything seriously religious or profound, it never came to that. In our city the church was always in use but I've never been in it.

As far as I can remember, my parents and my grandmother Ksenia were always working. From morning until six or seven at night they worked. By the way, my father didn't work regular hours. Sometimes he had to work the night shift, sometimes the day shift. Sometimes my mother would have to lock us in the house and leave, because there just wasn't anybody to look after us. This was before I started school at age seven. We had very kind neighbors who were like family, if we needed help when we were home.

When I was ready to start at the institute, I knew that the one I wanted to attend, which prepared students for teaching, would accept more of the indigenous population, so I decided not to apply there. Because it's the republic of Azerbaijan, Azerbaijanis are considered indigenous. The fifth line of my passport says Ukrainian because that is where my father was born. In the USSR you take your nationality from your father. My mother is Russian.

Baku is the capital of the republic of Azerbaijan. In the same way that you have fifty states in America, in the Soviet Union there are fifteen republics. Azerbaijan is one of three Caucasian republics—Armenia, Azerbaijan, and Georgia. Baku is an industrial city with around 2 million people in the city itself. The oil industry is very important there. During the war Hitler tried to take over the city because he needed it for oil. The city was not damaged during the war because he didn't get there. It would have been awful. The city just wouldn't have existed anymore.

There wasn't much differentiation between nationalities when I was a child. When I graduated from high school, I didn't have any comprehension of what an Armenian was or an Azerbaijani or a Georgian. That was my personal experience. Maybe I was just lucky in school. There was just a wonderfully friendly atmosphere. Our neighbors were those kinds of people. I didn't experience any nationalistic pressures. Maybe that's why when I met my husband there wasn't any sense that he was a Jew and I was not.

We met in 1977 in the store where I worked. I was the salesclerk and he was the customer. We introduced ourselves. He was with a friend, and we talked a bit. Then we went to a party together.

In general, of course, I think Sasha's mother wanted him to marry a Jewish woman. But I tried to adapt to things the way they were. When our son, Paul, was two months old, we had him circumcised. It was in our house, on the table. Usually a rabbi does the circumcision. I couldn't allow this, because I was worried that the rabbi's tools wouldn't be sterile. It's illegal to perform circumcisions at home, but I asked the doctor to do it; he did and I paid him. When Sasha's mother came, I think she said some prayers.

Mountain Jews are perhaps more stringent in their observance of the rituals. In Baku being Jewish is just a fact of nationality. Sasha never seemed different or foreign to me. His parents may have seemed a little more so, but he was raised just like other Soviet children. Maybe there were things his parents did that he didn't understand, but he accepted the obligations.

When we got married, of course, we didn't have any idea that we were going to leave. There weren't even any discussions about it. Our consciousness changed, and step by step we came to the decision that we had to leave. Lately, I hadn't even been sure that my children would have a future.

I think the decision to raise our children in the Jewish tradition came after we were married. I didn't really think in terms of Russian or Jewish. I thought we would combine everything together.

When they are sixteen, children get their internal passport. If we had stayed in Baku, my children's passports would say *Mountain Jew*. In principle, there is a regulation that children can take either their mother's or father's nationality. But people will know that their father is Jewish. Basically, if the father is Jewish, they're Jewish.

GLOSSARIES

HISTORICAL AND POLITICAL REFERENCES

Afghanistan War

Soviet attempt through political and military action to maintain a puppet regime despite stubborn Afghan rebel opposition, 1979–1989.

Andropov, Yuri

General Secretary of the Communist Party, 1982–84.

Begun, Yosef

Imprisoned several times for Jewish activism such as teaching Hebrew, was released in 1987 and emigrated to Israel.

Birobidzhan

Established 1934, in the distant Far East of the Soviet Union, as a Jewish Autonomous Province though remote from Jewish population centers and culture. Its leaders were purged between 1936 and 1938, further dimming any promise of a strong Jewish state.

Brezhnev, Leonid

General Secretary of the Communist Party, 1966–1982.

Cantonist

Jewish conscript in czar's army, forced to serve from age 12 for 25 to 30 years, often forcibly converted to Christianity.

Collectivization

The consolidation of many small farms into one large cooperative unit under government supervision, called a collective farm.

Cosmopolitanism

A term used officially beginning in 1948 to denounce Jews of the USSR, presumably because they were less loyal to Soviet society than to other countries.

Doctors' Plot

Announced in 1953, the alleged plan of the Kremlin doctors, most of whom were Jewish, to poison Soviet officials. After Stalin's death the accused were exonerated.

Erenburg, Ilya

Jewish journalist, war correspondent, poet and novelist who wrote in Russian, but was also concerned with Jewish themes and history. He published the novel, *The Thaw*, in 1954 during the hopeful period after Stalin's death.

Glasnost

Policy of government openness and honesty, instituted by Mikhail Gorbachev in 1985.

Gorbachev, Mikhail

Born 1931; General Secretary of the Communist Part of the Soviet Union, 1985–1991; resigned when the USSR dissolved after 74 years as a socialist state. His policies paved the way for greater cooperation with other nations and opened the flood gates of Jewish emigration.

Great Patriotic War

Soviet name for World War II.

Grossman, Vasily

Member of the Jewish Anti-Fascist Committee, war correspondent and author of several novels, including *Life and Fate* which gave a true picture of what went on in the USSR prison camps and the fate of the Jews during World War II. His books were read in *samizdat*, when they were banned.

Gulag

Harsh Soviet political prison system.

KGB

Soviet Secret Police, officially known as State Security Committee.

Khrushchev, Nikita

Head of USSR, 1958–64.

Kulaks

Prosperous peasants, in the czarist and early Soviet period. Under Stalin's plan for forced dekulakization they were deported in vast numbers to the north and to gulags during the 1930's, actions which contributed to widespread famine and death in 1932–1933.

Lenin, Vladimir Ilyich	1870–1924, born V. I. Ulyanov, revolutionary leader and first Chairman of the Council of People's Commissars of the new socialist state.
Leningrad Blockade	German siege of Leningrad during World War II in which supplies were cut off for 900 days. The death toll of hundreds of thousands required mass graves.
Mestechko	Pale of Settlement.
Mikhoels, Solomon	Producer, actor, member of Soviet Jewish Anti-Fascist Committee; assassinated in 1948.
Molotov-Ribbentrop Pact	Public non-aggression pact of 1939 between Russia and Germany pledging neutrality, which had a secret protocol that assigned vast tracts of land to Soviet Russia. These included Finland, Estonia, Latvia, Bessarabia and parts of Poland, partitioned for the plan. Later Lithuania was added. The arrangement permitted Germany to invade Poland, an act which triggered World War II.
NKVD	Early precursor to the KGB.
Ottepel'	The thaw, refers to easing of harsh regime after Stalin's death during Khrushchev's presidency. Also novel by Ilya Erenburg, published in 1954.
Pale of Settlement	Area in which Jews were restricted by czars to live and work.
Pamyat	Modern Anti-Semitic organization. The name means "Memory."
Perestroika	Economic restructuring program instituted by Gorbachev.
Pogrom	Organized massacre of helpless people, often against Jews.
Purges	The term used by Communists for expulsions, ruthless mass arrests, exile and execution of party members either through standard methods or by "show"

trial, the latter occurring prominently during the 1930's.

Sakharov, Andrei

1921–1989. Famed Russian physicist, father of Soviet hydrogen bomb; human rights activist; 1975 Nobel Peace Prize winner; tried and imprisoned for dissident activities. Exiled in 1980 to Gorky. Released in 1986.

Samizdat

Self-published writings, usually typewritten, of books that were banned in the USSR.

Shcharansky, Anatoly

Jewish Prisoner of Conscience, USSR, 1977 until release in 1986; he continues as an activist in Israel for human rights.

Six Day War

Six days in June 1967 when Israel retaliated for Arab threats and blockades by defeating Egyptian, Jordanian and Syrian armies.

Stalin, Joseph

1879–1953. Communist party leader; took key roles in the activities leading to the 1917 revolution overthrowing the czarist government. He grew more powerful and ruthless after Lenin's death and Trotsky's exile. By 1940 he was head of the USSR.

Trotsky, Leon

1879–1940, born Lev D. Bronstein, of Jewish parents; with Lenin he organized the October Revolution of 1917. Later he differed with party policy and was exiled in 1929 to Turkey. He was assassinated in Mexico in 1940.

Trotskyite

One who believed in Trotsky's views.

Vovsi, Dr. Miron

Prominent Kremlin physician, first cousin of Mikhoels, expert in military medicine, one of the nine physicians named in the Doctors' plot and forced under torture to confess his "guilt." He was freed almost immediately after Stalin's death.

Yevtushenko, Yevgeny

Prominent Russian poet whose poem, "Babi Yar," written in 1961, was the first published acknowledgment of the massacre of Jews outside of Kiev during WWII, breaking the "conspiracy of silence" about the Jewish Holocaust.

ZAGS

Soviet bureau of records.

RUSSIAN TERMS

Anketa	Application form.
Avtomatika	Automated systems; automation.
Babushka	Grandmother.
Blat	Influence or connections used to gain employment or other objective.
Dacha	Country house; summer cottage.
Farsi	Language of Eastern Iran.
"Five"	In school grading system, the highest possible mark.
Glina	Clay, as used in peasant huts.
Gold Medal	Awarded to students with straight Fives.
Grammatika	Award for perfection in class; grammar.
Gymnaziya	Secondary school.
Inkassator	Financial officer.
Kabarda; Kabardintsy	Region; natives of region, Kabardians, of the Kabardino-Balkarian ASSR.
Kabinet	Medical or dental examining room.
Khrushchovka	Small, compact apartment built en masse during Khrushchev's term of office.
Kolkhoz	Collective farm.
Kolkhozny	Adjective referring to a collective farm or worker.
Komsomol	Official Communist young adult group, ages 16–24.
Kulich	Traditional Russian Easter cake.

Mestechko	Pale of Settlement.
Obshchezhitie	Communal dormitory for students or workers.
Oktyabryata	Communist organization, for 5–7 year-olds, literally, children of October.
Ordinatura	Medical internship.
OVIR	Government agency for registering migration; travel permits were issued or denied here.
Prodavshchitsa	Saleswoman, shop assistant.
Refuseniks	Those refused official exit permits.
Silver Medal	Academic award just below Gold Medal.
Sistema Upravleniya	Administrative/management system.
Taiga	Sub-arctic coniferous forest.
Zhid, Zhidovka, Zhidy	Pejorative name for Jews; masculine, feminine, and plural.

YIDDISH AND HEBREW TERMS

Bar or Bat Mitzvah	Ceremony for which at age 13, boy or girl prepares, marking his or her ability for participation in Jewish rituals and ceremonies.
Braha	Blessing.
Brit	Ritual circumcision.
Davened	Past tense of daven, to pray.
Evrey, Evreya	Jew (masculine and feminine).
Haggadah	Book giving order of Passover Seder.
Hamantaschen	Triangular pastry filled with fruit, traditional Purim treat.
Hanukkah	Festival commemorating redemption of temple by Maccabees; also called Festival of Lights.

Heder	Jewish school for young children.
HIAS	Hebrew Immigrant Aid Society.
Hupa	Used at weddings, a portable roof.
Kashrut	Dietary laws for keeping kosher.
Kibbutz, kibbutzim	Communal farm(s) in Israel.
Kosher	Ritually pure for use by traditional and religious Jews.
Latkes	Pancakes made from potatoes or matzah meal.
L'haim	To life! A toast.
Matzah	Unleavened bread eaten at Passover.
Mazel tov	Good luck.
Megillat Esther	Story of Esther and the origin of the Purim celebration.
Menorah	Candelabrum used for Shabbat and holidays; a nine-branched one is used for Hanukkah, the Jewish festival of lights.
Mezzuzah	Case containing a scroll of blessing, placed upon the doorpost of a Jewish home.
Mohel	One who performs ritual circumcision.
Moreh, morah	Teacher, m.,f.
Passover	Jewish holiday commemorating Exodus from Egypt.
Seder	Ceremonial meal eaten on Passover holiday.
Shtetl	Small town or village of Eastern Europe, where Jews lived.
Shul	Synagogue or place to meet for study and prayer.
Simen tov	May this be a good omen; greeting at a Jewish celebration.
Simhat Torah	Celebration of the annual completion of reading of the Torah, following autumn

High Holy Days. Traditionally observed by marching and dancing while carrying Torah scrolls.

Sohnut

Israeli organization for helping Russian immigrants.

Sukkot

Autumn festival during which meals are taken in a shelter with a roof open to the sky.

Tanakh

Acronym for Torah, Nevi'im, (Prophets) and Ketuvim, (Writings), which include Psalms, Proverbs, Job and short works of poetry or prose such as Lamentations and the Song of Songs.

Tefillin

Phylacteries; small leather boxes containing slips with Hebrew scriptural passages, bound to the forehead and left arm during weekday morning prayers by observant Jewish men.

Torah

The Five Books of Moses, Old Testament of the Bible; also the sacred scroll which contains the scriptures.